TOTAL HISTORICAL REVENUE, SPENDING, AND NATIONAL DEBT (cont.)
inflation-adjusted to 2009 dollars (in billions)

gress	Administration	Revenue[1]	Spending			%
54	Grover Cleveland (1893–1897)	$38.07	$4...			%
57	William McKinley (1897–1901)[3]	$64.73	$66...			12%
-60	Theodore Roosevelt (1901–1909)	$93.17	$87.63	$45.94	$0.08	0%
62	William Howard Taft (1909–1913)	$59.49	$58.80	$47.37	$1.43	3%
-66	Woodrow Wilson (1913–1921)	$225.03	$451.45	$216.07	$168.70	356%
-68	Warren G. Harding (1921–1923)	$104.45	$92.73	$237.35	$21.28	10%
-70	Calvin Coolidge (1923–1929)	$258.83	$219.80	$178.25	−$59.10	−25%
72	Herbert Hoover (1929–1933)	$175.35	$184.49	$258.15	$79.90	45%
-79	Franklin D. Roosevelt (1933–1945)	$1,486.72	$3,196.77	$2,034.79	$1,776.64	688%
-82	Harry S. Truman (1945–1953)	$2,751.47	$3,626.87	$1,730.67	−$304.12	−15%
-86	Dwight D. Eisenhower (1953–1961)	$3,737.67	$4,077.31	$1,662.36	−$68.31	−4%
-88	John F. Kennedy (1961–1963)[3]	$1,680.60	$1,806.11	$1,715.57	$53.21	3%
-90	Lyndon B. Johnson (1963–1969)	$3,412.03	$3,636.65	$1,787.29	$71.72	4%
-93	Richard M. Nixon (1969–1974)[3]	$5,114.77	$5,380.00	$1,685.88	−$101.41	−6%
-94	Gerald Ford (1974–1977)	$1,790.88	$2,183.53	$1,901.18	$215.30	13%
-96	Jimmy Carter (1977–1981)	$4,378.01	$4,954.55	$2,048.45	$147.27	8%
-100	Ronald Reagan (1981–1989)	$10,249.65	$12,633.05	$4,196.60	$2,148.15	105%
−102	George H. W. Bush (1989–1993)	$6,160.01	$7,529.72	$5,670.78	$1,474.18	35%
−106	Bill Clinton (1993–2001)	$15,955.79	$16,436.76	$6,873.72	$1,202.94	21%
−110	George W. Bush (2001–2009)	$18,782.14	$20,947.96	$10,061.93	$3,188.21	46%
−114	Barack Obama (2009–2017)[4]	$20,123.30	$27,138.13	$17,222.90	$7,160.97	71%

...ite early termination of this administration, figures for the last budget year of this administration are credited to this administration.
Budgeted Revenue and Spending is included for 2017. The National Debt is estimated by the U.S. National Debt Clock (www.usdebtclock.org/) as of June of 2016.

FULL FAITH

AND

CREDIT

AND **CREDIT**

THE NATIONAL DEBT, TAXES, SPENDING,
AND THE BANKRUPTING OF AMERICA

ALAN AXELROD

FEATURING EDITORIAL CARTOONS BY
MICHAEL RAMIREZ

ABBEVILLE PRESS PUBLISHERS
NEW YORK   LONDON

DEDICATION

*To all who wish a brighter future for our children and grandchildren
and most especially to my father, Harry N. Abrams, and his mentor,
Harry Scherman, whose publishing contributions to the culture of
our country have been worth emulating.*

—Robert E. Abrams

For Anita and Ian
—Alan Axelrod

ACKNOWLEDGMENTS

It is a pleasure to thank my editor, Lynn Northrup, and also the
team at Abbeville Press who made this book possible: designer
Misha Beletsky and Abbeville vice president Will Lach. My special thanks to Abbeville's chief number cruncher, John Olivieri,
who collaborated with me on the tables used in the introduction
and the endpapers.

The idea for this book came from Robert E. Abrams, cofounder
and CEO of Abbeville Press. I have known Bob for many years as
a man with a passion for delighting, dazzling, enlightening, and
educating readers. His contributions to this book are very many.
More than a publisher, he has been a generous and demanding
collaborator.

—Alan Axelrod

NOTE: Wherever noted and in blue sidebars like this one, dollar figures for historical revenue, spending, and debt are in billions and have been adjusted for inflation
to 2009 dollars.

Editor: Lynn Northrup
Designer: Misha Beletsky
Compositor: Michael Russem
Production Manager: Louise Kurtz

First edition
10 9 8 7 6 5 4 3 2 1

Library of Congress Cataloging-in-
Publication Data available on request.

ISBN 978-0-7892-1283-2

For bulk and premium sales and for text
adoption procedures, write to Customer
Service Manager, Abbeville Press, 116
West 23rd Street, New York, NY 10011,
or call 1-800-ARTBOOK.

Visit Abbeville Press online
at www.abbeville.com.

CONTENTS

PUBLISHER'S FOREWORD By Robert E. Abrams 11
INTRODUCTION: THE TERRORISM OF DEBT 15

PART I

HOW WE GOT HERE

THE UNINTENDED CONSEQUENCES

OF ELECTED GOVERNMENT

GEORGE WASHINGTON TO THEODORE ROOSEVELT.........53

WOODROW WILSON TO FRANKLIN DELANO ROOSEVELT 83

HARRY S. TRUMAN TO RONALD REAGAN 105

4.

GEORGE H. W. BUSH TO BARACK OBAMA 129

PART II

THE TYRANNY OF GOOD INTENTIONS

SPENDING OUT OF CONTROL

5.

IN GOVERNMENT WE TRUST 147

6.

THE UNINTENDED CONSEQUENCES OF UNELECTED GOVERNMENT 169

7.

OUR CLIMATE OF MORAL HAZARD: FROM NEW DEAL TO RAW DEAL 195

PART III

SPENDING TOO MUCH FOR THE

COMMON DEFENSE

TRAPPED IN THE PUZZLE PALACE

8.

IKE'S FIRST DRAFT 227

9.

THE PENTAGON AND PORK CHOP HILL...........................249

PART IV

SPENDING TOO MUCH AT THE

CIVILIAN PORK BARREL

ONE MAN'S WASTE IS

ANOTHER MAN'S DINNER

FROM THE BOTTOM OF THE BARREL:
GRINDING THE POLITICAL PORK SAUSAGE...............279

11.

LET THEM EAT PORK:
HOW CONGRESS BUYS VOTES.............................301

PART V

WHAT TAXES

COST US

TAX PLANS AND POLICY CHOICES

12.

ABANDON ALL HOPE?......................................349

13.

WHEN SUBSIDIES AND PREFERENCES PASS FOR
TAXES..371

PART VI

SOLUTIONS

ASKING THE RIGHT QUESTIONS

HOW MUCH LONGER DO WE HAVE TO PERCH ON THIS PAINFUL TIPPING POINT? 389

15.

STAY CURIOUS, GET SKEPTICAL:
RESOURCES, REFERENCES, AND POLICY CHOICES.......... 413

The economies of the world remind me of a hamper full of dirty shirts. None are clean but the United States is the cleanest of the dirty bunch.

—Stephen Mauzy,
"The World's Cleanest Dirty Shirt"
Wyatt Investment Research
October 18, 2013

It is difficult to get a man to understand something, when his salary depends on his not understanding it.

—Upton Sinclair,
I, Candidate for Governor:
And How I Got Licked (1934)

Derivatives are like sex. It's not who we're sleeping with, it's who they're sleeping with that's the problem.

—Warren Buffett (2008)

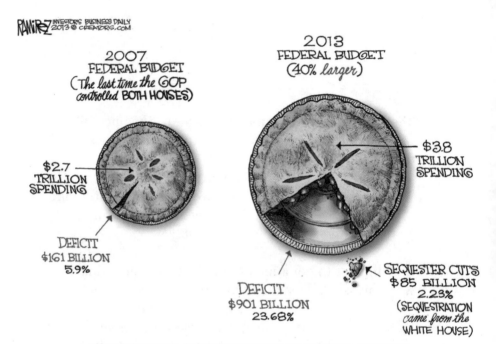

2007
FEDERAL BUDGET
(The last time the GOP
controlled BOTH HOUSES)

2013
FEDERAL BUDGET
(40% *larger*)

$2.7
TRILLION
SPENDING

$3.8
TRILLION
SPENDING

DEFICIT
$161 BILLION
5.9%

DEFICIT
$901 BILLION
23.68%

SEQUESTER CUTS
$85 BILLION
2.23%
(SEQUESTRATION
came from the
WHITE HOUSE)

The ILLUSTRATED SEQUESTRATION & BUDGET PIE CHARTS

PUBLISHER'S
FOREWORD

Each of us sees life through a personal lens. The lens distorts, biases, filters, and focuses. It selects. It refracts a large part of our character. The more we are aware of the nature of our personal lens, the more we can refine it, even alter it, if we want. The more we can learn.

My lens, in part, is that of a small, entrepreneurial businessman, among whose businesses is publishing. I like reaching an audience and helping talented authors and artists reach their audience—sometimes, oftentimes, a very small audience.

My hope is that, through Alan Axelrod's work, this book will reach a large audience. I hope that this book will help us all learn more about the economic aspects of our political and cultural environment here in the United States. I hope it will allow us to refract what we learn through our personal lenses, and then weigh our priorities, so that we can engage in a constructive and informed level of discussion about our best choices in the 2016 election and well beyond.

Managing businesses, employees, suppliers, and customers is hard. Some are better at it than others. I believe the larger the organization, the more complex it is to manage it adequately, let alone really well. *Full Faith and Credit* highlights the challenge of managing the $4.5 trillion-per-year enterprise called the federal government.

Some people feel that as long as "same-sex marriage" and "a woman's right to choose" are the law of the land, everything else will work itself out. Others feel just as passionately that these social issues are symptoms of the nation's moral decline. Although it can be argued that all politics is ultimately about social issues, *Full Faith and Credit* is not about *these* particular social issues. They are important, one way or the other, but addressing them— as voters, for instance—to the exclusion of other issues will not ensure the continued existence, let alone the well-being, of our nation.

There are 17 members in my immediate family, including children and their families, and we are all American citizens.

The chart on the endpapers of this book indicates that the federal government has made my family of 17 a guarantor, effectively a co-signor, and personally responsible for over $900,000 of our country's current debt.

That is my viewpoint through my personal lens.

Full Faith and Credit is about the political challenge of managing the largest single economic enterprise in the world. That is the political—and social—priority the author of this book has chosen to address. It is up to each reader to decide how he or she wants to prioritize that challenge of effectively managing this national enterprise. It is the responsibility of each reader to make informed choices among the available approaches.

Informed choices: Many extremely bright, hardworking people have devoted their lives to acquiring, analyzing, and evaluating the data that can inform rational choices. Building on their data, analysis, and evaluation, this book lays out some of the available options. The question remains: Will we pay attention? Will we examine the data, the analysis, the evaluation? Will we follow the money from source to expenditure to effect? And, having done all this, will we act to husband our resources and put our federal government on a sustainable basis for our present, our future, and the future of our children and theirs?

—Robert E. Abrams
Abbeville Press
New York City

At the heart of the American economy today is a national debt that is unsustainable—in fact, nearly unimaginable—and it is terrorism in a different form. The introduction diagnoses, defines, and quantifies our economic terror, its causes and its consequences. As for its victims, they are a mature generation today that is less well off than the generation before them, and a rising generation doomed to amputated aspirations and a compromised future—perhaps even worse. Although government numbers calculate the national debt as more than **$19 trillion** (July 3, 2016), some credible non-governmental but non-partisan economists believe it is actually closer to **$210 trillion**.

How did this happen to us? What can we do about it? The introduction outlines an approach to the answers.

INTRODUCTION

THE

TERRORISM

OF

DEBT

During the week of December 4–8, 2015, a CBS News/*New York Times* poll asked 1,275 Americans nationwide what they thought were "the most important problems facing this country today." For month after month, year after year, the top response had been "the economy."[1] But this time, it was "terrorism"—14% confessed themselves terrified over terrorism, versus 12% concerned about the economy. It seems that ISIS and its misbegotten brethren were not only invading territory in Africa and the Middle East, but also taking over a big piece of the American psyche.

This is understandable. Terrorism is fast, bloody, and indiscriminate in creating its victims. Terrorism is, well, terrifying—and not just for those directly impacted, those who actually hear the gunshots, feel the explosions, experience the loss. On some days, all 24 hours of the 24-hour cable news cycle are devoted to it. It is visual and therefore visceral. It bleeds, so it leads. ISIS makes threats, carries out threats, and creates homicidal followers who wear masks, tactical clothing, and suicide vests; carry assault weapons; and hurl pipe bombs.

The national debt? It's just a number! There is such a thing as the U.S. Debt Clock, and it tells us that, at the moment (4:11 EST on June 23, 2016), the number happens to be **$19.286 trillion**.[2] Can you hear it? Can you feel it? Does it send a chill of terror up your spine?

Probably not. And that is because the number alone, big as it is, does not paint a picture of the human cost of a failing economy: families imperiled, aspirations amputated, hopes of promising futures abandoned. Today, novels and films recall the Great Depression of the 1930s not by reciting the numbers, horrifying as they are, but by showing the searing, compassionate photographs taken by Dorothea Lange and Walker Evans, quoting from John Steinbeck's *The Grapes of Wrath,* or playing newsreel footage of threadbare figures shuffling, bone-tired, in breadlines.

These are things we can see and feel. But a trillion? What is it? How much is it? The easy answer is one million million or 10^{12} or a 1 with twelve zeros following it. But that hardly grabs the gut. A friend of mine tried to get beyond pure numbers by picturing something really big yet homely and measuring it with something familiar. The planet Earth is really big and we really live on it. If you measured its circumference in humble inches, surely you would at least learn what a trillion or even more inches *look* like. So, the circumference of Earth at its greatest girth, the equator, is 24,901 miles—which converts to 1,577,727,360 inches. On your hands and knees, measuring out with thumb and index finger one inch after another, crawling over desert and swamp and mountain range, floating over oceans, once around the equator ends up as 1.6 billion inches. With a "B." Repeat this journey about 634 times, and you finally come up to a trillion—with a "T." (Multiply that by 21, and then hear the news that at least some economists believe the real national debt is closer to **$210 trillion**.... But that is a story for later.)

Big numbers seem to switch off one part of the human brain while turning on another. That's a problem for this book, which deals with our unsustainable national debt (**$19.286 trillion** and counting—fast), the reasons behind it, and what we can do about it.

I'm hardly the first writer who has been faced with the task of uncovering the visceral reality behind complex systems and abstract theories. The great Victorian novelist Charles Dickens wrote fifteen major novels in his lifetime, totaling precisely 3,859,231 words. A great many of those words deal with the twisted plots and troubled lives of many individual characters caught up in or trod down by a society whose laws and economy failed them. But in just 26 words, one Dickens character, *David Copperfield*'s Mr. Micawber, cuts right to the visceral reality behind the other 3,859,205 words: "Annual income twenty pounds, annual expenditure nineteen pounds nineteen [shillings] and six [pence], result happiness. Annual income twenty pounds, annual expenditure twenty pounds nought [0 shillings] and six [pence], result misery."

Put it this way. Spend within your means, and you create happiness. Spend beyond your means, and you create misery. This turns out to be the story of our lives. More than that, it is the fate of our nation.

Big numbers get in the way of our grasping this simple principle. With eyes glazed over to the power of twelve, we lose contact with the "misery" that is unsustainable debt, so that I am reminded of something Joseph Stalin reputedly once said: "One death is a tragedy. A million deaths is just a statistic."

What is a trillion? 10^{12} or much, much more than the number of inches in a hands-and-knees trek along the equator. With that unsatisfying answer, let's move on to another question and another metaphor.

What is a sinkhole?

ANSWER #1 It is a hole in the ground that appears when the surface layer of that ground collapses. It may be no more than a yard wide by a yard deep or it may be as much as 2,000 feet across and 2,000 feet deep.

ANSWER #2 On Thursday, February 28, 2013, Jeff Bush, age 37, was in the bedroom of the home he shared with his brother Jeremy in Seffner, a suburb of Tampa, Florida. He was just turning in for the night. Later, Jeremy told CNN's *AC360* that he heard a crash and thought a car had hit the house. Next came Jeff's scream.

"I ran toward my brother's bedroom because I heard my brother scream," Jeremy told CNN. "Everything was gone. My brother's bed, my brother's dresser, my brother's TV. My brother was gone."

Jeremy Bush ran to get a shovel, leaped into the void that moments earlier had been the solid concrete slab forming the room's floor. He dug at the rubble until police officers arrived and rescued Jeremy as the void relentlessly grew to 20 feet across and 20 feet deep. "I couldn't get him out. I tried so hard. I tried everything I could. I could swear I heard him calling out."[3]

— ★ —

There are several definitions of the national debt, but we can begin by defining it in two ways.

DEFINITION #1 The United States national debt is the sink-hole on which we stand.

DEFINITION #2 The United States national debt is what we the people collectively owe to our government's lenders.

Let's break it down a bit. The gross national debt reported in President Obama's budget request for FY 2017, **$20.1 trillion** (compare the running count of the U.S. Debt Clock as of June 23, 2016: **$19.286 trillion**) includes debt held by so-called federal accounts, which are also known as "intragovernmental holdings." This is money the nation borrows from itself. Strange as that sounds, it works like this: The Treasury holds some 230 "trust funds," which are stacks of money collected for specific purposes designated by law. To take the biggest example, the payroll taxes withheld from our paychecks go into a trust fund to finance Social Security and Medicare. From time to time, the Treasury borrows money from one trust fund—primarily the big one, Social Security/Medicare—to deposit into another in order to fund some other expense. When the pizza guy appears at the door, I might reach into my pocket, come up short, and so take a few dollars from my cookie jar. I may or may not choose to replenish this cookie jar fund. After all, it's *all* my money. When the U.S. Treasury dips into one government cookie jar to replenish another, however, this is an act of borrowing from a legally constituted trust fund. This means it must, at some specified time, be paid back to finance the purpose or program for which the fund was created. So, it is an actual debt. But because it is a government debt owed to the nation itself and no interest is charged, it is not considered part of the "public debt," which consists of money owed to entities outside of the government. Sometimes, therefore, for statistical and planning purposes, the "intragovernmental holdings," or "federal accounts," are subtracted from the reported national debt. Based on the FY 2017 budget request, about 28% of the national debt, or **$5.4 trillion**, is owed to federal accounts, which leaves a balance of **$14.8 trillion** in public debt owed to investors and creditors outside of the government.[4] In this book, unless otherwise specified, *national debt* includes *public debt* and borrowing from *federal accounts*, and the term "national debt" is used in preference to "federal debt," with which it is synonymous.

The U.S. national debt is the largest in the world for a single country. It is about the same size as the debt of the entire European Union, a debt that consists of the combined national debts of all twenty-eight EU countries.

HOW THE NATIONAL DEBT

GOT SO BIG

Now that we know what the national debt is, we can ask how it got so big. Here goes.

Every year, the federal government takes in revenue, mostly in the form of taxes. When a country spends more in a given year than it has taken in during that year, it shows a budget deficit. The national debt is nothing more or less than the accumulation of annual budget deficits.

The United States came into being in 1776. Nearly 200 years passed before Congress enacted the Congressional Budget and Impoundment Control Act of 1974, the nation's *first* formal process for creating an annual budget. (You *cannot* make this stuff up.) The president of the United States, however, has been submitting to Congress a proposed budget (a budget request) every year since 1921 (thanks to the Budget and Accounting Act of 1921).

The federal government's fiscal year (FY) begins on October 1 and ends on September 30 of the following calendar year. On February 9, 2016, President Obama submitted his FY 2017 budget, requesting revenue of **$3.6 trillion** against requested outlays of **$4.1 trillion**, resulting in a deficit of **$503 billion**.[5] As Dickens' Mr. Micawber might put it: "Annual income 3.644 trillion dollars, annual expenditure 3.643 trillion dollars, result happiness. Annual income 3.644 trillion dollars, annual expenditure 4.147 trillion dollars, result misery." Except that the federal government calls this "misery" the "deficit." It is the difference between revenue collected during the fiscal year and money spent during that same period.

To cover the deficit—the shortfall in funds available to spend that year—the government borrows money. Because the deficit is added to the national debt each year, the debt grows even if there are no extraordinary expenditures such as a war. The interest on the growing debt must be "serviced" (paid) and so is added to the year's expenditures, which means that some or all of it is piled onto that year's deficit. Fiscal 2011 was a record year for interest on the debt: **$454 billion**. For FY 2015, it is "only" **$402 billion**, thanks to the lowest interest rates in history (see the discussion of Federal Reserve System excesses in Chapter 7).[6] The interest on the debt is expected to rise dramatically in the near term, however, equaling both defense and non-defense discretionary outlays by 2021 (about **$600 billion** each) and surpassing them by 2022, reaching nearly **$800 billion** by 2025.[7]

So far, investors in U.S. debt—buyers of Treasury securities (often called "Treasuries" for short)—have accepted low interest rates in return for the security of government-backed obligations. Why do they keep coming back? The short answer is that the United States, which guarantees its public debt with its "full faith and credit,"[8] is still regarded by many as a great, honorable, and stable country, and by even more as maybe not so great, but still a better bet than anyone else. You will find a somewhat longer answer when we ask "How high can our debt be piled?" later in this introduction. For now, however, it is important to realize that, at some point—and probably sooner rather than later—the growth of the national debt will finally spook certain investors, prompting them to worry about the government's ultimate ability to pay. This may drive some of them out of the market for Treasuries while moving others to demand higher interest payments to compensate for the perception of increased risk. If fewer Treasuries can be sold to investors or if the government is unable to pay higher interest rates on them, federal cash flow will decrease and federal expenses will increase over time. This, in turn, will increase the deficit while simultaneously making the cumulative debt that much more difficult to finance. Talk about a vicious cycle! The more that debt cries out to be paid, the more the debt itself will drive up expenses.

Finally, I have to tell you that the deficit figures reported by the government each year do not include the money borrowed from the Social Security Trust Fund. This is not an attempt to hide an obligation, but is a feature of the Twilight Zone called accounting, federal style: The government cannot post as a deficit money it owes itself. The full report of the national debt (not the annual deficit) does include this internal borrowing, so, in some ways, looking at the level or increase in the debt is a truer indication of the actual annual deficit.

THE NATIONAL DEBT BY

PRESIDENTIAL ADMINISTRATION[9]

Since the national debt is the accumulation of budget deficits, economists, politicians, and political pundits portray the growth of the debt by comparing the budget deficits during the terms of successive presidents. The dollar amounts in Table 1 (see following pages) are in billions of 2009 (inflation-adjusted) dollars. The per capita figures in Table 2 are in 2009 (inflation-adjusted) dollars.

Because federal revenues have been insufficient to pay for the nation's expenses throughout most of the modern era, the federal government borrows money from domestic and foreign investors by offering Treasuries. The most important of these are Treasury bills ("short-dated" securities, having less than five years to run before redemption) and bonds (long-term interest-bearing securities), which may be traded on the open market. Since the very first secretary of the treasury, Alexander Hamilton (in office September 11, 1789 to January 31, 1795), the United States has never defaulted on the national debt. Because Treasuries are promises made by the United States, they yield relatively low interest because purchasers believe they represent low risk. Foreign investors such as China and Japan (the two largest foreign financiers of the U.S. national debt) are eager to loan the U.S. Treasury money at relatively low rates because this allows the United States, a major importer, to buy the exports of these nations. Purchasing Treasuries also allows major exporters to keep their currencies low relative to the dollar.

In addition to selling Treasuries, the Treasury funds the expenses of the federal government by borrowing—interest-free—from the Social Security Trust Fund. The problem with this is that the funds borrowed came from the payroll taxes collected in the past from the baby boom generation. Because the borrowed funds were loaned to the Treasury at zero interest to pay for current expenses other than Social Security, they were unavailable for investment. This greatly diminishes the resources for paying the Social Security benefits of the boomers, who are now retiring. Every year, more and more retired boomers will begin drawing down more Social Security funds than are being replenished solely by current payroll taxes. The only way to make up the shortfall in the Social Security Trust Fund is by increasing federal taxes, decreasing the promised level of payments, raising the age of retirement, or introducing some combination of these. As of this writing, legislators have failed to agree on any plan to meet Social Security's future obligations.

In an effort to control the relentless growth of the national debt, a maximum debt level, or "debt ceiling," has been established by law. Because enforcing the debt ceiling could possibly cause the United States to default on its obligations, Congress has repeatedly voted to raise it.

UNSUSTAINABLE DEBT IS A BAD THING

Before we turn from *how* the national debt got so big to *why* it got so big, let's make sure we all have good reason to understand that an unsustainable national debt is a bad thing. Even though it doesn't tote an AK-47 or wear a suicide belt, unsustainable debt is, as Mr. Micawber would say, a bringer of misery.

To be perfectly clear, not all public debt is bad, and virtually every modern nation purposefully incurs some of it. In the short term, public debt is a fine way to raise the extra money needed to invest in economic growth, infrastructure projects, and social welfare benefits. In the case of the United States, public debt is a safe and attractive way for foreigners to invest because buying government-backed securities is less risky than "direct investment" in America through, for instance, foreign purchase of a minimum 10% interest in the nation's companies, businesses,

TOTAL HISTORICAL REVENUE, SPENDING, AND NATIONAL DEBT
inflation-adjusted to 2009 dollars (in billions)

Congress	Administration	Revenue[1]	Spending[1]	National Debt[2] Amount	National Debt[2] Change	%
1–4	George Washington (1789–1797)	$0.54	$0.57	$1.33	$–	0%
5–6	John Adams (1797–1801)	$0.61	$0.58	$1.38	$0.05	4%
7–10	Thomas Jefferson (1801–1809)	$2.00	$1.30	$1.02	−$0.36	−26%
11–14	James Madison (1809–1817)	$2.11	$2.69	$2.15	$1.13	111%
15–18	James Monroe (1817–1825)	$3.84	$3.36	$2.24	$0.09	4%
19–20	John Quincy Adams (1825–1829)	$2.35	$1.67	$1.59	−$0.65	−29%
21–24	Andrew Jackson (1829–1837)	$6.37	$4.03	$0.00	−$1.59	−100%
25–26	Martin Van Buren (1837–1841)	$2.47	$2.91	$0.08	$0.08	100%
27–28	William Henry Harrison/ John Tyler (1841–1845)	$2.07	$2.32	$0.55	$0.47	588%
29–30	James K. Polk (1845–1849)	$2.98	$3.60	$0.98	$0.43	78%
31	Zachary Taylor (1849–1850)	$0.76	$1.05	$1.33	$0.35	36%
31–32	Millard Fillmore (1850–1853)	$3.43	$3.16	$1.39	$0.06	5%
33–34	Franklin Pierce (1853–1857)	$5.90	$5.35	$0.62	−$0.77	−55%
35–36	James Buchanan (1857–1861)	$5.05	$6.49	$1.31	$0.69	111%
37–39	Abraham Lincoln (1861–1865)	$6.99	$30.48	$21.02	$19.71	1505%
39–40	Andrew Johnson (1865–1869)	$23.32	$31.88	$36.42	$15.40	73%
41–44	Ulysses S. Grant (1869–1877)	$49.51	$43.28	$41.12	$4.70	13%
45–46	Rutherford B. Hayes (1877–1881)	$25.20	$22.90	$42.00	$0.88	2%
47–48	James A. Garfield/ Chester A. Arthur (1881–1885)	$33.95	$24.24	$38.19	−$3.81	−9%
49–50	Grover Cleveland (1885–1889)	$34.68	$27.09	$36.93	−$1.26	−3%
51–52	Benjamin Harrison (1889–1893)	$40.19	$36.03	$35.26	−$1.67	−5%

1. Aggregate of amounts for all years of the administration. For any given year, amounts are as reported, or as interpolated between actual reported values or as budgeted estimate in US FY17 budget.
2. Level of debt for last full year of the administration. For any given year, amounts are as reported except for 2016, which is estimated by usgovernmentspending.c

TOTAL HISTORICAL REVENUE, SPENDING, AND NATIONAL DEBT *(cont.)*
inflation-adjusted to 2009 dollars (in billions)

ngress	Administration	Revenue[1]	Spending[1]	National Debt[2] Amount	National Debt[2] Change	National Debt[2] %
-54	Grover Cleveland (1893–1897)	$38.07	$41.27	$40.78	$5.52	16%
-57	William McKinley (1897–1901)[3]	$64.73	$66.49	$45.86	$5.08	12%
-60	Theodore Roosevelt (1901–1909)	$93.17	$87.63	$45.94	$0.08	0%
-62	William Howard Taft (1909–1913)	$59.49	$58.80	$47.37	$1.43	3%
-66	Woodrow Wilson (1913–1921)	$225.03	$451.45	$216.07	$168.70	356%
-68	Warren G. Harding (1921–1923)	$104.45	$92.73	$237.35	$21.28	10%
-70	Calvin Coolidge (1923–1929)	$258.83	$219.80	$178.25	−$59.10	−25%
-72	Herbert Hoover (1929–1933)	$175.35	$184.49	$258.15	$79.90	45%
-79	Franklin D. Roosevelt (1933–1945)	$1,486.72	$3,196.77	$2,034.79	$1,776.64	688%
-82	Harry S. Truman (1945–1953)	$2,751.47	$3,626.87	$1,730.67	−$304.12	−15%
-86	Dwight D. Eisenhower (1953–1961)	$3,737.67	$4,077.31	$1,662.36	−$68.31	−4%
-88	John F. Kennedy (1961–1963)[3]	$1,680.60	$1,806.11	$1,715.57	$53.21	3%
-90	Lyndon B. Johnson (1963–1969)	$3,412.03	$3,636.65	$1,787.29	$71.72	4%
-93	Richard M. Nixon (1969–1974)3	$5,114.77	$5,380.00	$1,685.88	−$101.41	−6%
-94	Gerald Ford (1974–1977)	$1,790.88	$2,183.53	$1,901.18	$215.30	13%
-96	Jimmy Carter (1977–1981)	$4,378.01	$4,954.55	$2,048.45	$147.27	8%
-100	Ronald Reagan (1981–1989)	$10,249.65	$12,633.05	$4,196.60	$2,148.15	105%
4-102	George H. W. Bush (1989–1993)	$6,160.01	$7,529.72	$5,670.78	$1,474.18	35%
3-106	Bill Clinton (1993–2001)	$15,955.79	$16,436.76	$6,873.72	$1,202.94	21%
7-110	George W. Bush (2001–2009)	$18,782.14	$20,947.96	$10,061.93	$3,188.21	46%
-114	Barack Obama (2009–2017)[4]	$20,123.30	$27,138.13	$17,222.90	$7,160.97	71%

spite early termination of this administration, figures for the last budget year of this administration are credited to this administration.
Budgeted Revenue and Spending is included for 2017. The National Debt is estimated by the U.S. National Debt Clock (www.usdebtclock.org/) as of June of 2016.

PER CAPITA HISTORICAL REVENUE, SPENDING, AND NATIONAL DEBT
inflation-adjusted to 2009 dollars

Congress	Administration	Population in Millions[1]	Revenue	Spending	Debt
1–4	George Washington (1789–1797)	4.44	$121.62	$128.38	$299.55
5–6	John Adams (1797–1801)	5.08	$120.08	$114.17	$271.65
7–10	Thomas Jefferson (1801–1809)	6.12	$326.80	$212.42	$166.67
11–14	James Madison (1809–1817)	7.79	$270.86	$345.31	$275.99
15–18	James Monroe (1817–1825)	9.80	$391.84	$342.86	$228.57
19–20	John Quincy Adams (1825–1829)	11.64	$201.89	$143.47	$136.60
21–24	Andrew Jackson (1829–1837)	13.84	$460.26	$291.18	$0.00
25–26	Martin Van Buren (1837–1841)	16.37	$150.89	$177.76	$4.89
27–28	William Henry Harrison/ John Tyler (1841–1845)	18.44	$112.26	$125.81	$29.83
29–30	James K. Polk (1845–1849)	20.85	$142.93	$172.66	$47.00
31	Zachary Taylor (1849–1850)	22.49	$33.79	$46.69	$59.14
31–32	Millard Fillmore (1850–1853)	23.92	$143.39	$132.11	$58.11
33–34	Franklin Pierce (1853–1857)	26.61	$221.72	$201.05	$23.30
35–36	James Buchanan (1857–1861)	30.06	$168.00	$215.90	$43.58
37–39	Abraham Lincoln (1861–1865)	33.10	$211.18	$920.85	$635.05
39–40	Andrew Johnson (1865–1869)	35.91	$649.40	$887.77	$1,014.20
41–44	Ulysses S. Grant (1869–1877)	41.29	$1,199.08	$1,048.20	$995.88
45–46	Rutherford B. Hayes (1877–1881)	48.26	$522.17	$474.51	$870.29
47–48	James A. Garfield/ Chester A. Arthur (1881–1885)	53.14	$638.88	$456.15	$718.67
49–50	Grover Cleveland (1885–1889)	58.19	$595.98	$465.54	$634.65
51–52	Benjamin Harrison (1889–1893)	63.54	$632.51	$567.04	$554.93

1. Average of population for all years of the administration.

Congress	Administration	Population in Millions[1]	Revenue	Spending	Debt
53–54	Grover Cleveland (1893–1897)	68.64	$554.63	$601.25	$594.11
55–57	William McKinley (1897–1901)[2]	74.80	$865.37	$888.90	$613.10
57–60	Theodore Roosevelt (1901–1909)	83.90	$1,110.49	$1,044.46	$547.56
61–62	William Howard Taft (1909–1913)	92.77	$641.26	$633.83	$510.62
63–66	Woodrow Wilson (1913–1921)	101.03	$2,227.36	$4,468.47	$2,138.67
67–68	Warren G. Harding (1921–1923)	108.44	$963.21	$855.13	$2,188.77
68–70	Calvin Coolidge (1923–1929)	115.19	$2,246.98	$1,908.15	$1,547.44
71–72	Herbert Hoover (1929–1933)	123.40	$1,420.99	$1,495.06	$2,091.98
73–79	Franklin D. Roosevelt (1933–1945)	131.56	$11,300.70	$24,298.95	$15,466.63
79–82	Harry S. Truman (1945–1953)	148.56	$18,520.93	$24,413.50	$11,649.64
83–86	Dwight D. Eisenhower (1953–1961)	169.11	$22,102.00	$24,110.40	$9,830.05
87–88	John F. Kennedy (1961–1963)[2]	183.89	$9,139.16	$9,821.69	$9,329.33
88–90	Lyndon B. Johnson (1963–1969)	193.38	$17,644.17	$18,805.72	$9,242.37
91–93	Richard M. Nixon (1969–1974)[2]	206.61	$24,755.67	$26,039.40	$8,159.72
93–94	Gerald Ford (1974–1977)	215.78	$8,299.56	$10,119.24	$8,810.73
95–96	Jimmy Carter (1977–1981)	222.91	$19,640.26	$22,226.68	$9,189.58
97–100	Ronald Reagan (1981–1989)	236.32	$43,371.91	$53,457.39	$17,758.12
101–102	George H. W. Bush (1989–1993)	250.46	$24,594.79	$30,063.56	$22,641.46
103–106	Bill Clinton (1993–2001)	269.62	$59,178.81	$60,962.69	$25,494.10
107–110	George W. Bush (2001–2009)	293.94	$63,897.87	$71,266.11	$34,231.24
111–114	Barack Obama (2009–2017)[3]	315.26	$63,830.81	$86,081.74	$54,630.78

. Despite early termination of this administration, figures for the last budget year of this administration are credited to this administration.
. No Budgeted Revenue and Spending is included for 2017. The National Debt is estimated by the U.S. National Debt Clock (www.usdebtclock.org/) as of June of 2016.

or real estate. For that matter, buying Treasuries is less of a risk than investing in America's public companies through the stock market.

As with any source of funding, public debt can be used to make important improvements in America's overall standard of living by providing for growth of infrastructure (roads, railways, public utilities, and so on) and financing real investments in the country's future.

We have to admit as well that deficit spending can temporarily boost economic growth, even as it adds to the national debt. Especially in times of recession, deficit spending injects cash—liquidity—into the economy. When people, companies, and the government itself buy more, demand is increased, production ramps up, jobs are created, consumers have more buying power, and, ultimately, the government can collect more revenue. During the 1930s, British economist John Maynard Keynes advocated government spending—deficit spending—as a means of lifting national economies out of the worldwide Great Depression. With the private sector down for the count, Keynes argued that only the public sector could spend sufficiently to stimulate economic output (production of goods and services) by creating demand. This, in turn, would increase employment, which would give more consumers more money to buy goods and services, thereby further increasing demand and production, thus lifting moribund economies out of their depression. Some critics of Keynes conceded that deficit spending might well be effective for the short run, but demanded to know *What about the long run?* Keynes's answer was simple: "In the long run, we're all dead."[10]

"He that dies pays all his debts." The quotation is from Shakespeare's *The Tempest,* and it is quoted by William Bonner and Addison Wiggin, the iconoclastic principals of Agora Financial, a publisher of financial newsletters and other investor analytics, in *The New Empire of Debt.* They go on to ask who pays the debts of the dead—and how. The short answer to who pays the debt, it turns out, is "someone else." And in the case of public debt—national debt owed to other countries—there are generally three possible "hows." "The currency in which the debt is denominated can be devalued against other currencies; the currency can be made less valuable through inflation; or the debt can be repudiated. One of these things—or all of them—is likely to happen." The United States, however, need not repudiate. Because the U.S. dollar is the world's reserve currency—the "anchor currency" the world's governments hold in large quantities for international transactions the way they used to hold gold—its public debt is denominated in dollars, the value of which the U.S. Treasury can do a great deal to control. As Bonner and Wiggin put it, "Having the world's reserve currency means you can stiff your creditors without ever having to say you're sorry."[11] America's creditors have long retained their faith in our democracy. They continually extend the United States credit by buying its debt in the form of Treasuries. Now, whereas a "father would not have dinner in a fine restaurant and send the bill to his son, nor would he say to the restaurateur: Hold the bill for my unborn grandson," the United States government does it all the time with respect to its public debt. "Generally, the public has only the dimmest, most remote idea of the kind of obligations that are being contracted on its behalf. If asked about them directly, many—if not most—would surely object. But who asks? Besides, the unborn don't vote. And neither do foreigners."[12] As for those who originally contracted the debt, they will be out of office, perhaps employed as lobbyists, by the time the bill comes due or when the dollar loses some of its luster as a reserve currency. And, in the long run, they will be dead.

After some eighty years of Keynesian deficit spending, Keynes's glib quip—"In the long run, we're all dead"—has worn thin. Public debt and deficit spending, it turns out, are like certain powerful medicines. They can treat some acute conditions, but in the long run, they are harmful or fatal if swallowed. Not only can interest rates rise when the federal government takes on a great deal of the economy's available credit, but the government may also see the value of the U.S. dollar fall relative to other currencies in order to create repayment dollars that are cheaper than the dollars borrowed. This strategy is initially attractive—until foreign governments and foreign investors slow their purchase of Treasuries, thereby forcing interest rates higher if the national debt continues to rise. Inflation usually follows and real wealth shrinks. While this can quickly become devastating to the private sector, the federal government may try to buy time for itself by printing more dollars, diluting the value of its currency even further.

When higher interest rates reduce the ability of businesses to finance the employment of workers, economic growth slows and unemployment increases. The result is stagflation, a crippling combination of a stagnant economy with inflation—bringing to businesses, families, and individuals the worst aspects of recession (or even depression) and inflation.

In addition to slower economic growth and weaker job markets, rising interest rates will force the government to allocate more of the federal budget to making interest payments, leaving fewer dollars to devote to the economically productive spending Keynes pinned his hopes on. As we will see in Chapter 5, the federal budget is broadly divided into discretionary and mandatory spending items. Discretionary spending is part of the budget Congress decides on in its annual appropriation process. It is from this portion of the budget that cuts can be most readily made. Mandatory spending is "mandated" by existing laws rather than determined by the annual budgeting process. No cuts can be made from this spending without major changes in the applicable existing law. Of the mandatory items, "entitlements"—namely, Social Security, Medicare, Medicaid, unemployment, and labor—are the biggest sources of spending. In projections for FY 2017, these items amounted to **$1.9 trillion**, 75% of spending on all mandatory programs.[13] Since this spending cannot be reduced without new legislation—most of it bound to be politically difficult—the government might be moved to increase revenues by raising taxes. Doing so, however, will take its toll on a population already challenged by inflation and a shrinking job market.

Since we have touched on the subject of Social Security, many authorities believe the greatest impact of debt on the American economy will be felt as more baby boomers retire and become eligible to collect Social Security. To fund payments owed to the aging boomers, the government will likely have to take some or all of the unpleasant steps mentioned earlier. Because the Treasury will probably no longer be able to borrow from the Social Security Trust Fund, taxes will almost certainly need to be raised to fund the shortfall and/or the government will have to reduce spending in other areas, including Social Security, Medicare, and Medicaid, as well as projects and programs financed by discretionary spending. Not only will this result in a reduction of government services, but it will also further reduce government spending on things that productively stimulate the economy to some extent. Pulling out of this grim situation will be difficult because a slowed economy reduces federal revenues, which, in turn, deepens the deficit in the short run and raises the debt in the long.

WHO "RUNS" AMERICA?

Another category of consequences is involved when you have a massive national debt. Understanding this begins by answering the question, *Who "runs" the United States of America?* A very satisfying answer is *We the people do.* (Or, at least, *We the 55% who pay federal taxes.*) Satisfying indeed, but not quite true. At best, we the people share "management" of our nation with others that own our national debt. These debt-owning fellow managers fall into two broad categories.

First, there are the *federal accounts,* also known as "intragovernmental holdings"—that debt the government has borrowed from itself and therefore owes itself. Based on the FY 2017 budget request, **$5.4 trillion** of the projected **$20.1 trillion** national debt is owed to federal accounts. Roughly, then, 28% of the debt is held by 230 federal agencies, of which Social Security (the Social Security Trust Fund and the Federal Disability Insurance Trust Fund) is the largest, at **$2.8 trillion**.[14]

Second, the remainder of the national debt, **$14.8 trillion**, roughly 70%, is owned by "the public." As of December 15, 2015, this included[15]:

- Foreign investors: **$6.2 trillion**
- The Federal Reserve: **$2.4 trillion**

(Many people do not realize that the Fed is *not* a department of the U.S. government, but an independent central banking system established by Congress on December 23, 1913. As such, the debt it holds is considered part of the public debt rather than an intragovernmental holding.)

- Mutual Funds: **$1.2 trillion**
- State and local governments, including their pension funds: **$710 billion**
- Private pension funds: **$481 billion**
- Banks: **$511 billion**
- Insurance companies: **$295 billion**
- Buyers of U.S. Savings Bonds: **$175 billion**
- "Other" (including government-sponsored enterprises, brokers and dealers, bank-held personal trusts and estates, corporate and non-corporate businesses, and other investors): **$834 billion**

It is that **$6.2 trillion**[16] owned by foreign investors, including foreign governments, that concerns many Americans. As already mentioned, foreign investment in the national debt is useful for facilitating trade and other relationships. But if a particular country (or group of countries) owns too much of our debt, they may be in a position to exert undue political and economic pressure on our sovereign policy choices.

For some years, China and Japan have been trading places with one another as the largest foreign holders of American national debt. As of March 28, 2016, China was the largest holder, with **$1.2 trillion**. Japan came next, with **$1.1 trillion**.[17] These holdings allow both countries to keep the value of the dollar high in relation to their own currencies. Doing this gives them a great advantage in exporting to their biggest international customer, the United States, by making their exports appear affordable to Americans. Thanks to a large export market anchored by the

United States, the Chinese and Japanese economies have a huge and reliable source of growth.

As a major investor in U.S. debt, China frequently feels emboldened to scold us, admonishing our leaders to take action to lower our national debt. Perhaps it's part of a power trip, or perhaps Chinese bankers and economists are genuinely fearful that sooner or later the United States will no longer be able to honor its financial obligations. Whatever is behind the warnings, China has so far kept right on buying Treasuries, as have other foreign governments and investors. Despite rising American debt, they persist in seeing U.S. government–backed securities as a relatively safe haven in an increasingly unstable economic and political world.

The top ten holders of the U.S. national debt are[18]:

Mainland China	$1,236.1 billion
Japan	$1,122.6 billion
Caribbean banking centers	$351.7 billion
Oil exporters	$292.5 billion
Ireland	$265.1 billion
Brazil	$254.8 billion
Switzerland	$231.9 billion
United Kingdom	$218.3 billion
Luxembourg	$200.5 billion
Hong Kong	$200.2 billion
TOTAL TOP 10	$4,383.7 billion

China is very competitive with the United States, strategically, geopolitically, and economically. This makes a lot of Americans squeamish over the stunning amount of our debt that China owns. They worry that China will, sooner or later, use its holdings against us.

IS THIS HEARTBURN JUSTIFIED?

In his 2012 book *The Debt Bomb,* former U.S. Senator Tom A. Coburn, M.D., quotes Admiral Mike Mullen, at the time the Chairman of the Joint Chiefs of Staff: "Our national debt," Mullen said on June 24, 2010, "is our biggest national security threat." Coburn goes on to present a hypothetical scenario in which a large Japanese investment firm—Coburn calls it Entrust—decides to sell its Treasuries before the severely over-leveraged "Americans have a chance to devalue their currency." Soon, holders of U.S. debt throughout Asia begin dumping their Treasury securities onto the market. As a result, the dollar, under siege, plummets. "Americans woke to the horrifying news.... Everything they owned—their life savings, retirement plans, and homes—had now lost a third of its buying power compared to other currencies. And there was no way to predict if we had hit bottom."[19]

In Coburn's scenario, within a week of a Wall Street crash, the value of the dollar was halved. The members of the G-20—representatives of the world's twenty major economies—offered a bailout that came with a stiff price in the form of sharp constraints on American spending, including immediately pushing back the retirement age for all entitlement programs to seventy-two. This is hard on the baby boomers, who feel massively cheated, and it is hard on all Americans, who feel the sovereignty of their country being chipped away. But, after three very tough years of austerity decreed by foreign powers, and with unemployment stuck at nearly 30%, the United States does begin to recover.

Two more years pass. China, which held onto its Treasury securities throughout the entire crisis, suddenly seizes Taiwan. When the U.S. president responds with threats of military action, the Chinese threaten to dump all of the U.S. debt they hold. Faced with this prospect, the president meekly backs down. And so the United States suffers a humiliating "military" defeat without anyone firing a shot.

Coburn's scenario is fiction, but it is far from implausible. A U.S. sovereign default may or may not have immediate military consequences, and bankruptcy need not mean national annihilation. What it does mean, however, is turning over control of finances to some nation or entity that is not responsive to any electorate. And to cede a nation's finances is to cede much of its economy, which means much of its sovereignty—a nation's power to decide its own policies and destiny. We have only to look at nations such as Ireland and Greece, which, virtually insolvent, were for a time compelled, in return for bailouts, to cede control of their finances, economy, and sovereignty to unelected officials of the European Commission. At present, amid mounting American spending, deficit, and debt, China grumbles to us from time to time, but its leaders know that owning U.S. Treasuries spurs badly needed growth in the Chinese economy by keeping the yuan weaker than the dollar. This means that products exported from China are cheaper than products made in America, both for international and American businesses and consumers. As for the United States, it benefits from having China as one of its biggest bankers. American businesses and consumers enjoy a wealth of inexpensive Chinese imports.

Selling debt is currently vital to financing many federal government programs while also keeping U.S. interest rates low. But there is a price to pay. In the case of China as a creditor, that price is the shift of the economic balance of power away from the United States. This gives China political leverage against the U.S. Nevertheless, should America's national debt reach a point that makes Treasury securities an undeniably risky investment, China (and other nations) will very likely decide to sell their holdings—or they might use the mere threat of such a sale to extort certain actions, behavior, or compliance from the American government.

There's no denying that we (and others internationally) are vulnerable. China currently enjoys a "profit" on its U.S. dollar "reserves," but it sells them anyway to prevent the yuan from depreciating too quickly. China has also accumulated more dollar debt. If it suddenly unloads its American debt, the value of the dollar would face a lot of pressure and possibly even collapse. The thing is, if the dollar collapses, every developed nation on earth, China foremost among them, will suffer. Knowing this, China continues to hold its Treasuries and enjoy the economic growth this investment brings. For now.

HOW HIGH CAN OUR DEBT BE PILED?

In his FY 2017 budget request, President Obama projected a gross domestic product (GDP) of **$19.303 trillion**. The national debt, as given in the FY 2017 budget, stands at close to the same number, **$20.149 trillion**. In other words, the value of all goods and services the nation is expected to produce in FY 2017 is approximately equal to the national debt. This is no idle coincidence.

In 2009, Princeton University Press published *This Time Is Different: Eight Centuries of Financial Folly,* by Carmen M. Reinhart (Professor of Economics and Director of the Center for International Economics at the University of Maryland) and Kenneth S. Rogoff (Thomas D. Cabot Professor of Public Policy at Harvard University). In this book, the authors examine 800 years of financial crisis in sixty-six countries across five continents. Among their conclusions is that there is a tipping point at which "financial folly" turns into economic, political, and social collapse. Throughout history, advanced economies that allow the ratio of debt to GDP to exceed 90% are uncommon. Why? Reinhart and Rogoff have a simple answer: because they do not survive.[20]

As of the first quarter of 2016, the United States' national debt is not 90% of GDP, but 105.72874% of GDP[21]. (By contrast, consider that in 1988, despite a stubborn recession, the ratio of debt to GDP was 50%.) If you are among the many of us who struggle to maintain a presentable FICO credit score, you have undoubtedly noticed that the greater your ratio of debt to income, the lower your score, and the harder it is to get credit—at least at anything resembling a reasonable interest rate. What is true for individuals in this case is true as well for nations. A high debt-to-GDP ratio tells would-be investors that the nation will have a hard time repaying its obligations. At some point, therefore, the nation will have trouble finding buyers for its debt—at least at anything resembling a reasonable interest rate. (Note the cruelly self-fulfilling prophecy. Nations that look like they can't repay their debt don't attract investment in their debt and, therefore, cannot repay their debt.)

According to Reinhart and Rogoff's research, when a nation's indebtedness reaches 90% of its GDP, it may be doomed to bankruptcy. Not everyone believes this, however. Some economists have called into question the validity of the 90% tipping point as an indicator of serious distress.[22] Business journalist Jacob Davidson pointed out in *Time* that there is "an ongoing controversy over whether a particular high debt watermark among advanced economies—such as a 90%-debt-to-GDP ratio—is broadly correlated with slower growth, or whether such thresholds are effectively arbitrary or too general to be of significance." Because "debt is such a partisan issue," Davidson remarks, "the debate has become heated at times." Professor Rogoff himself believes the 90% threshold is a warning sign, not a death sentence, and, referring to a discussion of the controversy published in *The Economist*, Davidson concludes "there may be more common ground than has generally been portrayed."[23]

On balance, and based on the 800 years of history Reinhart and Rogoff have reviewed, it is difficult to dismiss their thesis out of hand. Yet is also true that the United States is not bankrupt, even with indebtedness exceeding 105% of GDP. That it has thus far evaded the fate that has overtaken many nations over nearly a millennium is certainly partly due to America's record of incredible productive capacity and remarkable political and economic stability—at least compared to the rest of the world. Financial analyst, stockbroker, talk radio host, author, and sometime political candidate Peter Schiff puts it this way: "How do we get away with this? Why does anyone lend us money when they know we're only going to pay it back by borrowing, and that we're going to pay it back with dollars that are worth less than they are today?" The answer is our "dollar is considered the 'reserve currency' of the world...all major governments in the world hold dollars."[24] The value of a reserve currency is as a trusted medium of foreign exchange. Foreign countries are willing to take dollars because they know that other foreign countries take dollars. Of course, there is a limit to this universal confidence. If our foreign credit freezes up, we could lose our status as the issuer of the world's reserve currency. Lose that, and (as Schiff phrases it), we lose our ability "to buy things without really paying for them." In short, "the free ride ends."[25]

It is possible that, someday, some other currency will gain ascendency over the dollar as a contender for *the* global reserve currency. In 1969, the International Monetary Fund (IMF), an organization originally founded in 1944 to reconstruct the war-ravaged international payment system, introduced "special drawing rights," or the XDR, as a unit of account intended to serve as a "reserve asset" alternative to a reserve currency (then, as now, the U.S. dollar). The XDR came into being at a time when the United States, operating under a relatively conservative monetary policy, was disinclined to increase the quantity of dollars in existence. This orientation created a fear of an impending shortfall in U.S. dollars, which could well bring about a global liquidity crisis, especially among developing nations.

The value of the XDR is determined every five years by the value of a "basket" of international currencies the IMF considers key. Effective October 1, 2016, the basket consists of the U.S. dollar (44.73%), the Euro (30.93%), the Chinese yuan (10.92%), the Japanese yen (8.33%), and the British pound (8.09%).[26]

Although the IMF itself has recently characterized the practical role of the XDR as "insignificant" and has called it an "imperfect reserve asset," it periodically draws renewed attention whenever the dollar is weak or the global economy is under unusual stress.[27] In 2009 and 2011, in response to the global financial crisis of 2007–2010, the IMF allocated XDRs in an effort to provide added liquidity to in the world's system of exchange. In 2009, Zhou Xiaochuan, governor of the People's Bank of China, issued a provocative paper calling for a reform of the international monetary system that would include an expanded role for the XDR, and in 2011 the IMF published a paper on how the use of the XDR could be increased.[28]

The takeaway is this: Americans have no reason to feel complacent about the status of the U.S. dollar as the world's unassailable reserve currency.

WHY THE NATIONAL DEBT GOT SO BIG

Now that we have looked the national debt in the eye, have asked how it got so big (unsustainable, in fact), have agreed (I hope) that unsustainable debt is a bad thing, have seen who holds U.S. debt and thus who has a hand in the "running" of America, and have identified the tipping point beyond which debt can no longer be piled, it is time to move from the *how* to the *why*.

President Ronald Reagan is praised—and by some condemned—for having answered the *why* decades ago, in his 1981 inaugural address. Government is why. "Government is not the solution to our problem; government is the problem."[29] Government is the reason for the immensity of the national debt.

Many of Reagan's self-proclaimed disciples declare that *all* government is bad, and *big* government is plain awful. End of story. Some of Reagan's critics point to the quotation from the inaugural address as the essence of Reagan's reductionism. It's too simple, too pat. Period. In all fairness, what is most frequently quoted from the speech is not actually what President Reagan said.[30] He began the speech by laying out the situation into which, as president beginning in January 1981, he was walking. It was "one of the worst sustained inflations of our national history." After describing it in admirably sharp detail, he concluded, "In this present crisis, government is not the solution to our problem; government is the problem." That introductory clause is key, because it does not simply define government as *the* problem, but as the problem *"in this present crisis."* The necessary implication is that government does have a role to play—it *is* the solution—sometimes and in some things. Certainly, President Reagan's record in office bears this out. On his watch, this so-called advocate of small government presided over the nation's first national debt measurable in the trillions, personally adding **$1.9 trillion** (186%) to the Carter debt, thereby creating a national debt of **$2.8 trillion**, and raising taxes eleven times during his eight-year administration.

Government is not *the* problem, not always and not in all things. Big government isn't even *the* problem. But *unsustainably* big government is: "Annual income 3.644 trillion dollars, annual expenditure 3.643 trillion dollars, result happiness. Annual income 3.644 trillion dollars, annual expenditure 4.147 trillion dollars, result misery."

What makes big government *unsustainable* big government? I believe there are five causes, five reasons *why* the national debt got so big, unsustainably big.

CAUSE 1: **THE CONUNDRUM OF THE ADMINISTRATIVE STATE.** Mention "government" and what comes to mind for most of us are members of Congress, the president, and so on. But the total number of elected personnel in the federal government is actually relatively small. There are two in the executive branch, the president and vice president (though they come as a pair, so, practically speaking, there is just one). There are 100 in the Senate and 435 in the House, for a total of 535 in the legislative branch. Now, the president appoints and the Senate approves Supreme Court justices, cabinet members, ambassadors, and other officials. But the directly elected government consists of just 537 people. Contrast this with the portion of our government that is neither directly elected nor appointed by directly elected officials. It totals approximately 4,185,000 persons. Subtract from this number uniformed personnel in the armed forces and 606,900 U.S. Postal Service workers, and that (as of May 2016) leaves 2,172,500 civilian federal employees.[31]

So when we speak of democratic government, and mean by it democratically elected government, we are really talking about a government that is democratic only in no greater a ratio than 537 to 2,172,500. Little wonder that some conservatives contrast what they call the "Constitutional State" (the elected government) with the "Administrative State."[32] In recent years, *the Administrative State* has become a kind of buzz phrase, much as "big government" was during the Reagan years. But the phrase actually dates back at least to 1948, when it was used as the title of a book by political scientist Dwight Waldo.[33] In it, Waldo struggled to reconcile what was (and still is) officially called "public administration"—the unelected bureaucracy—with the elected government of a constitutional democracy. In contrast to the position of the far right today, many of whom clamor for dumping the whole bureaucracy, there was little talk in the postwar years of totally dismantling the Administrative State. There was, however, much discussion about getting the administrative bureaucracy to model itself on business administration by unambiguously setting as its goal scientific efficiency. That sounded (and still sounds) like common sense, but Waldo argued that the goal of the government bureaucracy could not be scientific efficiency because the purposes and priorities of government are not those of business. Rather, the purposes, priorities, and powers of government are those enumerated (and also perhaps implied) by the Constitution; therefore, the purposes, priorities, and powers of the unelected officials charged with managing units of the government must honor the Constitution and other democratic imperatives. Doing this may or may not promote or even allow scientific efficiency in a strict business sense.

Dwight Waldo was not arguing for inefficiency in government. But he did identify a still-unresolved tension between the elected and unelected government in our constitutional democracy. To the degree that the Administrative State puts scientific efficiency ahead of the Constitution, it creates an unelected government that is indeed incompatible with democracy. Yet, to the degree that the Administrative State puts the Constitution ahead of efficiency, it may create bureaucratic structures and processes that are inefficient and therefore costly. This inefficiency is a big part of what we will consider in Chapter 6, but, really, the problem of the Administrative State is at the heart of everything in this book and drives the other four causes of our unsustainable national debt.

CAUSE 2: **CAREERISM.** Dwight Waldo came of age during the multiple administrations of Franklin D. Roosevelt and the New Deal, which was the birth of truly big government, government capable of taking a hand in virtually every aspect of American life and business. New Deal government was not just big in size, it was gigantic in its reach and therefore required a massive expansion of the Administrative State. Waldo argued that this unelected bureaucracy endeavored to coexist constitutionally with the elected government—and therefore put the Constitution ahead of scientific efficiency. More recent, mostly conservative, critics of unelected government have argued that, far from conforming to the democratic mandates of the Constitution, chief among which is *limited* government, the Administrative State has effectively "infected" elected government. The members of the unelected government are government employees, who see themselves as engaged in government "careers."

The goals of most employees in any enterprise are first and foremost personal and not necessarily relevant to or always compatible with the goals of the employer. This, critics point out, is at least as true of government bureaucrats as it is of employees in the private sector. (Most critics argue that it is actually far worse in the public sector because a combination of civil service laws and public employee unions protect government workers from losing their jobs. In contrast, in the private sector, employees who consistently put their personal interests ahead of those of the company can be fired.)

The goals of a lifelong civil servant may have little to do with managing a fiscally responsible national government. Indeed, they may even run counter to this objective. As many critics of big government see it, the careerism that drives the bureaucrats of the Administrative State has spread to the elected government, making careerism an increasingly serious structural problem in our government. Legislators have increasingly come to see themselves as pursuing a government career, which has driven most to put their personal career priorities ahead of national priorities. Their prime directive is no longer the creation and maintenance of good government. It is the preservation and development of their career.

Whether among members of the elected or unelected government, careerism is an especially powerful force for suboptimization, an economic phenomenon discussed below in Cause 5. Indeed, the force of careerism is one of the most pervasive and potent causes of our unsustainable national debt.

CAUSE 3: FAILURE TO AGREE ON THE PROPER ROLE AND LIMITS OF GOVERNMENT. The leading theme of Chapter 5, "In Government We Trust," is our national failure to agree, even after 228 years and counting, on what the Constitution intended as the proper, legitimate, and lawful role of government. In two places, the Constitution mentions the topic of "the general Welfare." The Preamble defines the purposes of the Constitution itself as an instrument "to form a more perfect Union, establish Justice, insure domestic Tranquility, provide for the common defence, *promote the general Welfare*, and secure the Blessings of Liberty to ourselves and our Posterity," and Article I, Section 8 gives Congress the power to "*provide for* the common Defence and *general Welfare* of the United States" (italics added). What exactly does this "general Welfare" imperative mean? In creating and implementing the laws and programs of the New Deal in the 1930s, FDR successfully argued for the vast expansion of government in scope, authority, and spending. This interpretation has dominated American politics and policy ever since, and, ever since, it has been one of the leading causes of and rationales for what has now become an unsustainable national debt. Parts I and II consider this issue in detail.

CAUSE 4: FAILURE TO PRIORITIZE NEEDS, WANTS, AND THE SPENDING ON THEM. Thanks most directly and immediately to Causes 2 and 3 (careerism and the dispute over the role of government), the elected government has repeatedly failed to adequately prioritize spending. By the default of inaction, legislators often cede their constitutional authority over the federal purse to members of the unelected government. This failure is less familiar to the public than the instances of careerism (the imperative to achieve reelection quite literally at any cost) that prompt legislators to introduce bills promoting lobbyists and special interests or that provide special projects and funding to their districts and constituents. Chapters 9, 10, and 11 are all about how legislators buy votes through special-interest, pork barrel, and earmark spending.

CAUSE 5: SUBOPTIMIZATION. All four of the causes I've just discussed contribute to what we may call *the suboptimization of America*. The last thing any of us wants is to see our great nation become less than great: suboptimal. But the word *suboptimization* has a special meaning in economics. Suboptimization happens when prioritizing particular benefits—personal, political, or however defined—occurs without taking overall costs into account. That's Economics 101. Let's put it into humbler English. Picture a big old-fashioned department store in which the manager of the housewares department is the advertising manager's son-in-law. Not surprisingly, a disproportionate amount of the store's ad budget always gets allocated to promoting housewares. This creates some nice spikes in sales of pots and pans, but other departments end up turning in consistently flat performances. The undue focus on the success of one department has made the other departments less successful than they could be. To optimize performance in a single department, the performance of the entire store suffers suboptimization.

Big government is a huge organization. In any organization, coordination of departments and functions can be difficult to achieve, even when everyone is fully focused on the good of the entire organization. When elected legislators and unelected bureaucrats focus on their own fiefdoms, bailiwicks, constituents, and careers, determined first and foremost to see these prosper, they tend to direct spending in ways that economists call irrational with respect to the performance of the nation as a whole. For instance, if disproportionate spending on entitlements, even in the name of promoting "the general Welfare," contributes to the unsustainability of the national debt, that spending is irrational in that it causes the suboptimization of America itself. Put another way, spending to promote the general welfare is fundamentally irrational if it ultimately destroys the general welfare by bankrupting the nation.

WHAT'S AHEAD FOR OUR COUNTRY

Mr. Micawber's explanation of debt is simple. Make more than you spend—result, happiness. Spend more than you make—result, misery. These are the immutable rules for personal debt, the rules to which we all are individually subject. But are they the rules for government debt as well? Many economists say no. Nations carry a national debt, they say. It's what they do. It's how they roll.

And it is true that the United States has often carried a debt. It is also true that, since 1985, the United States has been a debtor nation. As *The New York Times* reported on September 16, 1985, "for the first time since World War I," America owed "foreigners more than they owe it."[34] It is also manifestly true that, more than thirty years later, we're still standing.

We will remain standing just as long as those "foreigners" keep buying our debt. There are costs to this situation. We do pay ever-compounding interest on the debt, and debt service is very expensive. But it is a bargain compared to the other cost of being a debtor nation, the cost in sovereignty lost, the need for foreign and even domestic policy to be slyly crafted, year after year, in the knowledge that the United States, like Tennessee Williams's hapless Blanche DuBois, must always depend on the kindness of strangers.

Any banker will tell you that debt becomes unsustainable when you can no longer service it, let alone pay it off. Actually, though, it becomes unsustainable long before it reaches that point. Debt is a killer. Its victim is liberty.

In strictly economic terms, a national debt creates inflation by reducing the pool of credit available to the private sector—businesses and individuals. As credit tightens and interest rates rise, the range of opportunities contracts, both for businesses and individuals. Employers pull in their horns or shut down entirely. Either way, people lose jobs. In broader, geopolitical terms, the range of opportunities for the nation likewise contracts. Indebted to this or that foreign power, the nation is no longer truly sovereign. To the degree that any nation is a debtor nation, it cannot be a land of liberty, sweet or otherwise, for its destiny is no longer its own. As the country becomes economically suboptimal, it also becomes politically suboptimal, in thrall to other nations.

CUI BONO?

If we do not act to reduce and ultimately eliminate the national debt, we will continue along a course of suboptimization. This is not the destination that our nation's founders envisioned or that our children deserve. Yet, year after year, as debt continues to expand and liberty continues to contract, nobody—no president, no legislator, no mob of angry villagers with pitchforks and torches—rises up to seriously confront the problem of debt.

Why not? What stops them? What stops us?

To answer these questions, we need to start by following the money—digging down to the tangled roots of the debt, spending, and taxes that are bankrupting America. And that means asking another question. According to the great Roman orator and politician Cicero (107–43 B.C.), a celebrated judge named Lucius Cassius always weighed the evidence and arguments of a case by asking *Cui bono?*—"Who profits?"[35] Since then, cops, detectives, prosecutors, grand juries, and judges have been starting investigations and judicial proceedings by asking the very same question.

Cui bono?

Opposing "small government" to "big government" is something of a false dichotomy or, at least, the wrong opposition. The objective is not to create a small or a big government, but the government that is the right size for what the people decide they want and need that government to do for them. Abraham Lincoln described the American government as "government of the people, by the people, for the people."[36] A government is too big not when it reaches a certain size, but when it is no longer of, by, and for the people.

Who profits from such a government, a government grown beyond Lincoln's ideal? Here's a short list:

1. *The government itself—in the form of the Administrative State.* A vast bureaucracy of some 2,172,500 full-time civilian federal employees in addition to untold numbers of political and technical consultants—the denizens of the Beltway, which traverses five of the ten wealthiest counties in America.[37] This unelected government not only constitutes a big government, it thrives on it, needs it, desires it, and will do all it can to keep from ever making it any smaller.

2. *The government itself—in the form of our incumbent elected federal officials.* Although they are elected by the people, our president, senators, and representatives do not most immediately serve the people. Most immediately, they serve the entities that furnish them the wherewithal to keep them in office, election cycle after election cycle. In both the unelected and elected governments, "government service"

is only incidentally about service. For those who make their living by it, so-called government service is first and foremost a *career in government.* The bigger that government, the more secure and lucrative the career. Cui bono? The incumbents.

3. *Big corporations and big organizations.* Although they are in the private sector, these entities thrive on big government, which provides the laws, regulations, international connections, and financial aid (tax exemptions, preferences, and tax expenditures, in addition to outright subsidies) that benefit them—typically at the expense of competition from smaller businesses and organizations. Cui bono? The incumbents.

4. *Big media.* It is fashionable these days to bash the "mainstream media"—so fashionable, in fact, that we no longer recognize the substance behind the bashing. And there *is* substance. Big media is, above all else, a big corporate business. What is the market for the media business? Who are its consumers? Are they the audience—"the people"? Well, yes, but this market is second in line. For major media, the most important consumer is the B2B customer; namely, the big corporations and organizations that pay media billions upon billions of advertising dollars. Media is a retail business that is nevertheless driven by its B2B customers, and it will do anything to support its B2B constituents through the entertainment and information products it sells into its retail market. Since big business supports its profit center in big government, big media does, too. True objectivity in news and other programming is not an option in this market. Cui bono? The incumbents.

In serving these four constituents before or even instead of the people, big government creates debt. For there is no other way to serve these constituents other than by producing debt. Each time our legislators fail to do much of anything meaningful to reduce the debt, they blame "partisan gridlock." The Democrats say the Republicans are obstructionists. The Republicans make the same accusation against the Democrats. In truth, both parties are allies within the same big government. In truth, all four constituents of big government—unelected government, elected government, big business, and big media—are allies in sustaining and defending the status quo. When it comes to dealing effectively with the national debt, neither the Democrats nor the Republicans are the enemy. The enemy is the status quo and the inertia it induces in us all.

WHAT'S AHEAD IN THIS BOOK

L iberals and conservatives argue bitterly and fruitlessly about big government versus small government, more government versus less government, more spending versus less spending.

This book also argues. It argues a case against big government—but it defines "big government" less by its size (which is an arbitrary definition) than by such a government's spectacularly wide departure from the Lincoln model: government of, by, and for the people. So defined, the case against big government, perforce, is also the case against inaction on the debt through capitulation to the four big profiteers from that debt. We will make this case in six parts:

PART I, **HOW WE GOT HERE,** is a "living autopsy" of the economically catastrophic growth of the American government, from George Washington's idea of "right-sized" government to the morbid obesity that makes our government sick today and threatens to kill us tomorrow.

PART II, **THE TYRANNY OF GOOD INTENTIONS,** explores the fundamental issue of our federal debt; namely, why and how we ran away from the exquisite model of small government—limited government—that the founders framed in the Constitution, embracing instead a mammoth model of interventional government that habitually bites off more than we the taxpayers can chew.

PART III, **SPENDING TOO MUCH FOR THE COMMON DEFENSE,** explores our addiction to military waste.

PART IV, **SPENDING TOO MUCH AT THE CIVILIAN PORK BARREL,** tucks into pork, which our legislators serve up for breakfast, lunch, *and* dinner in order to buy their reelection votes on the taxpayers' multibillion-dollar dime.

PART V, **WHAT TAXES COST US,** explains how the massive and ever-growing body of the IRS code and federal tax regulations generate the equivalent of covert and highly complex tax preferences to create economic advantages and weave de facto social safety-net programs while also providing middle- and upper-end entitlements and corporate welfare.

PART VI, **SOLUTIONS,** takes us to the tipping point of the national debt crisis and offers ideas on what to do about it. Now.

HOW WE GOT HERE

THE UNINTENDED CONSEQUENCES

OF ELECTED GOVERNMENT

We begin with George Washington as the inventor of the American presidency and what we call the "Father of Right-Sized Government." Unfortunately, the careers of most of the forty-three presidents who came after Washington—especially those generally considered the "greatest" or "most important"—present a wide deviation from the inventor's template of restraint.

Every American president comes into office with the best of intentions. Few, however, do the painful and unpopular work of weighing the costs of those intentions against their benefits. Jackson, Lincoln, and Theodore Roosevelt, each in his way, added to the imperial model of the presidency, creating taxation and spending policies accordingly.

CHAPTER 1

GEORGE WASHINGTON

TO

THEODORE ROOSEVELT

The Aequi were a powerful tribe in the Apennine Mountains of what is today central Italy. In 458 B.C., they closed in on Rome, intent on invading the Republic's capital. A panicked Senate responded by sending special emissaries to retired general L. Quinctius Cincinnatus. When they found the renowned warrior, he was quietly working the fields of his modest farm outside Rome. The emissaries told him the Republic urgently needed him to lead the Legions against the Aequi. He would be given dictatorial powers and absolute authority, they assured him. With that, Cincinnatus abandoned his plow where it stood, bade farewell to his wife, and directly led the Roman Legions to total victory against the would-be invaders. Within two weeks of his accepting the Senate's commission and bestowal of dictatorship, the crisis was ended. Without waiting another day, Cincinnatus summarily resigned his authority, disdained any glory or reward, and returned to his plow, which was exactly where he had left it.

After winning the American Revolution in 1783, George Washington promptly resigned his commission so that he might return to his "farm," the plantation called Mount Vernon. To the classically educated gentlemen of 18th-century America, this made him seem nothing less than the reincarnation of Cincinnatus.

GEORGE WASHINGTON:

THE FATHER OF RIGHT-SIZED GOVERNMENT

GEORGE WASHINGTON (NO PARTY, 1789–1797)
Revenue = $0.54, Spending = $0.057,
Debt = $1.33; Change = $ – / 0%

Six years after Washington retired to Mount Vernon, the Articles of Confederation (under which there was no chief executive) were replaced by the Constitution, and the United States suddenly needed its first president. The founding fathers persuaded Washington to accept the office, and, because there was no opposition, his election was a foregone conclusion. That Washington had not actively sought the presidency was all the proof voters needed of his suitability to it. (John Adams, who did have opponents, won election as vice president in a close vote.)

On April 14, 1789, Charles Thomson, secretary to Congress, called on Washington at Mount Vernon to notify him of his election. Two days later, the president-elect set off for New York, at the time the nation's capital city. In 1998, when President Bill

Clinton went to China, he traveled with "5 Cabinet secretaries, 16 members of Congress, 86 senior aides, 150 civilian staff (doctors, lawyers, secretaries, valets, hairdressers, and so on), 150 military staff (drivers, baggage handlers, snipers, and so on), 150 security personnel, several bomb-sniffing dogs, and many tons of equipment, including 10 armored limousines and the 'blue goose,' Clinton's bulletproof lectern." The visit required 36 U.S. Air Force large cargo aircraft, for a total cost of **$14 million.** Just flying Air Force One clocked in at **$34,000/hour.**[1] Two hundred nine years earlier, Washington traveled to his new job in his own rather plain coach—and he took his sweet time about it, too, stopping at every town and village through which he passed so that he might meet the people—or, more to the point, so that the people might meet him: a man riding, on the people's business, in his own coach, pulled by his own horses.

Washington was the nation's original "conservative" in the sense that he deliberately set an example of thrift and humility for the nation and for the other officers of its government. He was even more keenly aware that, as the very first to hold the office of president, his example would essentially create it—for the Constitution specified very little about the presidency. "I walk on untrodden ground," he remarked early in his first term. "There is scarcely any part of my conduct which may not hereafter be drawn into precedent."[2] The thing was, as of 1789, the year of Washington's first inauguration, the American people had known only kings and royal governors as chief executives. The example Washington set was of a man conducting himself as an *elected* head of state, commanding respect, power, and authority, yet not behaving like a king or, even worse, an emperor.

Washington established an open presidency, but one that was "open" only during specified business hours. Any "respectably dressed" man was welcome to call upon the president between three and four o'clock any weekday afternoon without an appointment. In this way, he mingled freely with the ("respectably dressed") masses but did so on his own timetable. The schedule made the relationship between executive government and the people remarkably straightforward. There were rules and, while strict, they were not onerous. The same straightforward-ness characterized the internal structure of the executive branch as President Washington designed it. The *cabinet* is one of the many things about the presidency that most of us today take for granted. But Washington had to invent it. Article II of the Constitution, which is devoted to the executive branch, says nothing about a cabinet and alludes only to the existence of "executive Departments," specifying that the president was empowered to require "the Opinion, in writing, of the principal Officer in each of the executive Departments, upon any Subject relating to the Duties of their respective Offices." After Washington's first term was already under way, it was Congress, not the president, that created the first three executive departments: State, Treasury, and War. Washington nominated Thomas Jefferson as secretary of state, Alexander Hamilton to head up the Treasury, and, as secretary of war, his own revolutionary comrade-at-arms, the general who had been in charge of the Continental Artillery, Henry Knox. The Senate approved all of the appointments. In addition to this three-department cabinet, Washington took it upon himself to appoint an attorney general, Edmund Randolph of Virginia. As Washington conceived it, however, the office of attorney general was not a cabinet-level department, just a legal advisory position.

The first president clearly intended the small size and struc-tural informality of the executive branch to be one of his bequests to the nation: a government neither arbitrarily small nor arbi-trarily large, but just big enough to enable efficient government—and no bigger. Small though it was, Washington did not intend the executive branch to be inconsequential. He took great pains in selecting his cabinet, each of whom was a man of formidable intellect, good judgment, and high esteem. Although Washington had worked with all of them in the past, none were cronies—and none were yes men. Indeed, they resembled what historian Doris Kearns Goodwin called Abraham Lincoln's cabinet, a "team of rivals." Jefferson and Hamilton, for example, represented oppo-site poles of American political thought at the end of the 18th cen-tury, and their arguments were often heated.

In Washington's day, before the advent of the civil service system, the president was also responsible for making a host of appointments to lesser government offices. (By the 19th century, these numbered in the thousands.) This presented a temptation to distribute administrative plums to friends and anyone else the president wished to put in his debt. Far from doing anything of the kind, however, Washington scrupulously avoided political patronage and generally avoided appointing friends and relations. This, too, was part of the template he created for the executive branch. He made it clear that the criteria by which he judged appointees included their character, standing in the community, and manifest support for the Constitution.

THE PRESIDENT AS "CHIEF MAGISTRATE"

A synonym for the American president, little used today, is "chief magistrate." The phrase neatly sums up Washington's concept of his office. He believed that the president's primary duty was to "faithfully execute" the laws passed by Congress. As Washington saw things, the president had no role in either originating or sponsoring legislation. Washington's example was one of limited executive authority over a limited central government. Perhaps the most dramatic demonstration of these limits was his refusal to serve more than two terms, an aspect of his legacy that endured until Franklin D. Roosevelt, whose first two terms spanned the Great Depression, sought and won an unprecedented third and then fourth term.

THE LEGACY OF WASHINGTON:

WHAT WENT WRONG?

George Washington is properly credited with "inventing" the American presidency. He also invented right-sized government, which meant a government as small as possible without being too small to conduct the business of the nation. Both were great inventions. Washington's template for the presidency has endured, although it has been modified, more or less, by his successors to the office.

His template for "small-enough" government? Not so much. In fact, not at all.

And since big government—wrong-sized government, *unnecessarily* big government, *dysfunctionally* big government—drives the evolution of our unsustainable national debt, we need to know what went wrong during the more than two centuries since Washington left office. Finding out is the purpose of Parts I and II of this book.

"COMMON AND CONTINUAL MISCHIEFS":

THE EMERGENCE OF POLITICAL PARTIES

JOHN ADAMS (FEDERALIST, 1797–1801)
Revenue = $0.61, Spending = $0.58,
Debt = $1.38; Change = $0.05 / 4%

Just as Washington was careful to create an example of structural, bureaucratic, and personal restraint in the office of the president and its associated "departments," he was anxious as well to prevent the presidency from becoming entangled with political parties, which, he believed, introduced harmful factionalism in the administration of government. In his Farewell Address, delivered on September 17, 1796, near the close of his second term, Washington called the "common and continual mischiefs of the spirit of party... sufficient to make it the interest and duty of a wise people to discourage and restrain it. It serves always to distract the Public Councils, and enfeeble the Public Administration. It agitates the Community with ill-founded jealousies and false alarms; kindles the animosity of one part against another, foments occasionally riot and insurrection."[4] Yet despite the president's popularity and prestige, parties not only became a dominant fact of American political life, they made their precocious appearance as early as the beginning of Washington's own second term. His decision not to stand for a third term put the election of 1796 into play, and, by this time, the parties were well established. They divided the nation sharply, even bitterly, between the faction (led by Thomas Jefferson) favoring a *weak* central government (many historians call this the Democratic-Republican Party, but most "members" called themselves Jeffersonians, and most modern political historians use the term "Jeffersonian Republicans"), and the faction (led by John Adams) supporting a *powerful* central government. This was the Federalist Party. With decentralized (Jeffersonian Republican) government versus centralized (Federalist) government at stake, the presidency now became as much a political prize as it was a national office.

Today's Americans would find a lot to recognize in the campaigns of 1796. They were ugly and supremely negative. The Federalists did not tout the virtues of John Adams nearly as much as they attempted to smear Thomas Jefferson as an atheist determined to destroy religion in the United States, a radical democrat who embraced the French Revolution (1789), and a reckless man who wanted to install government by mobocracy. For their part, the Jeffersonian Republicans condemned Adams as a "monarchist" who would likely sell out the United States to the British Empire. Come election day, Adams won by the narrowest of margins, winning 71 electoral votes to Jefferson's 68; that is, nine states supported Adams, while seven favored Jefferson. This split was regional, with New England and the Middle Atlantic states (save Pennsylvania) favoring Adams, and the South and West siding with Jefferson. Thus, Adams came into office without the full support of the country.

And it got even worse. Per the Constitution as it existed prior to ratification of the Twelfth Amendment in 1804, the electoral front-runner won the presidency, and the closest runner-up automatically became vice president. So a partisan President Adams was stuck with his partisan opponent as vice president, and his four years in office were turbulent and contentious. When, in 1798, it looked as if war might erupt between the United States and its erstwhile revolutionary ally France, Adams signed into law three pieces of legislation passed by the Federalist-controlled Congress: the Alien and Sedition Acts, which included the Naturalization Act (June 18, 1798), raising the residence prerequisite for citizenship from five to fourteen years' residence in the United States; the Alien Act (June 25, 1798), authorizing the president summarily to deport, without trial or hearing, all aliens he regarded as dangerous; and the Alien Enemies Act (July 6, 1798), authorizing the president, in time of war, to arrest, imprison, or deport subjects of any enemy power, again without resort to trial or hearing.

The Jeffersonian Republicans raised vehement objections to what they regarded as an unconstitutional power grab. The Naturalization Act, they said, was clearly partisan. Many of the supporters of the Jeffersonian Republican Party were recent immigrants; increasing the residency requirement excluded them from voting as well as from running for office, thereby reducing the constituency of the Federalists' rival party. The Alien Act and the Alien Enemies Act, the Jeffersonian Republicans claimed, gave the president unconstitutional authority by abridging the right to due process of law. But the Sedition Act (July 14, 1798), they asserted, was the most outrageous of all. Its prohibition of assembly "with intent to oppose any measure of the government" and of printing, uttering, or publishing anything "false, scandalous, and malicious" against the government were blatant violations of the Bill of Rights. Adams countered, lamely enough, by arguing that the president needed the authority to protect the nation against sedition and other threats and that the people would simply have to trust that the character and integrity of the occupant of the White House would be sufficient to restrain him from abusing the powers granted. Once again, Vice President Jefferson worked behind the scenes to undermine his president. He and James Madison took it upon themselves to covertly draft resolutions on behalf of the states of Virginia (Madison in 1798) and Kentucky (Jefferson in 1799) opposing the Alien and Sedition Acts as unconstitutional. Thanks to these, the unpopularity of the Alien and Sedition Acts became almost universal, John Adams lost popular support, and, in 1800, he became both the first victim of American partisan politics and the nation's first one-term president, losing his bid for reelection to Thomas Jefferson in 1800.

JEFFERSONIAN AMERICA

THOMAS JEFFERSON
(JEFFERSONIAN REPUBLICAN, 1801–1809)
Revenue = $2.00, Spending = $1.30,
Debt = $1.02; Change = $(0.36) / –26%

Adams offered the Federalist past and present, in which the government was dominated by the chief executive functioning as head of state, and in which governing power was concentrated at the national, rather than the state and popular, level. Federalist government was certainly representative government, but the elected leaders did not so much represent the perceived *will* of the people as they did the *best interests* of the people. And it was the leaders—president, senators, and representatives—who determined what those "best interests" were. Jefferson offered the Jeffersonian Republican future, in which the power of the central government, including that of the chief executive, was subordinated to the governing authority of the states and the people themselves. The Jeffersonian Republican emphasis on popular democracy constituted a kind of second American Revolution.

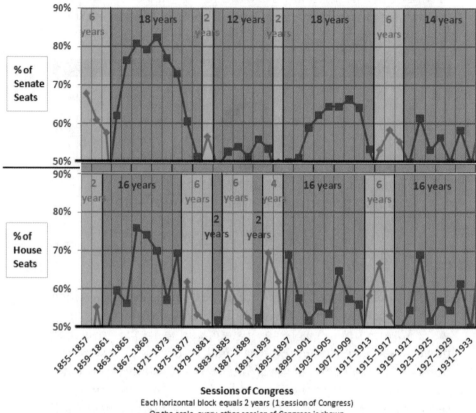

PARTY CONTROL OF THE U.S SENATE

AND HOUSE OF REPRESENTATIVES

Sessions of Congress

Each horizontal block equals 2 years (1 session of Congress)
On the scale, every other session of Congress is shown
(i.e.- 2009-2011, is all of 2009 & 2010, newly elected take office in January 2011; i.e.- 2007 is election year 2006)

Credit: Wikimedia Commons[5]

NOTE: From January 3 to January 20, 2001, with the Senate divided evenly between the two parties, the Democrats held the majority due to the deciding vote of outgoing Democratic Vice President Al Gore. Senator Thomas A. Daschle served as majority leader at that time. Beginning on January 20, 2001, Republican Vice President Richard Cheney held the deciding vote, giving the majority to the Republicans. Senator Trent Lott resumed his position as majority leader on that date. On May 24, 2001, Senator James Jeffords of Vermont announced his switch from Republican to Independent status, effective June 6, 2001. Jeffords announced that he would caucus

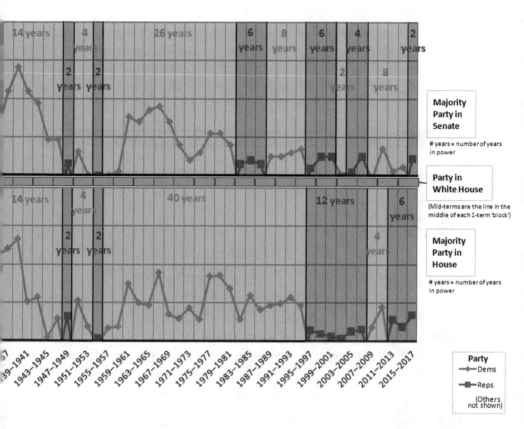

with the Democrats, giving the Democrats a one-seat advantage, changing control of the Senate from the Republicans back to the Democrats. Senator Thomas A. Daschle again became majority leader on June 6, 2001. Senator Paul D. Wellstone (D-MN) died on October 25, 2002, and Independent Dean Barkley was appointed to fill the vacancy. The November 5, 2002 election brought to office elected Senator James Talent (R-MO), replacing appointed Senator Jean Carnahan (D-MO), shifting balance once again to the Republicans—but no reorganization was completed at that time since the Senate was out of session.

And yet Jefferson also built into the political party a new intermediate layer of power between the people and "their" government. Jefferson was the first American president who also actively served as leader of his political party. This gave him, in effect, two constituencies: the people of the United States and the members of his party. Potentially, therefore, his leadership loyalties were divided between the good of the party and the good of the nation. Thus, the election of Jefferson represented both a revolutionary choice for more democratic and less republican government, yet it had the unintended consequence of elevating partisan politics to a powerful and enduring role in American government.

JACKSONIAN GOVERNMENT

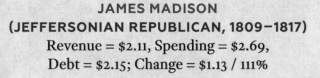

JAMES MADISON
(JEFFERSONIAN REPUBLICAN, 1809–1817)
Revenue = $2.11, Spending = $2.69,
Debt = $2.15; Change = $1.13 / 111%

JAMES MONROE
(JEFFERSONIAN REPUBLICAN, 1817–1825)
Revenue = $3.84, Spending = $3.36,
Debt = $2.24; Change = $(0.09) / 4%

JOHN QUINCY ADAMS
(JEFFERSONIAN REPUBLICAN, 1825–1829)
Revenue = $2.35, Spending = $1.67,
Debt = $1.59; Change = $(0.65) / –29%

ANDREW JACKSON (D, 1829–1837)
Revenue = $6.37, Spending = $4.03,
Debt = $0.00; Change = $(1.59) / –100%

T he three presidents who successively followed Jefferson—James Madison (1809–1817), James Monroe (1817–1825), and John Quincy Adams (John Adams's son, 1825–1829)—were all Jeffersonian Republicans. J. Q. Adams, however, was part of a splinter faction of that party, which was called the National Republican Party (or, sometimes, the Anti-Jacksonian Party) and which veered back toward the old Federalist idea of a strong central government. J. Q. Adams was opposed for reelection by Andrew Jackson, the first of what in today's politics are called "outsider candidates." Jackson rose from a humble log cabin birth in 1767 on the border of North and South Carolina, a frontier region remote from the long-settled eastern seaboard, the traditional center of power and wealth. Whereas Adams, father and son, as well as Jefferson, Madison, and Monroe had all served in the executive branch before becoming president, Jackson, who was briefly a representative, senator, and military governor of Tennessee, was far more famous as the daring and victorious general in the Battle of New Orleans during the War of 1812 and as an Indian fighter in the Creek War and the First Seminole War. He was a *popular* hero.

In the break-up of the Jeffersonian Republican Party, Jackson went with the faction today called the Democratic Party, and his election over the incumbent quasi-Federalist John Quincy Adams—like his father, doomed to be a one-termer—was a clear vote for popular democracy over republicanism. Even more than Jefferson, Jackson sought to limit the size and role of the federal government in the belief that this would spread opportunity to the expanding frontier. He put his foot down on the issue of federal funding of internal improvements (roads and canals), insisting that such matters were for states to decide and to finance. Although he had been a general, he reduced federal military spending, putting greater reliance on state militias. Partisans portrayed Jackson as the "people's tribune," thereby comparing him to the official elected by the Roman plebeians to protect their rights against abuse by the aristocratic magistrates. Not only did President Jackson feel obliged to defend the rights of the people against the other two branches of government, legislative and judicial, he laid claim to a relationship with the people that was even more direct than that of the representatives and senators in Congress.

Paradoxically, by diminishing the legislature while magnifying the executive branch, Jackson proposed to decentralize governing power. His boldest step in this direction was his dismantling of the nation's central bank. Since a central bank, in the form of the U.S. Federal Reserve, is key to modern American government and its fiscal policies, understanding Jackson's war against the Second Bank of the United States is a good place to begin the effort to follow the money that runs through our government today.

Secretary of the Treasury Alexander Hamilton championed the creation of the First Bank of the United States in 1791 as a means of stabilizing and improving the credit of the fledgling nation. In 1795, after Hamilton left office, his successor, Oliver Wolcott, informed Congress that the government needed to raise more money. To do so, he said, Congress could either raise taxes or sell the government's shares of stock in the bank.

Guess which alternative Congress chose?

The shares were duly sold and the bank dismantled. In 1816, under President Madison, a Second Bank of the United States was chartered for twenty years. In 1832, four years before the charter was set to expire, Representatives Henry Clay and Daniel Webster led their fellow National Republicans (now renamed the Whig Party) in passing a bill to recharter the Second Bank. Clay and Webster expected Jackson to veto the bill, and in fact they hoped he would, because they believed it would cost him votes in the upcoming election in which Clay would be the likely Whig candidate for president. Jackson did have constitutional objections to the bank, but mainly he believed that its tight credit policies deprived the "western" frontier—his power base— of much-needed funding for expansion and settlement there. He wanted to distribute the government's assets into various private banks. Not only did he veto the bill, he used the veto to marshal his anti-bank constituents to support him for reelection. They did, Congress could not muster the votes to override the veto, and Jackson finished off the Second Bank of the United States once and for all by withdrawing the government's deposits from it and redistributing them. In 1828, he was elected to a second term.

FROM PARTISANSHIP TO CAREERISM

Jackson's dismantlement of the Second Bank made him a hero among those opposed to strong central government. Yet, at the same time, he used his veto to assert his personal and presidential supremacy over Congress, for which his critics mocked him as "King Andrew." They had a point. Jackson took a radically new approach to the exercise of the presidential power of appointment throughout government. All of the presidents before him strove to create continuity in the non-elected federal bureaucracy by making appointments on a party-neutral basis and generally carrying the previous president's appointments into their own administrations, regardless of party. Jackson decided to use appointments to reward party loyalty and enforce party discipline. In 1829, the first year of his first term, he fired thousands of federal employees who had been appointed by Federalists and made no secret of his political motives for doing so. He then replaced them with loyal Democrats. Senator William L. Marcy (D-NY), famously (or infamously) observed that his party found "nothing wrong in the rule that to the *victor* belongs the spoils of the *enemy.*"[6] From that moment on, Jackson's presidential patronage system was known as the *spoils system*, and it transformed public *service* in government into a lucrative *career* in government. A crusader against the central authority advocated by the Federalists, Jackson nevertheless planted the seeds of big government and the culture of partisanship and careerism that go along with it.

THE NONENTITIES

MARTIN VAN BUREN (D, 1837–1841)
Revenue = $2.47, Spending = $2.91,
Debt = $0.08; Change = $0.08 / 100%

**WILLIAM HENRY HARRISON/JOHN TYLER
(WHIG, 1841–1845)**
Revenue = $2.07, Spending = $2.32,
Debt = $0.55; Change = $0.47 / 588%

JAMES K. POLK (D, 1845–1849)
Revenue = $2.98, Spending = $3.60,
Debt = $0.98; Change = $0.43 / 78%

ZACHARY TAYLOR (WHIG, 1849–1850)
Revenue = $0.76, Spending = $1.05,
Debt = $1.33; Change = $0.35 / 36%

MILLARD FILLMORE (WHIG, 1850–1853)
Revenue = $3.43, Spending = $3.16,
Debt = $1.39; Change = $0.06 / 5%

FRANKLIN PIERCE (D, 1853–1857)
Revenue = $5.90, Spending = $5.35,
Debt = $0.62; Change = $(0.77) / –55%

JAMES BUCHANAN (D, 1857–1861)
Revenue = $5.05, Spending = $6.49,
Debt = $1.31; Change = $0.69 / 111%

It is no accident that the presidents between Jackson and
Lincoln—Martin Van Buren (1837–1841), William Henry
Harrison (1841), John Tyler (1841–1845), James K. Polk

(1845–1849), Zachary Taylor (1849–1850), Millard Fillmore (1850–1853), Franklin Pierce (1853–1857), and James Buchanan (1857–1861)—seem rather small in comparison to those two giants. In his classic *Democracy in America* (1835–1840), French political thinker Alexis de Tocqueville wrote that Jackson had increased his own power, so that "in his hands the Federal Government is strong," but he predicted that it "will pass enfeebled into the hands of his successor."[7] Modify this so that it reads "to *many of* his successor*s*," and you have an accurate statement about the history of the presidency. The chief executives after Jackson and before Lincoln were what Harry S. Truman, in an essay unpublished during his lifetime, classified as "nonentity presidents."[8] Without offending *too* many people, we could also probably add to the list of nonentities those presidents who came after Lincoln and before Theodore Roosevelt: Andrew Johnson (1865–1869), Ulysses S. Grant (1869–1877), Rutherford B. Hayes (1877–1881), James A. Garfield (1881), Chester A. Arthur (1881–1885), Grover Cleveland (1885–1889), Benjamin Harrison (1889–1893), Cleveland—again (1893–1897)—and William McKinley (1897–1901).

Nobody, of course, would call George Washington a nonentity, yet he regarded the president's primary role as doing no more or less than faithfully executing the laws Congress enacted. Many conservatives today would approve. Indeed, in their iconoclastic *The New Empire of Debt: The Rise and Fall of an Epic Financial Bubble,* Addison Wiggin and William Bonner go so far as to call any American "president who does nothing a treasure." They single out William Henry Harrison as "a model national leader.... The poor man caught pneumonia giving his inaugural address. He was dead within 31 days of taking the oath of office."[9] But the fact is that most recent presidents have wanted to make their mark on the nation and on history. In this, they all have had the best intentions, yet, somehow, those intentions ended up leaving government bigger and costlier than it had been before each took office.

ABRAHAM LINCOLN

ABRAHAM LINCOLN (R, 1861–1865)
Revenue = $6.99, Spending = $30.48,
Debt = $21.02; Change = $19.71 / 1505%

Elected during of the greatest existential crisis the "United" States ever faced, Abraham Lincoln pushed the envelope of both the presidency and the federal government. On March 4, 1861, Lincoln was inaugurated president of a broken country in the throes of secession. In his inaugural address, he disclaimed any "purpose, directly or indirectly, to interfere with the institution of slavery in the States where it exists. I believe I have no lawful right to do so, and I have no inclination to do so." Thus he opened his presidency by affirming his primary duty as faithfully executing the laws of the United States, not creating new ones. "One section of our country believes slavery is right and ought to be extended, while the other believes it is wrong and ought not to be extended. This is the only substantial dispute," Lincoln explained. The South claimed that only secession could resolve the issue, but Lincoln argued that the people had not asked him to "fix terms for the separation of the States"; therefore, his only constitutional "duty [was] to administer the present Government as it came to his hands and to transmit it unimpaired by him to his successor." The people, not the president, must use the government to resolve their differences. The president's only role was to defend the Constitution and preserve the Union so that the people's justice could prevail.

Southerners, it turned out, did not believe that presidential power was as limited as Lincoln claimed it to be. They were certain that Lincoln would resort to force to end slavery, so they acted with preemptive force on April 12, 1861, by firing upon Fort Sumter in Charleston Bay. Thus, the Civil War began, and it did so when Congress was in recess. Lincoln chose not to call Congress into special session until July 4, 1861. This meant that he exercised executive authority, unchecked by legislative branch, from April 12 to July 4. He imposed a naval blockade on the South and expanded both the army and the navy. When rioters in Baltimore, the largest city in the border state of Maryland, threatened to block military reinforcements from passing into Washington to defend the capital, Lincoln suspended habeas corpus in regions still under federal control. This gave a whole range of civilian and military officials the authority to make arrests at will, not only without warrant but even without specific charge. (On March 3, 1863, Lincoln signed into law "An Act relating to Habeas Corpus, and regulating Judicial Proceedings in Certain Cases," by which Congress approved presidential authority to suspend habeas corpus.) Many northerners backed the president's actions, but others accused him of transforming the presidency into a military dictatorship. "If I wanted to paint a despot, a man perfectly regardless of every constitutional right of the people," Senator Willard Saulsbury (D-Delaware) proclaimed, "I would paint the hideous, apelike form of Abraham Lincoln."[10]

Other presidents before Lincoln had presided over wars, but the Civil War was the largest military conflict in the Western world since the end of the Napoleonic Wars in 1815 and prior to the outbreak of World War I in 1914. It was a war of large armies and industrial weapons—mass-produced muskets, innovative artillery, and the new iron and ironclad class of warships, as well as the military application of railroads and the telegraph. The men and the machines cost a great deal of money, and this war created unprecedented linkages between the government and business.

A hundred years after the Civil War began, President Dwight D. Eisenhower, in his televised farewell address of January 17, 1961, memorably warned his fellow citizens against the emerging "military-industrial complex." In fact, the original draft of the speech had called it the "congressional-military-industrial complex," but Eisenhower decided against possibly offending Congress and edited the speech accordingly.[11] It is the phrase "congressional-military-industrial complex" that most accurately describes what came into being under President Lincoln during the Civil War. It was the first true manifestation of *statism* in America, a situation in which the state assumes substantial control of a nation's commerce, industry, and economy. In "The High Cost of War," economic and business historian John Steele Gordon notes that during the 1850s, the federal government spent about $1 million per week. Early in the Civil War, by mid-1861, federal spending was **$1.5 million *per day*,** rising to **$3.5 million per day** by the time Lee surrendered at Appomattox Court House on April 9, 1865.[12] In January 1862, Congress authorized the president to seize control of the nation's railroads and telegraph lines, and the U.S. Military Railroad (USMRR) was created.[13] In the emergency that was the Civil War, seizing the railroads, telegraph system, and the economy itself may well have been appropriate. The problem is that the statist precedent outlasted the war, in varying degrees. Statism was a central feature of big government, and both statism and big government, created during the Civil War, never quite went away.

To finance the war, Lincoln successfully urged Congress not only to raise taxes, but to find new sources of taxation. First, import tariffs—long kept low by southern politicians—were raised, both to produce revenue and to protect northern industry. Second, the government laid taxes on items hitherto untaxed or lightly taxed, including legal documents, the gross receipts of businesses, and liquor. The most radical innovation was a graduated income tax, initiated in August 1861. A 3% tax was levied on annual incomes over $800, but the act was soon repealed and replaced in 1862 with a 3% tax on incomes between $600 and $10,000. Higher incomes were taxed at 5%, and in 1864 the law was amended to raise the rate to 5% on incomes between $600 and $5,000, 7.5% on incomes in the $5,000 to $10,000 range, and 10% on everything higher. The law was declared unconstitutional and repealed in 1872, but the seeds of a federal income tax were well planted.

The North derived 21% of its wartime revenue from taxes, whereas the South managed no more than 6%. But, both for the Union and the Confederacy, the far more important means of financing the war was by the sale of bonds. Selling government debt began in earnest another policy that would outlast the Civil War emergency: deficit spending. Using bonds, some two-thirds of the cost of the Civil War was pushed into the future. The result was the growth of the national debt from $**$1.31 billion** in 1861 to **$21.02 billion** in 1866 (adjusted for inflation to 2009 dollars). Whether in the 1860s or the 21st century, deficit spending ensures a future defined by debt.

Another expedient destined to spawn a counterpart in the latter third of the 20th century and thereafter was the printing of "greenbacks," fiat money that was legal tender but neither backed by gold nor convertible to gold. (The government itself did not accept it as a vehicle for paying taxes!) The Union printed $450 million in greenbacks, which touched off a wartime inflation of about 180% in the North. The Confederacy printed money to cover far more of its expenses—some 50%—creating a 700% inflation rate during the first two years of the war and a 9,000% rate by the end of it.

Financing the Civil War redefined the scale of government and spending, laid the basis for statism in America, created the precedent of deficit finance, and divorced currency from gold. These are defining features of our present national economic reality: *our* "normal." In the 1860s, however, all these things were considered *abnormal*, aberrant evils made necessary by a dire crisis that had broken the nation. "To do a great right, do a little wrong," Bassanio pleads in Shakespeare's *Merchant of Venice,* and so it seemed to many during the Civil War. Saving the nation required committing certain "wrongs"—extraordinary, outlandish shifts in economic policy—to "do a great right," namely defeat the Confederacy and restore the Union. What no one foresaw was that the end of the war would not erase the precedents that had been set.

AFTER LINCOLN

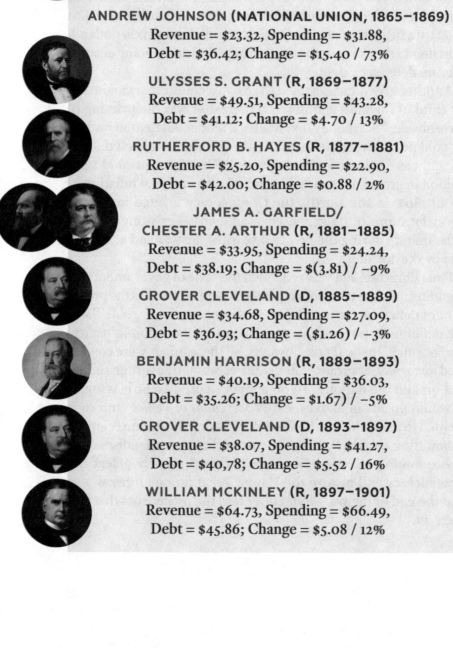

ANDREW JOHNSON (NATIONAL UNION, 1865–1869)
Revenue = $23.32, Spending = $31.88,
Debt = $36.42; Change = $15.40 / 73%

ULYSSES S. GRANT (R, 1869–1877)
Revenue = $49.51, Spending = $43.28,
Debt = $41.12; Change = $4.70 / 13%

RUTHERFORD B. HAYES (R, 1877–1881)
Revenue = $25.20, Spending = $22.90,
Debt = $42.00; Change = $0.88 / 2%

JAMES A. GARFIELD/
CHESTER A. ARTHUR (R, 1881–1885)
Revenue = $33.95, Spending = $24.24,
Debt = $38.19; Change = $(3.81) / –9%

GROVER CLEVELAND (D, 1885–1889)
Revenue = $34.68, Spending = $27.09,
Debt = $36.93; Change = ($1.26) / –3%

BENJAMIN HARRISON (R, 1889–1893)
Revenue = $40.19, Spending = $36.03,
Debt = $35.26; Change = $1.67) / –5%

GROVER CLEVELAND (D, 1893–1897)
Revenue = $38.07, Spending = $41.27,
Debt = $40,78; Change = $5.52 / 16%

WILLIAM MCKINLEY (R, 1897–1901)
Revenue = $64.73, Spending = $66.49,
Debt = $45.86; Change = $5.08 / 12%

Congress authorized most of the steps Lincoln took to conduct and finance the war, but he also made unprecedented use of executive orders. Before Lincoln, presidents issued executive orders almost exclusively to particular *executive* departments or *executive* officers. On rare occasions, they also issued various ceremonial proclamations, as when Lincoln himself issued his "Proclamation of Thanksgiving" (October 3, 1863), which set the precedent for our Thanksgiving holiday.[14] But on September 23, 1862, Lincoln used the proclamation format to execute one of the most important acts in American history, emancipating slaves on the legal theory they were a form of wartime contraband property and thus lawfully subject to confiscation. This was intended to circumvent Constitutional protections of slaves as property.

President Lincoln issued forty-eight executive orders, more than any of his predecessors. Except for Andrew Johnson (who issued seventy-nine), the presidents who came after Lincoln during the remainder of the 19th century did not seize upon the use of executive orders as a means of getting around Congress and the Constitution. But the second president of the 20th century, Theodore Roosevelt, did use them in this way—and with a vengeance, issuing no fewer than 1,081. Some historians have called T R's presidency the first "imperial presidency," a term that came to characterize the office itself in the modern era.

THEODORE ROOSEVELT

THEODORE ROOSEVELT (R, 1901–1909)
Revenue = $93.17, Spending = $87.63,
Debt = $45.94; Change=$0.8 / 0%

Although Theodore Roosevelt was thrust into the White House on September 14, 1901, by the assassination of William McKinley, under whom he served as vice president, he assumed office, unlike Lincoln, during a time of prosperity and peace. As a "progressive" Republican, Roosevelt believed that big business was the great engine of the American economy, but he disdained the traditional Republican policy of uncritical support for business at the expense of labor and consumers. He believed in a modified form of capitalism, in which the free market was reined in by what he considered and sometimes called *government stewardship*, but what moderns call *government regulation.*

In Roosevelt's progressivism may be found the origin not only of regulatory government, but of interventionist government, a form of statism in which the government attempts not only to oversee the relationship among business, labor, and consumers, but also intervenes in the economy with the purpose of "smoothing out" the peaks and troughs of boom-and-bust free-market capitalism. Andrew Jackson was no statist, but TR invoked his spirit, reviving the idea of the president as the "people's tribune" or, more specifically, as their "steward." TR believed that Congress had failed in this stewardship role because too many of its members had sold themselves to special interests—almost all related to big business—whose needs and wants they put before those of the people who elected them. Under Theodore Roosevelt—and often by means of executive orders—American government combined regulation and intervention to oppose control of government by powerful special interests.

Roosevelt regarded Jackson less as a populist democrat than as a strong chief executive. He therefore combined the Jacksonian model with that of the defunct party to which Jackson was most opposed: the Federalists. Whereas the Tenth Amendment specified that the "powers not delegated to the United States by the Constitution, nor prohibited by it to the States, are reserved to the States respectively, or to the people," TR emulated Alexander Hamilton's Arch-Federalist position, which was that the president could lawfully claim all governing authority not otherwise specifically barred by the Constitution. Yet TR saw his greatest authority as what might be called the molder in chief of public opinion. For him, the presidency itself served as what he called a "bully pulpit"—the adjective *bully* roughly meaning "damn good."

TR was the first president to package all of his domestic policies under a single compelling label, the Square Deal, a set of legislative initiatives and presidential policy directives intended to curb the abuses of big business while simultaneously shielding big business from the demands of what he called the radical fringe of labor. The Square Deal provided a precedent Woodrow Wilson would follow in his "New Freedom," Franklin D. Roosevelt in his "New Deal," Harry S. Truman in the "Fair Deal," John F. Kennedy with the "New Frontier," and Lyndon Johnson with what he called the "Great Society." All were huge packages containing big government.

As TR took government into business, he also took it into labor and was the first president to articulate a set of the legal rights of labor, thereby creating an enduring precedent for the involvement of the chief executive in labor disputes and other industrial issues. His interest in labor extended to government workers, and civil service reform played a major role in his progressive program. He built on the existing Civil Service Commission to firmly establish a merit-based system of federal appointments that significantly reduced political patronage on the federal level. This also had, however, the unintended consequence of increasing the autonomy and power of the nation's unelected "Administrative State."

Theodore Roosevelt introduced government regulation not only in business, labor, and among the unelected personnel of government, but he also brought government into the regulation of public lands and the natural environment. Not only did he preach "conservation" (what we would today call environmentalism) from his bully pulpit, he promoted an unprecedented program of conservation legislation, including laws that set aside some 43 million acres of national forest to be protected either entirely or in part from commercial exploitation. TR's environmental agenda ultimately collided with congressional representation of farmers and industrialists (who needed water power and other resources), prompting Congress to enact legislation in 1908 transferring from the president to Congress the authority to create future national forests in certain western states. Undaunted, the president circumvented Congress by using executive orders to implement many of his conservation initiatives.

As sweeping as Roosevelt's domestic agenda was, the enduring effects of his global agenda may be even more profound. He believed that the 1898 Spanish-American War, in which he had achieved fame leading the volunteer "Rough Riders" in a victorious charge up San Juan Hill, had permanently elevated the United States to the status of world power. In his first annual address to Congress on December 3, 1901, he declared that the United States now had "international duties no less than international rights." Convinced that the nation should lead construction of the Panama Canal, he persuaded Congress to ratify the Hay-Herrán Treaty with Colombia (which at the time included Panama), granting the United States the right to build a canal through a 10-mile-wide strip of land across the Isthmus of Panama in return for a $10 million cash payment and an annuity. When the Colombian senate held out for more money, Roosevelt actively incited a revolution by which Panama became an independent republic. Ninety minutes after the new nation declared its independence, Roosevelt proclaimed U.S. recognition of it and, shortly afterward, the new Panamanian government duly approved a canal treaty.

In 1823, President James Monroe put the nations of Europe on notice that the United States would tolerate no interference from the Old World in the affairs of the New. In 1904, in the "Roosevelt Corollary to the Monroe Doctrine," TR asserted the right of the United States to intervene in the affairs of Latin American states that failed to pay their debts to European lenders. He spoke of U.S. exercise of "an international police power" to keep errant Latin American nations in line. Under TR, the United States became what it had never been before, an imperialist power, and, ever since his administration, presidents who have dared to retreat from this stance have been derided as "isolationists."

LINCOLN AND ROOSEVELT:

UNINTENDED CONSEQUENCES

N either Abraham Lincoln nor Theodore Roosevelt embarked upon the presidency with sinister intentions, yet their activism had unintended consequences for the institution of the American presidency and government. In financing the war, Lincoln persuaded Congress to approve bond issues that multiplied the federal debt and inaugurated what would become an American addiction to deficit spending. The most radical of Lincoln's new taxes was levied on income. Found to be unconstitutional after the war, this income tax nevertheless inspired Woodrow Wilson to push for and obtain the income tax system authorized by the Sixteenth Amendment (ratified in 1913). Over the years, many have objected to federal taxation of incomes and have called for the repeal of the Sixteenth Amendment. Some see its graduated structure, with percentage taxed pegged to income level, as a fundamentally undemocratic wealth redistribution scheme. Even those who support taxation of income decry the byzantine complexity of the tax code, susceptible to all manner of manipulation by taxpayers and the unelected body of the IRS as well.

Even those who deplore the unintended consequences of Lincoln's executive innovations are inclined to excuse him for taking extreme measures in a time of utmost extremity. In the case of Theodore Roosevelt, however, aggrandizement of executive authority seems more an act of pure will. The reforms to political patronage and the civil service system were popular and, given the level of partisan corruption as well as the disadvantages of discontinuity in the staff of the federal bureaucracy, they were warranted. Yet they contained the seeds of today's runaway Administrative State.

The injustices of the era of the "robber barons," the exploitation of labor, the dangers certain food products and patent medicines posed to consumers, and the reckless exploitation of public lands and natural resources were very real in America's so-called Gilded

Age (roughly 1870s–1900). President Roosevelt gave government a role in regulating various aspects of business and the financial industry. The 26th president meant to curb the corrupting force of political patronage and to protect workers, consumers, and the natural legacy of the United States. He did not mean to create, in the process, a careerist monster and a class of unelected functionaries with often enormous regulatory powers that have the force of law without the checks and balances of the legislative process. Yet this is what came to birth in the age of Theodore Roosevelt. Today, the unelected government of the Administrative State consists of some 2,172,500 civilian federal employees, many of them engaged in regulating business, commerce, and other activities of the private sector. The Competitive Enterprise Institute (CEI), a libertarian think tank, annually publishes *Ten Thousand Commandments*, a survey of the size, scope, and cost of federal regulations. The 2015 edition notes that federal regulation and intervention cost American consumers and businesses an estimated **$1.9 trillion** in 2014 in lost economic productivity and higher prices, not to mention the administrative costs of regulation and enforcement. I will more fully address the impact of regulation on the national debt in Chapter 6, but consider here this additional CEI data about the current (figures for 2014) cost of regulation:

- If U.S. federal regulation were a country, it would be the world's tenth largest economy, ranking behind Russia and ahead of India.
- Economy-wide regulatory costs amount to an average of **$14,976** per household—around 29% of an average family budget of $51,100. (Although not paid directly by individuals, this "cost" of regulation exceeds the amount an average family spends on health care, food, and transportation.)
- The "Unconstitutionality Index" is the ratio of regulations issued by unelected agency officials compared to legislation enacted by Congress in a given year. In 2014, agencies issued 16 new regulations for every law—that's 3,554 new regulations compared to 224 new laws.

- Many Americans complain about taxes, but regulatory compliance costs exceeded in 2013—by more than **$160 billion**—what the IRS collected in both individual and corporate income taxes for that year.
- Some sixty federal departments, agencies and commissions have 3,415 regulations in development at various stages. The top six federal rule-making agencies account for 48% of all federal regulations. These are the departments of the Treasury, Commerce, Interior, Health and Human Services, and Transportation and the Environmental Protection Agency.
- The 2014 Federal Register (the official journal containing government agency rules, proposed rules, and public notices) contains 77,687 pages, the sixth highest page count in its history. Among the six all-time-high Federal Register total page counts, five occurred under President Obama.
- The George W. Bush administration averaged sixty-two major regulations annually over eight years, while the Obama administration has averaged eighty-one major regulations annually over six years.[15]

By no means does every source agree with the CEI's data. *The New York Times* and *The Washington Post* dispute the **$1.9 trillion** figure, and the Office of Management and Budget (OMB), which serves the executive branch, shows a net benefit of the regulatory regime in 2014.[16] Nevertheless, both the CEI and OMB data reflect a metastasis of the Administrative State that Theodore Roosevelt never contemplated when, with the best of intentions, he put the federal government into the regulation business. Nor did he intend to weaken America, burden it with ultimately unsustainable debt, and sacrifice many thousands of American men and women on distant battlefields when he announced to Congress on December 3, 1901, that the United States had "international duties no less than international rights." His expansionist global view set the United States on a course of becoming a world power, the builder of an empire, and self-appointed policeman to the world. We have been living with the unintended effects of this internationalism ever since.

The sequence of intensifying statism from Jackson through Lincoln and Theodore Roosevelt reached its apotheosis in the New Deal administration of Franklin D. Roosevelt, which permanently transformed the American government into a mechanism of wealth transfer.

CHAPTER 2

WOODROW WILSON

TO

FRANKLIN DELANO

ROOSEVELT

William McKinley had served less than seven months of his second term when he was fatally wounded, which meant that Theodore Roosevelt served more than three-quarters of McKinley's unfinished presidency before being elected in his own right in 1904. For all the charges of imperial ambition rivals leveled against him, TR declined even the appearance of breaking the two-term tradition of George Washington. He chose not to run for a second elected term, but he did handpick a successor, William Howard Taft, whom TR believed capable of continuing his own progressive agenda. Once in office, however, Taft proved so non-progressive that Roosevelt chose to run against him on the new Progressive ("Bull Moose") Party ticket. This 1912 campaign turned out to be a four-way race, in which, remarkably,

TR's third-party bid garnered 27.4% of the popular vote for a second-place finish ahead of the Taft (23.2%) and labor leader Eugene V. Debs (6.0%), who ran on the Socialist ticket. The victor, however, with 41.8% of the popular ballot, was Woodrow Wilson.

WILLIAM HOWARD TAFT (R, 1909–1913)
Revenue = $59.49, Spending = $58.50,
Debt = $47.37; Change = $1.43 / 3%

PROGRESSIVELY WILSONIAN

WOODROW WILSON (D, 1913–1921)
Revenue = $225.03, Spending = $451.45,
Debt = $216.07; Change = $168.70 / 356%

Although he was a Democrat, Wilson was more progressive than either Taft or Roosevelt. Not content to be the mere "steward" of the people's welfare, he thought of himself as the very brain of the nation. His role was to think through problems and opportunities and formulate policy, educating the people to that policy and thereby gaining their understanding and support. Wilson attempted to remodel American government along the lines of the British cabinet system, in which he was a kind of prime minister and the members of Congress the Parliament. Thus, in contrast to Theodore Roosevelt, he approached Congress not as an adversary but as a partner.

During his first term, he persuaded Congress to enact a comprehensive program of progressive reform, including the introduction of a federal income tax with ratification of the Sixteenth Amendment (1913); the lowering of import tariffs; passage of the Federal Reserve Act of 1913; sweeping currency and banking reforms; new anti-trust legislation with the passage of the Federal Trade Commission Act and the Clayton Anti-Trust Act; and labor reform with the Adamson Act, giving railway workers an 8-hour day, and the Child Labor Act, which curtailed children's working hours.

The income tax, with incremental rates pegged to income, was very popular and essentially put government into the business of redistributing wealth. The Federal Reserve Act vies with the income tax as Wilson's most profound reform. It created a new central banking system and a new currency, the Federal Reserve Note, and was a far more radical move toward introducing greater stability to free-market capitalism than anything Theodore Roosevelt had introduced. Potentially, the Federal Reserve board had enormous power to act preemptively to level the "natural" cycles of business, which was often a punishing roller-coaster ride of booms and busts. Although the Federal Reserve initially showed considerable restraint in its early years, the pressures of the Great Depression (Chapter 7) and, later, President Nixon's departure from the gold standard (Chapter 3) would move it to exercise more and more of its potential power. When Alan Greenspan served as the Fed's thirteenth chairman (under presidents Reagan, George H. W. Bush, Clinton, and George W. Bush), the institution became the single most powerful instrument by which the federal government shaped—or deformed—the free market.

Wilson's domestic initiatives were packaged under what he called the "New Freedom," which supplanted Roosevelt's Square Deal and New Nationalism. Instead of using laws to force the break-up of existing monopolies (called "trusts"), the New Freedom sought to create a new national economic environment, in which business would no longer have the capacity to create trusts in the first place. Tariff reform protected domestic businesses of whatever size, and the Federal Reserve effectively freed up credit for businesses—again, regardless of size. New antitrust legislation (the Clayton Anti-Trust Act and the Federal Trade Commission Act, both of 1914) did not break up trusts (TR's approach), but barred the "unfair" business practices that made trusts possible. Under the New Freedom, the law did not punish monopolies so much as it protected competition.

Implementing the New Freedom required a whole new set of federal administrative appointees, and, under Wilson, the Administrative State grew by leaps and bounds. Although his natural inclination was to make the appointments on a nonpartisan merit basis, Wilson's single-minded need to enforce Democratic Party discipline moved him to partially reinstate much of the old patronage system, distributing many federal appointments as rewards for party loyalty—a tradition that, despite the civil service system, remains alive to this day (Chapter 6).

Wilson's impact on the domestic aspects of our national government was enormous, but his embrace of TR's expansion of the role of the United States in the world and of the role of the U.S. president as a world leader is even more consequential. Wilson was an internationalist idealist, determined to use his influence to bring "enlightened" government to the planet. He used the U.S. military to intervene in the internal politics of Mexico during 1914–1917, and, although he ran for reelection in 1916 on a platform of continuing to keep the U.S. out of the "Great War" (World War I, which Americans at the time called the "European War"), he marched the nation into that war in 1917.

Germany presented no existential threat to the United States, so America was not compelled to fight. It is true that business interests favored entering the war; American financial and industrial firms were heavily invested in the Allies (principally Britain and France) and were eager to protect their investments by ensuring an Allied victory. But Wilson asked Congress for a declaration of war on purely idealistic, ideological grounds, namely to "make the world safe for democracy." In his war message to Congress, he admitted that "it is a fearful thing to lead this great peaceful people into war, into the most terrible and disastrous of all wars, [but] the right is more precious than peace, and we shall fight for the things we have always carried in our hearts." He said "that America is privileged to spend her blood and her might for the principles that gave her birth and happiness and the peace which she has treasured."[1]

Ideological war is war fought not to defend against a demonstrated existential threat to the nation, but in the name of an ideology. Wilson's decision to enter the "European War" set the precedent for all the budget-busting wars that followed World War II—a war whose very outbreak disproved Wilson's contention that World War I would "make the world safe for democracy" and be "the war to end all wars." U.S. involvement in the Korean War (1950–1953), the Vietnam War (1955–1975), the Persian Gulf War (1990–1991), the Iraq War (officially 2003–2011, but ongoing), and the War in Afghanistan (officially 2001–2014, but ongoing) were all ideological wars, wars of choice rather than of necessity. They were also wars decreed by the president, not declared by Congress.

Wilson *intended* none of this, of course—the costs, the precedents, the inexorable transformation of democratic government. All of these were the unintended consequences of Wilson's interventionist, internationalist government.

And it really stuck.

Forty-four years later, in his 1961 inaugural address, John F. Kennedy offered his countrymen a proposition almost identical to Wilson's. "We will pay any price," JFK proclaimed, "bear any burden, meet any hardship, support any friend, oppose any foe, in order to assure the survival and the success of liberty."[2] Hearing this, did the throng gathered outside the Capitol portico that cold January 1961 morning gasp and demand a recount, a recall, an impeachment, a revolution? Not at all. The proposition had a ring to it: "Ask not what your country can do for you. Ask what you can do for your country."[3] *Really?* Yet the people were down with it, just as they had been in April 1917, when they cheered America's entry in Europe's war.

WAR CREATES ANOTHER BIG GOVERNMENT

American involvement in World War I created emergency legislation and executive orders of all kinds. Conscripting, training, equipping, and transporting an American army of unprecedented size required all the nation's resources to be directed toward creating and maintaining a vast military machine. The industrial economy was put under federal control. Wilson acquired a broad range of presidential powers, including (through the Lever Food and Fuel Control Act of 1917) total control of the importation, manufacturing, warehousing and stockpiling, mining, and distribution of practically everything, from commodities to food to manufactured goods. The wartime powers Wilson amassed dwarfed those Lincoln had claimed during the Civil War, creating a model for the office as it would exist during World War II and remain influential ever since.

For the size, scope, and authority of the Administrative State—the unelected bureaucracy—entry into the war proved to be a potent growth hormone. A remarkable example was the Committee on Public Information (CPI), essentially a ministry of propaganda charged with overseeing a program of "voluntary" censorship while simultaneously flooding the media with news from official government sources in a comprehensive effort to manage the war information that reached the public. Authorized by an executive order issued on April 14, 1917, the CPI became a complex assemblage of functions that, before the end of the year, employed more than 100,000 persons—some paid, others volunteers. It was a massive, instant bureaucracy, whose explosive growth spawned departments and bureaus that might be created in the morning and closed down or merged with others by the afternoon.[4] As for the army, it exploded from 133,000 men to more than four million by the end of the war, thanks to military conscription enabled by the Selective Service Act of 1917.

The Administrative State was not the only threat to democracy introduced to make the world safe for democracy. On June 15, 1917, Wilson signed into law the Espionage Act of 1917 and, little less than a year later, on May 16, 1918, the so-called Sedition Act of 1918 (actually an amendment to the 1917 Espionage Act). The Espionage Act defined *espionage* as obtaining or attempting to obtain "information respecting the national defence with intent or reason to believe that the information to be obtained is to be used to the injury of the United States, or to the advantage of any foreign nation." The act also prohibited disseminating false information "with intent to interfere with the operation or success of the military or naval forces of the United States or to promote the success of its enemies and whoever when the United States is at war." Punishment for each count of offense was a fine of $10,000 and up to two years in prison.[5]

The Espionage Act did not end with the armistice of November 11, 1918. It was used throughout the 20th century and, most recently, was the basis for charges filed in June 2013 against Wiki-Leaks leaker Edward Snowden.[6] Similarly, while most of the wartime agencies and bureaus were dismantled after World War I, their creation served as templates for a new bureaucracy during World War II and may be seen as the ancestors of the USA PATRIOT Act, signed into law by President George W. Bush on October 26, 2001, and extended under Barack Obama on May 26, 2011. Within little more than a month of the terrorist attacks of 9/11/2001, the legislation created a new cabinet department, Homeland Security, which employs (as of 2015) some 240,000 persons[7] and (per FY 2017 budget request) has a budget of **$40.6 billion** in addition to **$6.7 billion** for the Disaster Relief Fund.[8]

THE TURN AGAINST WILSON, INTERNATIONALISM, AND BIG GOVERNMENT

American intervention in World War I brought victory to the Allies, yet a majority of the American people ultimately rebelled against Wilson, his costly and intrusive idealism, and his ideological presidency. Wilson believed that America's sacrifice in Europe's war would buy the nation—

and, more to the point, himself—a seat at the conference table at which the postwar destiny of the world would be decided. He intended to lead the Allied powers in crafting a treaty that would rebuild Europe and preempt virtually all future wars, thanks to a League of Nations, in which international disputes would be settled by negotiation rather than bullets, bombs, and poison gas.

Unfortunately, what Wilson had not understood is that Britain, France, and Italy wanted none of this. All they truly wanted was to punish and neuter Germany by crushing it economically, politically, and militarily. For the most part, the terms of the Treaty of Versailles (into which Germany was permitted no input) reflected precisely these objectives. This is hardly the outcome Wilson intended, but he acquiesced, attempting to mollify the American people with the naïve assertion that the League of Nations would provide a platform from which he personally could repair the defects of the Treaty of Versailles and, in the end, bring justice to the world.

Yet while Wilson was in Europe for six months, hammering out a treaty so punitive that it would produce the unintended consequence of creating an environment that made a *second* world war virtually inevitable, he lost touch with the rapidly changing mood of America. The country he had left was not the same as the country to which he returned. The American electorate had put a Republican majority in both the House of Representatives and the Senate, and Wilson had high-handedly refused to consult with any Republicans concerning the treaty or the League of Nations. In response, Wilson's longtime nemesis, Senator Henry Cabot Lodge (R-Mass.), led Republican opposition to the League of Nations. Since ratification of the Treaty of Versailles required acceptance of the League of Nations, the Senate indicated that it would reject both. Instead of negotiating with the Republicans in this dispute, Wilson took his case directly to the people. He embarked on a grueling 9,500-mile transcontinental whistle-stop speaking tour, which brought about his physical collapse on September 25, 1919, after speaking in Pueblo, Colorado. Rushed back to Washington, he suffered a massive stroke a week later. It left him partially paralyzed, totally unable to carry on the fight for the Treaty and the League.

With Wilson largely out of the picture, the nation, in the presidential election of 1920, overwhelmingly rejected the Democratic ticket of James M. Cox and Franklin D. Roosevelt, who were pledged to support the League of Nations, and elected instead Warren G. Harding, a nondescript product of the Republican political machine. Harding's chief campaign promise was to bring about a national "return to normalcy," by which he meant a return to the isolationism that had marked the period following the Spanish-American War. After Harding's death in office of a cerebral hemorrhage on August 2, 1923, his vice president, Calvin Coolidge, took over. Coolidge was a hands-off, minimal-government president—an approach sufficiently welcomed by voters to gain him election in his own right, by a landslide, in 1924. The party wanted him to run again in 1928 but he declined, and Herbert Clark Hoover, who had been secretary of commerce under both Harding and Coolidge, was tapped, despite his lack of military experience.

THE CALL FOR THE RETURN OF

BIG GOVERNMENT

WARREN G. HARDING (R, 1921–1923)
Revenue = $104.45, Spending = $92.73,
Debt = $237.35; Change = –$21.28 / 10%

CALVIN COOLIDGE (R, 1923–1929)
Revenue = $258.83, Spending = $219.80,
Debt = $178.25; Change = $(59.10) / –25%

HERBERT HOOVER (R, 1929–1933)
Revenue = $175.35, Spending = $184.49,
Debt = $258.15; Change = $79.90 / 45%

The election of three presidents, Harding, Coolidge, and Hoover, was a popular revolt against Wilson and the internationalist, interventionist big government he stood for. Yet when the massive Great Depression struck, beginning with the stock market crash of October 29, 1929, poor Hoover, eight months in office, took much of the blame—not for having caused it, but for being helpless to end it. Even historians have criticized him as clueless. In truth, Hoover was far from oblivious to the crisis. He introduced a program of federally financed public works projects in an effort to create employment and stimulate the economy. The Hoover Dam, often cited as one of the crowning achievements of Franklin Roosevelt's New Deal, was actually begun by Hoover, who also called for the reduction of taxes on low-income Americans (Congress did not respond) and the closure of some tax loopholes that favored the wealthy (this was mostly accomplished). He even advocated government-funded $50-per-month pensions for those over 65 (Congress failed to act).

What he drew a hard line against was the notion that the federal government should directly dole out money and other aid to citizens. He encouraged the states to do this (even though the coffers of many were empty), but he argued that *federal* handouts would forever demoralize the people, transforming the democratic, free-market culture of the United States into a culture of perpetual dependency and entitlement. Ironically, even tragically, the three federal interventions that Hoover *did* champion were just awful. The Smoot-Hawley Tariff was intended to protect domestic industries but had the unintended consequence of severely damaging international trade with Europe and China. This, along with retaliatory tariffs enacted by several U.S. trading partners, severely deepened the Depression. Sharp increases in the top personal income tax bracket, from 25% to 63%, and increases in corporate taxes did produce a balanced budget in 1933, but at the cost of discouraging both consumer buying and investor finance of new businesses. Together, these effects drove down already depressed levels of employment.

A NEW PRESIDENCY,

A NEW DEAL

FRANKLIN D. ROOSEVELT (D, 1933–1945)
Revenue = $1,486.72, Spending = $3,196.77,
Debt = $2,034.79; Change = $1,776.64 / 688%

P robably any Democrat would have defeated Herbert Hoover when he ran for reelection in 1932, but the huge margin of Franklin Delano Roosevelt's electoral victory—472 to 59—gave this particular Democrat a popular mandate to do whatever he deemed necessary to pull the nation out of the quagmire. FDR's initial program was aimed less at long-term recovery than immediate relief. Even this, however, required him to redefine the role of government as expressed in the Declaration of Independence and the Constitution. FDR proposed that the job of modern government was to defend economic welfare as an "unalienable right" on a par with life, liberty, and the pursuit of happiness. Whereas Hoover had invoked the American tradition of self-reliance as a reason for refraining from using federal resources to directly assist individuals, Roosevelt argued that, in this economic crisis, America's cherished rugged individualism had to give way to working on behalf of the common good. People would have to make individual sacrifices, but the government would, in return, provide *direct* help and support.

Although he did not use the phrase, Franklin Roosevelt announced the creation of a *welfare state.* To lead it, he assumed unprecedented executive power. Moreover, like his fifth cousin, Theodore Roosevelt, FDR defined himself as the direct representative of the people, the principal agent of democratic government over and above both the legislative and judicial branches. Terrified and desperate, a large majority of the electorate was receptive to this redefinition of the presidency and the government. In his speech accepting the Democratic Party nomination on July 2, 1932, FDR pledged himself to "a new deal for the American people."[9] Directly following his inauguration on March 4, 1933, that "New Deal" came into being in a flood of executive orders. FDR bypassed Congress by issuing an order proclaiming a Bank Holiday intended to halt a rash of runs and bank failures. During the first "Hundred Days" of the Roosevelt administration, FDR not only issued executive orders, he successfully urged Congress to create the Federal Deposit Insurance Corporation to guarantee bank deposits, to expand the powers of the Federal Reserve Board, to establish the Home Owners' Loan Corporation, and to pass a Federal Securities Act, requiring companies to fully disclose financial information on new stock issues. To combat unemployment, Roosevelt called on Congress to appropriate **$500 million** for relief programs and to create job programs, the best known of which was the Civilian Conservation Corps (CCC). To stimulate industry, FDR asked Congress to pass the National Industrial Recovery Act (NIRA). The act established the Public Works Administration (PWA) and forced industrial leaders to enact codes of fair practices, allowing them in turn to set prices without fear of antitrust prosecution, thereby institutionalizing a key element of crony capitalism. Minimum wages and maximum work hours were set under NIRA, and workers were given the right to bargain collectively. In addition, NIRA established the National Recovery Administration (NRA), which drafted business codes and labor regulations. At the same time, labor unions used the NRA to accumulate more clout and attract more members.

The Great Depression had hit the agricultural sector first and hardest, and Roosevelt prevailed on Congress to create the Agricultural Adjustment Administration (AAA) in May 1933, which imposed production limits and provided federal subsidies to raise agricultural prices to "parity" with the prices farmers had enjoyed when agriculture was in its best years. This was (and, for many economists, remains) among the most problematic, even egregious, of the New Deal measures. With the outbreak of World War I in 1914, American agricultural output came into great demand by the European nations. The demand increased tremendously when the United States entered the war in 1917 and was sustained after the war, when America became the breadbasket of a war-ravaged Europe. The "best years" of American agriculture were therefore a boom period created not by normal demand but by wartime scarcity. The hard fact is that the severity of the depression in the agricultural sector, coupled with a massive natural disaster—a drought that transformed much of the lower Midwest and parts of the West into a "Dust Bowl"—retarded the economic recovery in farming states. Nevertheless, the aim of the agricultural price and production controls and subsidies was to restore the agricultural sector not merely to viability but to an artificially prosperous level, and farmers came to rely on federal support long after the Great Depression came to an end. What politician, author, and director of Ronald Reagan's Office of Management and Budget David Stockman calls a "Hayseed Coalition"[10] was created, and it has endured to this day as the crony capitalism of massive federal agricultural subsidies.

The Hundred Days also witnessed the birth of the Tennessee Valley Authority (TVA), an agency responsible for broad social and public works programs within the Tennessee River Valley region. Hydroelectric plants, nitrate manufacturing for fertilizers, soil conservation, flood control, and reforestation were all aspects of a program covering parts of seven states.

EFFECTIVENESS

AND UNINTENDED CONSEQUENCES

OF THE NEW DEAL

 oubtless, the New Deal made people feel better. Yet, in 1934, despite its measures, nine million people were still out of work. The most memorable New Deal employment program, the Works Progress Administration (WPA), left its most lasting mark on America in the cultural and social sphere, with its Federal Theater Project, Federal Writers' Program, and Federal Art Project, rather than creating an enduring economic stimulus. Indeed, despite the volume of cash injected into the economy by New Deal programs, the Great Depression continued little abated. That Roosevelt was elected to a second term (1936) and an unprecedented third term (1940), David Stockman believes, is evidence that, by 1936, the New Deal was thickly shrouded in a popular mythology. Stockman argues that the Depression was already beginning to lift during the Hoover administration and might even have improved earlier than it did if Roosevelt had not meddled:

> The New Deal hagiographers never mention that 50% of the huge collapse of industrial production, that is, the heart of the Great Depression, had already been recovered under Hoover by September 1932. The catalyst for the Hoover recovery was not Washington-based policy machinations but the natural bottoming of the severe cycle of fixed-asset and inventory liquidation after 1929. By mid-1932, the liquidation had finally run its course because inventories were virtually gone, and capital goods and durables production could hardly go lower. Accordingly, nearly every statistic of economic activity turned upward in July 1932.[11]

David Stockman is foremost among FDR's modern critics who believe a majority of the American voters saw in the president an economic messiah when he was actually nothing more than a very determined man with a wrecking ball, whose New Deal "shattered the foundation of sound money and inaugurated a régime of capricious fiscal and regulatory activism that inexorably fueled the growth of state power and the crony capitalism which thrives on it."[12]

Even in the midst of the New Deal, Republicans denounced Rooseveltian Big Government. Government spending was about 5% of GDP when Roosevelt took office in 1933 and was still less

INITIALS	DATE CREATED	FULL NAME
AAA	1933	Agricultural Adjustment Administration
CCC	1933	Civilian Conservation Corps
CWA	1933	Civil Works Administration
DRS	1935	Drought Relief Service
DSH or SHD	1933	Subsistence Homesteads Division
EBA	1933	Emergency Banking Act
FAA	1933	Federal Aviation Administration
FAP	1935	Federal Art Project (part of WPA)
FCA	1933	Farm Credit Administration
FCC	1934	Federal Communications Commission
FDIC	1933	Federal Deposit Insurance Corporation
FERA	1933	Federal Emergency Relief Administration
FHA	1934	Federal Housing Administration
FLSA	1938	Fair Labor Standards Act
FMP	1935	Federal Music Project (part of WPA)
FSA	1935	Farm Security Administration
FSRC	1933	Federal Surplus Relief Corporation
FTP	1935	Federal Theatre Project (part of WPA)
FWA	1939	Federal Works Agency
FWP	1935	Federal Writers' Project (part of WPA)
HOLC	1933	Home Owners' Loan Corporation
NIRA	1933	National Industrial Recovery Act
NLRA	1935	National Labor Relations Act
NLRB	1934	National Labor Relations Board/The Wagner Act
NRA	1933	National Recovery Administration
NYA	1935	National Youth Administration
PRRA	1933	Puerto Rico Reconstruction Administration
PWA	1933	Public Works Administration
RA	1935	Resettlement Administration
REA	1935	Rural Electrification Administration
SEC	1934	Securities and Exchange Commission
SSA	1935	Social Security Administration
SSB	1935	Social Security Board
TVA	1933	Tennessee Valley Authority
USHA	1937	United States Housing Authority
USMC	1936	United States Maritime Commission
WPA	1935	Works Progress Administration

than 10% in 1939.[13] The numbers, however, tell only part of the story. It is the alphabet soup of new agencies, bureaus, and programs, not their cost, that laid the predicate for big, interventionist government.

One unintended consequence of the New Deal was the sheer profusion of government agencies. The list above consists of 37. Some three-quarters of a century later, the spring 2015 edition of the twice-annual *Unified Agenda of Federal Deregulatory and Regulatory Actions* lists 60 agencies, the Administrative Conference of the United States pegs the number at 115, the online *Federal Register Index* currently shows 257 (Senator Chuck Grassley [R-Iowa] puts the number at more than 430, if departments and subagencies are counted), FOIA.gov lists 252, the *United States Government Manual* takes a stab at 316, and Regulations.gov weighs in with a modest 89.[14]

Today, the short answer to the question, "How many government agencies are there?" is "Nobody really knows." Clyde Wayne Crews Jr., policy director of the Competitive Enterprise Institute, calls these literally numberless agencies sources of "regulatory dark matter," which is "made possible by Congress' perpetual delegation of lawmaking power to agencies." He quotes Robert A. Rogowski's 1989 description of the function of regulatory bureaucracies as an "impressive underground regulatory infrastructure [that] thrives on investigations, inquiries, threatened legal actions, and negotiated settlements." Thanks to the obscurity of regulatory dark matter, "Many of the most questionable regulatory actions...escape the scrutiny of the public, Congress, and even the regulatory watchdogs in the executive branch."[15]

The New Deal's "alphabet soup" agencies were the progenitors of today's Administrative State and regulatory dark matter, into which Chapter 6 will venture. But size is only one dimension of big government. To be sure, the profusion of agencies and their regulations is costly and crippling, and the obscurity of multiple agencies makes transparency in government an impossible dream. Yet, as founded in the New Deal, the bigness of big government reaches well beyond the overcrowded corridors of Washington itself. The New Deal created expectations that, as the much-derided Herbert Hoover feared, did make people chronically dependent on government. The New Deal government's well-intentioned but ultimately ineffective manipulations of the free market led to the political culture of crony capitalism that afflicts us today. The alphabet soup of regulatory and economic stimulant agencies made success in business dependent on developing "special relationships" between business leaders and political leaders. Legal permits, licenses, government grants, tax breaks, and incentives created a new economy of scarcity. Those businesses that received these valuable commodities succeeded. Those that were left out—well, they were left out. This is the essence of crony capitalism as it was institutionalized by the Roosevelt's New Deal.

ANOTHER WORLD WAR

Even those sympathetic to the achievements of the New Deal admit that, in the end, it was the economic stimulus created by military spending in the run-up to World War II, and not the New Deal, that ended the Great Depression in America. Unlike World War I—the "European War"—World War II did pose an existential threat to the United States. Once Pearl Harbor was attacked on December 7, 1941, the nation had no choice but to go to war. Nevertheless, in the run-up to war and to U.S. entry into it, FDR confronted the reluctance of a wary Congress to increase America's global engagement. He responded by summarily assuming unilateral control over foreign policy. FDR chose sides, beginning with the implementation of embargos to halt the export of U.S.-made weapons to nations *he* deemed dangerous. When the 1936 embargo was challenged in the Supreme Court (*United States v. Curtiss-Wright Export Corporation*), the justices ruled in favor of the president, effectively affirming what some earlier presidents had only asserted, namely that the president is the supreme authority in the conduct of foreign policy.[16] Beginning in September 1939, Roosevelt used his court-bolstered authority to methodically align the United States with Great Britain and the other Allied powers as they fitfully struggled to stem the tide of Nazi conquest. Throughout the 1930s, he steered Congress away from neutrality and on September 2, 1940, he concluded a destroyers-for-bases deal with Britain's prime minister, Winston Churchill, whereby the U.S. Navy would "lend" 50 obsolescent World War I–vintage destroyers to the Royal Navy in return for leases on British naval bases in the Caribbean. Implemented entirely by executive order, this paved the way for the far more expansive Lend-Lease Act (March 11, 1941) by which Congress authorized the president to furnish materiel to any nation whose security he deemed essential to that of the United States and to supply these items on any basis the president saw fit, whether for cash payment, on credit, on exchange, or simply as a grant or loan.[17] It was a spectacular concession of legislative branch authority to the executive branch. The military merits of Lend-Lease are beyond dispute, but within this legislation were the seeds of the postwar practice that would make World War II (so far) the last war Congress, in compliance with the Constitution, declared.

In his prewar and wartime conduct of foreign relations, President Roosevelt not only routinely circumvented Congress, he often bypassed even his own cabinet. Much of his diplomacy—most notably that conducted with Winston Churchill—was strictly personal. As FDR transformed diplomacy into a matter of personal partnership, so he tended to bring all aspects of foreign policy into the White House itself. Functions traditionally performed by the Department of State and overseen by the secretary of state were increasingly assumed by non-cabinet-level presidential advisers who passed in and out of the president's inner circle. This consolidation of foreign affairs in the White House would become a common feature of all the postwar presidencies. Even as the size of government sprawled, the bureaucracy becoming increasingly unwieldy and the volume of agencies multiplying into numbers that have yet to be definitively tallied, foreign relations became increasingly personal, informal, and ad hoc. Government simultaneously sprawled *and* contracted—to a central point at 1600 Pennsylvania Avenue.

Ever since Abraham Lincoln, U.S. presidents have assumed some extraordinary powers in times of war. Like President Wilson before him, FDR extended executive authority over wartime domestic economic and social affairs, including matters of war production, allocation of resources, and rationing, and the institution of special regulations to prevent espionage and sabotage, including the establishment of secret military tribunals. His most egregious domestic exercise of wartime authority was, of course, the removal of some 100,000 U.S. citizens of Japanese descent from their homes and businesses along the West Coast to "relocation camps" situated inland. This mass dispossession and internment was instituted on February 8, 1942, by Executive Order 9066, without congressional action (although members of Congress overwhelmingly approved of the action).[18] When challenged in the Supreme Court, the legality of this unprecedented affront to the Fourth and Fifth Amendments was upheld on the grounds of "military necessity."[19]

THE FINAL UNINTENDED

CONSEQUENCE

D espite the unintended consequences of so much of what Franklin Delano Roosevelt introduced into the American government, the American economy, and American life, he is persistently cited by historians as one of the greatest of American presidents. The 2014 survey of the 162 members of the American Political Science Association's Presidents and Executive Politics section asked them to rank the U.S. presidents. Franklin Roosevelt came in third, one step above Theodore (ranked fourth), and one step below George Washington, who was ranked second to Abraham Lincoln.[20]

Number 3 FDR broke the seemingly inviolable precedent established by Number 2 Washington by running for a third term in 1940 and a fourth in 1944. To that fourth term, America elected a physically spent, very sick man. He was felled by a cerebral hemorrhage on April 12, 1945. This left Vice President Harry S. Truman in charge. Not only was FDR the toughest of tough acts to follow, he had shared almost no information or counsel with his vice president, who had to learn the office from scratch. Fortunately for the nation, Truman proved himself up to this Herculean task. But Congress had had enough of the presidency as potentially an office for life. It passed the Twenty-Second Amendment on March 21, 1947, and, on February 27, 1951, after ratification by the requisite thirty-six of the then forty-eight states, it became law: "No person shall be elected to the office of President more than twice, and no person who has held the office of President, or acted as President, for more than two years of a term to which some other person was elected President shall be elected to the office of the President more than once."

A term limit applied to the presidency by constitutional amendment was the final unintended consequence of the Roosevelt presidency. The objection most frequently raised against term limits is that they are inherently undemocratic in that they deprive voters of choosing the incumbent. The counterargument is that incumbents often run unopposed or opposed only by a token candidate with virtually no chance of winning. Indeed, even though Americans consistently voice dissatisfaction with Congress, House incumbents get re-elected 94% of the time.[21] It is, proponents of term limits say, the incumbency advantage that is undemocratic. Term limits would give voters more choices. This may be true, but the most compelling reason for term limits is to curb careerism in government. Term limits would tend to make a career in elected government impossible, which would be a good thing. Serving in government should be just that, serving. To the degree that it becomes a career, doing everything one can to maintain that career becomes a motive that tends to displace all others. Service to the people recedes as a priority. Keeping one's job ascends. The governors of thirty-six states and four U.S. territories are subject to term limits, as are legislators in fifteen states. A handful of local governments also impose term limits on mayors. In the federal government, the idea of term limits for representatives and senators has been floated frequently since the

Twenty-Second Amendment was ratified, but, so far, it has not advanced to law. Nevertheless, a Gallup Poll conducted in January 2013 found that 75% of adults "would vote for term limits" (21% were opposed, 5% undecided). Fully 82% of Republicans favored term limits, with Independents next (79%), and Democrats third (65%).[22] The inescapable conclusion is that there exists in America substantial sentiment against one of the dominant features of big government: careerism. So far, however, except with regard to the presidency, any suggestion of a popular movement remains dormant. As for the other aspects of big government and the unsustainable debt it both feeds and feeds on, the subject is often raised, but government, since World War II, only continues to grow.

BEARING FRUIT

The post–World War II presidencies of Harry S. Truman, Dwight D. Eisenhower, and John F. Kennedy were the last fiscally responsible administrations of the 20th century. With the best intentions, Lyndon Johnson doubled down (and then some) on the New Deal, mortgaging the nation itself to finance the Great Society, only to simultaneously charge into the cataclysm of the Vietnam War. In the process, Johnson created the economic climate in which his successor, Richard M. Nixon, cut the dollar loose from gold, and the major economies of the world found themselves tethered to a floating reserve currency.

This chapter concludes by narrating the deficit-driven and debt-bound careers of the three presidents who followed Nixon, the last of whom, Ronald Reagan, apostle of small government, managed to break the trillion-dollar debt ceiling by nearly **$2 trillion**.

CHAPTER 3

HARRY S. TRUMAN

TO

RONALD REAGAN

Everyone knew Harry S. Truman was no FDR insider, and when the three-term president succumbed to a cerebral hemorrhage on April 12, 1945, little more than three months into his fourth term, there were doubts about Truman's ability to see World War II to victory. There were, however, few doubts about how he would follow up on his fallen chief's New Deal programs. It was generally assumed that he would not. FDR was a liberal New Yorker, HST a far more conservative Missourian. But on September 6, 1945, with World War II just won, President Truman introduced what he called the "Fair Deal," designed to make permanent most of the New Deal provisions that had been implemented during an economic emergency that no longer existed. Truman felt bound, he explained, to fulfill a vision for a postwar economy that embodied

what FDR had called a "Second Bill of Rights," with guarantees
of the opportunity to enjoy adequate employment, good medical
care, decent housing, and a good education. Yet even as Truman
moved to enshrine the New Deal forever in American life, the
old-fashioned Missourian in him injected a dose of old-school
fiscal orthodoxy. And when he took the nation into war against
Soviet-backed Communist North Korea, which invaded the
democratic South on June 25, 1950, he insisted on financing it
the old fashioned "honest" way—not by borrowing and deficit
spending, but by raising taxes. It was painful and it was unpopular, and Truman maturely accepted these political downsides as
part of the cost of war.

HARRY S. TRUMAN (D, 1945–1953)
Revenue = $2,751.47, Spending = $3,626,87,
Debt = $1,730.67; Change = $(304.12) / 15%

Of course, what was decidedly *not* old school was fighting a war
without a congressional declaration. Truman believed that a formal declaration would be a de facto recognition of North Korea
as a sovereign nation, and he also feared that formally declaring war would force the Soviets and perhaps even the Chinese
to reciprocate formally, escalating the Korean "conflict" into a
new world war. Despite these rational motives for bypassing
Congress, an unconstitutional precedent was set for the conduct
of major wars in Vietnam, Iraq (twice), and Afghanistan. These
undeclared wars defined American life and deformed the American economy for at least ten years of the post–World War II 20th
century—and who knows for how many more of the 21st.

Truman served out FDR's fourth term and defied pollsters
and pundits by achieving election to a term in his own right in
1948. He chose not to run in 1952, and Dwight D. Eisenhower,

former Supreme Allied Commander in Europe and newly minted Republican, trounced Democrat Adlai Stevenson. Eisenhower was a fiscal conservative who doubled down on Truman's economic orthodoxy when he declared that balancing the budget was his top economic priority. Despite his lofty military pedigree, Ike slashed the military budget with his "New Look" defense strategy, which sharply reduced conventional forces and invested instead in building up a thermonuclear deterrent.

DWIGHT D. EISENHOWER (R, 1953–1961)
Revenue = $3,737.67, Spending = $4,077.31,
Debt = $1,662.36; Change = $(68.31) / –4%

GREAT SOCIETY?

Although John F. Kennedy was elected in 1960 as an activist president who wanted to shake America out of the purported complacency of the two-term Eisenhower era, he was actually an economic conservative who took up most of Eisenhower's insistence on fiscal discipline, including the U.S. commitment to the Bretton Woods system.

JOHN F. KENNEDY (D, 1961–1963)
Revenue = $1,680.60, Spending = $1,806.11,
Debt = $1,715.57; Change = $53.21 / 3%

Created by an agreement reached during July 1–22, 1944, among representatives of the forty-four World War II allies gathered at the Mount Washington Hotel in Bretton Woods, New Hampshire, the "Bretton Woods system" was a set of rules, institutions, and procedures intended to regulate the postwar international monetary system. The system, which established both the International Monetary Fund (IMF) and the International Bank for Reconstruction and Development (IBRD), included an agreement among the United States, Canada, Western Europe, Australia, and (later) Japan to adopt national monetary policies that maintained the exchange rate among them by tying each of their currencies to gold, with the IMF functioning to bridge any temporary imbalances of payments. As finally implemented, the agreement stipulated that the currencies of the signatories be pegged both to gold and to the U.S. dollar, since the United States held more than two-thirds of the world's gold. JFK's commitment to Bretton Woods, therefore, was above all a conservative commitment to the gold-based dollar.

The assassination of President Kennedy on November 22, 1963, put into office Lyndon Baines Johnson, who engineered passage of the landmark Civil Rights Act of 1964 and the Voting Rights Act of 1965, aspects of his "Great Society" programs that had as their goal the elimination of poverty and racial injustice in America. The civil rights legislation was long overdue, and these acts were understandably linked to the problems of poverty. But it was one thing to cast government in the role of promoting racial justice and quite another to require it to shoulder virtually the entire responsibility for eliminating poverty. But LBJ had come of age politically in the era of the New Deal, and under him, the Great Society became a reincarnation of Rooseveltian presidential government, in which both the day-to-day administration of the government as well as its long-range strategic planning was concentrated in the White House through a plethora of programs, task forces, and presidential commissions. This had the unintended consequence of removing much of the Great Society—intended as a monument to democracy—from the democratic process.

LYNDON B. JOHNSON (D, 1963–1969)
Revenue = $3,412.03, Spending = $3,636.65,
Debt = $1,787.29; Change = $71.72 / 4%

The breadth of Great Society legislation was extraordinary. Under the "War on Poverty" were programs reminiscent of the New Deal, including the Job Corps, VISTA (Volunteers in Service to America, a kind of domestic Peace Corps), Upward Bound, and the Food Stamp program (authorized by the Food Stamp Act of 1964). Education programs, beginning with the Elementary and Secondary Education Act of 1965, ended the unspoken taboo barring federal involvement in and funding of public education. This was augmented by the Higher Education Act of 1965, which appropriated funding for universities and created low-interest scholarships. In the area of health, the Social Security Act of 1965 created Medicare, providing federal funding of the medical costs of older Americans, and Medicaid, which funded medical care for low-income individuals and families regardless of age. In addition to health, new Social Security legislation substantially expanded welfare benefits across the board. Consumer protection was enhanced as part of the Great Society, as were a thick deck of environmental programs.[1] The unintended but inevitable consequence of all this was explosive expansion of the administrative and regulatory state (see Chapter 6).

Housing, rural development, and labor were also affected by the Great Society. The most enduring legacies in these areas are fair housing and non-discrimination laws in housing, and raises in the federal minimum wage.

SOME GOOD LUCK

Although Johnson became president as a result of violence, he had the good fortune to enter office during a period of economic growth and declining unemployment. Despite moderately rising inflation (reaching nearly 5% by 1968, his final year in office), between 1963 and 1968, real GDP increased by 29%, or by 5.2% per year on average, and the rate of unemployment declined from 5.7% in November 1963, the start of the LBJ presidency, to 3.4% in January 1969, when he left office.[2]

In 1960, the official poverty rate was 22%. In 1969, when Johnson left office, it stood at 13%. Infant mortality among the poor had barely declined between 1950 and 1965, yet it fell by one-third in the decade after 1965, quite likely due to the expansion of federal medical and nutritional programs. Before Medicaid and Medicare, 20% of the poor were never examined by a physician. When Johnson left office, that number had fallen to 8%.[3]

These social benefits are real. But also real was the performance of the economy during 1963–1968, which was likely attributable more to good luck and the Eisenhower-JFK traditional approach to the economy than it was to the work of Johnson-era policy-makers. It is also difficult to determine to what extent the reduction in poverty during the LBJ presidency was the result of the Great Society programs of the War on Poverty or the robust economy. Yet even assuming that at least some of the reduction in poverty during the Johnson years was due to the Great Society programs, the 13% poverty rate of 1968 was measured at 14.9% in 2014,[4] and the conservative Heritage Foundation has calculated that the total cost of the Great Society has, over the years, amounted to **$22 trillion** in current dollars, rising "by about $1 trillion a year as more than 80 overlapping means-tested federal programs sap resources the country does not have."[5]

GUNS OR BUTTER VERSUS GUNS AND BUTTER

Now, let us step back in time for a moment. In 1946, congressional legislation created the Council of Economic Advisers (CEA) to advise presidents on economic policy. The CEA worked independently from the secretary of the treasury and introduced a series of academic economic "advances" in the making of policy. The cornerstone of these was the abandonment of a "cyclical model" of the economy—the idea that the economy was subject to "natural" cycles about which little could *or should* be done—and the adoption instead of a "growth model," which held that much could *and should* be done to actively manage the national economy. The CEA set performance targets for the economy and made policy recommendations accordingly.

In 1949, CEA chairman Edwin Nourse had a showdown with council member Leon Keyserling. Nourse held that the nation had to choose between "guns or butter"; that is, whether to gear national investment toward defense *or* civilian goods. You can't do both, Nourse argued. Keyserling countered that the postwar economic expansion allowed for a "guns *and* butter" approach: substantial defense expenditures without the necessity of pinching the standard of living. Swayed by advisers, the normally conservative Truman agreed with Keyserling, who replaced Nourse as CEA chairman. The guns and butter economic model was not, however, implemented by Truman's successor, Eisenhower. Kennedy, Ike's successor, presided over a White House in which the secretary of the treasury, C. Douglas Dillon, a fiscally conservative Republican and a former member of the Eisenhower State Department, countered the expansive CEA and its new chairman, Walter Wolfgang Heller. Together with CEA member James Tobin, Heller persuaded Kennedy in 1962 to advocate tax cuts for the purpose of stimulating the economy. Wall Street had generally favored Eisenhower's insistence that no tax cuts should be made when the government was in deficit. In 1962, the federal deficit stood at **$7.146 billion**.[6] Nevertheless, Wall Street surprised President Kennedy by enthusiastically welcoming the tax cut *and* the increased deficit spending that would come with it. Going against the advice of Secretary Dillon, JFK included the cut in his 1963 budget message to Congress.

What alarmed Secretary Dillon was Heller and Tobin's proposal that the United States step back from Bretton Woods by suspending the "gold window" (the figurative teller window at which Bretton Woods system nations could, on demand, redeem their dollars for gold), cutting domestic interest rates, and negotiating a "long-term borrowing arrangement" with Europe.[7] The benefit to the U.S. economy in doing these things, Heller and Tobin argued, was the avoidance of paying off short-term dollar claims held by foreign central banks by renegotiating them over the long term. Dillon warned that doing this would be profoundly destabilizing while also merely putting off fixing the U.S. balance of payments problem. Dillon declared that "no country can run a consistently large balance of payments deficit," and Federal Reserve Board Chairman William McChesney Martin Jr. warned that suspending the gold window would be seen by "world financial markets as a declaration of U.S. insolvency."[8]

The gold window suspension was tabled, but the CEA succeeded in pushing the 1963 tax cut. To describe the CEA at this point as a politburo-in-the-making is provocative, yet not unreasonable. The tax cut legislation of 1963 was a major step toward a policy in which the free-market economy was to be prodded and pulled by raising or lowering tax rates on presidential command—based on the analysis of White House economists. "In convincing Kennedy to take the first fateful step down the slippery slope of deficit-financed tax cuts," David Stockman writes, "the [CEA] professors were paving the way for the eventual transformation of the tax code into a tool of national prosperity management. They were also offering it up as a piñata to be battered endlessly by crony capitalist lobbies."[9]

THE TRIUMPH OF GUNS AND BUTTER

S enate Republicans held up the tax cut bill in committee, denouncing it as reckless, but the shots fired in Dallas on November 22, 1963, proved sufficient ammunition for President Johnson to get the bill passed. With that, willful non-emergency, peacetime deficit finance went from taboo to just one more tool in the federal economic policy toolbox.

In the short term, what were now called "the Kennedy tax cuts" seemed to have nothing but a salutary effect: Real GDP rose by 5.3% in 1964 and 5.9% in 1965, yet inflation rose only at a modest 1.5% during each of these years. But this did not last long. By the spring of 1967, inflation was at 5% and rising.[10]

Of course, by 1967, the overwhelming national issue was not the "butter" of the Great Society, but the "guns" of the Vietnam War. This is not the time or place to re-litigate the murky complexities of the infamous Tonkin Gulf Incident of August 2, 1964. Suffice it to note that the Johnson White House inflated a highly questionable report of attacks on two U.S. destroyers operating off the coast of North Vietnam into an urgent reason for escalation of the Vietnam "conflict" into the Vietnam War. As in the Korean War, Congress abrogated its constitutional responsibility to declare—or to *refuse* to declare—war. In the case of Vietnam, Congress even more fully capitulated to the executive branch by passing the Tonkin Gulf Resolution, which gave the president a blank check to conduct the war in Vietnam without seeking congressional approval.[11] And now that deficit finance was a fact of American economic life, LBJ also had in hand a more literal blank check for use in financing the war.

But he wanted to do more than that. He insisted that the United States was prosperous and powerful enough not only to foot the bill for an expanded war, but also to continue to finance, unabated, the Great Society. Moreover, he intended to do guns *and* butter without taking the unpopular step of raising taxes.

Unfortunately for LBJ and the nation, rising inflation had already reduced domestic demand for goods, and the trade surplus of 1964 had by 1968 evaporated in the heat of the Vietnam War at its height. As dollars piled up in offshore markets, upward pressure on the gold price mounted, and the Federal Reserve used currency swap lines to bring home dollars to prevent their being traded on the London gold market or hauled in wheelbarrows to the gold window. The Bretton Woods swap lines were intended as short-term emergency means of creating liquidity in order to smooth bumpy markets in a crisis. They were intended as strictly short-term (ideally, overnight) agreements between the central banks of Bretton Woods nations to keep a supply of their country's currency available to trade to one another *at the going exchange rate.* Now, however, LBJ began using swap lines routinely to patch what was becoming a widening structural crack in the U.S. economy itself, namely the lopsided U.S. balance of payments as the government struggled to pay for both butter and guns. The swaps were at best a short-term palliative drug and not a cure. Foreign claims on dollar-denominated assets continued to build, soon expanding at an annual rate larger than the gold holdings of the United States. Any trigger event might cause a panic in the global market capable of creating a run on America's dwindling gold.

The eruption of the Arab-Israeli "Six-Day War" in June 1967 turned out to be that trigger. The panic hit the UK first but reverberated worldwide because, back on November 1, 1961, the U.S. Federal Reserve and seven European central banks had agreed to cooperate in maintaining the Bretton Woods system of fixed-rate convertible currencies by defending a gold price of $35 (U.S.) per ounce. They would use the London gold pool to counter upward or downward deviations from the $35 valuation on the London gold market. The United States was on the hook for 50% of the required gold supply in the pool. When the Six-Day War closed down the Suez Canal, UK global trade was hit hard as the international money market speculated fiercely against the pound.

What could Britain do? The Conservative approach would have introduced domestic austerity by increasing the Bank of England discount rate and slashing the government budget. Instead, the Labour government tried to borrow its way out of the crisis, drawing on its currency swap lines with the U.S. Federal Reserve and other central banks. It proved hopeless. On November 17, 1967, the pound was devalued by 14%, unleashing a tsunami of speculation in the London gold market that drained **$600 million** from the London gold pool inside of a week. Members of the pool rushed to make up the deficit, the United States Treasury even calling on a U.S. Air Force cargo transport aircraft to ferry Fort Knox bullion to London. When December brought another run on gold—**$400 million** gone in three days—LBJ did what he could not bring himself to do in Vietnam: He surrendered. He announced that he would request from Congress a 10% surtax and introduce other popularly unpalatable measures to bring the budget closer to balance. Still, the gold continued to flow out of the London pool.

In March, the new chairman of the CEA recommended that President Johnson slam shut the gold window if Bretton Woods members did not act to sell their gold on an uncovered basis to bolster the U.S. dollar. Fortunately, the Senate preempted this rash action by voting to repeal the law requiring that Federal Reserve notes be backed 25% by gold. Now the U.S. Treasury could access *all* of the nation's remaining gold stock, some **$12 billion** (already down from the **$22 billion** 1959 high). The conservative approach at this point would be to support sound money by using the gold to uphold the $35 gold/dollar parity. Once the run on gold was stopped, a conservative president would increase taxes and cut spending. This was the only chance to save the Bretton Woods system such that the world's major currencies would remain tied to a fixed value.

But that is not what the president did. Instead, on March 14, 1968, he announced the closure of the London gold pool. This triggered a global dumping of the dollar for other currencies. Two weeks later, on March 31, LBJ announced that, having personally become an unwillingly divisive force and an obstacle to peace in Vietnam, he would not seek reelection as president of the United States.

Following LBJ's unconditional withdrawal from the 1968 presidential race (March 31, 1968), the assassination of Robert F. Kennedy (June 6) during the primaries, and the riot-torn Democratic National Convention in Chicago (August 26–29), the Democratic Party's presidential candidate Hubert H. Humphrey was soundly defeated in the November 1968 elections, and Richard Nixon became the nation's 37th president.

RICHARD M. NIXON (R, 1969–1974)
Revenue = $5,114.77, Spending = $5,380.00,
Debt = $1,685.88; Change = $(101.41) / –6%

LBJ's closing of the gold pool cut the cord connecting the U.S. dollar with London's free market in gold. This teed up for the new president the possibility of a radical new direction in the management of the economy. By the time Nixon was sworn in on January 20, 1969, U.S. gold reserves had dwindled to **$10 billion**, whereas short-term dollar liabilities held by foreign central banks totaled some **$20 billion**. In short, the United States, issuer of the world's "reserve currency," could not cover with gold the dollar debt it owed to foreign nations and interests. The Vietnam War and the Great Society—guns *and* butter—had overdrawn the American bank account. With the United States now its deadbeat dad, Bretton Woods languished in its death throes throughout 1969–1970.

Early in 1971, West Germany withdrew from Bretton Woods, thereby boosting the German economy. Americans saw the dollar drop a sharp 7.6% against the Deutsche Mark. Next, Switzerland and France redeemed their dollars for gold, to the tune of **$50 million** and **$191 million,** respectively, prompting Congress to recommend devaluation of the dollar to protect it against "foreign price-gougers."[12] At this same time, August 1971, Switzerland quietly withdrew from the Bretton Woods system.

The drumbeat in Washington intensified: It was high time for the United States, linchpin of Bretton Woods, to make its exit. On August 13, 1971, Federal Reserve Chairman Arthur Burns, newly appointed Treasury Secretary John Connally, and Paul Volcker, future chairman of the Fed and, at the time, Undersecretary for International Monetary Affairs, secretly convened at Camp David with President Nixon and a dozen other top economic advisers. The most boisterous among them all was John Connally, the former Texas governor who had survived grievous wounds received in the assassination of John F. Kennedy. He advised permanently shutting the gold window and thereby ending Bretton Woods once and for all. To preempt the inflationary effects of cutting the dollar loose from gold, Connally also recommended freezing wages and prices for ninety days and, to ward off a run on the dollar, imposing an immediate 10% surcharge on all imports. He was confident that these steps would stabilize the economy and reduce both the 6.1% unemployment rate and the 5.84% inflation rate.[13]

Nixon agreed. On August 15, he closed the gold window and imposed the ninety-day freeze on wages and prices—the first time the federal government had intervened in this way since the days of rationing in World War II—and announced a 10% import surcharge. Cut loose from gold, the world's reserve currency was set adrift on a free float.

In the short term, most Americans enthusiastically approved the step. The Dow jumped 33 points on the Monday following the speech—at the time a record one-day gain. President Nixon ended the import surcharge in December, and in March 1973, the fixed exchange rate system officially became a floating exchange rate system. In the long term, the departure from Bretton Woods and gold triggered or exacerbated the stagflation of the 1970s, a brutal situation in which inflation is high while the growth of the economy is "stagnant," with slow growth and high unemployment. Nevertheless, Nobel laureate liberal economist Paul Krugman sees advantages in a dollar tied to nothing and in a Federal Reserve that "can print as much or as little money as it deems appropriate," responding "to actual or threatened recessions by pumping in money." Krugman believes that this flexibility prevented (for example) the stock market crash of 1987 from touching off a depression, as the crash of 1929 had done.[14] On the other hand, he points out that "freely floating national money... can create uncertainties for international traders and investors." Krugman concedes that the "costs of...volatility are hard to measure...but...must be significant."[15]

FROM GUNS AND BUTTER TO BUTTER AND EGGS

Paul Krugman wrote, "a system that leaves monetary managers free to do good also leaves them free to be irresponsible..."[16] To say the least, holding a license to print money is a tough test of character, and not everyone involved is a dedicated public servant.

The Chicago Mercantile Exchange, better known as the Merc and today called CME Group, was founded in 1898 as an agricultural commodities exchange with the homely name of the Chicago Butter and Egg Board. Its purpose for the first seventy-three years of its existence was trade in farm commodity futures, and, in this, it performed a vital function in the agricultural sector. For investors, agricultural futures trading is about making lucrative investments. For farmers and sellers, however, it is a means of locking in fall harvest prices before that harvest is planted in the spring. It is thus an indispensable risk-reducing, seasonal smoothing mechanism. The abandonment of Bretton Woods and the gold standard gave both elected and unelected government officials unprecedented power to shape (and deform) economic policy. It also gave one Leo Melamed, chairman of the Merc, an unprecedented inspiration. He would apply the William McKinley–vintage farm futures concept to the Tricky Dick

Nixon–vintage value of free-floating global currencies. One year after Camp David, in 1972, Melamed founded the International Monetary Market (IMM) under the auspices of the Merc. It was the world's first financial futures exchange.

Speculating on the future value of global currencies was entirely a creature of Camp David. Before the secret meeting there, when exchange rates were fixed, with most major currencies pegged to gold, those whose businesses depended on international exchange—on export and import—had no need to hedge their future purchases. What was based on $35/ounce gold in April would be based on $35/ounce gold in November. After Camp David, however, such hedging became essential.

But that is not all. Financial futures trading for its own sake, as strictly speculative arbitrage, became an even more compelling motive to invest in futures than hedging the currency risk involved in the business of importing or exporting actual goods. What IMM started in 1972 is now a global market with daily trade volume estimated at **$4 trillion**. The daily *merchandise* trade— trade in actual "stuff"—is a mere **$40 billion**. International currency speculation has become an end in itself. Paul Krugman remarked that the costs of the volatility of free-floating currency "are hard to measure...but...must be significant."[17] Stockman identifies these costs as "dead-weight losses to society" itself, a "massive churning" that is "a profound deformation of capitalism,...[consuming] vast resources without adding to society's output or wealth [because it] flush[es] income and net worth to the very top rungs of the economic ladder—rarefied redoubts of opulence which are currently occupied by the most aggressive and adept speculators."[18] Thus the signature economic "achievement" of the Nixon administration not only permanently destabilized world currencies and economies, it enabled and promoted the concentration of wealth among those we now call "the 1%."

THE NIXON SHADOW

lthough voters widely accepted the break with gold as a "necessary" and even "unavoidable" response to an international economic crisis, the unemployment rate nevertheless rose from 3.9% in January 1970 to 6.1% in December of that year, remaining around 6% through 1971 before declining to 5.2% by December of 1972. During 1973, unemployment generally hovered just below 5%, only to rise sharply through 1974, ending the year at 7.2% and hitting a peak of 9% in May 1975.[19] Inflation rates averaged 5.7% in 1970, falling to 4.4% and 3.2% in 1971–1972, when President Nixon introduced the wage and price freezes, but the number hit 6.2% in 1973 (the controls having been lifted) and stood at 11% for 1974, having peaked in December of that year at 12.3%.[20]

GERALD R. FORD (R, 1974–1977)
Revenue = $1,790.88, Spending = $2,183.53,
Debt = $1,901.18; Change = $215.30 / 13%

Taking a chainsaw to Bretton Woods is not the "crime" for which Richard Nixon was hounded into resignation on August 9, 1974. Watergate overshadowed what could have been called (in retrospect, of course) Bretton-gate, or, even more accurately, Default-gate. Assuming the presidency upon Nixon's resignation, Gerald Ford inherited stagflation and was defeated for election in his own right in 1976 by Democrat Jimmy Carter. As governor of Georgia, Carter was not widely known nationally, and he may be seen as the first of the modern era's "outsider" candidates, a new broom in the White House that Johnson and Nixon, each in their own way, had soiled.

JIMMY CARTER (D, 1977–1981)
Revenue = $4,378.01, Spending = $4,954.55,
Debt = $2,048.45; Change = $147.27 / 8%

President Carter sought to end what critics of Nixon termed "the imperial presidency," an administration of high-handed authoritarianism and secretiveness. He debuted on the national stage with the disarming informality of a genuine political outsider. This played well with voters, but not so well after the president was actually in the Oval Office. The most widely lampooned lapse in presidential image was his television appearance in a cardigan sweater rather than a suit to give a talk on energy conservation, in which he asked the American people to turn down their thermostats at home, just as he himself had in the White House. The talk was made necessary by the skyrocketing energy costs that would contribute to an inflation rate that averaged 5.8% in 1976, 6.5% in 1977, 7.6% in 1978, and a truly alarming 11.3% in 1979.[21] Yet the very idea of offering a cardigan and a lowered thermostat as the answer to persistent stagflation, the critical state of the energy markets, and the hostility of the Arabs who controlled much of the oil supply was off-putting. In his zeal to undo the imperial presidency, Jimmy Carter came off as prosaic and even feckless. His difficulty working with Congress—in which both chambers had two-thirds Democratic majorities—compounded the public perception of weak leadership. The deepening energy crisis brought on by the sharp increase in oil prices imposed by OPEC (Organization of Petroleum Exporting Countries) was beyond Carter's control, to be sure, yet Americans' anger over high gas prices and shortages was laid at the doorstep of the White House. Similarly, when Islamic revolutionaries stormed the U.S. embassy in Tehran and took much of the embassy staff hostage on September 4, 1979, Carter was blamed for his inability to secure their release.

Just when things, it seemed, couldn't possibly get worse, President Carter managed to make them worse by delivering, on July 15, 1979, a televised speech on the energy situation in which he told the nation that it faced "a crisis in confidence." It was a speech so pessimistic that commentators reported that it described Americans as suffering from a "malaise." Carter himself had not used that term, but it was attributed to him nonetheless, and it became the perfect foil against which Carter's opponent in the election of 1980 defined himself.

MORNING IN AMERICA

RONALD REAGAN (R, 1981–1989)
Revenue = $10,249.65, Spending = $12.633.05, Debt = $4,196.60; Change = $2,148.15 / 105%

In so many words, Republican presidential candidate Ronald Reagan told voters to stop whining about a "malaise" and, what is more, to stop turning down their thermostats. Instead, he asked them to return themselves to their birthright of greatness by voting for a candidate who would cut both taxes and the size of government and who would "get government off our backs." Candidate Reagan explained that these goals could be achieved by cutting out much of the regulatory Administrative State and rolling back the welfare state. The only area of government he proposed enlarging was the military, which needed to be bigger and stronger in order to win, once and for all, the Cold War. When he ran for reelection in 1984, his campaign featured a TV commercial officially titled "Prouder, Stronger, Better," but it became known as the "morning in America" ad, after its opening line:

It's morning again in America. Today, more men and women will go to work than ever before in our country's history. With interest rates at about half the record highs of 1980, nearly 2,000 families today will buy new homes, more than at any time in the past four years. This afternoon, 6,500 young men and women will be married, and with inflation at less than half of what it was just four years ago, they can look forward with confidence to the future. It's morning again in America, and under the leadership of President Reagan, our country is prouder and stronger and better. Why would we ever want to return to where we were less than four short years ago?[22]

Not malaise in America but morning in America is what Reagan had not only offered in 1980 but, the 1984 ad asserted, had also delivered. The sun had been made to rise just as soon as government was forced to stop holding it down. In his January 20, 1981, inaugural address,[23] Reagan had made precisely this point: "We suffer from the longest and one of the worst sustained inflations in our national history. It distorts our economic decisions, penalizes thrift, and crushes the struggling young and the fixed-income elderly alike. It threatens to shatter the lives of millions of our people." Clearly, he understood the human dimension of the crisis: "Idle industries have cast workers into unemployment, human misery, and personal indignity." And he put the blame not where his predecessor had put it, on Americans who turned their thermostats too high, but on government:

Those who do work are denied a fair return for their labor by a tax system which penalizes successful achievement and keeps us from maintaining full productivity.

But great as our tax burden is, it has not kept pace with public spending. For decades we have piled deficit upon deficit, mortgaging our future and our children's future for the temporary convenience of the present. To continue this long trend is to guarantee tremendous social, cultural, political, and economic upheavals.

The press would call Ronald Reagan "the Great Communicator," and a speech like this was why: We suffer, he said, because we are overtaxed even as the profligate "public spending" of the government means that no amount of taxation will ever be enough.

"In this present crisis," the new president proclaimed, "government is not the solution to our problem; government is the problem. From time to time we've been tempted to believe that society has become too complex to be managed by self-rule, that government by an elite group is superior to government for, by, and of the people. Well, if no one among us is capable of governing himself, then who among us has the capacity to govern someone else? All of us together, in and out of government, must bear the burden. The solutions we seek must be equitable, with no one group singled out to pay a higher price." We "hear much of special interest groups," he went on. "Well, our concern must be for a special interest group that has been too long neglected. It knows no sectional boundaries or ethnic and racial divisions, and it crosses political party lines. It is made up of men and women who raise our food, patrol our streets, man our mines and factories, teach our children, keep our homes, and heal us when we're sick—professionals, industrialists, shopkeepers, clerks, cabbies, and truck drivers. They are, in short, 'We the people,' this breed called Americans."

REAGANOMICS

There it was. In a handful of lines from an inaugural address—not the most poetic in American history, but surely one of the best—there was the promise, whole and entire: minimal government, minimal regulation of the private sector, lower taxes, reduction in public spending, an end to deficit spending—no more mortgaging our children's future—and an end to the costly influence of special interests. As distilled into what was popularly called "Reaganomics," it was an approach built on four pillars:

1. Reducing the growth of government spending
2. Reducing both the federal income tax and capital gains tax
3. Reducing government regulation
4. Tightening the money supply to reduce inflation

Reaganomics was founded on supply-side economics, which held that growth is most effectively achieved by investing in capital and lowering barriers on the production of goods and services. This requires implementation of pillars 2 and 3, lowering marginal tax rates and reducing government regulation. The benefits to consumers are more goods and services at lower prices. The benefit to working people is a reduction in unemployment because stimulated businesses will hire more of them.

TAXES UNDER REAGAN

To implement Reaganomics, the president signed the Economic Recovery Tax Act of 1981, which included a decrease in the marginal income tax rates by 23% over three years and reduced the top rate from 70% to 50%, the bottom rate from 14% to 11%, cut estate taxes, and sharply reduced corporate taxes. In 1982, however, he rolled back the corporate tax cuts and, to a lesser degree, the individual income tax cuts, reversing the total 1981 cut by about a third. In 1984, the president sent Congress a bill to close a variety of tax loopholes. As tax historian Joseph Thorndike observed, the 1982 and 1984 legislation transformed the president who had run on a promise of lowering taxes to get government off our backs into the president who introduced "the biggest tax increase ever enacted during peacetime."[24] Moreover, the bipartisan Tax Reform Act of 1986, further reducing the top marginal rate, removed various write-offs, preferences, and exceptions, thereby raising revenue by about 4%.[25] In the end, the Reagan-era taxes were generally reduced on higher earners and on capital gains on existing investments; however, payroll taxes rose, as did taxes on new investments. The president raised taxes eleven times, taking back 50%

of the original 1981 tax cut, but also lowering top marginal rates dramatically.[26]

PUBLIC SPENDING UNDER REAGAN

Reducing public spending was a mighty pillar of Reaganomics and a prominent passage in the president's 1981 inaugural address. During President Reagan's two terms, public spending actually increased significantly, mostly in the area of defense, with Department of Defense expenditures rising (in constant 2000 dollars) from **$267.1 billion** in 1980 to **$393.1 billion** in 1988. This represented an increase from 4.9% of GDP and 22.7% of public expenditure to 5.8% of GDP and 27.3% of public expenditure.[27] Nor did deficit spending end. On the contrary, the federal deficit topped out in 1983 at 6% of GDP in 1983, falling to 3.1% in the president's final budget.[28] Although the rate of growth in spending (adjusted for inflation) fell from 4% under Carter to 2.5% under Reagan, the deficit as a percentage of GDP was up from 2.7% at the end of the Carter years.[29]

It has been argued, often quite convincingly, that President Reagan's prodigious military spending was the secret weapon of the final, victorious battle of the Cold War. Under Reagan, the military budget ante was repeatedly upped until the Soviet Union went broke trying to keep up. If this was the last battle of the Cold War, it was won at high cost but without firing a single shot or losing a single soldier. Yet even admirers of Ronald Reagan must find stunning, especially given the sentiments he expressed in his first inaugural address concerning borrowing, the rise under Reagan of the national debt (in non-inflation-adjusted dollars) from **$997 billion** (with a B) to **$2.9 trillion** (with a T).[30] This transformed the nation, one cloudy morning in America, from the world's largest global creditor to the planet's greatest debtor.[31] In the years following Reagan, it only got worse.

HOW REAGAN LEFT US

Addison Wiggin and William Bonner provide a concise reading of what Reaganomics left us with.[32] The GDP grew at an annual average rate of 3.2% throughout the eight years of Reagan's two terms, a modest improvement over the 2.8% average gain in the eight years before, but substantially better than the 2.1% in the eight years (four of George H. W. Bush and four of Bill Clinton) that followed. Yet it hardly felt like morning in America, since growth was slower than in the 1960s, after Kennedy's 30% tax cut went into effect in 1964 and produced 5% annual GDP growth. It is true, however, that real median household income rose from $37,868 in 1981 to $42,049 in 1989, but this also lacked sticking power after Reagan left office.

The failure of even the modest improvement in the economy to endure suggests that the heart of Reaganomics, the emphasis on stimulating the *supply* side, failed in the long term. The increase on the *demand* side, however, did pick up. Federal government receipts fell from 20.2% of GDP in 1981 to 18.6% in 1992; however, spending during that period rose from 22.9% in 1981 to 23.5% in 1992. Obviously, borrowing increased. Adjusted for inflation to 2009 dollars, by the end of 1992, the federal debt was **$4.2 trillion**. In 1981, it had been **$2.1 trillion**.

No wonder George H. W. Bush, when he ran against Reagan in the 1980 Republican primaries, called his opponent's financial promises "voodoo economics."[33] President Reagan cut nominal tax rates, yet, because government borrowed, government consumed more resources. In the short term, lower tax rates stimulated consumer spending. People spend more when they feel richer. But for "every tax-cut dollar that a citizen spent, the federal government had to borrow as much as $1.18 (with interest)."[34]

The debt-burdened and debt-burdening reigns of the post-Reagan presidents are covered here, highlighting the ideological opposites, George W. Bush and Barack Obama, who together managed to take the federal debt to **$19.286 trillion**—*if not, indeed, something like ten times this amount, as some economists calculate it.*

CHAPTER 4

GEORGE H. W. BUSH

TO

BARACK OBAMA

fter serving as vice president through Ronald Reagan's two terms, George H. W. Bush won election to the presidency in 1988. Early the year before, *Time* had run an article by Robert Ajemian titled "Where Is the Real George Bush? The Vice President must now step out from Reagan's shadow." But Bush never really did, and in that article he unintentionally revealed why he never would. Ajemian reported that when a friend of Bush's suggested he go to Camp David to think through his plans for a Bush presidency, the candidate replied impatiently, "Oh, the vision thing."[1] George H. W. Bush came off as a competent manager, the president as technocrat. He made no radical changes to what Reagan had bequeathed to the economy, but oil prices spiked mightily during Operations Desert Shield/Desert Storm (the "first" Gulf War, 1990–1991), and unemployment climbed from about 5.4% in January 1989 to more than 7.3% in January 1993.[2]

GEORGE H. W. BUSH (R, 1989–1993)
Revenue = $6,160.01, Spending = $7,529.72,
Debt = $5,670.78; Change = $1,474.18 / 35%

AN END TO "THE VISION THING"

BILL CLINTON (D, 1993–2001)
Revenue = $15,955.79, Spending = $16,436.76,
Debt = $6,873.72; Change = $1,202.94 / 21%

The S&P 500 Index dipped during the Gulf War, but recovered quickly. It stood at 285.0 on January 1, 1989 and at 453.23 on January 1, 1993.[3] But Wall Street isn't Main Street, and Main Street felt left out. In 1992, Bill Clinton, the young Democratic governor of Arkansas defeated Bush with an economic policy some called "Clintonomics." It was a "New Democrat" policy, with four principal objectives that combined at least some of the pro-market orientation of the Reagan years with such perennial Democratic concerns as progressive income distribution and concern for the environment:

1. To create fiscal discipline, including balancing the budget
2. To maintain low interest rates that would encourage private-sector investment

3. To promote free trade by eliminating protectionist tariffs
4. To build America's human capital through education and advanced research

To achieve these objectives, Clinton promised to redesign government itself, making it less wasteful, more responsive, smaller, and friendlier to business while giving state and local jurisdictions more authority. The problem was that the Republican-Democratic hybrid did not always sit easily with Republicans—*or* Democrats, for that matter. Certainly, Clinton had a great deal of trouble obtaining congressional agreement on his 1993 budget. Although both the House and the Senate had Democratic majorities, Clinton was a moderate "New Democrat," at odds with more liberal legislators. In the end, he was able to sell Congress on what has been called "progressive fiscal conservatism." The 1993 budget combined policies of redistribution (the progressive part) with budget discipline (the fiscal conservative part) by including significant spending reductions and tax increases—which, however, were concentrated on upper-income taxpayers. The budget also expanded the Earned Income Tax Credit, Head Start, and other government programs that benefitted lower-income earners. Still, Clinton's emphasis on fiscal discipline narrowed the range within which policy-makers could create or expand programs. The Clinton budgets of FY 1990, FY 1993, and FY 1997 tightened up on discretionary spending, but also allowed income tax cuts—provided that these were offset by reductions in entitlement spending or increases in other taxes. Tax cuts were often precisely targeted to increase their effect while restricting their application. Many were aimed at education and environmental research and development.

The "small bore" nature of many of Clinton's initiatives and reforms brought scorn from some Republicans and Democrats alike. Seeking to achieve something bolder, President Clinton assigned Vice President Al Gore the task of chairing the National Performance Review (NPR), a key feature of Clinton's program to "reinvent government" (REGO) by streamlining it. In September 1993, Gore's NPR issued proposals designed to save **$108 billion** over five years by eliminating more than a quarter-million federal jobs and introducing many other systemic innovations, the most stunning of which was the creation of a "customer service contract" between the federal government and the American people.

Despite some Republican congressional scorn for a presumptuous invasion of President Reagan's ideological stomping grounds, the public liked REGO, but the leadership of Clinton's own party gave the initiative little support, thereby demonstrating the ultimate limits of any president's power to create changes in spending habits. Moreover, the president also had difficulty balancing domestic with international policies. His successful promotion, in his first term, of the North American Free Trade Agreement (NAFTA), which created free trade with Canada and Mexico, remained controversial, and his abrupt withdrawal of U.S. forces from the chaos of Somalia in October 1993,[4] made him look weak and inept in his management of global affairs. The electorate expressed their unease over Clinton's apparently unsteady command of foreign trade and military affairs by sending Republican majorities to both houses of Congress. Immediately, the new Republican speaker of the House, Newt Gingrich, seized on the midterm electoral rebuff of the Democrats to promulgate a "Contract with America," which trumped Gore's "customer service contract" and which sought to preempt relations between the presidency and the people by interposing Republican congressional pledges to eliminate federal programs, cut taxes, and generally reduce regulatory "burdens."

Like George H. W. Bush, Bill Clinton seemed destined to be a one-term president. But always at his best in adversity, Clinton doubled down on his "New Democrat" initiatives, taking fresh aim at taxes, crime reduction, welfare reform, and budget cutting in his boldest moves yet to encroach on the traditional Republican issues. He refined the aim of his economic policy to appeal to the middle class by promoting a balanced budget that did not require rolling back such New Deal and Great Society institutions as Social Security, Medicaid, Medicare, education initiatives, and environmental protection. Two years after taking a beating in the midterms, Clinton trounced Republican challenger Bob Dole in the 1996 general elections.

During the year of his reelection bid, *The New York Times* offered "Mr. Clinton's Economic Scorecard," asking, "How has he done?" The *Times'* answer was, "The record is mixed...." Having put "deficit reduction above all else, [Clinton] had no new money to spend. Once the Democratic leaders in Congress scuttled his plans to shift money away from their vested interests and toward new training and education initiatives, Mr. Clinton's invest-in-people strategy became little more than rhetoric." Nevertheless, "When Mr. Clinton was cautious—budget, trade, regulation—he was sensible and modestly successful. When he was bold—health care and welfare—he failed."[5]

From the backward-looking perspective of the economic disasters of his successor's two terms, a majority of Americans concluded that Clinton had presided over an economic boom and had also balanced the budget. Others, however, pointed out that the seeds of the implosion that took place during the administration of George W. Bush were planted by the Clinton administration. Clinton took a hands-off approach to Wall Street and took no action to counter the rising stock bubble of the late 1990s. The bursting of that bubble in 2000–2002 was the prelude to what was at the time the longest period without job creation since the Great Depression. Unfortunately, the nation recovered from the collapse of the stock bubble by pumping up another bubble, this one in housing. When that burst in 2008, it did so with even more catastrophic consequences than the downturn of 2000–2002.

Some suggest that the stock bubble, more than Clinton's tax increases and spending cuts, created the budget surpluses he left for George W. Bush to squander. In 1995, the Congressional Budget Office projected a deficit equal to between 2.7% and 3.1% of GDP for 2000.[6] As many see it, it was the capital gains generated by the tax bubble that created the tax revenue that led to the surplus. Undeniable is that the so-called Glass-Steagall Act—more accurately, the provisions in the Banking Act of 1933 that rigorously separated commercial and investment banking—was repealed under President Clinton in 1999 by the Gramm-Leach-Bliley Act. This tore down the legislative walls between the commercial and investment banking sectors, thereby blurring the strict distinctions between banking and securities products. With the walls down, the tracks were greased for banks to make the kind of risky and highly speculative investments that led to yet another bubble, in housing, which created a hot market for derivative subprime mortgage investment bundles. When these soggy paper bags soaked through, the bottoms fell out, and the massive financial crisis of 2007–2008 plopped down upon the nation and the world. It must be noted that Glass-Steagall, enacted as banking reform at the nadir of the Great Depression, had been subject to a long decline, which began even before the end of the Depression, and the effect of the legislation was increasingly diluted by court cases during the 1960s and 1970s. Glass-Steagall's repeal during the Clinton presidency had been a long time coming.

We may also see in NAFTA and other Clinton trade policies drivers of today's massive U.S. trade deficit, which has, in turn, contributed substantially to the budget deficits that came in the wake of the Clinton presidency.

MISSION ACCOMPLISHED

Bill Clinton's highest approval rating stood at 73% in the Gallup results of December 19, 1998 (his lowest was 36% on May 26, 1993, and his average for two terms was 55.1%). His immediate predecessor, George H. W. Bush, received a high of 89% just after the Gulf War (February 28, 1991), but the number fell as low as 29% (July 31, 1992) and averaged out over his single term at 60.9%. Ronald Reagan, who attained a kind of sainthood among many Republicans, did climb to 68% (as reported on May 16, 1986) but hit a low of 35% (January 28, 1983) and averaged below Clinton at 52.8%.[7]

Thus, subjectively, Bill Clinton was judged to be a good president. By the numbers, he increased the federal debt by 21%, adding **$1.2 trillion** to bring it to **$6.9 trillion**. This, however, was less of an increase in terms of percentage than the single-term increase under George H. W. Bush (+35%, a **$1.5 trillion** increase to **$.7 trillion**) and much less than under Ronald Reagan (+105%, an addition of **$2.1 trillion**, which brought the federal debt to **$4.2 trillion**).[8] More tangibly, under Clinton, the budget deficit dropped from **$290 billion** when he entered office to a budget *surplus* of **$128 billion**—a sum critics point out that came from taxing capital gains generated by the financial bubbles of the 1990s.[9]

GEORGE W. BUSH (R, 2001–2009)
Revenue = $18,782.14, Spending = $20,947.96,
Debt = $10,061.93; Change = $3,188.21 / 46%

With fewer popular votes than opponent Vice President Al Gore, George W. Bush became Clinton's successor in an electoral contest so close that it came down to a highly controversial 5–4 Supreme Court decision concerning the disputed vote count in a few counties of a single state, Florida. "It's amazing I won," Bush candidly confessed at a press conference on June 14, 2001. "I was running against peace, prosperity, and incumbency."[10]

Once in office, Bush made short work of the Clinton budget surplus. At the end of FY 2001 (October 1, 2000–September 30, 2001), the budget surplus was **$128 billion**. During the Bush presidency, it shifted into deficit[11]:

YEAR	RECEIPTS	OUTLAYS	DEFICIT
	(IN MILLIONS OF DOLLARS)		
2002	1,853,136	2,010,894	−157,758
2003	1,782,314	2,159,899	−377,585
2004	1,880,114	2,292,841	−412,727
2005	2,153,611	2,471,957	−318,346
2006	2,406,869	2,655,050	−248,181
2007	2,567,985	2,728,686	−160,701
2008	2,523,991	2,982,544	−458,553

First came the Bush tax cuts of 2001, 2002, 2003, 2004, 2005, and 2006. The Congressional Budget Office (CBO) reported declines in total federal revenues in 2001 (down **$10 billion**), 2002 (down **$138 billion**), and 2003 (down nearly **$71 billion**). Revenues turned up in FY 2004, but didn't reach pre-tax-cut levels until FY 2005.[12] This is at odds with some Republican claims, such as that of Senator Jeff Sessions (R-Alabama), that "revenue went up every single year after those tax cuts."[13] The CBO, in November 2012, released data showing that the expiration of the Bush-era tax cuts would have minimal negative impact on the economy while generating significant federal revenue.[14] Indeed, Mark Thoma, writing for *Business Insider,* called the Bush cuts a "test of [Republican] claims about supply-side economic policies.... We were promised that cutting taxes on the wealthy would result in much higher economic growth and broadly shared prosperity" and that "the cuts wouldn't cost us anything. Growth would be so strong that the tax cuts would more than pay for themselves.... The reality, of course, has been quite different. There is little evidence that the Bush tax cuts, or any other tax cuts directed at the so-called job creators, have had a noticeable effect on economic growth."[15] The U.S. Census Bureau's September 2009 report, "Income, Poverty, and Health Insurance Coverage in the United States: 2008," revealed that the median household income in 2007 was lower than it had been in 2000.[16] In testimony to the Senate Budget Committee (November 15, 2011), CBO director Douglas Elmendorf advised extending all of the Bush tax cuts *except* those exclusively targeting high-income taxpayers.[17]

It is crucially important to note that the Bush tax cuts are not simply "to blame" for projected long-term deficits. Entitlement costs certainly dwarf their effect.[18] Nevertheless, the net cost of those cuts in federal receipts was amplified by a failure to make significant cuts in outlays. The fact is that, of the tax cuts, all but the first were made while the country was at war. The terrorist attacks of September 11, 2001, prompted the Bush administration to take the nation into two wars—undeclared by Congress, of course—one against the Taliban in Afghanistan and the other against Saddam Hussein's Iraq. As innumerable critics have pointed out, both of these wars were wars of choice rather than of necessity. As was the case when the United States went to war against Germany and its allies in World War I, neither the Taliban nor (even less) Iraq posed a direct existential threat to the United States. Let's not, however, further argue here the merits of these wars, but simply point out their staggering cost, a cost incurred in the midst of a relentless series of what the National Priorities Project termed "heedless tax cuts"[19]:

FISCAL YEAR	COST (IN BILLIONS OF DOLLARS)
2001–2002	20.8
2003	67.7
2004	90.4
2005	105.5
2006	120.6
2007	170.4
2008	185.6
2009	155.0
2010	171.7
2011	169.4
2012	121.1
2013	98.7
2014	92.3
2015	73.3
TOTAL	$1642.5

The conclusion is inescapable. Like Lyndon Johnson, who was committed to maintaining a guns *and* butter economic policy, President Bush was unwilling to risk making the wars against Afghanistan and Iraq unpopular by obliging American taxpayers to dig deeper to pay for them.

Aside from contributing to the digging a very deep hole, did the Bush tax cuts accomplish anything of value—other than warding off a popular revolt against the wars? In conservative Republican hands, tax cuts are often seen as tools to forcibly reduce the size of government by "starving the beast." Yet government spending increased significantly since the Bush tax cuts, from 17.6% of GDP in 2000 to 20.2% of GDP in 2008, a period during which both the presidency and the House were in Republican hands.[20]

Did the tax cuts at least stimulate the economy, making American lives better and more prosperous? Compared to the ten administrations before him, that of George W. Bush saw the lowest employment growth and the lowest growth in disposable income. Consumer confidence during the Bush presidency was also low. Compared to the six previous administrations during which consumer confidence was evaluated, only Jimmy Carter fared worse than Bush.

In terms of economic growth, as measured by the Dow Jones Industrial Averages, Bush left office with the stock market down 2.3%, annualized, over eight years.[21] Of the presidents since John F. Kennedy, George W. Bush, ranks below all.[22]

COLLAPSE: WHO'S TO BLAME?

Blame for the collapse of the housing and subprime mortgage bubbles in 2007–2008 and the economic meltdown this brought on is often laid at the feet of George W. Bush. He hardly deserves all the blame, and, in fact, as early as 2001, President Bush began warning of what were described as "the systemic consequences of failure to reform GSEs"—government-sponsored enterprises, including mortgage lenders Freddie Mac and Fannie Mae. Congress either ignored or rejected these calls for reform in 2001, 2002, 2003, 2004, 2005, 2007, and 2008.[23] Moreover, the kind of imprudent financial deregulation that enabled reckless lending and the excesses of the derivatives market had their origin in the Clinton, if not even earlier. It is a contention of this book that the regulatory functions of the Administrative State are at present increasingly oppressive, costly, and counterproductive to economic growth. Yet *less* supervision is not the same as *lax* supervision. It is probably fair to say that appropriate leadership has been missing since President Nixon untied America's currency from the discipline of gold. Since this time, investors at every level have been subject to decreasing regulation. As financial instruments have become increasingly complex and increasingly based on derivatives—that is, defined by contracts that are based on the performance of underlying entities—the need for investors to perform due diligence has become more and more urgent, especially in the absence of much meaningful government oversight. This is especially true when the underlying entities are not tangible assets, but the likes of indexes and interest rates. But even where highly tangible assets have been involved, namely bundles of mortgages (which are loans collateralized by earth, brick, and mortar), investors—including giant banks and venerable investment institutions—demonstrated extraordinary recklessness and even an absence of the most basic fiduciary responsibility.

As the Federal Reserve "managed" the money supply to keep interest rates unnaturally low, the man and woman on the street could no longer think of a savings account as a place to put their money. Stocks were an obvious choice, but increased volatility often made them unsuitable for small investors. With low interest rates, lax lending requirements, the mortgage interest federal tax deduction, and policies promulgated both in the Clinton and Bush presidencies designed to increase home ownership by making ownership "affordable," *buying a home* became *investing in real estate.* To many, in fact, home ownership seemed the only worthwhile investment. For the first time in history, a home was less a place to live and raise a family than it was a fast-growth commodity in which to invest. This transformation began before George W. Bush entered the White House, as President Clinton inflated the national housing bubble through subsidy and easy loan programs offered by the Department of Housing and Urban Development, Fannie Mae, Freddie Mac, and Ginnie Mae. The Clinton mandates were embraced by the Bush administration, under which the bubble inflated even faster and bigger.[24] Add to this a regulatory regime so lax as to be virtually vestigial and corrupt private-sector credit rating agencies (CRAs) that failed to audit the creditworthiness (indeed, unworthiness) of the mortgages that were being packaged and sold to investors, and the subprime mortgage crisis and financial collapses of 2007–2008 were inevitable.

MISSION IMPOSSIBLE

On March 16, 2003, President George W. Bush issued an ultimatum to Saddam Hussein: "All the decades of deceit and cruelty have now reached an end. Saddam Hussein and his sons must leave Iraq within 48 hours. Their refusal to do so will result in military conflict, commenced at a time of our choosing."[25] When the deadline passed, on March 19, President Bush took the United States to war. Two and a half months later, on May 2, 2003, the president dramatically landed in a Lockheed S-3 Viking anti-submarine jet on the deck of the aircraft carrier USS *Abraham Lincoln* anchored just off its San Diego base. Emerging from the two-man craft in full flight suit, the smiling president waved to the carrier's assembled crew, went below, and changed into a business suit and tie. A short time later, he mounted a podium set up on the flight deck, a huge banner emblazoned with the phrase "Mission Accomplished" festooning the ship's superstructure "island" in the background.

"Admiral Kelly, Captain Card, officers and sailors of the USS *Abraham Lincoln*, my fellow Americans," President Bush began. "Major combat operations in Iraq have ended. In the Battle of Iraq, the United States and our allies have prevailed."[26]

Up to the moment of this declaration, the post-9/11 wars had cost **$88.5 billion**. After the "Mission Accomplished" declaration, they would cost an *additional* **$1.5 trillion**.[27] Mission accomplished? It was just getting started.

Then came 2008, an election year and, as it turned out, a day of reckoning the likes not lived through since 1929. We will explore the 2008 subprime mortgage "meltdown" and its consequences in Chapter 7, but this is how matters stood on September 30, 2008, little more than a month before the election: The federal deficit for FY 2008 was projected at $438 billion in October, but by the 2008 elections predictions ran much higher. Operations in Iraq were consuming nearly $12 billion per month.[28] The president responded with deep cuts or funding freezes in domestic programs, including the elimination of grants for firefighters' assistance, low-income schools, family literacy, and rural housing and economic development. The national debt passed the $10 trillion mark, representing nearly $33,000 per U.S. resident. Under pressure of the wars in the Middle East, gasoline prices exceeded $4 per gallon by July.[29] The crisis in the mortgage industry metastasized with stunning speed and aggression, becoming a meltdown, it seemed, of the global economy itself. To rescue the hemorrhaging financial sector, the federal government sliced open its own veins and let an estimated $22 trillion flow out of government coffers, credit accounts, and the economy itself.

THE BATTERED BATON IS PASSED

BARACK OBAMA (D, 2009–2017)
Revenue = $20,123.30, Spending = $27,138.13,
Debt = $17,222.90; Change = $7,160.97/ 71%

Barack Obama was elected over Republican John McCain by a substantial margin, 52.9% of the popular vote versus 45.7% (365 electoral votes versus 173). During the interval between Obama's election in November and his inauguration in January, President Bush seemed to recede into the background, and President-elect Obama took center stage in the economic crisis. "The markets are saying that George Bush is irrelevant to the economic future of the country, and they want to hear from Obama," New York University professor Paul Light told McClatchyDC. "Obama doesn't have much choice but to reassure the markets as best he can. The ball is in his court whether he likes it or not."[30]

The new president entered the White House with a popular wind at his back. Since the current state of the economy in general and the federal debt in particular are the subjects of this book, Barack Obama's two terms will come under close scrutiny throughout it. For now, let us merely observe that economic policy under George W. Bush was burdened by an overabundance of optimism or a paucity of realism. Maybe both. Bush slashed taxes during a costly war. Now, with revenue throttled, Barack Obama was faced with financing two ongoing wars and massive bailout and "stimulus" initiatives.

We can assume that President Obama, like every chief executive before him, accepted this battered baton with the best of intentions. But recall an incident unrelated to the economic crisis. On Christmas Day 2009, Northwest Airlines Flight 253, bound for Detroit from Amsterdam, was nearly blown out of the sky by a terrorist with a bomb sewn into his underpants.[31] At a press gaggle aboard Air Force One on January 4, 2010, "Deputy Press Secretary Bill Burton told reporters that President Obama's focus on national security in the wake of the Christmas Day bombing attempt will not take his focus away from increasing employment levels and other issues. 'When you're President of the United States you've got to be able to walk and chew gum at the same time, so you can anticipate there's going to be a very heavy push to get Americans back to work,' Burton said." He added, "in addition to working 'to get the economy as strong as it can be,' the White House would remain focused on passing 'health care [reform], financial regulatory reform, things like that.'"[32]

Walk and chew gum. Whereas President Bush had tried to finance a bailout while borrowing the money to fight two wars, President Obama not only enhanced the bailout but continued the wars (while also winding them down) *and* pursued a "hope and change" agenda that entailed even more ambitiously stimulating the economy and multiplying an already unsustainable burden of entitlements by adding the Patient Protection and Affordable Health Care Act ("Obamacare") to them. Moreover, he approached this feat of simultaneous perambulation and mastication in the manner of every president after the dour Jimmy Carter. Whereas Carter donned a cardigan and scolded the electorate to turn down their thermostats, Ronald Reagan, George H. W. Bush, Bill Clinton, George W. Bush, and now,

Barack Obama, proposed to offer more than could possibly be paid for and to fix absolutely everything, without the necessity of sacrifice or pain.

A 2010 Pew Research survey found that only about a third of Americans knew that the main government bailout program—the Troubled Asset Relief Program (TARP)—had been signed into law by George W. Bush, not (as 47% of those Pew questioned mistakenly believed) Barack Obama.[33] Part of the reason for this error was that most Americans are notoriously uninformed about the nation's politics. But, arguably, a more direct cause was that the Obama administration eagerly doubled down on TARP. Like his four most immediate predecessors, Barack Obama ensured that, whatever course his administration embraced, there would be nary a cardigan in sight and the thermostat would be set to "nice and toasty."

Bush's guns and butter spending plus TARP and the rest added **$5.8 trillion** to the federal debt. Obama put the guns and the butter and the vigorous continuation of TARP together with the American Recovery and Reinvestment Act of 2009. ARRA was an $831-billion hyper-Keynesian stimulus package that created and continues to create significant controversy as to its impact on employment and economic output and its costs versus its benefits. The IDM Forum poll conducted by the University of Chicago Booth School of Business in 2012 found that 29% of experts "strongly agreed" and 51% "agreed" that unemployment at the end of 2010 was lower because of ARRA. Asked, however, whether the "benefits will end up exceeding costs," only 12% "strongly agreed," 34% "agreed," and 27% were "uncertain," whereas 5% "disagreed" and 7% "strongly disagreed" (2% had "no opinion"). Asked these same questions in 2014, more respondents were willing to conclude that "benefits will end up exceeding costs": 20% "strongly agreed," 36% "agreed," 23% were "uncertain," and 5% "disagreed," but now 0% "strongly disagreed" (0% had "no opinion").[34]

It has been a whole lot of chewing and a whole lot of walking—Barack Obama's statist project to achieve a total economic reset by adding to the Bush bailouts a massive stimulus (that even committed neo-Keynesians like Paul Krugman criticized as *insufficiently massive* to "jumpstart the economy"[35]). The result (in current dollars) was an OMB-projected **$8.5 trillion** added to the debt, a 72.8% increase over the Bush monster, to an OMB-projected **$20.1 trillion**. (As of 4:11 p.m. EST on June 23, 2016, the debt stood at **$19.286 trillion**, according to the U.S. Debt Clock.[36]) The consequences of such a number, intended and unintended, are virtually unfathomable.

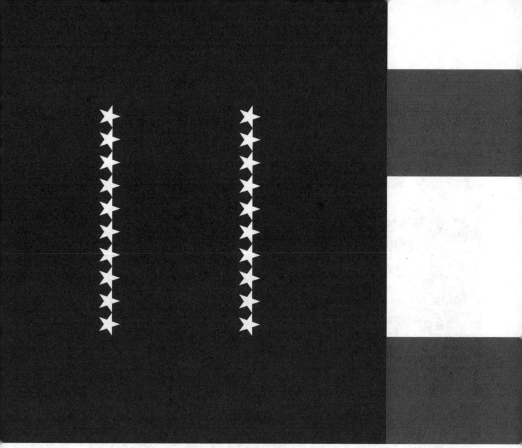

THE TYRANNY
OF GOOD INTENTIONS
SPENDING OUT OF CONTROL

These days, people love to tell pollsters how little they trust their government. Nevertheless, as this chapter shows, they trust it all too easily and far too much. The failure to question government, to get curious and to be skeptical, has allowed government not merely to grow but to metastasize. This chapter charts that malignant growth through fraud, waste, and abuse, yes, but mostly through the very best of intentions implemented inefficiently, unrealistically, or both.

CHAPTER 5

IN

GOVERNMENT

WE TRUST

The Preamble to the Constitution assigns just six duties to government, among which is promotion of "the general Welfare." Common sense alone tells us that setting fiscal policies that balance benefits against costs is essential to our nation's *general welfare*. Yet, as this chapter details, creating this balance was ignored only in extraordinary times during our first hundred-plus years, but throughout most of the 20th century and now into the 21st, breathtaking disregard for benefit-cost analysis has become a matter of policy and routine. The consequence of this quite literal ignorance is the purchase of a general welfare state at the cost of the general welfare itself.

Gallup and the Pew Research Centers are the top brand names in American polling. Yet they rarely agree. Gallup tends toward the right, Pew toward the left. So it's newsworthy, maybe even remarkable, when these two public opinion titans come to the same conclusion: Americans are losing faith in their government.

True, as of June 2015, Gallup reported a slight uptick in Americans' confidence in each of the three branches of government. But the keyword is "slight," and the key context is that the previous poll, in 2014, showed confidence at an all-time ("historic") low. In the June 2015 poll, 33% of Americans had "a great deal" or "quite a lot" of confidence in the presidency (up from 29% in 2014), 32% reported comparable levels of confidence in the Supreme Court (up from 30%), but just 8% expressed the same sentiments about Congress (up from 7%).[1]

In November 2015, Pew reported that a mere 19% of Americans said that they trusted the government "always/most of the time," that "20% would describe government programs as being well-run," and that 55% believed "'ordinary Americans' would do a better job of solving national problems" than the government does.[2]

The dismal numbers unmistakably trend downward. In 1991, confidence in the presidency was at 72%, in the Supreme Court at 48%, and in Congress at 30%, according to Gallup. In 2005, it was at 44% for the presidency, 41% for the Supreme Court, and 22% for Congress.[3] Pew tracked overall confidence in government from a high of 77% in October 1964, when Lyndon Johnson was president, to a steep dip in March 1980, 27%, during the Carter presidency, to 42% in March 1991 under George H. W. Bush, and to 31% in September 2005 under George W. Bush.[4]

Judging by the numbers, Americans did not always distrust their government. But they do now.

Or at least they say they do—and they presumably believe they do. But if we dig deeper into the Pew research, the picture becomes more complex.[5] While it is true that 74% of those Pew questioned in 2015 reported their opinion that "most elected officials put [their] own interests ahead of the country's" and 55% thought that "ordinary Americans would do a better job solving problems," respondents had a mixed and generally more positive view of both the role of government and its performance in specific areas:

AREA	MAJOR ROLE FOR GOVERNMENT	GOVERNMENT DOING A GOOD JOB
Keeping country safe from terror	94%	72%
Responding to natural disasters	88%	79%
Ensuring safe food and medicine	87%	72%
Managing immigration system	81%	28%
Maintaining infrastructure	76%	52%
Protecting the environment	75%	59%
Strengthening the economy	74%	51%
Ensuring access to high-quality education	70%	52%
Ensuring basic income for 65+	69%	48%
Setting workplace standards	66%	76%
Ensuring access to health care	61%	56%
Helping people get out of poverty	55%	36%
Advancing space exploration	47%	51%

If we calculate the average grade for government performance based on this area-by-area breakdown, we find that 56.3% of Americans—a fairly solid majority—believe the government is doing a good job. Perhaps even more significantly, we find that 72.5% believe government should play a major role not only in defense and immigration, but in disaster response, regulation (in the areas of food, medicine, and the environment), infrastructure, economic stewardship, the workplace, education, and welfare (for seniors, for access to health care, for addressing poverty). The only area a slim majority of Americans (53%) want the government to move out of is space exploration.

THE DISSONANT STATES OF AMERICA

sychologists have a name for what the Pew research reveals. It is *cognitive dissonance,* a state of mental stress experienced when a person holds two or more contradictory beliefs, ideas, or values at the same time. When asked *in a general way* how they feel about government, a large majority of Americans these days are very negative. When asked this question in terms of *specific areas* or topics, however, these same Americans are far more approving. In fact, well over half feel that the government is doing a good job in most areas, and nearly three-quarters believe that government has a role to play in a wide array of fields.

For some time now, the country has been divided pretty evenly between those who identify themselves on the conservative end of the spectrum and those who call themselves liberals or progressives. In terms of these self-applied labels, the nation is divided approximately 50/50. Asked what they think of the federal government generally, just 19% of Americans across this 50/50 divide say that they feel confidence, and only 20% say that government programs are well run. Yet the far more positive responses elicited when pollsters ask more detailed and specific questions about government also cut across the 50/50 divide. It is no surprise to hear a self-identified *liberal* opine that government properly has many roles to play and that the government performs quite well in them. What is surprising is that a significant fraction of self-identified *conservatives* also believe that government has a place in numerous fields and that it generally does a good job in them.

Since at least the rise of the Tea Party movement following Barack Obama's 2009 inauguration, it has been generally assumed that a vocal minority of voters was attracting a growing majority in at least questioning, if not outright condemning, "big government" and calling for sharp cuts in spending across many areas and the complete withdrawal of the federal government from others. During 2009–2010 especially, self-identified Tea Party members often showed up at "town meetings" convened by various political leaders, including President Obama. They used these forums to protest a variety of initiatives, but especially health-care reform. As reported in *The Huffington Post* in September 2009 (and updated in May 2011), the president told one town hall crowd that he "got a letter the other day from a woman.

She said, 'I don't want government-run health care. I don't want socialized medicine. And don't touch my Medicare." An attendee at another town hall, this one held by a Republican, Representative Robert Inglis of South Carolina, warned the congressman to "Keep your government hands off my Medicare." Inglis told *The Washington Post* that he "had to politely explain that, 'Actually, sir, your health care is being provided by the government.' But [the irate speaker] wasn't having any of it."[6]

Liberals have cited the "Keep your government hands off my Medicare" admonition so often that it has become an Internet meme. They use it to mock the Tea Party and others who rail against big government even as they covet the bounty big government provides. But such patronizing mockery misses the point. It is not that those who distrust government are misinformed. It is not that those who believe the government has become too big and too costly are wrong. It is not even that many Americans just don't know what it is they really want from their political leaders. It is that many Americans are genuinely conflicted. Their impulse is to distrust and disdain big government. Yet, when, prompted to examine, piece by piece, the responsibilities of that government, many are reluctant to ask for, let alone demand, change.

America's cognitive dissonance when it comes to big government is neither ignorant nor hypocritical. It is irrational—or, more precisely, it is beyond rationality. Call it non-rational.

In the great 1982 movie *The Verdict,* Paul Newman, on the verge of losing his client's case, has one last chance: the summation to the jury. "You know," he tells them, "so much of the time we're just lost. We say, 'Please, God, tell us what is right; tell us what is true.'... In my religion, they say, 'Act as if ye had faith...and faith will be given to you.'"[7] To call faith irrational sounds like a condemnation. Call it, rather, non-rational.

The essential non-rationality of simultaneously condemning and praising big government is a product of faith—faith in government, our government, which is *big* government. For a majority of Americans, it is a faith that survives both argument and evidence. Faith, after all, is non-rational. Incredibly enough, however, it is also a faith that survives even one's own deep feelings of dissatisfaction and outright anger: *The government? The government is too big, too incompetent, too inefficient, too corrupt, too biased, too expensive! Ordinary people could do a better job than the politicians we elect!* Yet: *When it comes to fighting terrorism, looking after our seniors, giving people access to health care, helping folks out of poverty, taking care of the environment—yes—government does have a responsibility and it actually does a pretty good job. But, hey, just keep your big government hands off my Medicare!*

Judging from the Pew results, most Americans say they distrust government, yet they act as if they had faith in it...and—Glory, hallelujah!—faith has been given to them.

Faith is essential to every religion. There are at least 4,300 different faith groups in the world,[8] and people rarely choose their faith as a result of persuasion through logical argument. Typically, their choice is a matter of birth and upbringing, but any sustained allegiance to a faith is, again typically, a matter of faith. Faith can survive the onslaught of logic, pragmatic convenience, counter-argument, the evidence of life experience, and sometimes even coercion and outright persecution. Although faith is essential to every religion, faith has no constitutional role in government, including in the evaluation of government. The First Amendment to the United States Constitution guarantees freedom *of* religion (Congress is barred from making any law "prohibiting the free exercise of" religion) but also freedom *from* religion ("Congress shall make no law respecting an establishment of religion..."). Undeniably, faith has long played an important part in American life, but in writing the First Amendment, James Madison simultaneously obligated Congress to respect religion *and* remove the business of government from religion. Before any of us can intelligently and effectively judge our government—its roles, its priorities, its management of finances—we must abandon our faith in government and base both our support and our criticism on evidence, analysis, and informed opinion. What we decide has to make sense on rational grounds. Democracy is perfectly compatible with faith, but no democracy can survive on faith alone or on faith that is unempirical and unthinking.

THE CONSTITUTION:

SHORT, SWEET, AND SUBJECT TO CORRECTION

Fortunately for us, our American democracy comes with a set of rules and a statement of values written in concise form by admirably rational authors. I refer, of course, to the Constitution. Although some politicians compare it to the Bible as the sacred book of American government, it is not *the* Bible or even *a* bible, and it was never intended as such. It is, rather, a set of principles and precedents that "constitute" the government. The Constitution is a guide—a *firm* guide—written by men who had participated in the government of the colonies, who had read widely in the history and philosophy of government, and who had contemplated what today would be called the "best practices" of both existing and historical governments (especially that of the ancient Roman Republic).

But how do we actually know that the framers of the Constitution did not think of it as holy writ and final word?

First, there is its distinctly unbiblical brevity. The King James Version of the Holy Bible contains 783,137 words. At about 4,400 words, the Constitution is by far the briefest constitution of any major government in the world. Yet it is also the oldest—in other words, the most durable. Doubtless, one of main reasons for its longevity is also the second feature that tells us its authors did not think of it as final. Article V provides for "amendment" of the Constitution. Now, *amendment* is a very interesting word. At its simplest, an "amendment" is a change in the words and, often, the meaning of a document, especially the text of a law. But in the late 18th century, when the Constitution was written, the word *amendment* more specifically meant (according to the *Oxford English Dictionary*) "The removal of faults, correction, reformation." Even today, to *amend* is to both change *and* improve—"to put right" (in the phrase *Merriam-Webster* uses). We still speak of "making amends" as a gesture of apology and compensation for a loss, injury, slight, rudeness, or other wrong we may have inflicted.

A document that provides for its own amendment confesses itself to be manifestly imperfect and therefore certainly far from biblical. With Article V, the framers of the Constitution acknowledged not only that they might be mistaken in their own time, at the moment, but also that times do change and so the government's constitution might also have to be changed accordingly. Without this provision, the Constitution would be today, like the Articles of Confederation it replaced, nothing more than a historical document. Those Articles, by the way, included no formal provision for amendment.

Nevertheless, Article V intentionally makes the process of amendment difficult and demanding. A two-thirds majority of both houses of Congress must first propose the specific amendment, which is then submitted to the legislatures of the states. Only after three-quarters of the state legislatures ratify the amendment does it become part of the Constitution. As an alternative to congressional action, two-thirds of state legislatures may call "a convention for proposing amendments." In either case, whether originated by Congress or by a constitutional convention, any proposed amendment must be ratified by three-quarters of the state legislatures before it becomes part of the Constitution. In the nearly 230 years since the ratification of the Constitution in 1788, an estimated 11,000 attempts have been made to amend it—an average of nearly fifty attempts a year. But just twenty-seven amendments have been passed and ratified—ten of those bundled together in the Bill of Rights (written in 1789 and ratified in 1791). Clearly, while the framers owned up to imperfection, they did not intend for change to be undertaken lightly, expediently, or for the sake of transitory convenience.

A GOVERNMENT OF LAWS,

NOT OF MEN

In the Constitution, the framers embodied the values they believed should be the enduring foundation of the nation's government. All laws had to conform to the Constitution and, therefore, all laws would flow from these enduring values. Like the Constitution itself, those laws were not necessarily permanent in the sense of being absolute and timeless, but they were more enduring than the particular people who wrote them at a particular time, in a particular situation, and moved by particular thoughts and passions. No role of the Constitution was more important than the promotion of what John Adams, in the 1780 Constitution of Massachusetts, called "a government of laws, and not of men."[9]

In a 1789 letter to fellow founding father Roger Sherman, John Adams wrote, "Power naturally grows. Why? Because human passions are insatiable. But that power alone can grow which already is too great; that which is unchecked; that which has no equal power to control it."[10] Two years earlier, in writing to Thomas Jefferson, Adams declared "that neither Philosophy, nor Religion, nor Morality, nor Wisdom, nor Interest, will ever govern nations or Parties, against their Vanity, their Pride, their Resentment or Revenge, or their Avarice or Ambition. Nothing but Force and Power and Strength can restrain them."[11]

Adams and Jefferson disagreed on much and did so in much the same way as Republicans and Democrats disagree today. But they agreed absolutely on the force and power of a government of laws to harness, guide, and check the force and power of insatiable human passions. The difference between them was chiefly this: Whereas Adams feared unchecked power in human beings themselves, Jefferson feared unchecked power in human beings acting through unchecked government. Whereas Adams believed that people were subject to an insatiable lust for increase of power at the expense of others, Jefferson believed that it is in the nature of government, if unchecked, to feed, to abet, to enable, and to magnify that lust.

Both Adams and Jefferson were in Europe—Adams as ambassador (minister) to Great Britain and Jefferson as ambassador (minister) to France—when James Madison led the drafting of the Constitution, so neither man took a direct part in its creation. On December 20, 1787, Jefferson wrote to Madison to tell him what he liked and did not like about the proposed document. He had two specific objections and one that was more general. The first was the "omission of a bill of rights"—an objection others shared and an omission that would be swiftly remedied. The "second feature I dislike," he wrote, "and greatly dislike, is the abandonment in every instance of the necessity of rotation in office, and most particularly in the case of the President." Jefferson wanted a strict one-term limit on all federal elective offices. In the case of the president in particular, he feared that otherwise "the first magistrate will always be re-elected if the Constitution permits it. He is then an officer for life."[12]

This second objection was related to Jefferson's more general confession that he was "not a friend to a very energetic government" because such government "is always oppressive." Commenting on Shays' Rebellion, an armed protest mainly against aggressive tax and debt collection in Massachusetts (August 1786–June 1787), Jefferson observed to Madison that the uprising created "more alarm than I think it should have done. Calculate that one rebellion in 13 states in the course of 11 years, is but one for each state in a century & a half. No country should be so long without one."[13] Some ten months earlier, Jefferson had written to Madison, "I hold it that a little rebellion now and then is a good thing, and as necessary in the political world as storms in the physical.... It is a medecine [sic] necessary for the sound health of government."[14] But Jefferson himself did not rebel against the proposed Constitution, assuring Madison, "If they approve the proposed Convention [Constitution] in all it's [sic] parts, I shall concur in it chearfully [sic], in hopes that they will amend it whenever they shall find it work wrong."[15]

Neither Adams nor Jefferson would have had any reason to criticize the Preamble to the Constitution. In admirably concise prose, it identifies the authority for government, the allowable functions of government, and the purpose of the Constitution itself:

> We the People of the United States, in Order to form a more perfect Union, establish Justice, insure domestic Tranquility, provide for the common defence, promote the general Welfare, and secure the Blessings of Liberty to ourselves and our Posterity, do ordain and establish this Constitution for the United States of America.

The Preamble identifies "the People" as the authority for the Constitution and therefore of the government as well. (Today, those who fume at "*the* government" need to remember that they are railing against "*their* government" and act accordingly.) The Preamble then goes on to enumerate four roles for the government as defined by the Constitution for the purpose of achieving two ends. The government is to function to 1) establish justice, 2) ensure domestic tranquility, 3) provide for the common defense, and 4) promote the general welfare; and it is to do so for the purpose of 1) forming a more perfect union, and 2) securing the "Blessings of Liberty" for the present and the future. The rest of the Constitution establishes a framework and basic rules (with the force of law) for carrying out these four roles and achieving these two ends. Within the framework and the basic rules, it is the task of legislators, the president, and the judiciary to figure out permissible ways to execute the responsibilities of government. To the legislature also falls the task of finding the means to fund execution of the functions of government.

Section 8, Clause 18 of Article I of the Constitution gives to Congress the power "To make all Laws which shall be necessary and proper for carrying into Execution the foregoing Powers, and all other Powers vested by this Constitution in the Government of the United States, or in any Department or Officer thereof." James Madison believed that this so-called "Necessary and Proper Clause" empowered Congress (and thereby the federal government) while also defining the limits of its power (by restricting it to what is "necessary and proper"). A number of the states wanted the limits of government power to be stated more explicitly and therefore asked for an amendment to be added using language borrowed from the Articles of Confederation: "Each state retains its sovereignty, freedom, and independence, and every power, jurisdiction, and right, which is not by this Confederation expressly delegated to the United States, in Congress assembled." Madison at first objected, arguing that Article I, Section 8, Clause 18 already implied this by limiting Congress to the powers variously enumerated in Article I and adding only the power to make "necessary and proper laws" for the execution of those "enumerated powers." But when several states conditioned their ratification of the Constitution on the inclusion of an amendment making explicit the limitation of federal authority, Madison agreed, provided that the word "expressly" was deleted lest it be interpreted as rejecting the federal powers implied by the "Necessary and Proper Clause." The Tenth Amendment thus became the final amendment in the Bill of Rights: "The powers not delegated to the United States by the Constitution, nor prohibited by it to the States, are reserved to the States respectively, or to the people."

SO WHAT'S TO ARGUE ABOUT?

The brevity of the Preamble and the entire Constitution, together with the "Necessary and Proper Clause" and the Tenth Amendment, would seem sufficient to make clear the intention of the framers of the Constitution to establish a sharply limited government. Henry David Thoreau began his iconic 1849 essay "Civil Disobedience" by announcing "I heartily accept the motto: 'That government is best which governs least...'"[16] Over the years, many have assumed that Thoreau was quoting Jefferson. The problem with this assumption is that nobody has ever been able to find the quotation in Jefferson's published or unpublished writings. Still, the motto accurately reflects what most people think of as the "Jeffersonian point of view" and, what is more, encapsulates the spirit of a *brief* Constitution and a *sweeping* Tenth Amendment: *Establish justice, ensure domestic tranquility, provide for the common defense, promote the general welfare. Do these things—and do no more.*

And yet, at last count, as of May 2016, the federal government of the United States employed 2,779,000 persons. Subtract from this number the 606,900 U.S. Postal Service workers, and you have 2,172,500 civilian federal employees.[17]

This does not seem like the staff "necessary and proper" to run a sharply limited government. But, then, **$4.1 trillion**, the budget for FY 2017, doesn't seem like the "necessary and proper" sum of money required for a government to perform four sharply limited roles. It's about 21% of the entire U.S. economy. Is it really "necessary and proper" for a constitutionally limited government to suck up more than a fifth of the GDP? Apportioned among the entire U.S. population, the budget costs about **$12,000** for every man, woman, child, and infant in the nation. As it is, in nature, newborns get a rude awakening when they enter the world. In addition to this, some, probably, are still thumped on the backside. Do they also deserve to be shaken down by the government for twelve grand before the birth certificate is even filled out?[18] Is this "necessary and proper"?

Chapters 1 through 4 have traced the history of our long drift from the fifty-two simple words of the Preamble to the Constitution to the vast Administrative State of today. The rest of this book will dive into the present and the future in an effort to understand how the elected and unelected government has created and continues to add to our unsustainable national debt. But before we can understand the debt, we need to understand the structure of the federal budget. It always addresses three broad areas: discretionary spending, the interest on the federal debt, and mandatory spending.[19]

Discretionary spending is the part of the budget Congress decides in its annual appropriation process. The president sends a requested budget to Congress each year, but it is Congress that finally sets the spending levels. In FY 2017, the biggest portion of the nation's **$1.15 trillion** in discretionary spending is devoted to the military: **$622.6 billion**, roughly 54% of discretionary spending. The rest of the discretionary budget is divvied up this way:

> Food and agriculture: $12.8 billion, 1%
> Transportation: $24.7 billion, 2%
> Science: $30.7 billion, 3%
> Social Security, unemployment, and labor:
> $31.7 billion, 3%
> Energy and environment: $41.3 billion, 4%
> International affairs: $41.4 billion, 4%
> Medicare and health: $58.6 billion, 5%
> Housing and community: $68.5 billion, 6%
> Education: $72.8 billion, 6%
> Veterans' benefits: $75.4 billion, 7%

Another thick slice—$69.0 billion, 6%—goes to simply running the government.

Before we move on to mandatory spending, let us note that in the FY 2017 budget, **$303 billion**, 7% of the budget, is devoted to servicing the interest on the federal debt. Although this item is not classed as "mandatory," neither is it "discretionary," since the nation's debts are backed by the "full faith and credit" of the United States. Seven% of the *total* budget, this item is a third of a trillion dollars unavailable to finance any other function or service in 2017.

Mandatory spending is based on—*mandated* by—existing laws rather than on the budgeting process. It is not, therefore, part of the annual appropriations process. Its biggest program and expense is Social Security. (Note that some Social Security expenditures are subject to annual appropriations, so they fall under discretionary spending; most of the spending, however, is based solely on the eligibility rules for Social Security. This spending is mandated by existing law and therefore is classified as mandatory spending.)

In the FY 2017 budget request[20], mandatory spending was nearly **$2.8 trillion**, of which Social Security, Unemployment, and Labor spending totaled **$1.4 trillion**, 49.5% of all mandatory spending. Next highest was Medicare and health, at **$1.2 trillion**, 41.5%. (As with Social Security, some Medicare and health spending is subject to annual appropriations and so is also included among the discretionary items.) Additional mandatory spending for FY 2017 is divided among:

> Food and agriculture: $125.2 billion, 4.47%
> Veterans' benefits: $103.6 billion, 3.7%
> Transportation: $84.3 billion, 3%
> Housing and community: $21.5 billion, <1%
> Education: $12.2 billion, <1%
> Energy and environment: $9.7 billion, <1%
> International affairs: $3.6 billion, <1%
> Science: $1.3 billion, <1%

"Entitlement programs" include Social Security, Medicare, Medicaid, most Veterans Administration programs, federal employee and military retirement plans, unemployment compensation, food stamps, and agricultural price support programs. Entitlement programs provide "individuals with personal financial benefits (or sometimes special government-provided goods or services) to which an indefinite (but usually rather large) number of potential beneficiaries have a legal right...whenever they meet eligibility conditions that are specified by the standing law that authorizes the program."[21] Most mandatory spending is devoted to entitlements, which means that close to two-thirds of the *total* federal budget is dedicated to funding entitlements.

As we will see throughout this book, entitlements are not the only source of heavy federal spending. But they are a whopper— bigger than anything else. And they are also expenditures that many people and politicians most often challenge as crossing the boundaries of the "necessary and proper" role of government.

As simple, concise, and clear as the Preamble seems to make itself when it lists the four essential roles of government, there is one that has consistently created controversy. We have a good idea of what establishing justice, ensuring domestic tranquility, and providing for the common defense mean. But what, exactly, does it mean to "promote the general welfare"? The phrase is used not only in the Preamble, but is also echoed in Article I, Section 8 (using the word "provide," which is an even stronger word than "promote"): "The Congress shall have Power To lay and collect Taxes, Duties, Imposts and Excises, to pay the Debts and *provide for the* common Defence and *general Welfare* of the United States" (italics added).

Liberals and Conservatives continue to wrangle over the meaning of "the general welfare."

The very phrase "*To Promote the General Welfare*" is the title of an enlightening collection of essays that "make the case for big government." In the preface to the collection, the editor, Steven Conn, contends that all of the essays in the volume "demonstrate just how central the federal government has been in creating the kind of society Americans have wanted across the decades. As they [the essays] make clear, those efforts have been far from perfect, nor do they suggest that the federal government is the answer to all our problems. But taken together, they make the case for 'big government' by reminding us how seriously the federal government has taken its constitutional task: To Promote the General Welfare."[22]

Conn takes the phrase at face value as the enumeration of one of government's constitutional tasks. In his collection of conservative articles, *American Contempt for Liberty,* Walter E. Williams challenges this kind of face-value interpretation of the "general welfare" phrase by inviting us to "look at what the men who wrote the Constitution had to say about" it. He quotes a letter from James Madison (the "father of the Constitution") to Edmund Pendleton, who had led the conventions in which Virginia declared independence (1776) and ratified the U.S. Constitution (1788): "If Congress can do whatever in their discretion can be done by money, and will promote the General Welfare, the Government is no longer a limited one, possessing enumerated powers, but an indefinite one..." Madison continued, "With respect to the two words 'general welfare,' I have always regarded them as qualified by the detail of powers connected with them. To take them in a literal and unlimited sense would be a metamorphosis of the Constitution into a character which there is a host of proofs was not contemplated by its creators." Indeed, as the nation's fourth president, Madison vetoed the Bonus Bill of 1817, which would have used federal money to finance certain "internal improvements"—chiefly canals, bridges, and roads. In his veto message, Madison wrote that he could not reconcile the bill with the Constitution because "it does not appear that the power proposed to be exercised by the bill is among the enumerated powers" in Article I, Section 8, Clause 1. The 1817 bill, he wrote, "would have the effect of giving to Congress a general power of legislation instead of the defined and limited one hitherto understood to belong to them, the terms 'common defense and general welfare' embracing every object and act within the purview of a legislative trust."[23] Williams bolsters Madison's position by quoting Jefferson, who said, "Congress has not unlimited powers to provide for the general welfare, but only those specifically enumerated."[24]

TO FIND THE RIGHT ANSWER,

ASK A DIFFERENT QUESTION

Concise, even elegant, the United States Constitution, like all truly profound documents, becomes complex when its words are actually applied to the business of living and governing. Little wonder that its 4,400 words have spawned an entire field of legal and academic study, Constitutional law. Little wonder, too, that some people debate the words of the Constitution in the manner of theologians and biblical scholars.

So it is well to remind ourselves again that the Constitution is not the Bible. Not only does it admit its own fallibility and provide for correcting itself through amendment, but the Constitution also contains very few outright commandments and even fewer "thou shalt nots." It does provide rules and further authorizes the making and enforcement of laws to set limits that are, for the most part, intended to temper unwise action and to contain human failings—especially human failings that may be magnified by government itself. In this sense, the Constitution truly provides the foundation of a government of laws and not men. In the end, however, the framers were keenly aware that they were writing a Constitution for imperfect human beings to act upon. They assumed that future generations who followed what they had written would do so with common sense, exercising judgment in applying to the present those principles that had been set down in ink dried by the passage of years.

What does "promote" (or "provide for") "the general welfare" mean? The liberal interpretation holds that it implies the exercise of powers not specifically enumerated in the Constitution. This interpretation is defensible—at least in the abstract. The conservative interpretation holds that the phrase (as Madison put it) is "qualified by the detail of powers connected with them" and cannot be reasonably interpreted in "a literal and unlimited sense." This reading is also defensible—again, in the abstract.

But we cannot make actual use of abstract definitions. For the purposes of creating good government, we need to ask and answer concrete, real-world questions. Not "What does 'promote the general welfare mean'"? But "What does it mean for us, at this time, in this nation, and in this world?" We need to decide and to define just what aspects of "the general welfare" we would like our federal government to promote (or provide for) and how much of what we would like it to do can be realistically afforded.

After all, avoiding unsustainable levels of debt—damaging, crippling, even lethal debt—is of the essence in promoting or providing for the general welfare. Incurring any debt has an opportunity cost. If we have $XXX and we spend $XX on Y, we will have only $X to fund Z. To some degree, the opportunity cost may actually erode the general welfare. Incurring not just any debt, but unsustainable levels of debt, rapidly erodes and will soon destroy the general welfare as more and more opportunity vanishes.

The same index of common sense must be applied to the three other roles enumerated in the Preamble. What can reasonably, rationally, and affordably be done to establish justice, ensure domestic tranquility, and provide for the common defense? The vital question is not "What *must* be done?" Or, even less, "What did the framers of the Constitution *want* us to do?" Instead, we need to begin and end by asking "What things *can* be done with what we have?" And "Which things are most important to do with what we have?"

Judging frankly from the sheer size of our government, its unsustainable cost, and the unsustainable debt it continues to accrue, we have no rational choice but to conclude that the federal government has often tried to do too much—that is, more than it can hope to pay for.

It is time to stop repeating the mistake of endlessly arguing over the definitive or absolute meaning of "general welfare." It is time instead to do the essential work of studying, debating, and determining a *working* definition of "general welfare" that we as a nation can live with and prosper by. It cannot be a definition that requires our throwing trillions of dollars at the impossible. It must be one based on rational decisions about what is doable, worth doing, and affordable.

Does making and acting upon such decisions require a big government or does it instead demand a small one?

We don't need to answer this question. We do not have to answer whether small government or big government is better. Nor do we have to answer whether our government is bigger or smaller than the ideal government. Nobody knows the ideal size of government for the simple reason that the ideal government does not exist. The only questions that are both relevant and unavoidable are "What size government can we *afford*?" and "What size government can we *tolerate* in order to get from it what we want and need?"

DON'T LET THE 1% DISTRACT YOU FROM THE 1.5%

Well, wait a minute. There *is* another question we should ask at this point: Why are five of the ten wealthiest counties in America suburbs of Washington, D.C.?[25]

Asked by a newspaper reporter why he robbed banks, safe-cracker Willie Sutton (1901–1980) reputedly answered, "That's where the money is." It doesn't matter that Sutton himself denied ever having said any such thing.[26] It is still the best answer to the reporter's question—and to ours.

Why are five of the ten wealthiest counties D.C. suburbs?

"That's where the money is."

No doubt about it, the Washington area is home to a lot of prosperous people, including, we must assume, a number of those 1-percenters—the people we 99% cordially hate but sure wouldn't mind being counted among. Over the years, various political candidates have advocated passage of a "soak the rich tax" with a top marginal rate reaching 90%. The problem is that levying confiscatory rates on the 1% will not produce sufficient revenue to fund current, let alone expanded, entitlements and other social programs. If anything, making the tax code less progressive by holding down top marginal rates shows more promise of actually increasing the tax revenues paid by the rich.[27] In fact, a 2015 study from the Brookings Institution answers with an unequivocal *No* the question "Would significant increase in the top income tax rate substantially alter income inequality?"[28]

And while we are at it, we should not be so quick to assume that salary inequality is both catastrophic and blatant. The AFL-CIO published data in 2015 that dramatized the gap between CEOs and workers, citing the difference between what Walmart CEO Doug McMillon earns per hour—$9,323, by the union's calculation—versus $9 for starting employees.[29] University of Michigan-Flint professor Mark J. Perry cites this very comparison as an example of what is wrong with this view of pay inequality. It creates a biased ratio by "using only the top 1% of the highest paid CEOs in the U.S." and compares them to some of the lowest-paid workers. "Using the BLS average of $216,100 for all American CEOs of "companies and enterprises" in 2014...and the AFL-CIO's estimate of worker pay ($36,134 in 2014) would produce a 'CEO-to-worker pay' ratio of only 6-to-1, far, far below the AFL-CIO's 373-to-1 biased ratio."[30] (And even farther below the 1,000-to-1 case of McMillon versus an entry-level employee.)

But there is another 1%—more precisely, 1.5%—that makes a far greater impact on the national economy than that created by the wealthiest among us. The U.S. Census Bureau estimated the population of the United States at 322,762,018 in January 2016.[31] The total number of nonfarm workers in the United States was 143,894,000 in May 2016.[32] Federal government spending in 2015 was 20.55% of GDP.[33] For FY 2016, it is expected to rise to 21% of GDP.[34] Figure, then, that 2,172,500 civilian federal employees (plus 537 elected officials)—about 1.5% of the American nonfarm workforce—are effectively responsible for roughly 21% of GDP. This leaves the rest of us (141,721,500 people) with the other 79% of GDP to allocate among ourselves while we are saddled with the obligation to finance—on *our* full faith and credit—the profligacy, inefficiency, and waste of the Administrative State.

Indeed, a 2015 CATO Institute study showed that federal pay, after a federal wage freeze enacted during the George W. Bush years slowed growth from 2011 to 2013, is very much on the rise. In 2014, federal employee wages rose 2.9%, compared with 1.7% in the private sector. The federal government in 2014 had the fourth highest-paid workers in the United States (average salary $119,934), behind mining ($135,003), utilities ($137,055), and management of companies ($143,809).[35] Salary is only one dimension of government employee compensation. Health-care benefits and pensions are generally far more generous than such benefits in the private sector.[36]

We the 99% would do better to rebrand ourselves as we the 98.5% and, as such, work toward beginning to reclaim a degree of responsibility for government, to seize from the 1.5% at least some of the leadership in prioritizing our national needs, desires, and means. Whatever else the framers of the Constitution expected from us—the people of their "posterity"—surely they expected, or at least hoped, that we would have the good sense and wisdom to arrange our needs and wants in order of importance, in relation to their cost, and in the context of our available means.

Mention "government," and most people picture their elected representatives and the president. But the bulk of the government in our democracy is peopled by an unelected bureaucracy of some 2,172,500 persons. Of these, more than 300,000 are assigned to formulate, write, and enforce rules and regulations that are not enacted by Congress, yet have all the coercive force of federal law. Our unelected federal government is an "Administrative State" that outnumbers the elected federal government 2.2 million to 537. Moreover, thanks to civil service law, enacted with the very best intention of insulating the federal bureaucracy from the power-seeking whims of party politics, the members of the Administrative State are almost impossible to fire.

This chapter details the regulatory operations of the Administrative State. Although the impulse behind regulation is often laudable, the result is often an unelected bureaucracy behaving badly in service to an ethos of waste.

CHAPTER 6

THE UNINTENDED

CONSEQUENCES OF

UNELECTED

GOVERNMENT

It is a federal crime to sell "turkey ham" as "ham turkey" or to print the words *turkey* and *ham* in different fonts— 21 United States Code §461 & 9 Code of Federal Regulations. Let your pet make a noise that scares the wildlife in a national park, and you (not the pet) are in violation of federal law—18 USC §1865 & CFR §2.15(a)(4). Selling onion rings made from *diced* onion such that they resemble onion rings made from *sliced* onion and then failing to announce that you have done this puts you in criminal violation of federal law—21 USC §333 & CFR §102.39. When you ride a moped into Fort Stewart, Georgia, without wearing long trousers, it is literally a federal case—18 USC §1382 & 32 CFR §636.28(g)(iv).

It is a federal crime to skydive while drunk—49 USC §46316(a) & 14 CFR §105.7(a). You may be permitted to hunt doves and pigeons, but to do so using a machine gun or a "stupefying substance" is a violation of federal law—16 USC §707, 50 CFR §§20.21(a) & 20.11(a). A statute at 40 USC §1315(c)(2) & 45 CFR §3.42(e) makes it a federal crime to skateboard—at least on the grounds of the National Institutes of Health.

Taking home milk from a quarantined giraffe or any animal that "chew[s] the cud" puts you in violation of 7 USC §8313, 9 CFR §§93.400 & 93.414. It is a federal crime to sell anti-flatulent drugs unless you stipulate that "flatulence" is "referred to as gas"—21 USC §§333, 352 & 21 CFR §332.30(b). If you say something so annoying to someone that it provokes that person to strike you in a national forest, *you* are guilty of a federal crime—7 USC §1011(f) & 36 CFR §261.4(b). And here are two more federal crimes: selling wine with a brand name that includes the word *zombie*[1]—27 USC §207, §205(e) & 27 CFR §4.39(a)(9)— or attempting to change the weather without informing the secretary of commerce—15 USC §§330a & 330d.

All of this (and more) was reported by FreedomWorks blogger Jason Pye from the Twitter account "A Crime a Day." At 12:01 p.m. on July 17, 2015, @CrimeADay informed its followers: "Today, @CrimeADay will have tweeted a federal crime every day for a year. By some estimates, it will only take ~800 years to tweet the rest."[2]

The examples here are real laws, laid down in both the U.S. Code and the Code of Federal Regulations. Break them, and you are guilty of a federal crime. Yet none of them was directly enacted by the members of Congress, the men and women we elect to represent us and to be accountable to us in the creation of our laws. Instead, these are regulations created by some 300,000 unelected personnel of federal agencies that act under congressional authority but do not answer to the electorate. They are, for the most part, members of the civil service, the constituents of the Administrative State, or, more specifically, the regulatory state within that Administrative State. The regulations they enact have the full force of law. We must obey them and, as taxpayers, we must pay directly for the costs of their enforcement. As consumers and as stakeholders in companies (owners, employees, investors), we also pay for the costs they impose on various aspects of business. In some cases, the benefits outweigh the costs. In other cases, they surely do not.

HOW RULES AND REGULATIONS

BECOME LAWS

It works like this. The Constitution, our nation's supreme law, established three branches of government—legislative, executive, judicial—and no more. Neither the Administrative State nor the regulatory state within it is one of these branches. In Article I, the Constitution gives the legislative branch the power to lay and collect taxes; to regulate "Commerce with foreign Nations, and among the several States"; and to make all "Laws...necessary and proper for carrying into Execution" those first two powers. Article II assigns all executive power to the president, who is the chief of the executive branch. The president's principal duty is to "take Care that the Laws be faithfully executed." Article III vests the "judicial power...in one supreme Court, and in such inferior Courts as the Congress may from time to time ordain and establish." All of these powers of the three branches are relevant to the Administrative State, as is the Tenth Amendment to the Constitution, which states that the "powers not delegated to the United States by the Constitution, nor prohibited by it to the States, are reserved to the States respectively, or to the people."

Congress (legislative branch) makes laws. The president (executive branch) sees to their faithful execution (*execution*, after all, is a job for an *executive*). The courts (judicial branch) adjudicate both the laws and their execution.[3]

On paper—or parchment, in the case of the Constitution—this looks cut, dried, and elegant. In practice, it gets a lot messier. Presidents "see to" the execution of the laws, but it is a practical impossibility for one person to personally execute them. This is a job for specialized agencies. In some laws, Congress itself specifies the functions of relevant agencies and the goals they are to meet. The Clean Water Act, for instance, mandates reductions in specifically defined waterborne contaminants. In other laws, Congress endows an agency with broad powers, leaving it up to the agency to determine what should be regulated and how. The Occupational Safety and Health Act requires OSHA (the Occupational Safety and Health Agency, created by the law) to formulate and issue "occupational and health standards." The act does not specify what these are; however, the standards OSHA sets embody the authority of Congress and thus carry the full force of federal law—even though Congress never votes on any given standard.

The judicial branch entered into this picture early in the 20th century. Here's how.

Throughout the late 18th century, all of the 19th, and into the early 20th century, the courts unanimously interpreted the separation of powers laid down in the first three articles of the Constitution as pretty nearly absolute. Legal decisions affirmed that Congress could not delegate its legislative powers to the executive branch. This "non-delegation doctrine" was taken as a bedrock constitutional principle until 1928, when the Supreme Court (*J. W. Hampton, Jr. & Company v. United States*) decided that Congress *could* delegate power if the statute in question included an "intelligible principle": an unambiguous standard to guide the responsible agency's rule-making.

In 1946, Congress decided to preempt further judicial debate on delegation by passing the Administrative Procedure Act (APA), which established standing procedures for executive rule-making. In effect, Congress created a template for rule-making that was intended to apply to virtually all legislation. This was a means of permanently avoiding the accusation of delegation. Congress passed the APA not to shirk its constitutional responsibility, but on the assumption that technocrats in the executive branch, although unelected, had the expertise to make decisions on the complex technical issues often at the heart of regulatory legislation. In an era of increasingly sophisticated technology, this argument seems even stronger today than in

1946. In short, at present, the unelected personnel of the executive agencies generally enjoy a wide margin of discretion in making rules that have the force of federal law. We tend to take this for granted, and the more we do, the more distant we feel from government. Rather, it is as if we live among two governments, one that is elected and one that is not.

In addition to agencies that are part of the executive branch, so-called independent regulatory agencies or commissions (IRCs) administer some regulations independently of *any* branch of government. The Federal Communications Commission (FCC) and the Commodity Futures Trading Commission (CFTC) are examples of IRCs in that they are not formally attached to any constitutionally specified branch. IRC members are certainly governed by law. The makeup of each IRC must reflect a balance of the political parties. Each commissioner is appointed by the president to a specific term, and each appointment must be confirmed by Congress. This said, the actions of IRCs are not subject to regulatory review by the president. In this sense, they are truly independent.

Although, as we saw at the start of this chapter, some regulations have resulted in laws that seem bizarre, frivolous, and arbitrary, the APA lays out rigorous procedures for rule-making. Even though the regulatory agencies themselves are not directly answerable to voters and are staffed by unelected members of government, regulations, in most cases, do not go into effect without a public hearing. The APA requires agencies to provide broad public notice of a proposed regulation by publishing it in the *Federal Register,* which is accessible online and elsewhere. The notice period may range from 30 to 120 days, depending on the complexity of the regulation. For some proposed regulations, the agency involved might negotiate the details with stakeholders directly impacted by the regulation. In addition, the Office of Information and Regulatory Affairs (OIRA—discussed later in this chapter) reviews the proposal under authority of the White House Office of Management and Budget (OMB). If the regulation impacts small business, the Small Business Office of Advocacy also has an oversight role. Additionally, when the regulatory jurisdictions of different agencies overlap, they consult to work out any conflicts before the regulation is finalized.

While it is true that Congress does delegate considerable authority to regulatory agencies, it monitors their activities via oversight committees, and, since Congress holds the purse strings, it can reduce an agency's budget or even forbid an agency to use its money in certain ways. In addition, a series of laws passed during the last twenty years of the 20th century and early in the 21st provide Congress with additional regulatory review authority. Yet it is evident that Congress does not always exercise its review authority and responsibility. In *Chevron U.S.A. v. Natural Resources Defense Council, Inc.* (467 US 837 [1984]), the U.S. Supreme Court decided that courts are obliged to defer to regulatory agencies' interpretation of ambiguous laws, provided that their interpretation is "reasonable." This decision, informally referred to as the "*Chevron* doctrine," has contributed to what has been called the "emergence of an almighty Administrative State filled with unelected federal bureaucrats who have the ability to effectively implement, interpret and create laws." Recently, interpretation of laws relating to everything from FCC rules concerning "net neutrality" to EPA regulations relating to the "Clean Power Plan" and Department of Education and Department of Justice requirements concerning transgender bathroom facilities have rested on the "*Chevron* doctrine" and have therefore gone largely unexamined, let alone challenged, by Congress. The interpretations in these cases are not necessarily bad, but they are most assuredly undemocratic, amounting to law created by unelected government bureaucrats absent the voice of the people. [4]

STATES, MUNICIPALITIES,

AND FEDERALISM

Our feeling of alienation from government is amplified by the fact that inexplicably burdensome or just plain silly regulations and rules are not confined to federal jurisdiction. In a 2010 roundup of "12 Ridiculous Government Regulations That Are Almost Too Bizarre To Believe," *Business Insider* reported[5] on a Texas law forcing computer repair technicians to obtain a private investigator's license—something that requires a criminal justice degree or a three-year apprenticeship with a licensed PI. Violate the law, and you can be fined $4,000 to $10,000 and possibly spend a year in jail.[6] Texas also forbids interior decorators to call themselves "interior designers" or even to use the term "interior design" without acquiring a license from the state. Bloggers in Philadelphia must purchase a $300 "business privilege license."[7] Monks who sell handmade wooden caskets in Louisiana must become fully licensed as funeral directors *and* convert their monasteries into licensed funeral homes. In Lake Elmo, Minnesota, selling pumpkins or Christmas trees grown outside the city limits is punishable by a $1,000 fine and a 90-day jail sentence. If you want—or simply must—go out of business in Milwaukee, you need to buy a "costly and burdensome license to tell the public your business is closing [and] complete an avalanche of paperwork (certified by a CPA) about [your] inventory, and then pay a sliding scale fee based on the duration of the sale, plus $2 for every $1,000 worth of inventory [you] seek to sell."[8]

And so on.... Bizarre? Yes, until you look closely and discover that virtually all seemingly unnecessary local regulations require people to give the city, county, or state money for a license or permit.

The broad authority of states and municipalities to enact regulations comes from the well-intended Tenth Amendment to the Constitution, which grants to the "States...or to the people" those powers not constitutionally delegated to the federal government. The idea behind this federalism, as it is called, is to create diversity of laws, instill a certain degree of productive competition among the states, and enable local responsiveness and self-determination by the states. Indeed, in 1932, Supreme Court Associate Justice Louis Brandeis identified federalism as a vehicle of innovation in government, something that allows "a single courageous State…, if its citizens choose, [to] serve as a laboratory; and try novel social and economic experiments without risk to the rest of the country…"[9]

To some degree, the Tenth Amendment may be seen as conflicting with Article 1, Section 8, Clause 3 of the Constitution itself, the so-called Commerce Clause, which explicitly gives Congress the power "to regulate commerce with foreign nations, and among the several states, and with the Indian tribes." The purpose of the clause is to prevent states from enacting burdensome taxes on interstate commerce, in effect setting up "import/export" trade barriers between one state and another. In the landmark 1942 case of *Wickard v. Filburn,* the Supreme Court found that certain apparently local activities affect interstate commerce and are therefore subject to federal jurisdiction as specified in the Commerce Clause.[10] Subsequent Supreme Court decisions have reinforced this interpretation, and so *federal* regulation often permeates and pervades daily life.

AN ENVIRONMENT OF INTENSIVE AND

PERVASIVE REGULATION

You may find reading descriptions of "bizarre" or "ridiculous" instances of regulatory overreach alternately amusing, outrageous, disgusting, or infuriating, even as you may believe that none of it has encroached on you in particular. But accompany the authors of *Regulation: A Primer*[11] on a tour of "A Day in the Life of a Regulated American Family," and you will discover federal regulation in virtually every minute of *your* day. Consider just the morning: The clock radio that wakes you up draws its programming from airwaves regulated by the Federal Communications Commission (FCC) and is powered by electricity regulated by the Federal Energy Regulatory Commission (FERC). The types of lightbulbs in your bedroom and bathroom (and everywhere else in your house) are specified by U.S. Department of Energy (DOE) regulations, and the very mattress you've just arisen from bears a label mandated by the Consumer Product Safety Commission. You shower with products subject to Food and Drug Administration (FDA) regulations, and if the water pressure in that shower is not quite what you'd like it to be, blame Department of Energy (DOE) water conservation regulations—the same regulations that limit the volume of water per toilet flush. The quality of that water is regulated by another entity, the Environmental Protection Agency (EPA). As for breakfast, the *Primer* authors point out that FDA regulations require nutritional labeling and regulate what the food company can and cannot say about the health benefits of its product. Both the FDA and U.S. Department of Agriculture have a regulatory say in your coffee and sugar, and the hedging of investments in trading these commodities is regulated by the Commodity Futures Trading Commission. If you include some fresh fruit on your breakfast plate, know that it is subject to grading standards set by the USDA, which also purchases (using taxpayer money) certain categories of produce in order to stabilize prices by "correcting" imbalances in supply and demand. "The USDA even regulates the size of the holes in the Swiss cheese you grate into your omelet."

ECONOMIC AND SOCIAL REGULATION

And so it goes throughout the rest of your day. By any measure, ours is an intensive and pervasive regulatory environment. The regulations are broadly divided into economic and social categories. Economic regulation constrains the decisions of "economic agents"—usually businesses. Most economic regulations are specific to a particular industry. The

Securities and Exchange Commission (SEC), for instance, regulates the entire securities industry; the Federal Communications Commission (FCC) regulates interstate communications by radio, television, wire, satellite, and cable; and so on.

Economic regulation typically works in four dimensions:

1. *Price.* A regulator may set a maximum (to curb monopolists and price gouging) or a minimum (to bar predatory pricing aimed at knocking out competitors).
2. *Quantity.* A regulator may set limits to production or may require that all demand be met by a certain regulated price (this is common with regulated utilities).
3. *Service quality.* A regulator may establish minimum standards of service, typically for regulated utility providers.
4. *Number of firms.* A regulator may limit new entrants into a market or industry or may bar existing firms from exiting a market.

The intention of economic regulation is to ensure for consumers a price equal to the *competitive* market price, but any time the free market is subject to outside manipulation, things can go wrong. Force prices below competitive market levels, and shortages will result. Fix prices above competitive levels, and consumption may be reduced. Regulation may discourage innovation and entrepreneurship by removing incentives to lower costs, improve quality, and develop new products and services. These effects are the result of errors in judgment by regulators, but there is also a distortion that is inherent in all regulation. Inherently, regulation is a means of transferring wealth. When wealth transfers are made available by regulation, firms will spend money to acquire them. For instance, they will spend money to ensure that they retain monopoly profits. Such expenditures do nothing to improve goods and services, to create more value for consumers, or to promote innovation. From the perspective of society, they represent wasted investment of resources.

Social regulation generally applies in the areas of health, safety, and the environment. Whereas the rationale for economic regulation is the correction of "market failures," the justification for social regulation is to address "externalities" or "information asymmetries." In economics, an externality is a cost or benefit that affects a party that did not choose to incur the cost or benefit. In our time, environmental pollution is perhaps the most frequently encountered externality. Factory A dumps waste in a nearby stream, which carries it downstream where folks who want to fish or swim must either bear the cost of clean-up or forgo fishing and swimming. The consumers of Factory A's product bear none of the cost. One regulatory solution is to impose on the polluter (Factory A, in this case) a tax per unit of pollution and thereby internalize the externality. This is known as a Pigouvian tax, after A. C. Pigou, the economist who first proposed it. Another solution is to define property rights such that Factory A can negotiate directly with the folks downstream. Regulators can impose one or the other approach.

The Latin phrase *caveat emptor*—let the buyer beware—describes the typical relationship between a seller and a buyer, which is a relationship in which (normally) the seller has more information than the buyer. The seller may know something about a defect or a design flaw or the fact that the price he asks is higher than what the seller down the street asks. The difference between the seller's and buyer's command of information is called an "information asymmetry." Much recent social regulation requires sellers to reduce or eliminate information asymmetries through labeling that discloses comparative energy efficiency, caloric content of food, nutritional value of food, and so on.

Where safety is concerned, regulators must typically first assess the risks inherent in a product or service. Using science, regulators establish the health and safety effects of a product or a manufacturing process. Once the risks are assessed, they must be managed by weighing policy alternatives to choose the most appropriate (efficient and cost-effective) regulatory action. Management choices may range from no regulation (when the risk is assessed as being of little or no consequence) to barring the use or even manufacture of some product or substance; most regulatory solutions fall somewhere between these extremes.

THE BEST OF INTENTIONS—

AND THEIR COST

Upton Sinclair's *The Jungle*, an early-20th-century novel set in Chicago's notorious meatpacking district, has long been a staple of high school history and social studies reading lists.[12] It vividly dramatizes "the need" for government regulation of a rapacious and delinquent food industry at the turn of the 19th century and has indoctrinated generations of young history and civics students in the power of socially conscious literature. President Theodore Roosevelt read the novel when it came out in 1906. Its harrowing depiction of a meatpacking industry more interested in cutting corners than in slicing wholesome beef prompted T R to fire off a message to the Department of Agriculture, which replied to him that the meatpacking industry was closely inspected and its product was safe. When the president wrote an angry letter to Frank Doubleday, founder of the publishing house that bore his name, charging that he had published a false and sensational book, Doubleday responded by explaining how his company had meticulously confirmed the accuracy of Sinclair's descriptions. This prodded the president into launching his own investigation, and when he received the investigators' report, he publicly revealed that it confirmed that the meatpacking industry was using methods that posed a danger to health. He announced, however, that he would not make the report public—at least not yet.

Roosevelt was well aware that Congress was debating a pure-food-and-drug bill at the time, a piece of legislation he enthusiastically supported. The bill had been languishing under pressure from food and drug industry lobbyists when Sinclair's novel stirred a public demand for action. By the end of February 1906, the Senate voted it up 63 to 4. Because the bill failed to address meat inspection, however, Senator Albert Beveridge, a progressive Republican from Indiana, introduced a meat bill, and President Roosevelt extorted its passage from a reluctant Senate by threatening to release the report he still held. The Senate ultimately obliged, enacting what Beveridge himself called "the most pronounced extension of federal power in every direction ever enacted."[13] But when the bill went to the House, Representatives diluted it, and the president retaliated by releasing the report. Still, the House held out for at least some compromises: The costs of inspection would be borne by the taxpayer, not the meatpackers, and canned meat did not have to carry the date stamp required by the Senate version. On June 30, 1906, just six months after publication of *The Jungle*, TR signed both the Meat Inspection Act and the Pure Food and Drug Act into law, declaring their enactment "a noteworthy advance in the policy of securing Federal supervision and control over corporations."[14]

Most Americans would agree that there are important benefits to a presumably objective, knowledgeable, and diligent regime of food and drug safety standards, testing, and inspection. Yet the remarks of both Senator Beveridge and President Roosevelt sound eerily menacing today: extending "federal power in every direction" and "securing Federal supervision and control over corporations." The problem is that, in recent years, so much regulation accumulates on a daily basis that the 2014 printed version of the *Federal Register,* the repository of all federal regulations, now consists of 77,687 pages.[15] To say the least, becoming aware of, let alone fully understanding and implementing, the regulations that apply to any particular activity or business is a daunting task.

Clyde Wayne Crews of the Competitive Enterprise Institute (CEI) reported in his 2015 *Ten Thousand Commandments: An Annual Snapshot of the Federal Regulatory State* that:

- Federal regulation and intervention cost American consumers and businesses an estimated **$1.98 trillion** in 2014 in lost economic productivity and higher prices.
- Economy-wide regulatory costs amount to an average of **$14,976 per household**—around 29% of an average family budget of $51,100. Although not paid directly by individuals, this "cost" of regulation exceeds the amount an average family spends on health care, food, and transportation.

- The "Unconstitutionality Index" is the ratio of regulations issued by unelected agency officials compared to legislation enacted by Congress in a given year. In 2014, agencies issued 16 new regulations for every law—that's 3,554 new regulations compared to 224 new laws.[16]

In 2014, the National Association of Manufacturers (NAM) published its own study, *The Cost of Federal Regulation to the U.S. Economy, Manufacturing and Small Business,*[17] which concluded that total federal regulatory costs reached **$2 trillion** in 2012 (as calculated in 2014 dollars). NAM estimated that U.S. manufacturers spend on average **$19,564** per employee per year to comply with federal regulations. Manufacturers with fewer than fifty employees carry the greatest per-employee burden, an estimated **$34,671**. (The annual per-employee average for *all* U.S. businesses, including manufacturing, was calculated at **$9,991** annually, with the greatest burden again falling on small businesses, **$11,724** per employee.) The **$2 trillion** 2012 total breaks down to the following costs of federal regulations by type of regulation:

- Occupational Safety and Health and Homeland Security (OSHHS): **$92 billion**
- Tax compliance: **$159 billion**
- Environmental: **$330 billion**
- Economic costs: **$1.4 trillion**

The direct regulatory costs on manufacturers in 2012 is estimated at (in 2014 dollars):

- Operations and maintenance: **$10.7 billion**
- Capital equipment/tangibles/offsets: **$18.6 billion**
- Outside advisers: **$12.1 billion**
- Subject of federal compliance activity: **$2.4 billion**
- Full-time equivalents (FTEs) devoted to compliance: **$94.8 billion**
- Total direct compliance expenditures: **$138.6 billion**

While many Americans complain about taxes, Crews explains, "The cost of regulatory compliance costs exceed what the IRS is expected to collect in both individual and corporate income taxes for last year [2014]—by more than $160 billion."[18] Based on Office of Management and Budget (OMB) data, it may be calculated that the benefits of economically significant regulations issued between roughly FY 2003 and FY 2013 are between **$141 billion** and **$700 billion** per year, with taxpayer costs of between **$43 billion** and **$67 billion**. This said, the Small Business Office of Advocacy estimates that compliance with federal regulations costs businesses and consumers **$1.8 trillion**.

GROWTH OF THE WORLD'S

"10TH-LARGEST ECONOMY"

The 113th Congress (January 3, 2013–January 2, 2015) enacted 296 laws. The 114th Congress (January 6, 2015–ongoing as of March 16, 2016) has so far enacted 134. The 113th Congress currently holds the record as the least productive ever.[20] Quite likely, the 114th will break that record.

Contrast this performance with the sixty or so federal departments, agencies, and commissions that (as of May 8, 2015) had "3,415 regulations in development at various stages in the pipeline." Nearly half of this production came from six rule-making agencies: the departments of the Treasury, Commerce, Interior, Health and Human Services, and Transportation, plus the Environmental Protection Agency. "If U.S. federal regulation was a country, it would be the world's 10th-largest economy, ranking behind Russia and ahead of India."[21]

No question that federal, state, and local governments employ a lot of people: 22,042,000 folks in February 2016, of whom the federal government (excluding the military but including postal workers) employed 2,769,000. (Just by way of comparison, the manufacturing sector at this time employed 12,327,000, little more than half the number of all government employees.)[22] Of the roughly 2.8 million federal workers, about 300,000 "are devoted to issuing and enforcing regulations."[23] While the current federal government actually employs the fewest workers since the mid-1960s,[24] the 300,000 who deal specifically in regulation represent a five-fold increase in regulatory employees over that same period. In 1960, the federal government spent **$3.4 billion** on writing, administering, and enforcing regulations. For FY 2013, the expenditure approached **$60 billion**.[25]

Up to the 1960s, regulation was mostly economic in nature, aimed for the most part at controlling prices. During the 1970s, regulation of prices and quality applied to businesses declined due to policies of deregulation. Most economists believe that this bow to free-market forces has been largely beneficial. During the same decade, however, regulators increasingly turned their attention to "social" matters, the protection of health, safety, and the environment. It was during the 1970s that the Environmental Protection Agency (EPA), the Occupational Safety and Health Administration (OSHA), the Consumer Product Safety Commission (CPSC), and the National Highway Traffic Safety Administration (NHTSA) were created. These new agencies, together with the socially focused operations of established agencies, were responsible for the growing volume of regulation. After September 11, 2001, another regulatory category suddenly burgeoned to generate regulations pertaining to "homeland security." When the cabinet-level Department of Homeland Security was created in 2002, it took on the combined regulatory budgets of the numerous existing agencies it incorporated: about **$8 billion**. Little more than a decade later, that regulatory budget has grown to about **$25 billion**.[26]

We can expect that, during the next several years, the effect of two pieces of legislation enacted in 2010, the Patient Protection and Affordable Care Act (also known as Obamacare) and the Dodd-Frank Wall Street Reform and Consumer Protection Act, will not only increase the volume and cost of regulation as well as the number of regulators, but will also to some extent swing the pendulum back toward varying forms of economic regulation. Obamacare has issued stacks of regulations to control both the price and the quality of health care, and Dodd-Frank has unleashed many regulations affecting financial markets and has even created five brand-new regulatory agencies[27]:

- Consumer Financial Protection Bureau
- Financial Stability Oversight Council
- Office of Financial Research and Federal Insurance Office
- Investor Advisory Committee and Office of Housing Counseling
- Office of Minority and Women Inclusion

Another development that promises to impact the Administrative State is ongoing globalization, which requires harmonizing trade and environmental regulations with a variety of global partners, especially the European Union. It is uncertain whether this will further grow the U.S. regulatory apparatus or perhaps shrink it. The chief problem with differences and conflicts between national regulatory regimes is that they may become costly trade barriers that serve no purpose. Eliminating these may well streamline some agencies.

So, is the regulatory regime destined to grow? Or can the smaller-than-Russia-but bigger than-India-sized regulatory state be tamed?

In his classic 1989 study, *Bureaucracy: What Government Agencies Do and Why They Do It,* James Q. Wilson argues that there are three types of regulatory bureaucrats. There are careerists, who expect and want lifelong employment in an agency; would-be politicians, who regard working in the regulatory sector principally as a means of garnering the support of interest groups in order to gain advancement, either within the unelected Administrative State or in elective politics; and professionals, who derive personal fulfillment from developing and exercising their knowledge and expertise. While the motives may differ, all three types of employees want to ensure that the agencies within which they work continue to expand. Expansion ensures employment or career advancement or the continuation of fulfilling professional opportunities.[28] Doubtless, many regulatory employees want to do good in the world, improve the national economy, protect Americans, and "promote the general welfare." Nevertheless, the natural tendency of those employed in any organization, public or private, is to pursue their own individual interest above all else. In short, all employees of the regulatory state are motivated to enlarge their domain.

OIRA: AN ATTEMPT TO REGULATE REGULATION

It is naïve to assume that of 300,000 employees, the vast majority are so altruistic or patriotic that they will willingly work themselves out of a job in order to reduce the extent of the regulatory bureaucracy. Indeed, it is only natural that those who work in a complex organization tend to focus on their immediate work environment rather than take in, each and every day, the bigger picture. Within the bureaucracy, turf is expanded and defended. Even among the best-intentioned regulators, there is a tendency to extol one's own mission above those of all others and, as Justice Stephen Breyer wrote, regulators and agencies may become single-minded in the pursuit of some particular mission or goal such that (for example) "the regulatory action imposes high costs without achieving significant additional safety benefits."[29]

Congress passed the Paperwork Reduction Act of 1980 and, fifteen years later, the Paperwork Reduction Act of 1995. The first (among other things) created and the second enhanced the Office of Information and Regulatory Affairs (OIRA) within the Executive Office of the President. The best description of its function was provided by one of its former administrators, Susan E. Dudley:

> Its role, like that of the budget divisions, is to provide the president with a tool to check agencies' natural proclivity to want more (whether it's more budget resources or more regulatory authority). This institution of regulatory oversight is important but, not surprisingly, not always appreciated by

the agencies being overseen. The office scrutinizes agencies' planned regulations and collections of information, along with the analysis supporting them.[30]

Part of a law mandating the reduction of burdensome "paperwork," OIRA attempts to police the regulatory process and the regulatory state. Its go-to "weapon" is benefit-cost analysis, which, correctly done, is not only a nonpartisan approach to predicting and understanding the likely effects of regulation, but also a sufficiently objective approach to have a shot at overcoming the "natural proclivity" of some 300,000 regulators "to want more." While benefit-cost analysis can be quite complex, its objective is to answer an elementary question: Does regulating *a* using *b* produce a benefit *x* greater than cost *y*? OIRA seeks to purge subjectivity from regulation. Either the numbers reveal more benefit than cost, and the regulation deservedly lives, or they reveal more cost than benefit, and the regulation is just as deservedly killed.

That, at least, is the aim. But as Susan Dudley learned in her two-year tenure as OIRA administrator, "The pressure to regulate is powerful," such that even "administrations perceived to believe in free markets find themselves under pressure to support more restrictions on private sector activity. The [George W.] Bush administration issued some of the most far-reaching regulations addressing air quality, food labeling, and (of course) homeland security." Politicians "face strong incentives to 'do something,' and issuing regulations demonstrates action. Whether the regulatory action ultimately produces the desired outcome is less important" than having done something, "in large part because those effects are not immediately apparent, but also because action simply appears more constructive than inaction."[31]

While others have seen the inexorable growth of the regulatory regime as the product of careerism among unelected bureaucrats— as surely, to some extent, it is—Dudley attributes it in significant measure to a feeling among "politicians and party officials, regardless of party" that "they owe something to their constituents—those who helped them attain their positions of influence."[32] Thus the unelected regulatory state becomes a means by which members of the elected government promote and defend their own careers. The careerism of the unelected feeds the careerism of the elected. Dudley observes that the special interest constituency the Democrats serve is conventionally seen as labor unions, environmental groups, and so on. Conventional wisdom, she points out, also perceives Republicans as inherently less regulatory than Democrats because Republicans look out for business interests, which are believed to generally oppose regulation. Dudley argues, however, that "the evidence suggests otherwise."

> For decades, economists who study regulation have observed that regulation can provide competitive advantage, so it is often in the self-interest of regulated parties to support it. During my tenure at OIRA, I saw tobacco companies supporting legislation requiring that cigarettes receive Food and Drug Administration pre-marketing approval, food and toy companies wanting more regulation to ensure their products' safety, and energy companies supporting cap-and-trade for greenhouse gas emissions. Particularly when regulatory demands appeal to popular interests, politicians and policy officials find pursuing them hard to resist.[33]

Thus, according to the former commissioner of the regulatory agency essentially in charge of policing other regulatory agencies, the regulatory state runs heavily on crony capitalism. That is, legislators, whether Democratic or Republican, routinely use the regulations and regulatory agencies created by their legislation to support the special interests that support them. Some of these special interests are advocacy groups (for instance, those with an environmental agenda). Some are businesses, industries, and the associations representing them (such as cigarette manufacturers who actually *want* FDA pre-marketing approval). Such support of business by government is not always inherently harmful, of course. But it may be. For example, suppose a toy that meets all federal regulatory requirements injures a child. The government's certification, even if it proves to be in error, may well preclude a successful lawsuit against the manufacturer. To complicate matters further, some would argue that this is a benefit, because it protects businesses that follow the rules from liability they cannot foresee. Others will counter that the government regulation unfairly interferes with consumer rights, including the right to seek civil relief for an injury. Full-blown crony capitalism manifests itself in cases in which businesses use the regulatory regime to block competition. Dudley enumerates instances of:[34]

- Biotechnology companies that join with food safety activists to encourage stricter regulation of new foods involving genetic engineering; such regulation may block new competition into the biotech sector.
- "U.S. testing laboratories [arguing] aggressively on safety grounds against European requests to permit manufacturers of low-risk workplace electrical products to self-certify compliance with regulations rather than subject them to [fee-based] third-party testing."
- "U.S. cruise lines and associated worker organizations [that] lobbied for regulations restricting foreign-owned cruise line operations." (So far, they have been unsuccessful.)
- "Energy companies [that] have joined with national environmental organizations to push for cap-and-trade, which will confer financial benefits on the holders of grandfathered emission allowances."
- A push for renewable fuels coming from agricultural interests, which support regulations requiring the use of such fuels *and* federal subsidies for their use. Until recently, some environmental organizations supported this same regulation; however, that support has faded as questions concerning the life-cycle environmental effects of ethanol fuels have emerged.

REGULATION IN THE BALANCE

Although some will argue that the true intention of government regulation is neither more nor less than increasing the power of the government, most believe that government regulation means well and is aimed at promoting "the general welfare." Those who hold this view may point to powerful moral arguments in support of government regulation of the private sector; namely, the regulation of business:[35]

1. *Corporations are creatures of the state.* Because corporations are chartered by government authorities, they are creatures of the state and therefore should be regulated by the state, whose "dependents" they are.

2. *Failures of free markets.* Even passionate advocates of government regulation of business tend to believe that a free market *usually* creates the environment that promotes maximum efficiency while encouraging both responsible conduct and production of goods and services of genuine value to consumers. Nevertheless, free markets can fail in important ways. They sometimes waste resources. This is a principal argument for the regulation of utilities. Free-market competition fosters wasteful duplication of services and infrastructure, regulatory advocates argue; therefore, the government should regulate (i.e., restrict) competition among utility companies. It is also possible that markets may fail to serve real needs—such as medical care, workplace safety, employment fairness, availability of businesses in certain areas (for instance, poor neighborhoods may become "food deserts," underserved by supermarkets). The remedy is regulation through zoning ordinances, safety and health codes, minimum wage laws, special business licensing requirements, and so on.

3. *Protection of rights.* Free markets, many argue, do not protect rights. Because it is a function of the government to protect rights, government must regulate the free market to ensure that rights are protected there. A free market is not inher-

ently required to provide a safe working environment, "fair" wages, Social Security, and other benefits deemed by some governments to be rights. A free market is not inherently required to warn consumers of potential hazards of products or to provide labeling with such information as health benefits and dangers, nutritional content, value-oriented information to objectively assist in purchasing decisions, and so on. Government watchdog regulators, therefore, are required to protect rights.

4. *Judicial inefficiency.* Opponents of government regulation—or advocates of minimal regulation—argue that problems the free market fails to address can be quite effectively addressed by civil and criminal courts. Even in the absence of regulation, the makers of a product that fails to perform as advertised or that causes injury can be sued. The prospect of such litigation encourages businesses to take positive steps to avoid costly liability by ensuring that their products are safe. Even advocates of regulation concede the validity of this position—except in the case of an area such as pollution. Often, pollution harms victims who cannot be specifically identified. Often, too, individual polluters cannot be identified as having caused a particular person's injury. When culprit and victim cannot be brought together in court, there is "judicial inefficiency." For this reason, pollution (and therefore polluters—polluting industries) must be regulated.

Arguments for deregulation countering those for regulation include:

1. *Corporations are creatures of the state.* Businesses may be incorporated under state authority, but they do not *have* to be. They were so incorporated because the states have assumed the authority to incorporate them. If a community decides that corporations can create themselves entirely on their own authority, so be it. In effect, the "creature of the state" argument is an accident of history, and it is not enshrined in the Constitution.

2. *Failures of free markets.* Even though markets may fail at certain times and in certain circumstances, it does not follow that regulation creates superior efficiencies and benefits. A state that protects a monopolistic utility on the grounds of efficiency must also prohibit (by regulation) labor strikes, which are, arguably, far more injurious to efficiency. If regulation substantially erodes freedom, isn't it preferable to accept some degree of market inefficiency?

3. *Protection of rights.* Any regulatory advocacy based on an appeal to a "right" must justify defining the individual "right(s)" at issue. For instance, the Constitution does not enumerate a right to a *fair* wage. As amended by the Thirteenth Amendment, it does prohibit slavery. But it would be an unacceptable stretch to interpret this as a *right* to a certain level of wage. Moreover, paying workers to produce a certain product for a certain wage (to which they claim a right) requires consumers to pay a price above a certain level. Why not make the counterclaim that consumers have the "right" to *fair* prices? Do this, and regulations defending the right to a fair wage will come into conflict with the consumer's right to a fair price, and thus workers and consumers will become captives of one another's "rights." The mechanism of a free market resolves such conflicts far more efficiently than regulation can. The *spurious* assertion of rights creates a *false* need for regulation, which introduces severe inefficiencies.

4. *Judicial inefficiency.* In the case of pollution, there may be no sound alternative to a wise regime of regulation; however, a more draconian alternative is a policy of quarantine, whereby the courts address harms inflicted by polluting industries with injunctions that cut back production, force relocation, or find the polluter simply too dangerous to continue operating at all.

The preceding pros and cons are not intended to resolve the issue of regulation one way or another. They are intended, however, as an argument against automatically falling back on the regulatory state (on the one hand) *or* the absolute purity of free markets (on the other). As our system of criminal justice is based on an assumption of innocence, so our approach to regulation should be based on an assumption that individual welfare, common sense, and free markets are optimally efficient at solving most problems. Therefore, in most cases where regulation *could* be introduced, it is likely that it should *not* be introduced. In considering the need for regulation, this assumption should be the equivalent of the assumption of innocence when trying a criminal case.

On the other hand, there are bound to be exceptions—almost certainly numerous—in which regulation is desirable or even urgently necessary. In these cases, both intended and unintended consequences must by anticipated and evaluated. The principal responsibility of the regulatory apparatus should not be regulation, but the skeptical evaluation of the need for regulation, such that:

- The benefits of a proposed regulation demonstrably and compellingly outweigh costs.
- The manifest benefits to society outweigh any damage to business, enterprise, and commerce.
- Undue, unfair, and harmful instances of crony capitalism are avoided.
- No unconstitutional, non-constitutional, extra-constitutional, or pseudo-constitutional "rights" are fabricated, especially "rights" that will inevitably provoke the fabrication of conflicting "rights."

This is the only way to roll back the Administrative State, whose unelected status continually threatens conflict with our constitutionally mandated representative government. The outlook, at present, is not very bright. The George W. Bush administration averaged 62 major regulations annually over eight years, while the then six-year-old Obama administration averaged 81.[36]

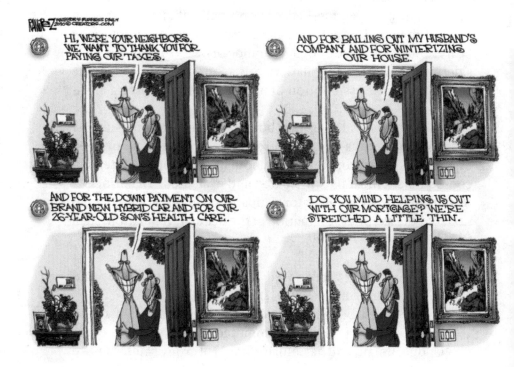

From the headwaters of the Depression-era New Deal, two torrents of government spending continue to flow: social entitlements *and* public-sector "insurance" for private-sector banking and other enterprises. *The first has become unsustainable—by one measure, to the tune of* **$210 trillion** *and counting. The second has been putting every single American taxpayer on the hook for the moral hazard created by everyone from the wolves of Wall Street to the families who snapped up a mortgage offered on a house they could not possibly afford. In the end, this chapter is about another mortgage, the mortgage today's adults have put on the future of their children.*

CHAPTER 7

OUR CLIMATE OF

MORAL HAZARD:

FROM NEW DEAL

TO RAW DEAL

By 2016, the Great Depression was rapidly slipping from our living memory. Fewer than 6 million Americans remained—less than 2% of the 2016 population—who had actually lived through it.[1] Yet we "know" it from "recorded" history. Or believe we do. Certainly, the website of cable TV's History Channel paints a plausible nutshell:

The Great Depression (1929–1939) was the deepest and longest-lasting economic downturn in the history of the Western industrialized world. In the United States, the Great Depression began soon after the stock market crash of October 1929, which sent Wall Street into a panic and wiped out millions of investors. Over the next several years, consumer spending and investment dropped, causing steep declines in industrial output and rising levels of unemployment as failing companies laid off workers. By 1933, when the Great Depression reached its nadir, some 13 to 15 million Americans were unemployed and nearly half of the country's banks had failed. Though the relief and reform measures put into place by President Franklin D. Roosevelt helped lessen the worst effects of the Great Depression in the 1930s, the economy would not fully turn around until after 1939, when World War II kicked American industry into high gear.[2]

By the numbers, the GDP—the monetary value of all the finished goods and services a country has produced within a specified period—fell from **$98.4 billion** in FY 1930 to a low of **$58.3 billion** in FY 1933, the year commonly considered the "nadir" of the Depression. Federal receipts, which were 4.1% of GDP in 1930 (**$4.058 billion**), fell to 3.4% (**$1.997 billion**) in 1933, whereas 1930 federal outlays rose from 3.4% of GDP (**$3.320 billion**) to 7.9% (**$4.598 billion**) in 1933.[3] Unemployment statistics for the period present a stark picture.[4] (See table.)

Alan Brinkley, the distinguished Allan Nevins Professor of History at Columbia University, expresses the consensus view of the Great Depression as "the worst economic crisis in American history by a very large margin," explaining that "it's almost impossible to convey the dimensions of such a terrible economic crisis."[5] And—by the numbers—it's hard to argue with this consensus view. That is why the Great Depression and the radical manner in which the New Deal transformed the very concept of government in response to it are seen as benchmarks, normative precedents, historical road signs pointing to the terrible consequences of laissez-faire economic policy on the one hand and the miraculous salvation of government intervention on the other.

Despite persistent dissenting voices, the Great Depression is regarded by some as a failure of free-market capitalism, and the New Deal is widely hailed as a collection of best practices for dealing with it. Yes, the Great Depression hit America and the rest of the world hard. No question. But for those historians today who actually studied the experiences of Depression-era Ameri-

YEAR	POPULATION	LABOR FORCE	UNEMPLOYED	PERCENTAGE OF LABOR FORCE
1929	88,010,000	49,440,000	1,550,000	3.14
1930	89,550,000	50,080,000	4,340,000	8.67
1931	90,710,000	50,680,000	8,020,000	15.82
1932	91,810,000	51,250,000	12,060,000	23.53
1933	92,950,000	51,840,000	12,830,000	24.75
1934	94,190,000	52,490,000	11,340,000	21.60
1935	95,460,000	53,140,000	10,610,000	19.97
1936	96,700,000	53,740,000	9,030,000	16.80
1937	97,870,000	54,320,000	7,700,000	14.18
1938	99,120,000	54,950,000	10,390,000	18.91
1939	100,360,000	55,600,000	9,480,000	17.05
1940	101,560,000	56,180,000	8,120,000	14.45
1941	102,700,000	57,530,000	5,560,000	9.66

cans—or, better yet, talked to them—the 1930s do not emerge as Armageddon, and the New Deal does not look like a manmade miracle.

AN AMERICAN MYTHOLOGY

John Steinbeck's 1939 novel *The Grapes of Wrath* and the 1940 film adaptation by John Ford are great works of American popular culture, so compelling as imaginative evocations that they are responsible for much of the picture we who did not actually live through the period have of the Great Depression. The problem is that neither Steinbeck nor Ford was a historian, sociologist, or economist. They were literary and cinematic artists. Their works are fiction, not documents of history, sociology, or economics. Commenting on Steinbeck's saga of the desperate Dust Bowl journey of the Joad family from Oklahoma to California, James N. Gregory, University of Washington professor of history, points out that "much of what we think that migration was all about is wrong, starting with the name. The whole concept of a Dust Bowl migration is a wonderful misnomer. Most of the people had nothing to do with the Dust Bowl region. Most really weren't victims of the [1930s prairie] drought either. A lot of them weren't even farmers." The late American demographer Ben Wattenberg adds that most of the Dust Bowl–era migrants came from areas east of the drought-stricken region and that "just 43%...were farmers or farm laborers. Almost one in six was a professional, a proprietor, or a white-collar employee. About two in five were blue-collar workers." While a third of the migrants did go to the still-fertile agricultural valleys of California, two-thirds, according to Gregory, went "into the cities, especially Los Angeles, where they found industrial jobs. And some of them were white-collar workers. So the imagery is misleading. It's much too negative. It creates an impression of great misery, when there were certainly difficulties and there were people who suffered tremendously, but the majority's story is much more positive." Wattenberg observes that, for most, "the journey itself, the great westward exodus, was not the hard road described in Steinbeck's novel," but (as Gregory reports) "two days with camping along the way or stopping at motels in Arizona, and for many people, not unpleasant days at all, any more than it is today. For those who ran out of money, of course, there could be difficulties. But for most people, it's just a drive."[6]

The popular view paints Franklin Roosevelt as a national savior and his New Deal as the nation's salvation. There is no question that FDR's most vocal supporters thought of him in such terms. Unfortunately, the numbers are difficult to pin down because there was no organized national polling in 1932 and 1933. We do have, however, evidence from the very first question the newly founded Gallup organization asked in 1935: "Do you think expenditures by the government for relief and recovery are too little, too great, or just about right?" Just 9% of those asked responded "too little," 31% thought the expenditures were "just right," but 60% believed them "too great." Six in ten Americans were not sold on the New Deal. Yet, in December 1935, three months after this first question was asked, Gallup asked respondents if they were in favor of government old-age pensions for the needy. This time, a decisive 89% answered yes, and only 11% no.[7]

Doubtless, the two dramatically different results say as much about what a question asks as they say about how people actually feel. Asked if too many of their tax dollars are being spent on something, they will tend to respond yes. But asked if they want the benefits of that expenditure, they will neglect the cost and focus on the benefits. Saying that too much is being spent but we want the benefit is a position loaded with cognitive dissonance, but it is nevertheless a valid expression of popular sentiment. During the Great Depression, most Americans approved of most of the New Deal most of the time, provided that they were prompted to consider only the benefit and not the cost.

Not even the harshest critics of the New Deal, both in the 1930s and today, dispute FDR's charisma and power of persuasion. At the very least, he made people feel better. He gave them hope—which is no small thing—and this is also reflected in the early Gallup data. Despite the New Deal programs, unemployment remained in double digits through 1940 and did not *steadily* decline from 1933 to 1939. Nevertheless, when asked throughout the Depression, about 50% of those polled expected general business conditions to improve over the next six months. Just 29% expected things to get worse. Even more people—60%—consistently believed that opportunities for getting ahead were better (45%) or at least as good (15%) as in their father's day. And this is yet more telling: Even while they were still in the throes of the Depression, 54% of Americans said that if another depression should hit, the government would do best to follow FDR's example in responding to it. A substantial minority, however—34%—disagreed with this.[8]

Partisans of Roosevelt and the New Deal point to the results of the November 1936 general election, in which FDR defeated Republican Alf Landon with 27 million votes to Landon's 16 million, as definitive proof of a mandate for New Deal statism. Another way to look at this, of course, is that 37% of the electorate, nearly four in ten Americans, objected to the New Deal or at least had serious doubts.

The objections from the Supreme Court, many Americans forget today, were far more absolute. In 1935, the high court found the National Recovery Administration (NRA) to be unconstitutional, and in 1936 likewise declared the Agricultural Adjustment Act (AAA) unconstitutional, holding that it violated Tenth Amendment federalism by usurping powers "reserved to the States respectively, or to the people." The high court also struck down other key New Deal legislation: the Agricultural Adjustment Act, Federal Farm Bankruptcy Act, Railroad Act, Coal Mining Act, and the National Industrial Recovery Act. The reason for the decisions was always roughly the same: The legislation encroached on the authority of the states in contravention of the Tenth Amendment, which gives to the states (or to the people) those powers not delegated to the federal government by the Constitution.

Still, the mythology of the New Deal goes beyond an estimate of overwhelming popular approval. The mythology holds that, yes, some aspects of the New Deal may have pushed the constitutional envelope, but it was urgently needed in any case. The historical data on federal receipts versus outlays as well as on the stubborn unemployment rate fail to provide evidence of the efficacy of the New Deal. No matter. This failure of fact barely makes a dent in the mythology of New Deal success. In the long history of civilization and civilizations, mythology has served to impart normative status to some set of beliefs, collective policy, or course of action. This is precisely the function of the mythology surrounding the New Deal. It has been the basis of Truman's Fair Deal, Kennedy's New Frontier, LBJ's Great Society, Clinton's "Clintonomics" with its "investment in human capital," Obama's promise of "Hope and Change" with Obamacare, and, before him, even George W. Bush's "compassionate conservatism." Behind all of these approaches, programs, policies, and promises is the unquestioned or little-questioned assumption that the New Deal *really worked*, not only delivering benefits, but delivering benefits that were greater than their cost. Shrouded in mythology, the New Deal is enshrined as a governing and economic best practice.

DEMYTHOLOGIZING THE NEW DEAL

The New Deal was far from simple, and so is its heritage. We, however, do not have to translate its alphabet of programs and agencies or labor to untangle its legacy. All we have to do is understand that from its experiments in statist, interventionist, and all-pervasive government, two major sources of spending flowed and continue to flow—in an ever-gathering torrent.

The first is *entitlements,* defined as government programs guaranteeing a specified group or groups access to some benefit or benefits based on rights established by the Constitution or other legislation. Depending less on objectively ascertainable fact than on the mindset and worldview we bring to them, entitlements may be seen as proceeding, like interventionist government itself, from the very best and noblest of intentions, or we may regard them as more or less cynical instruments of politics, benefits intended to transform a skeptical electorate into unquestioningly loyal constituents. We may regard entitlements as a new form of what the 1st-century Roman satirist Juvenal denounced as *panem et circenses,* "bread and circuses," popular favors that pass for responsible public policy but are really the use of taxpayer money to buy votes. In either case, under either interpretation, entitlements have grown beyond any hope of economic sustainability and represent the largest single category of cumulative public debt.

The second major source of spending created by the New Deal is *public-sector "insurance" for certain private-sector enterprises, most notably banking.* The Banking Act of 1933, also called the Glass-Steagall Act, created, among other things, the Federal Deposit Insurance Corporation (FDIC) to insure depositor accounts in member banks. The main idea behind the FDIC was to restore badly battered faith in the nation's banks after about one-third had failed in the early years of the Depression.[9] Senator Carter Glass (D-Virginia), former Secretary of the Treasury under Woodrow Wilson, and Representative Henry B. Steagall

(D-Alabama) were by no means radical New Dealers. The FDIC deposit insurance in their legislation was capped at $2,500 per ownership category (soon increased to $5,000) and was financed not by public funds, but by insurance dues paid by the insured banks, which pay into a pool, today called the Deposit Insurance Fund (DIF). Nevertheless, the FDIC was initially funded by $289 million in federal loans (which were eventually paid back with interest).

As originally conceived, the FDIC was a relatively modest confidence-building measure, and the Banking Act of which it was a part strictly separated commercial banking (relatively low-risk) from investment banking (relatively high-risk), so that taxpayers were at little risk. Since the original legislation, the FDIC coverage amount has grown to $250,000 per ownership category (established by the 2011 Dodd-Frank Wall Street Reform and Consumer Protection Act). Far more significant than the growth in this particular coverage is the establishment of the precedent of government as a hedge on free-market risk. Not the FDIC itself, but the precedent it created, was the acorn from which the mighty oak of moral hazard did grow. "Moral hazard" is defined as a situation in which one party takes more or greater risks because another party has agreed to bear the burden of them. In 2008, we discovered just how prodigiously that acorn had grown, as, under the Emergency Economic Stabilization Act of 2008, the Secretary of the Treasury was authorized to spend up to **$700 billion** to "bail out" banks that had invested heavily in mortgage-backed securities—bad debt that had turned "toxic" (that is, had lost most its value on a mark-to-market basis).

Many Americans, of course, believe these two "New Deal" redefinitions of government's role—entitlements and public sector insurance for the private sector—are positively progressive and that whatever excesses they have produced in recent years are symptoms of the poor execution and excessive application of essentially laudable principles. In this view, the unsustainability of our entitlements is a kind of toxic mutation, and the massive bailouts of 2008 as well as other egregious examples of corporate welfare are freaks, aberrations that should not and need not happen again. Those, however, who now regard the New Deal as the first step down a very slippery slope see the runaway entitlements and irrational commitment to moral hazard not as mutations or freaks, but as the inevitable destiny created by the New Deal—especially once this set of emergency measures became institutionalized in American law and policy as virtually aspects of a birthright.

The New Deal created the basis for an economic and political culture built on entitlements and the embrace of moral hazard. Some believe this is preferable to the free-market alternatives. Some believe it is not. Others are undecided and so would say the New Deal has given us these things "for better or worse." Spoiler alert: This chapter concludes that the New Deal precedents have been decidedly for worse. The entitlements have proven unsustainable. Presenting them as a form of pay-as-you-go insurance has proven fraudulent. As for that other form of taxpayer-funded "insurance"—public sector bailout of the private sector—it has proven itself a license for unreasonable risk and an acceptance of unacceptable moral hazard.

Justifying these conclusions requires that we address the assertion that the impulse behind the New Deal was good, even if its eventual development, execution, and application have gone awry. In this view, the New Deal is a kind of religion. It requires faith that transcends reason. When atheists, agnostics, or even religious skeptics ask the true believer why a God of infinite good allows the existence of evil, the reply is not a rational argument but an appeal to embrace a faith that provides a peace that passeth all understanding. The problem is that while it is possible to regard the New Deal as a religion, it is not a religion, but a set of policies. As such, it has no claim to adherence by faith. It must be required to live or die by reason. As the great management guru William Edwards Deming famously quipped, "In God we trust, all others bring data."[10]

So let us bring data. The New Deal was introduced in 1933. Federal receipts that fiscal year stood at 3.4% of GDP (which was **$58.3 billion**) and outlays at 7.9% (a deficit of −4.5% of GDP). Now, let's look at the rest of the Depression years:

YEAR	GDP*	RECEIPTS**	OUTLAYS**	DEFICIT**
1933	58.3	3.4	7.9	−4.5
1934	62.0	4.8	10.6	−5.8
1935	70.5	5.1	9.1	−4.0
1936	79.6	4.9	10.3	−5.4
1937	88.9	6.1	8.5	−2.5
1938	90.2	7.5	7.6	−0.1
1939	90.4	7.0	10.1	−3.1

*in billions of dollars　　　　　**percent of GDP

Although the GDP rose from its 1933 level of **$58.3 billion**, it did not regain even the 1930 level of **$98.4 billion**, despite the New Deal, which produced federal outlays that averaged 9.15% of GDP during 1933–1939 versus average federal receipts of 5.54% of GDP for that same period. From 1933 to 1939, the annual deficit averaged 3.814% of GDP.[11] As for unemployment, as the table reproduced at the beginning of this chapter shows, unemployment between 1933 and 1939 remained in double digits, far above pre-Depression levels, averaging 19.037% for the period, despite the federal job and economic stimulus programs of the New Deal.[12]

UNEMPLOYED PERCENTAGE OF LABOR FORCE DURING 1929–1941	
YEAR	PERCENTAGE OF LABOR FORCE
1929	3.14
1930	8.67
1931	15.82
1932	23.53
1933	24.75
1934	21.60
1935	19.97
1936	16.80
1937	14.18
1938	18.91
1939	17.05

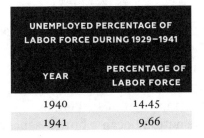

UNEMPLOYED PERCENTAGE OF LABOR FORCE DURING 1929–1941	
YEAR	PERCENTAGE OF LABOR FORCE
1940	14.45
1941	9.66

It was the onset of defense spending with the approach of World War II, not the programs of the New Deal, that finally lifted the nation out of the Depression. There is nothing new or original about this conclusion, which, in fact, is a standard observation in most histories of the period, except for the works of revisionists such as Fed chairman Ben Bernanke.[13] David Stockman is particularly harsh in his criticism, calling the New Deal "a Chinese menu with little rhyme or reason" and emphasizing crony capitalism with "endless special interest legislation sought by unions, the housing industry, and other organized lobbies." Even most of the programs that "provided humanitarian relief and a [social] safety net," he argues, "either retarded recovery or were abandoned before they could do much harm." Interestingly, in Stockman's judgment, nothing in the New Deal "resembled full-strength Keynesian demand stimulus like the **$800 billion** plan that Larry Summers, the chief economic advisor in the first years of the Obama administration... claimed to have channeled from FDR in February 2009." Nevertheless, Stockman does note that "a few" New Deal innovations—industrial union legislation, universal social insurance, Fannie Mae, bank deposit insurance, and farm price supports—"lived on to cast a heavy and debilitating shadow over the distant future."[14]

To many who were engulfed in the Great Depression, it must have seemed like bearing witness to nothing less than the failure of free-market capitalism itself, a sudden and apparently inexplicable loss of "domestic 'demand' that was somehow recoverable through enlightened macroeconomic policies." In fact, the president whose policies are often blamed for either bringing on the Depression or making it worse than it already was, Herbert

Hoover, diagnosed it less hysterically and more accurately as an event "rooted in the collapse of global trade."[15] Neither FDR nor his economic advisors stepped back to take in the international picture and America's central place in it.

The crash of 1929 had its origin in 1914 and the outbreak of World War I, which brought a spectacular export boom to the United States. The nation became both arsenal and breadbasket to the world, especially to the combatant nations. As a neutral country in the war, the United States had both the opportunity and the obligation to trade with both sides. At first, it did just that, but the volume of export also rapidly transformed America into the planet's biggest creditor, and U.S. financiers increasingly came to see the Western Allies—France, the UK, and Italy—as both better customers, with access to swifter and safer shipping routes, and better credit risks than the Central Powers (Germany, Austria-Hungary, Bulgaria, and the Ottoman Empire). While propaganda, Wilsonian democratic ideology, and (though least of all) actual German aggression and brutality served increasingly to align the United States with the Allies and against the Central Powers, it was trade and credit above all else that finally brought an end to American neutrality. U.S. banks and financiers *demanded* the defeat of Germany and its allies. So America went to war in 1917–1918. As for the export boom, it continued unabated, but was now augmented by a tremendous domestic demand for armaments and other industrial war materiel. After the armistice (November 11, 1918), food, machinery, and consumer goods saw heavy worldwide demand, which retreated, briefly though steeply, during 1920–1921, but resumed and continued throughout the 1920s—both domestically and globally.

With the end of the war, demand for American export goods of all kinds inflated a bubble, providing a prosperity that also accelerated domestic demand. The bubble finally burst—both domestically and globally—when demand shrunk even as overheated industrial producers continued to churn out goods at the same levels that had been selling out since the start of the war. In the context of decreasing demand, output and GDP reached unsustainable levels, and the crash of October 1929 pricked a bubble from which the oxygen was already escaping. The point is that nothing the New Deal did or could have done was capable of changing the natural and inevitable consequences of a burst bubble of planetary proportions. Neither FDR nor anyone else could have reheated demand to its former overheated levels. This being the case, it is doubtful that much, if any, of the tepid and wavering recovery between 1933 and 1939 can be honestly attributed to the programs of the New Deal.

But this fact has not stopped the mythmakers from trying. As Yaron Brook and Don Watkins wrote in *Forbes* in 2012, "The growth of government intervention over the last century was built on the back of a handful of myths." Among the longest-standing of these, Brook and Watkins point out, was the "dominant myth… that free markets caused the Great Depression." More recently, however, a new "key myth" has emerged to explain the collapse of financial markets in 2008. It is the myth that financial deregulation caused the implosion.[16]

This 2008 myth is linked to another New Deal myth, this one of vintage 1933. It holds that, say what you might about the New Deal, it did produce an undeniable good in the Glass-Steagall Act, which insured bank depositors even as it erected an unbreachable Chinese wall between commercial (low-risk) and investment (high-risk speculative) banking. During the Bill Clinton administration, passage of the Gramm-Leach-Bliley Act partially repealed Glass-Steagall, freeing up financial holding companies to own both commercial and investment banks. As Brook and Watkins note, "regulatory evangelists including Nobel Prize economist Joseph Stiglitz cite this act of deregulation as instrumental in the economic crisis that came to a head in 2008." By implication, the repeal must also be seen as the lethal betrayal of a piece of time-tested New Deal orthodoxy. The problem with this view is the existence of "zero evidence" that the repeal "unleashed the financial crisis. If you tally the institutions that ran into severe problems in 2008–2009, the list includes Bear Stearns, Lehman Brothers, Merrill Lynch, AIG, and Fannie Mae and Freddie Mac, *none of which would have come under Glass-Steagall's restrictions.*" Even President Obama has recently acknowledged that "there is no evidence that having Glass-Steagall in place would somehow change the dynamic."[17]

"'Wall Street has betrayed us,' John McCain declared just one day after Lehman's collapse. 'This is a result of excess and greed and corruption.... And we've got to fix it and we've got to update our regulatory system.'" In this, the senior senator from Arizona proved only that he, like many others, still bought into the New Deal mythology. "The definitive history of the financial crisis remains to be written," note Brook and Watkins. "But one thing is for sure: it shouldn't be written by those who have a quasi-religious conviction that the freedom to pursue profits is the cause of all the world's problems, and that government regulation is the unfailing elixir."[18]

UNSUSTAINABLE ENTITLEMENTS

Let's return to the numbers: GDP growth or decline, unemployment growth or decline, outlays versus receipts. What these tell us is that the radical and costly measures of the New Deal did little to ameliorate, let alone end, the Great Depression. If we nevertheless concede even the possibility that the New Deal paved the way for a "natural" recovery, we must also recognize that it did so under decidedly "unnatural" circumstances, namely the orgy of government expenditures to ramp up to and then to fund World War II. As Stockman and others have argued,[19] the notion that the New Deal was a bold experiment in Keynesian reflation of a depressed economy is largely mythical because, on the whole, the New Deal did not inject sufficient levels of government funding into the economy to move that economy. The truly massive injections John Maynard Keynes himself called for were not forthcoming until the 1940s, when the war demanded them. And, by the way, unlike World War I or the American wars of the *second* half of the 20th century, World War II posed a true existential threat to the United States. The nation *had* to borrow and the nation's treasure *had* to be spent as a matter of national life or death. Outlays as a percentage of GDP were absolutely breathtaking during 1941–1946:

YEAR	PERCENTAGE OF GDP
1941	11.7
1942	23.8
1943	42.6
1944	42.7
1945	41.0
1946	24.2[20]

And they *needed* to be. It is these "Keynesian" levels of government spending that put a period on the Great Depression. That punctuation certainly did not come for free. The resulting deficits during 1941–1946 were:

YEAR	DEFICITS	PERCENTAGE OF GDP
1941	$4.941 billion	−4.3
1942	$20.503 billion	−13.9
1943	$54.554 billion	−29.6
1944	$47.557 billion	−22.2
1945	$47.553 billion	−21.0
1946	$15.936 billion	−7.0[21]

Far in excess of the deficit spending during the New Deal, these deficits were part and parcel of the "war effort," and while they were necessary, nobody would have argued that they were desirable, normal, or sustainable.

Federal spending in the New Deal was excessive for what it accomplished, yet inadequate to accomplish its Keynesian mission. Nevertheless, we might concede that a majority of the American people demanded a federal response to the economic crisis of the Great Depression and the New Deal programs were an earnest attempt to deliver that response in what was a grave emergency during an epoch in which the democracies of the world cowered in the shadow of such "great dictators" as Sta-

lin, Mussolini, and Hitler. Yet what many today believe to have
been the crowning and most enduring achievement of the New
Deal, Social Security, had "virtually nothing to do with ending
the depression, and if anything it had a contractionary impact."[22]

Social Security is funded by payroll taxes. These, however,
did not begin until 1937, and regular Social Security benefits did
not commence until 1940. By then, industrial production in aid
of embattled democracies and in preparation for the defense of
America had already ended the Depression. So the Social Security Act of 1935 cannot share with the other economic legislation
of the 1930s the excuse of having been born to make an instanta-
neous response to crisis.

Conservative commentator Mark Levin calls Social Security
an example of "utopian statism,"[23] and David Stockman describes
it as having created a "fiscal legacy [that] threatens disaster in
the present era because its core principle of 'social insurance'
inexorably gives rise to a fiscal doomsday machine. When in the
context of modern political democracy the state offers universal
transfer payments to its citizens without proof of need, it offers
thereby to bankrupt itself—eventually."[24] These are dire judgments, but they are not unreasonable condemnations. Stockman
sagely points out that "a minor portion of the 1935 legislation"
actually introduces precisely the opposite of a scheme of "universal transfer payments," namely a "means-tested [social] safety net
offered through categorical aid for the low-income elderly, blind,
disabled and dependent families." Means testing for aid in specific categories of need creates a social safety net with less risk of
casting it indiscriminately over the entire population now and for
all time. Stockman additionally advocates a strictly cash-based
social welfare plan rather than what Social Security claims to be,
"social insurance," a welfare model that is not only indiscriminately regressive, but inherently inefficient—introducing a great
deal of complexity (as of 2012, the *Social Security Handbook* had
"2,728 separate rules governing its benefits"[25])—and "explosively
expansionary" because it "enlist[s] and mobilize[s] the lobbying
power of providers and vendors of in-kind assistance, such as
housing and medical services."[26]

So the concept of Social Security as a means-tested, cash-only social safety net is both humane and, for a prosperous and advanced nation, sustainable. In contrast, Social Security and other entitlements of this class, as they actually exist, are not only unsustainable, but also unfair and ultimately unbearable—especially in a prosperous and advanced nation. They now claim the single biggest slice of the federal budget, having overtaken defense spending in 1993. What is more, far from being the social lifeline it might have been, Social Security is a huge and growing financial burden on those working Americans as yet too young to enjoy its benefits. As for the unborn, they will also inherit our burden—only it will be much greater. During World War II, payment of Social Security benefits represented just 0.22% of federal outlays.[27] In 2015, these payments amounted to 24% of the federal budget—**$888 billion**, providing monthly retirement benefits averaging **$1,342** to 40 million retirees (December 2015). In 2015, Social Security also paid benefits to 2.3 million spouses and children of retirees, 6.1 million surviving children and spouses of deceased workers, and 10.8 million disabled workers and their eligible dependents (December 2015).[28] Dependents, survivors, and the disabled were not included in the original 1935 Social Security Act.

Lyndon Johnson's Great Society legislation, inspired by the political success of Social Security, created the additional welfare entitlements of Medicare and Medicaid, the Bill Clinton years introduced the Children's Health Insurance Program (CHIP), and the Obama presidency brought Affordable Care Act (ACA) marketplace subsidies. Together, these four post–New Deal, post–Social Security health insurance programs accounted for 25% of the federal budget in 2015: **$938 billion**. More than 60% of this, **$546 billion**, went to Medicare. Medicaid and CHIP provide, in a typical month, health care or long-term care to some 72 million persons—aid that also consists of matching payments made by the states. ACA subsidies were provided to 8 million of the 11 million people enrolled in health insurance exchanges during 2015.[29] Taken together, social welfare entitlements accounted for 49% of the FY 2015 federal budget.

"Stein's Law" was promulgated by economist Herbert Stein in the 1980s in reference to the U.S. balance-of-payments deficit, not the cost of entitlements. But it is a simple law: "If something cannot go on forever, it will stop."[30] And it surely applies to this statement made by the Social Security and Medicare Boards of Trustees in the Social Security Administration's 2015 Annual Reports:

> Social Security's total expenditures have exceeded non-interest income of its combined trust funds since 2010, and the Trustees estimate that Social Security cost will exceed non-interest income throughout the 75-year projection period. The Trustees project that this annual cash-flow deficit will average about $76 billion between 2015 and 2018 before rising steeply as income growth slows to its sustainable trend rate after the economic recovery is complete *while the number of beneficiaries continues to grow at a substantially faster rate than the number of covered workers.*[31]

The report goes on to explain that "Interest income and redemption of trust fund assets from the General Fund of the Treasury" will offset cash-flow deficits for just eighteen more years (from 2016), until 2034, when depletion of trust fund reserves will be "total." After this depletion, "tax income is projected to be sufficient to pay about three-quarters of scheduled benefits through the end of the projection period in 2089."[32]

As for Medicare, the trustees say that its Hospital Insurance (HI) Trust Fund will be depleted in seventeen years (from 2016), 2033, at which time "dedicated revenues will be sufficient to pay 86% of HI costs," falling to 80% in 2050 and then rising gradually to reach 84% in 2089. The trustees conclude: "Lawmakers should address the financial challenges facing Social Security and Medicare as soon as possible. Taking action sooner rather than later will permit consideration of a broader range of solutions and provide more time to phase in changes so that the public has adequate time to prepare."[33]

For what, exactly, should the public "prepare"? At best, benefits cut by 25%. In the 2015 report, the trustees project that the trust fund reserves on which the program depends to fill the widening gap between a shrinking workforce paying into Social Security and the growing pool of beneficiaries drawing from it will be depleted and go negative in 2033. From that year on, the Social Security trust funds will show an annual "unfunded obligation," which will reach **$11.1 trillion** by 2089, the end of the 75-year projection that was made in 2014.[34] Thus, Social Security faces what economist Laurence Kotlikoff calls a "fiscal gap," which is the difference between the present value of the government's financial obligations, including future expenditures and debt service, and the present value of projected revenue. Social Security's fiscal gap is part of the nation's fiscal gap, which is discussed in "The Mortgaged Future," later in this chapter. Taken by itself, however, the fiscal gap in the Social Security system is 33%, meaning that it is 33% underfinanced.[35] Moreover, since the fiscal gap encompasses future obligations and interest payments, the longer the gap remains unaddressed, the wider it grows—at an alarming rate.

So what is the "range of solutions" to cope with this dire situation? As Mark Levin puts it, they consist of "several unpleasant scenarios":

> Benefits will be slashed, benefits or other income will be heavily taxed, the retirement age will be pushed back further, and/or the federal government will eliminate other spending or go further into debt. Inasmuch as those retiring today will receive less than they "contributed" over the years into the system, it is difficult to see how younger people will be left with anything but horrendous debt and broken promises.[36]

FRAUDULENT ENTITLEMENTS

We have all been outraged by media reports of Medicaid fraud, which prompted the Government Accountability Office (GAO) to single out Medicaid as a program that is at high risk for improper payments due to fraud, waste, and abuse.[37] The U.S. Office of Management and Budget (OMB) estimated that improper payments made under the Medicaid program, including fraud, waste, and abuse, amounted to **$29.1 billion** in 2015, nearly 10% of the total cost of the program. This comes in the context of "improper payment amounts" across all major entitlement programs, totaling in FY 2015 nearly **$140 billion** in fraud and other errors for Medicaid in addition to all Medicare programs and for the School Lunch program; Supplemental Security Income (SSI); Pell Grants; Unemployment Insurance (UI); Retirement, Survivors, and Disability Insurance (RSDI); Public Housing/Rental Assistance; Earned Income Tax Credit (EITC); Supplemental Nutrition Assistance Program (SNAP); and other unspecified entitlement programs.[38]

Seventeen billion—let alone **$140 billion**—is a lot of unaddressed fraud each year, but it is ultimately less harmful than the inherent fraud at the very heart of Social Security. The government has always described Social Security as an "insurance" program. That is how it was and continues to be "sold" to American taxpayers and wage earners. In truth, Social Security is by no means insurance. This fiction is the fraud at its heart.

Social Security is a program of "massive generational transfer payments,"[39] in which the payroll taxes of workers (the young, relatively speaking) are *not* used to pay the putative "premiums" for their fictional "insurance," but to finance payments to current beneficiaries (the old, relatively speaking) as well as some of the government's other expenses. The government routinely borrows from the Social Security Trust Fund to pay expenses that have nothing to do with Social Security. Since the Trust Fund earns no interest on these loans, the growth of the fund is diminished, and the fiscal gap widens that much more rapidly. If the management of a private-sector insurance company dipped into its trust fund to pay, say, executive bonuses, people would go to prison. For the government, however, it's standard operating procedure.

Since it is an immutable actuarial fact of life that the ratio of workers to beneficiaries continues to drop (from 159 workers for every beneficiary in 1940 to 2.1 by 2035),[40] it is all but certain that (even in the best-case scenario) these younger people will receive less in benefits than they paid in payroll taxes. Moreover, the payroll taxes are regressive, with the same percentage withheld from every paycheck regardless of whether it is that of a minimum hourly wage burger flipper or the salary of a rising Fortune 500 executive. Currently, workers pay 6.2% of their first $117,000 of earnings as payroll taxes, with the employer paying an additional 6.2%. The self-employed foot the entire 12.4% total. Originally, the total levy was just 1%—and it did not reach 3% until 1960.[41] As noted, given the unsustainability of the Social Security entitlement, benefits will almost certainly be reduced and the retirement age will continue to be pushed further back. Finally, to add insult to injury, beneficiaries are required to pay income tax on the benefits they receive. This puts the final nail in the coffin of the lie that Social Security is insurance. Actual insurance settlements are not taxed as income.

UNREASONABLE RISK

In addition to social entitlements, including fraudulent social "insurance," the New Deal introduced the concept of federally backed "insurance" on bank deposits. The FDIC has become so much a part of ordinary Main Street financial life that deposit insurance seems like a no-brainer or, at least, a government service that can safely be taken for granted. This attitude might be justified if what was being insured were piles of cash sitting in a vault. But, in reality, the FDIC insures deposit money used as loans. If banks make excessively risky loans, they put their depositors' money at risk. The FDIC, in effect, guarantees that even the stupidest of bank decisions will be made good to depositors.

Objections raised to deposit insurance when it was under debate in 1933 were focused on two things. First, why should the government put itself (that is, taxpayers) on the hook for the consequences of stupid credit decisions in the private sector? (True, as originally legislated, the FDIC insurance pool was funded by the dues of member banks, not the taxpayer; however, the government ultimately backed this self-funded system with the "full faith and credit of the United States.") Second, critics of the FDIC argued that the free market provided the best incentive to fiscal and fiduciary discipline by holding over bankers' heads the imminent threat of deposit withdrawals or even a bank run if too many bad loans were made.

In answer to at least the first objection concerning moral hazard, the Glass-Steagall Act added restrictions on banking designed to reduce the risk borne by depositors and by the FDIC. Foremost among these regulations was the separation of investment and commercial banking, as well as tight restrictions on the quantity of illiquid holdings a bank might hold (restrictions on real estate assets and on holdings of corporate securities). Under Glass-Steagall, checking accounts, by their nature the most fluid of bank deposits, could not bear interest. This barred banks from making loans using funds deposited into checking accounts. Finally, a provision of the law known as Regulation Q placed a ceiling on interest rates on bank deposits. This was designed to discourage aggressive loan-making practices that would be funded by the money of more depositors lured by interest rates higher than those of competing banks. The unintended consequence of Regulation Q was to send huge numbers of depositors out of insured banks altogether and into higher-yield but uninsured and inherently riskier money market funds. Thus, insurance and regulations that were intended to promote depositor security sent depositors flocking to uninsured, less-regulated, and non-regulated investments.

Beginning in 1987, the restrictions of Glass-Steagall were gradually dismantled, and in 1999, the act was repealed entirely—except for deposit insurance. Although the FDIC continued to insure only deposit accounts, the holding companies of the banks themselves were now permitted to run both commercial and investment operations, thereby putting even the most conservative depositor at risk—a risk covered by the FDIC, eventually up to a quarter-million dollars.

UNACCEPTABLE MORAL HAZARD

Deposit insurance in 1933 got the foot of government in the banker's door, but it did so in the context of restrictive regulations that hedged at least some of the taxpayer's direct risk. With the repeal of Glass-Steagall, the restrictions were largely removed, but the taxpayer's insurance obligation remained. This created an unacceptable moral hazard, putting the consequences of risk on the shoulders of the federal government and those who paid taxes to it.

But the moral hazard was actually far greater than the direct liability of the FDIC. In 2008, that federal foot in the door materialized into the full-body presence of the government in private-sector banks, investment houses, mortgage companies, and even insurance providers. That figure of Uncle Sam barged in bearing sacks of money, lots of money, to cover so-called investments in colossally corrupt and utterly fraudulent mortgage-backed securities outrageously rubber-stamped by the gilt-edged credit rating agencies (Moody's, Standard & Poor's, and Fitch). The New Deal precedent became a compulsion. Promoted to the electorate during the Great Depression—and probably sincerely—as financial "protection for the little guy," deposit insurance suddenly mutated seventy-five years later into a bailout of hitherto unimaginable proportions. Far from being a helping hand extended to the "little guy," it was a spectacular potlatch sacrifice made in the name of crony capitalism and heaped upon the altar of certain financial concerns deemed "too big to fail."

Was Wall Street properly chastened by the collapse of 2007–

2008? Are you frickin' kidding me? In 2006, the New York City Security Industry Bonus Pool contained **$34.3 billion**, and the average bonus was **$191,360**. In 2007, the pool contained **$33 billion** (–4%), from which bonuses averaging **$177,830** (–7%) were paid. In the *annus horribilis* of 2008, the pool was sucked down to **$17.6 billion** (–47%), and the average bonus paid was a mere $100,850 (–43%). Come 2009, post-bailout, the bonus pool rose to **$22.5 billion** (28%), bringing the average bonus to a more palatable **$140,620** (39%). The year 2010 saw a modest rise to **$22.8 billion** (2%) but a dip in the average bonus to **$138,970** (–1%), followed by a stiffer retrenchment in 2011 to **$18.5 billion** (–19%), from which bonuses averaging **$111,430** (–20%) were paid, but in 2012 the pool surged to **$23.2 billion** (26%) and bonuses averaged **$142,860** (28%). In 2013, the bonus pool stood at **$27.6 billion** (19%), and the average bonus was **$169,820** (19%). The years 2014 and 2015 saw modest retreats, with the average 2014 bonus hitting **$160,280** (–6%) and that for 2015 declining to **$146,200** (–9%).[42] The headline of a *Washington Post* story on the 2015 bonus reads, "Why $146,200 is a terrible bonus for Wall Street," and goes on to note that bonuses "are still much bigger than they were during the financial crisis, but smaller than they were 10 years ago," citing the **$191,360** paid in 2006 as the "all-time high." New York State Comptroller Thomas P. DiNapoli fretted that state and city budgets, which "depend heavily on the securities industry," will suffer if there are fewer industry jobs. But Bart Naylor, a financial policy advocate for Public Citizen, observed that "New York's declining Wall Street bonus pay shows movement in the direction of sanity, but there are still one too many zeros."[43]

As for the derivatives market—the sector of investment bank activity that gave us the mortgage-backed security bundles filled with toxic subprime mortgages—there is perhaps reason for more hope. In 2011, the U.S. Commodity Futures Trading Commission formulated rules for the creation of derivatives clearing organizations (DCOs). The DCO reduces the risk of derivatives trading by enabling "each party to an agreement, contract, or transaction to substitute...the credit of the DCO for the credit of the parties." The DCO "arranges or provides, on a multilateral basis, for the settlement or netting of obligations . . . or otherwise provides clearing services or arrangements that mutualize or transfer credit risk among participants."[44] Put more simply, the DCO stands between parties to a derivatives trade by generally ensuring creditworthiness, thereby reducing the risk of any of the parties failing to honor their financial obligations.

BUT THE 2008–2009 "BAILOUT"
WAS A GOOD INVESTMENT...WASN'T IT?

On September 25, 2008, nervously looking on as Congress angrily argued over authorizing an unprecedented **$700 billion** bailout package demanded by Secretary of the Treasury Henry Paulson, President George W. Bush got up on his hind legs to deliver a warning: "If money isn't loosened up, this sucker could go down." Paulson himself rushed to the Capitol to plead with House Speaker Nancy Pelosi (D-California). Bending down on one knee before her, the supplicant beseeched the lady not to "'blow it up' by withdrawing her party's support for the package." She responded to the kneeling man: "I didn't know you were Catholic," and then continued: "It's not me blowing this up, it's the Republicans."[45]

Maybe we would all be better off if they actually *had* blown it up. In the end, however, panic prevailed, and the bailout of 2008—along with those that followed—were passed, to the tune, ultimately, of **$8 trillion**.[46]

It was a staggering investment, but was it really a necessary investment? Was it even a good investment? Was it an expenditure worth groveling for?

The rationale behind the bailouts of 2008–2009 was ultimately the same as that for the stimulus programs of the New Deal era. It is the idea, championed by John Maynard Keynes in 1936, that a massive injection of government spending will stimulate a languishing and imperiled economy. As President Obama put it seventy-three years later, in February 2009, the **$789 billion** American Recovery and Reinvestment Act would "revive our economy" and "create 3.5 million jobs."[47] The secret sauce that fueled this promise was the *multiplier effect*, which is "the idea that an initial amount of government spending leads to a change in the activity of the larger economy":

> In other words, an initial change in the total demand for goods and services (what economists term aggregate demand) causes a change in total output for the economy that is a multiple of the initial change. For example, if the government spends one dollar and, as a result of this spending, the economy (as expressed by the Gross Domestic Product, or GDP) grows by $2, the spending multiplier is 2. If the economy grows by $1.50, the spending multiplier is 1.5. However, if the economy only grows by 50 cents (a loss from the original $1 spent), the spending multiplier is 0.5.[48]

As a little-noticed 2010 study points out, while the "theory sounds pat, ... economists have been debating aspects of government spending multipliers for years. One crucial debate centers on how to measure a multiplier's value. Some economists find spending multipliers that are smaller than 1. Other economists, however, assert that spending multipliers are much larger. Still others argue that multipliers can't even be credibly measured."[49] The multiplier that was used to estimate the benefit of the 2009 stimulus package predicted 3.5 million new jobs within two years of the expenditure. As of July 2010, the date of the study, 3.8 million jobs had been not created but lost, and the authors concluded that the multiplier the Congressional Budget Office used to predict the benefit of the stimulus overestimated it by nearly a factor of two. "Thus, while the stimulus may appear to be a wise investment, it is really no wiser than a junk-rated mortgage-backed security; though the investment claims a good rate of return, in reality the return isn't worth it because money is lost." A better means of stimulating the economy might be strategic tax cuts, which (a 2007 study concluded) create a multiplier of about 3, so that $1 of tax cuts raises GDP by about $3.21.[50] As the authors of the 2010 study conclude, "the economy might get more bang for the buck with tax cuts rather than spending hikes."[51] Put another way, the multiplier effect of private-sector productivity, stimulated by appropriate tax cuts, is greater than the multiplier effect created by even massive government spending.

THE MORTGAGED FUTURE

On February 25, 2015, Laurence J. Kotlikoff, professor of economics at Boston University, testified before the United States Senate Budget Committee. After politely acknowledging that he was "honored to discuss" with the committee "our country's fiscal condition," Professor Kotlikoff got (as he said) "right to the point." "Our country is broke," he announced. "It's not broke in 75 years or 50 years or 25 years or 10 years. It's broke today. Indeed, it may well be in worse fiscal shape than any developed country, including Greece."[52]

Kotlikoff acknowledged that, with the public debt officially reported at 74% of GDP, the country did not yet *appear* insolvent. He went on to explain, however, that "the federal debt is not an economic measure of anything" and that the only meaningful "measure when it comes to fiscal sustainability and generational policy" is "the infinite-horizon fiscal gap," which "tells us whether the government has, over time, enough receipts to cover its projected spending. It equals the present value of all projected future expenditures less the present value of all projected future receipts." The infinite-horizon fiscal gap puts everything on the books, regardless of how they are labeled, as either outlays or receipts. If the resulting balance sheet yields a positive fiscal gap, it "means the government is attempting to spend, over time, more than it can afford." A "positive fiscal gap is a direct measure of the unsustainability of current fiscal policy."[53]

The infinite-horizon fiscal gap enables *generational accounting,* which allows us to understand *today* "the fiscal burdens our kids could face from the fiscal gap," as adults, in the *future.* Generational accounting reveals the "fiscal burden that will be imposed on today's and tomorrow's children if current adults don't pay more or receive less from the government."[54]

Although numerous economists disagree,[55] Kotlikoff argues that the infinite-horizon approach, by enabling generational accounting, is required to accurately understand a most inconvenient truth—that unsustainable entitlements and the moral hazard created by government insurance of private-sector financial decisions have mortgaged our children's future to finance our debts *today*. Financial storms come and go; the economic *weather* changes. *Climate*, however, endures, and we, today, are creating a climate of moral hazard in which our children will have to live and work for a long time, maybe their whole lives, as well as those of *their* children. Beyond that, who knows?

Looking at our national fiscal condition through the prism of the infinite-horizon fiscal gap, we discover that what we label as "the national debt" is not a mere **$19.3 trillion**, but **$210 trillion**. Kotlikoff calculates that our **$210 trillion** fiscal gap represents 58% of the present value of projected future taxes; therefore, the federal government is underfinanced by 58%. Detroit, an icon of governmental and societal failure, was 25% underfunded at the time it declared bankruptcy. In this view, therefore, the United States is more than twice as bad off as bankrupt Detroit, which was described in 2013 as 139-square-mile city in which "large chunks...have literally vanished: Of Detroit's 380,000 properties, some 114,000 have been razed, with 80,000 more considered blighted and most likely in need of demolition."[56]

How to reverse a national fiscal slide that has already outrun devastated Detroit?

By the numbers, Kotlikoff testified that Congress would have to eliminate the fiscal gap with a 58% permanent tax hike or cut spending on all expenditures except for servicing the official national debt. This means a 38% spending cut.

Nobody said this would be easy. Moreover, either the tax hike or the spending cut has to be done immediately. Any delay necessitates levying even greater tax hikes or enduring even deeper spending cuts. Between 2003 and 2015, the fiscal gap exploded

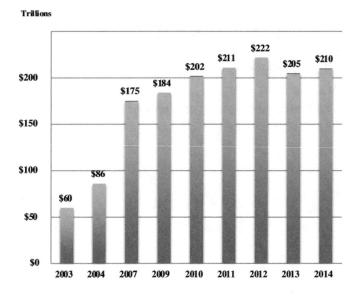

Trillions

HISTORICAL U.S. FISCAL GAPS, SELECTED YEARS[57]

This graph shows what happens when the fiscal gaps are calculated using infinite-horizon budget accounting. The magnitude of increase in the fiscal gap becomes alarming when one folds future values of assets and liabilities into present projections.

from **$60 trillion** to **$210 trillion** due mainly to increases in Medicaid and Medicare benefit levels, additional defense spending, and the introduction of Medicare Part D prescription coverage. Of the four causes, three are entitlement increases, and they widen the fiscal gap with astounding speed.

Taking the generational view by measuring the infinite-horizon fiscal gap forces us to confront the unsustainability of the fiscal gap we call the national debt, and forces us further to confront its least sustainable core; namely, entitlements. As Professor Kotlikoff testified to the members of the Senate Budget Committee, "we don't need to abandon any generation, we don't need to eliminate social insurance, and we don't need to discard the poor to turn things around. What we do need is to understand the fiscal hole we've placed ourselves and our children in and start digging ourselves out in a sensible, efficient, and humane manner."[58] It promises to be hard labor that involves pain and self-sacrifice— you know, the kind of thing parents have been doing for their children since human beings first began to walk the earth.

SPENDING TOO MUCH
FOR THE COMMON DEFENSE

TRAPPED IN THE PUZZLE PALACE

BEATING SWORDS INTO FOOD STAMPS.

On January 17, 1961, three days before he turned the White House over to John F. Kennedy, Dwight David "Ike" Eisenhower broadcast his farewell address. It contained a warning to his countrymen: "Guard against the acquisition of unwarranted influence, whether sought or unsought, by the military-industrial complex." What Ike originally intended to put into his farewell address, however, was military-industrial-Congressional complex, *but, before he faced the TV cameras, he decided he couldn't risk offending Congress.*

He had it right the first time. This chapter goes to the heart of our irrational military spending in modern America. It is all about pounding swords into pork and pork into votes, while in the process surrendering to the president an unconstitutional license to make war after war after war.

CHAPTER 8

IKE'S

FIRST

DRAFT

In 1796, outgoing president George Washington bade farewell to his fellow citizens with a speech that included four profound admonitions: shun political partisanship, "steer clear of permanent alliances with any portion of the foreign world," beware of "the accumulation of debt," and "avoid the necessity of...overgrown military establishments."[1] One hundred sixty-five years passed before another American president delivered a farewell address with advice so pithy. Unlike Washington, that president figures on no historian's list of "the greatest" chief executives, but, just like Washington, he was a retired general—and a great one at that. Where Washington spoke of "overgrown military establishments," President Dwight D. Eisenhower, the victorious supreme Allied commander of Europe during World War II, entreated his fellow citizens to "guard against the acquisition of unwarranted influence, whether sought or unsought, by the military-industrial complex."[2]

These two presidents who had been top generals felt themselves compelled to warn not against military power per se, but against the power of military institutions. Washington's warning came in a list of admonitions, but Eisenhower focused singularly on the "the military-industrial complex" and elaborated on it. It is well worth reading his famous quotation in that context of elaboration. "Until the latest of our world conflicts," the outgoing president explained, "the United States had no armaments industry. American makers of plowshares could, with time and as required, make swords as well. But now we can no longer risk emergency improvisation of national defense; we have been compelled to create a permanent armaments industry of vast proportions. Added to this, three and a half million men and women are directly engaged in the defense establishment. *We annually spend on military security more than the net income of all United States corporations.*"[3] As Washington well knew, the American Revolution had been, in part, a rebellion against a king and parliament who dared to maintain a standing army in their colonial subjects' midst. By 1961, with the nation spending more on "military security" than the net income of the producers of America's peacetime bounty, the former five-star general expressed his deep concern over something that clearly seemed to him out of balance in American life. Calvin Coolidge, one of the nation's Republican interwar presidents who pursued an unapologetically isolationist course, famously declared that "the business of America is business." But Ike Eisenhower, the nation's second Cold War president, was in no position to say the same thing. Just what "the business" of America had become was hardly as clear to him, in 1961, as it had been to Coolidge in the 1920s. The military and a policy of global military intervention were now inextricably bound to a defense industry. There was no telling where national military policy ended and private-sector business began.

In what he said next Eisenhower sounded somewhat at a loss, overwhelmed, even: "This conjunction of an immense military establishment and a large arms industry is new in the American experience. The total influence—economic, political, even spiritual—is felt in every city, every Statehouse, every office of the Federal government. We recognize the imperative need for this development." A necessary evil, perhaps. "Yet we must not fail to comprehend its grave implications. Our toil, resources, and livelihood are all involved; so is the very structure of our society." And so, therefore: "In the councils of government, we must guard against the acquisition of unwarranted influence, whether sought or unsought, by the military-industrial complex. The potential for the disastrous rise of misplaced power exists and will persist."

THE INCREDIBLY HIGH COST OF

THE MILITARY-INDUSTRIAL-CONGRESSIONAL

COMPLEX

Let's linger a moment over this. After all, when a general-become-president expresses deep concern over the national military as a potential source of "misplaced power," we need to listen and to contemplate.

Ike Eisenhower was never a particularly eloquent man or a confident public speaker, and, like all modern presidents, he leaned heavily on speechwriters. It was Ralph E. Williams, a White House staffer and speechwriter, who drafted the farewell address, doing so in consultation with Ike's own brother, Johns Hopkins University president Milton Eisenhower, and a political science professor at that university, Malcom Moos. Among them, this trio came up with the phrase "military-industrial complex," but Ike himself penciled into his draft a reference to the role of Congress. Their "military-industrial complex" became his "military-industrial-Congressional complex." Yet when it came time to actually deliver the televised speech, the president omitted his own addition. When brother Milton asked him why he dropped the reference, Ike replied frankly: "It was more than enough to take on the military and private industry. I couldn't take on the Congress as well."[4]

Pity, leaving that out. For it is the *total* triad—military, industry, Congress—that gives fullest substance to the rest of Ike's warning: "We must never let the weight of this combination endanger our liberties or democratic processes. We should take nothing for granted. Only an alert and knowledgeable citizenry can compel the proper meshing of the huge industrial and military machinery of defense with our peaceful methods and goals, so that security and liberty may prosper together."

Early in the 20th century, defense budgets hovered around 1% of GDP, spiking to 22% at the height of U.S. mobilization toward the end of World War I. The postwar rush to demobilize, to "return to" what President Warren G. Harding famously called "normalcy," took military budgets down to between 1 and 2% of GDP during the 1920s, rising to 2 to 3% during the 1930s. World War II brought the military budget to an all-time high of 41% of GDP, followed by a retreat to the neighborhood of 10% during the most intense periods of the Cold War. By 1980, defense authorizations hovered between 3 and 5%, spiking to 6.8% in the 1980s during President Ronald Reagan's military spending binge. As the Soviet Union lurched toward decline and breakup, defense budgets dipped to 6% in 1990 and then, with the Cold War at an end, settled below 4% in 1996 and stood at just 3.5% of GDP in 2001.[5]

In terms of actual dollars, Department of Defense budgets were far from trivial between 1980–2001[6]:

YEAR	DOD BUDGET
1980	$133.995 billion
1981	$157.513 billion
1982	$185.309 billion
1983	$209.903 billion
1984	$227.411 billion
1985	$252.743 billion
1986	$273.373 billion
1987	$281.996 billion

YEAR	DOD BUDGET
1988	$290.360 billion
1989	$303.555 billion
1990	$299.321 billion
1991	$273.285 billion
1992	$298.346 billion
1993	$291.084 billion
1994	$281.640 billion
1995	$272.063 billion
1996	$265.748 billion
1997	$270.502 billion
1998	$268.194 billion
1999	$274.769 billion
2000	$294.363 billion
2001	$304.732 billion

The terrorist attacks of September 11, 2001, on the United States brought defense authorization increases, first to 4.6% of GDP by 2005 during the U.S. invasion of Iraq and the wars there and in Afghanistan, and then to 5.0% in 2008 to finance the troop "surge" in Iraq to bolster the failing war effort there. It was, by the way, a war that Secretary of Defense Donald Rumsfeld told reporters on November 15, 2002, would last "Five days or five weeks or five months, but it certainly isn't going to last any longer than that." In fact, the Iraq War officially spanned March 20, 2003 to December 18, 2011, at which point the military budget authority had increased to 5.7% of GDP, partly due President Obama's increased effort in Afghanistan.[8] The total cost of the Iraq War at its official end was **$1.7 trillion**. Add to that **$490 billion** in benefits owed to war veterans, and expenses could grow to more than **$6 trillion** over the next four decades counting interest, a study by Brown University's Watson Institute for International and Public Affairs reported in 2013.[9] The actual direct defense outlays for the Iraq War years, 2003–2011, are:

YEAR	DOD BUDGET
2003	$404.733 billion
2004	$455.813 billion
2005	$495.294 billion
2006	$521.820 billion
2007	$551.258 billion
2008	$616.066 billion
2009	$661.012 billion
2010	$693.485 billion
2011	$705.554 billion

To date and beyond:

YEAR	DOD BUDGET
2012	$677.852 billion
2013	$633.466 billion
2014	$603.457 billion
2015	$589.564 billion
2016	$604.452 billion
2017	$616.981 billion (estimated)
2018	$598.965 billion (estimated)
2019	$600.221 billion (estimated)
2020	$605.951 billion (estimated)
2021	$612.440 billion (estimated)[10]

In 1980, the Department of Defense was allocated, for military programs, 21.0% of the federal budget authority, the amount of money Congress allows a federal agency to spend. During President Reagan's military spending spree, this rose to 26.2% in 1982, 27.5% in 1983, 28.0% in 1984, 27.9% in 1985, 27.8 in 1986, 27.0 in 1987, and was at 26.0% during his last year in office. After descending through the 1990s from 22.8% in 1990 to 15.9% in

2000, the DoD defense budget authority generally rose following the 9/11 attacks and during the wars in Iraq and Afghanistan:

YEAR	PERCENT OF FEDERAL BUDGET AUTHORITY
2001	16.3
2002	16.5
2003	19.4
2004	19.6
2005	18.7
2006	19.2
2007	21.1
2008	20.3
2009	16.4
2010	20.0
2011	19.7

The DoD slice of the federal budget has declined since 2011, and
DoD military programs are currently projected to receive 11.9%
of federal budget authority in 2019.[11]

In March 2013, automatic spending cuts were imposed across
the federal budget as part of a "sequestration" mandated by the
Budget Control Act of 2011 (BCA).[12] In defense spending, outlays were reduced 6.4%, from **$670.3 billion** in 2012 to approx-
imately **$627.6 billion** in 2013, and were reduced another 5.5%,
to **$593.4 billion**, in 2014. Defense spending was, however, set
to rise gradually from **$593 billion** in 2014 to **$714 billion** by
2023. This 2.1% annual growth rate during 2014–2023 was in step
with the inflation rate the Congressional Budget Office (CBO)
projected.[13]

These cuts in military spending programs represent at least a
modicum of fiscal sanity; however, there is another major source
of defense-related spending that does not show up on the DoD
budget, but has a budget line all its own: "Veterans' Benefits and

Services (Veterans Affairs)," which includes four major "subfunctions"—income security for veterans; veterans' education, training, and rehabilitation; hospital and medical care for veterans; and veterans' housing—plus "other" veterans' benefits and services. In 1980, the same index year we used in analyzing the DoD budgets, Veterans Affairs was authorized at **$21.194 billion**. See how it has grown from there:

YEAR	VETERANS AFFAIRS
1990	$30.499 billion
2000	$45.420 billion
2001	$47.513 billion
2003*	$59.033 billion
2010	$124.444 billion
2011**	$123.124 billion
2012	$124.524 billion
2016	$169.322 billion (estimated)
2019	$192.648 billion (estimated)[14]

*start of the Iraq War   **last official year of the war

Viewed as a percentage of federal budget authority, Veterans Affairs is authorized at:

YEAR	PERCENTAGE OF FEDERAL BUDGET
1980	3.2%
1990	2.4%
2000	2.5%
2001	2.5%
2003	2.6%
2010	3.6%
2011	3.5%
2012	3.5%

YEAR	PERCENTAGE OF FEDERAL BUDGET
2016	4.1% (estimated)
2019	4.0%[15] (estimated)

Here is a snapshot of the combined budget authority of the Department of Defense and Veterans Affairs, a combination that gives a more accurate picture of U.S. defense-related spending:

YEAR	BUDGET (DOD + VETERANS AFFAIRS)	PERCENT OF FEDERAL BUDGET (DOD + VETERANS AFFAIRS)
1980	$165.053 billion	24.2 percent
1990	$333.752 billion	25.2 percent
2000	$349.424 billion	18.4 percent
2001	$382.218 billion	18.8 percent
2003	$515.016 billion	22.0 percent
2010	$845.632 billion	23.6 percent
2011	$840.159 billion	23.2 percent
2012	$805.947 billion	21.8 percent
2016	$738.498 billion	17.4 percent
2019	$787.048 billion	15.9 percent[16]

WHY THE

MILITARY-INDUSTRIAL-CONGRESSIONAL

COMPLEX MAKES WAR

As of this writing, in 2016, more than 17% of the federal budget is dedicated to the military (Department of Defense plus Veterans Affairs), some **$738.498 billion**. This is a great deal of money, especially when we consider that the United States is in a severe fiscal crisis, is burdened with trillions of dollars in debt, may actually be broke,[17] and has, in any case, officially withdrawn from major combat in two costly wars, one in Iraq and one in Afghanistan—the latter having officially spanned 2001 to 2014, making it the longest war in U.S. history. World War II posed an existential threat to the United States, and military spending rose to 41% of GDP. The threat posed by the Soviet Union was at least arguably existential as well, and the fifty-year "Cold War" that followed the end of World War II spawned numerous "brushfire" conflicts and two major hot wars, one in Korea (1950–1953) and the other in Vietnam (1955–1975, with most direct U.S. involvement from 1964–1975). Hot as these two wars were, it is difficult to argue that they posed to the United States anything remotely approaching an existential threat. In any case, the Korean and Vietnam wars are long ended, as are the Cold War, the very existence of the Soviet Union, and the two recent conventional wars in the Middle East.

Of course, the United States, like many other countries, now faces threats from terrorist attacks. Frightening, disruptive, costly, and sometimes deadly as these can be, they do not threaten the existence of the United States. The deadliest and most destructive, the terrorist attacks of September 11, 2001, took 2,977 lives (not counting the nineteen suicide terrorists). And yet, they were not the work of the massive army of some hostile nation, but of al-Qaeda, a stateless organization of indeterminate size, but probably no more than 30,000 fighters at its height in the early 2000s.[18] The attacks of 9/11/2001 were carried out not by 30,000 soldiers, but by nineteen terrorists. More recently, what has been characterized as a "terrorist" attack in San Bernardino, California, on December 2, 2015, claimed fourteen lives—and was carried out by two perpetrators, husband and wife. Moreover, although the 2001 attacks motivated a U.S. military response against the Taliban regime in Afghanistan, that response principally employed small special forces units, not large conventional forces. (President George W. Bush and others in his administration subsequently linked Saddam Hussein's Iraq to the attacks and launched a larger war against the Saddam regime. In short order, however, it became apparent that neither Saddam nor others in Iraq had played a direct role in 9/11 or posed an immediate threat to the United States.) Ultimately, the immediate response to 9/11 was mostly a matter for local, state, and federal law enforcement, not the military. In the case of San Bernardino, the entire incident was handled by county and state law enforcement officials, with the FBI entering later in an investigative capacity. No troops, aircraft carriers, bombers, or missiles were required.

The truth is that since the end of World War II, the United States has faced no *active* enemy that actually threatened its existence in the way that Japan, Germany, and their allies had. Since the end of the Cold War and the almost simultaneous demise of the Soviet Union, the United States has faced no *potential* enemy with the capacity to overthrow the government or defeat its military. In short, since 1945—or, *perhaps*, 1991—there has existed no justification based on actual military need for what George Washington would surely have condemned as the "overgrown military establishment" that the United States has maintained for more than seventy years now. Throughout American history up to and including World War II, the nation mobilized its military only to meet major threats. After each threat had been vanquished— Mexico defeated in the U.S.-Mexican War, the rebellion crushed in the Civil War, Spain vanquished in the Spanish-American War, an armistice declared in World War I—mobilization was instantly reversed as demobilization and most of the warriors sent home. Americans could not abide "standing armies" in their midst.

But the period following World War II was radically different, as political scientist Rebecca Thorpe, author of *The American Warfare State,* correctly observes. Even after specific threats had "ebbed and receded, policy-makers advanced new rationales to maintain military readiness. For the first time in the nation's history, congresses consistently supported larger defense budgets..."[19] The most recent military budgets are about the same spent after the September 11, 2001 attacks and at the apogee of the Cold War. In inflation-adjusted dollars (not percentage of GDP), recent and current annual military and defense-related budgets have been greater than any since World War II. Put it this way: The United States currently spends as much on its military as the rest of the world's nations—combined.

Such an investment in the military is not part of the "American tradition." In fact, it goes against the American grain and is "historically unparalleled."[20] In warning against runaway spending on overgrown military establishments, George Washington was not offering innovative, let alone radical, advice. He was merely echoing the intention and the thoughtful work of the framers of the Constitution. The system of checks and balances this document embodies was in no small part intended to prevent the creation of any sizable permanent military. Such a force was deemed essentially undemocratic. It would create heavy tax burdens, saddle citizens with military service obligations, and divert precious resources from productive peacetime investment to wasteful military expenditures. In addition, the very existence of a standing military force would empower presidents to go to war essentially of their own volition—since they would not be obliged to seek massive funding from Congress to mobilize an army from scratch. By eschewing any substantial standing national army and by constitutionally dividing military authority between the president and Congress, the framers intended to discourage the waste of war—to make war something on which the nation embarked only by way of self-defense against genuinely existential threats.

One can make a persuasive argument that the Constitution is, in essence, a pacifist-leaning document.

The presidents are given authority to conduct peaceful diplomacy, but when it comes to waging war, the Constitution requires them to secure a declaration, as well as funding, from Congress. The framers of the Constitution assumed that the members of Congress would, by virtue of their offices, be naturally more immediately responsive to the people of their local constituencies and so would be reluctant to recruit them into potentially deadly wars and to levy upon them burdensome war taxes unless there were overwhelmingly compelling reasons to do so. At the same time, by making the *president* commander in chief of any army that *Congress* authorized and paid for, the framers recognized that strategic command had to be exercised not by a disputatious body of lawmakers, but by a single strong executive. Once the people's representatives had voted to go to war, they had to, for practical reasons, yield democracy to the extent of placing their trust in a commander in chief to lead the nation to victory. But getting to that point required overcoming a distrust of standing armies and centralized command of them, a distrust built into the very idea of American independence and enshrined in the Constitution.

Americans still celebrate their independence every July Fourth, and they continually resort to and rely on the Constitution to assert, claim, safeguard, and defend their rights. Yet, today, even without imminent military threat, the United States devotes nearly a fifth of its annual budget to maintaining the costliest and most powerful military in the history of the planet.

Six trillion dollars in costs! For what? Was going to war an honest mistake on the part of George W. Bush, Donald Rumsfeld, and Dick Cheney? Was it all a spectacular—but well-intentioned—misjudgment concerning the role of Saddam Hussein in 9/11 and his harboring "weapons of mass destruction"?

No. There *was* error. There *was* misjudgment. But going to war was not unintentional. Both the president and the Congress wanted to go to war. The question we need to ask is why.

Why does the military-industrial-Congressional complex make war?

It is the obvious question to ask, given the context of the post–World War II military-industrial complex Dwight D. Eisenhower described—and, even more, the military-industrial-*Congressional* complex he originally intended to describe. In this context, the military spending since 1945 and the American wars that opened the 21st century do not appear aberrant, accidental, or irrational. They appear to be what they truly are: the products of a radical redefinition of American government brought about by the nation's experience of World War II, the first American war fought not by the military, but by the military-industrial-Congressional complex.

Look back to the American Civil War (1861–1865). Whatever else it resolved, the Civil War demonstrated the war-winning edge that superior industrial capacity, a larger economy, and more access to more credit confers on one combatant over another. The Union military wedded itself to Northern industry, Northern production capacity, and a sovereign creditworthiness that the breakaway rural and slaveholding South simply did not and could not possess. Not for nothing is the Civil War often called the first major war of the Industrial Age, and the linkage to industrial innovation and production applies even more pervasively to World War I. The United States entered that conflict in 1917, three years after it had started in Europe in 1914. Late as the U.S. entry was, it enabled the Anglo-French victory not just because it injected into the conflict two million fresh fighters, but, even more, because it applied to it the output of a huge industrial base now tooled up for war. Twenty years later, from the perspective of the United States, World War II became the grand opera to which the two earlier conflicts, the Civil War and World War I, had been mere overtures. World War II was the ultimate product of an industry and an economy totally mobilized for total war. The world had seen nothing like it before—nothing like the United States of America dedicating all it had to the largest conflict humanity had ever fought.

And when that war was over and won, the mindset and the machinery and the money that had won it refused to retreat, declined to demobilize. This refusal was unique in American history. Based on historical research and the construction of unique economic maps, political scientist Rebecca Thorpe concluded that the profound American shift from distrust and avoidance of standing armies and centralized military power came in large part because "World War II military mobilization extended benefits [so] widely."[21] It funded war production not only in the established urban industrial centers, but in rural areas. In what had been prairie, field, and woods, war plants were built where no factories of any kind had stood before. Once the local economies of many country towns and hamlets and entire counties and congressional districts became reliant on military industry, legislators were motivated to maintain those industries at high levels of production—long after World War II had been won. Moreover, primary military contractors and their host communities were not the only beneficiaries of a war-driven economy that consumed 41% of GDP. Because primary contractors were permitted to choose their own subcontractors for parts, subassemblies, specialized services, and so on, the benefits of military contracts were widely disbursed. Unlike traditional pork barrel politics, where a particular state or, even more often, a specific congressional district is the sole beneficiary of some piece of legislation, the demands of military production benefits specific localities while also broadcasting secondary benefits far more widely. This gives legislators promoting particular weapons projects enormous political leverage. "Building weapon X will be just great for my district" is not a persuasive argument for budgeting a project. But "Building weapon X will be great for my district—and for yours, and yours, and yours" is. The template created by World War II military-industrial-Congressional mobilization and production has proven to be incredibly durable:

> The data suggest that the military industry is at least as integral to the economic landscape in the early 21st century as

when Eisenhower delivered his warning. Military spending [today] is higher than it was at the height of the Cold War, despite the absence of any comparable enemy investment. While the geographic scope of the national military mobilization in World War II was already extensive, defense dollars are also more widely dispersed. Defense contracts and subcontracts not only flow to every state and a preponderance of congressional districts, but also have systematically spread into more rural and semirural areas where defense jobs account for disproportionate levels of local jobs and revenue. Excessive economic vulnerabilities in areas with a large proportion of defense facilities relative to other industries encourage legislators to press for continued military spending and prioritize defense-sector growth.[22]

As discussed in Chapter 7, even outright fans of the New Deal concede that the ramp-up of war production in the months leading up to U.S. entry into World War II did more to end the Great Depression than any New Deal program did. But step through the looking glass of statist economic theory and gaze out from the other side. The fact is that the war machine—the rapidly forming military-industrial-Congressional complex—did not take the place of the New Deal, it operated in concert with it, synergistically. Both the war machine *and* the New Deal ran on the Keynesian fuel of massive federal spending, government wage subsidies, and corporate welfare in the form of tax breaks and direct subsidies. Military contracts typically underwrote and thereby guaranteed cost-plus earnings. The contractor couldn't lose. Moreover, before the war, the FDR administration sold the New Deal's assault on free-market capitalism as a patriotic necessity in a time of urgent and unprecedented crisis. During the war, selling patriotic necessity was suddenly a lot easier. The war required sacrifice, to be sure, but it also brought the benefits of well-paid employment, which, coupled with the patriotic need to defend the homeland and win the war, suppressed virtually all objection to government intervention, regulation, work rules, and price controls. Look closely, and you discover that the New Deal and the military-industrial-Congressional complex are cut from the very same cloth.

HOW CONGRESS WON

BY SURRENDERING TO THE PRESIDENT

There is yet another dimension to the current highly developed, thoroughly entrenched military-industrial-Congressional complex. As mentioned, the framers of the Constitution took great pains to divide the making of war between two branches of government, the executive and the legislative. Article I, Section 8 of the Constitution vests in Congress the "power to...declare War," to "raise and support Armies... and...a Navy." Moreover, it is Congress and Congress alone that "lays and collects taxes," that borrows money on the credit of the United States, and that holds the national purse strings. Acting on their own, presidents can do none of this. Indeed, to make sure that no president can decide to go to war, the Constitution specifies that funds appropriated to raise and support armies cannot be used longer than two years. Thus, presidents will not have a de facto standing army to send to war without the authorization of Congress. Clearly, the framers intended that this authorization would be in the form of a declaration of war; however, in all of American history, Congress had declared war only five times: the War of 1812, the U.S.-Mexican War (1845–1848), the Spanish-American War (1898), World War I (1917–1918), and World War II (1941–1945)—the last formally declared war the United States fought. All conflicts since then—Korean War (1950–1953), intervention in the Lebanon Crisis of 1958, Vietnam War (1955–1975), participation in the Multinational Force in Lebanon (1983–1984), Bosnian War (1992–2004), Second Liberian Civil War (2003), Haitian Coup d'état (2004), Persian Gulf War (1991), War in Afghanistan (2001–2014), Iraq War (2003–

2011), and the Libyan Civil War (2011)—have been authorized by congressional legislation or resolution and sometimes, initially, by a United Nations Security Council resolution (typically U.S.-instigated) that is subsequently confirmed by Congress.

(President George W. Bush described the attacks of September 11, 2001, as the beginning of the "first war of the 21st century."[23] They were not, however, the beginning of America's first "war on terror." During 1801–1815, presidents Jefferson and Madison waged war against the so-called Barbary states of Tunis, Algiers, and Tripoli because their Islamic governments conducted state-sanctioned piracy against the shipping of "Christian nations" in the Mediterranean. These states demanded protection money ["tribute"] from European nations as well as the United States in exchange for safe passage in waters they controlled. Both Jefferson and Madison chose to fight rather than pay the tribute. Like the modern wars in Afghanistan and Iraq, the Barbary Wars were not declared by Congress. Unlike the modern wars, however, the action against the Barbary states was highly successful, stopping the piracy and enhancing the prestige as well as the perception of sovereignty of the young American Republic.)

Why has the legislative branch surrendered so much of its constitutional authority to the executive branch? "The various explanations—a heightened security environment, legislative atrophy, executive initiative, changes in political culture, expansive constitutional interpretations of executive power—either fail to apply consistently throughout the post–World War II era or fail to account for historical variations during earlier periods of development."[24] For presidents, the capitulation of Congress has been a huge gain in precisely the executive war-making power the framers of the Constitution had labored so assiduously to prevent.

The rise of the military-industrial complex during *and after* World War II gave presidents unheard-of power to make war. The rise of the military-industrial-*Congressional* complex did even more. It put Congress in a position to perpetually provide the funds for presidents to use, at will, in order to possess the standing military forces they were never intended to have. Since the Korean War (1950–1953), Congress has never allowed defense funding to fall below a baseline of **$300 billion** (adjusted for inflation). In the 1970s, President Nixon was simultaneously winding down the Vietnam War even as he faced the military build-up of a resurgently hostile Soviet Union governed by superannuated Cold War hardliners at whose head was Leonid Brezhnev. Yet Congress provided more funding for the military during the post-Soviet Clinton era than it had during the Nixon presidency.

It is clear what the presidency gained from the authority Congress ceded. It is less immediately clear what Congress gained. "New research," Rebecca Thorpe explains, shows that...

> the scale, scope, and political geography of the World War II effort gave rise to large military industries located in rural and semirural areas that lack diverse economies.... Congress members representing these communities have powerful political incentives to press for ongoing military expenditures regardless of actual or perceived national security threats. These members face weak resistance because military spending benefits numerous geographic constituencies, while policy has shifted most of the costs of military spending and war onto political minorities who volunteer to fight, foreign populations where U.S. wars take place, and, ultimately, future generations of taxpayers.[25]

FORCE-FED ON GENETICALLY MODIFIED PORK

On the face of it, post–World War II military appropriations have become an endless, often outrageous, pork barrel bazaar, and we will walk through that bazaar in the very next chapter. On its surface, military pork barrel appropriations are just like those used in any other pork barrel corrupt political enterprise. That is, first and last, they are legislative bids to buy votes. Often, this cynically corrupt motive is barely disguised. How else, for example, to explain why "Congress failed to eliminate a single weapon-production line after the fall of the Soviet Union, despite testimony from secretaries of Defense, Joint Chiefs of Staff, and presidents that many of these weapons programs were no longer necessary"?[26]

But it is urgently important that we get past the face and below the surface and turn our cynicism into outrage.

These days a lot of people are fearful of GMOs—genetically modified organisms—especially when they are used in producing food.[27] Are GMOs safe? Will they harm the health of those who consume them? Will they affect human *genetic* health, perhaps creating birth defects and mutations in the offspring of GMO consumers?

Nobody knows for sure. But we do know this: Military pork is not the ordinary pork that legislators have been routinely trading for votes presumably since the 1st Congress. Military pork is the political-economic equivalent of genetically modified pork, and the danger it poses is mutation not only of the national economy, but of the Republic itself.

David Stockman titles his epic study *The Great Deformation: The Corruption of Capitalism in America*.[28] That term, *deformation*, is the perfect GMO label for a careerist legislative culture that swaps the constitutional responsibility for making, regulating, *and restraining* war in order to purchase constituent votes. Such a corrupt culture, such a corrupt practice, is a deformation of the economy, a deformation of national defense and security, a deformation of international relations, and a deformation of the very structure of our democracy. It puts in jeopardy our collective economic well-being as well as the economic future of our children. It endangers our security and it weakens our defense by hijacking decisions that should strictly concern critical military needs and priorities and making them instead to divert financial benefits to some subset of a congressional constituency. This deformation of democracy cheats and imperils our allies and potentially provokes our enemies. Most of all it betrays the Constitution to its core—its very DNA—mutating and mutilating a political and ethical legacy unique in history, a revolutionary gift purchased through generations of sacrifice, a parcel that we have received intact and that we are morally obligated to pass down, intact, to our children as whole and as perfect as it was passed down to us.

Chapter 8 is about the causes and context of wasteful military spending. This chapter gets down to cases and explores just how irrational defense spending has institutionalized, perhaps even enshrined, the astronomical costs of our military-industrial-Congressional complex. The results may be summed up in a variation on the acronym that described the Cold War doctrine of Soviet and American nuclear deterrence. Mutually Assured Destruction, it was called: MAD. Absent a national will to end the waste and abuse floating in the great military pork barrel, we as a nation are doomed to a doctrine of PAD—Perpetually Assured Debt.

CHAPTER 9

THE PENTAGON

AND

PORK CHOP HILL

T he United States military reported spending **$53 million** on marketing and advertising contracts with sports teams during the period 2012–2015. More than **$10 million** of those dollars went directly into the coffers of teams of the National Football League (NFL), Major League Baseball (MLB), National Basketball Association (NBA), National Hockey League (NHL), and Major League Soccer (MLS). Recruiting for the all-volunteer force (AVF) has a price tag, and, arguably, **$53 million** was money well spent, including the roughly 20% of that sum that went to the major league teams. After all, many sports fans are of prime military age and can be expected to possess the competitive, aggressive, yet team-oriented traits the military looks for.

Oh, but there are at least two worrisome details here—details that would never escape even the most basic due diligence practiced in private-sector business. Detail number one is that the Department of Defense cannot quite fully account for how every dollar of this money was used—or even to what or to whom much of it went. Detail number two is that **$6.8 million** of this chunk was spent to buy displays and demonstrations of "sincere" patriotism presented as gestures the teams offered spontaneously, voluntarily, and on their own dime. It was stuff like inviting color guard contingents to march the field at half-time, pseudo-impromptu enlistment and reenlistment ceremonies, ceremonial first pitches, ceremonial puck drops, even special performances of the national anthem. For the privilege of honoring the troops, the teams collected **$6.8 million** from the American taxpayer.

Ultimately embarrassed by the whole thing, the Department of Defense ended the practice of paying for patriotism.[1] Score one for us taxpayers.

But leave us not get too cocky.

In 2015, the DoD's celebrated Defense Advanced Research Projects Agency (DARPA)—the same outfit that financed the development of stealth technology in the 1980s and the forerunner of the Internet in the 1960s—spent **$2 million** on a project to teach robots how to play jazz. The project was given a *name* (Music Improvising Collaborative Agent, or MUSICA) and given a *goal* (to create a machine "capable of musically improvising with a human player").

A *purpose*? Not so much. The best that musician and University of Arizona Fred Fox School of Music associate professor Kelland Thomas, one of the beneficiaries of this DoD contract, could come up with was, "I think DARPA's interested in a program that will interact with humans." That is supposed to take about five years.[2] (*Historical note:* The Pentagon—once the world's biggest office building—was designed and built in eighteen months. The atomic bomb, which won World War II, was theorized, designed, built, and successfully tested all within a month shy of three years.)

The DoD sunk **$40 million** (or 20x its investment in robotic jazz) into a contest to see who could create the best "emergency rescue robot." In 2015 alone, DoD spent **$13.6 million** on its stupendous DARPA Robotics Challenge (DRC). Some of this dough was divvied up among the creators of the winning entries. That might have been money well spent—had any of the twenty-four robots actually completed the eight basic tasks they were assigned: Drive a vehicle, get out of said vehicle, push a door open and then move through the open doorway, twist a valve, drill a hole in drywall, navigate a rubble-strewn patch of ground, walk up some stairs, and then pull off a surprise task that would be introduced on the day of the competition. All twenty-four robotic entries performed so miserably that *Popular Science* pronounced the DRC "unimpressive," "bumbling," "fizzled," and "a bust." No matter, a **$2 million** grand prize was duly presented, as were a **$1 million** second-place award and a **$500,000** prize for third. "This was a contest whose entries were so incompetent, at least compared to humans," *Popular Science* noted, "that simply opening that door counted as a legitimate victory."[3]

With somewhat less grandeur of vision, the DoD Office of Naval Research threw **$2.5 million** into what it called a "Human Surrogate Interaction program." After three years, this endeavor managed to produce a "robot lobby greeter," which was stationed for some weeks during 2015 in the lobby of the Institute for Simulation and Training at the University of Central Florida. Described by one eyewitness as "resembling a hybrid of...Michael Myers from *Halloween* and Freddy Krueger from *A Nightmare on Elm Street*," the machine did succeed in greeting people who passed through the lobby, but it failed to be a robot, since it could not function autonomously but had to be operated by a human being stationed—well, stationed somewhere other than the lobby.[4] For **$2.5 mil**, Uncle Sam bought a remote-controlled dummy.

Mercenary patriotism and a motley collection of Robots without a Cause are certainly a *waste of money* and probably a *waste of time* as well, but spending more than **$700,000** on urgently needed military and medical supplies only to let them rot in a costly warehouse is nothing more or less than *waste*, period. The supplies were intended to aid Yemen in fighting terrorism, but—

apparently due to a breakdown in communications between the U.S. Department of State and authorities in Yemen, and between State and the DoD—they never even got out of Virginia. Stockpiled in 2007, the supplies were periodically shipped from one warehouse to another within in the state, but no further. None of these venues were DoD facilities. They were commercial warehouses, which have been billing taxpayers for storage over the past nine years and counting. Many of the items, such as medicines, have expired, while a consignment of explosives is no longer considered stable or viable, and a large shipment of batteries is almost certainly depleted if not dead. Also part of the urgent shipment was a collection of "special solvents," which are now classified as hazardous waste and must be disposed of at whatever it costs to safely and legally dispose of waste that has become hazardous.[5]

Everything, they say, is relative. The **$700,000** (and growing) spent on once urgently needed goods now rotting in a warehouse seems like chump change compared to the **$110 million** the DoD spends every year to maintain (that is, to light, heat, and repair) more than 360 "empty, unused, and excess" buildings in Afghanistan. The Special Inspector General for Afghan Reconstruction (SIGAR) reported to Congress in 2015 that the "old buildings were supposed to be disposed of, but the Afghan ministries receiving security aid hung on to many of the old structures." The SIGAR pointed out that while money was being squandered on heating and lighting unused buildings, "Afghan soldiers in Kandahar had no lights or heat for three nights." That's a bad three days and nights, but the SIGAR report also noted that a $14.7 million warehouse was never used because of construction delays. Nevertheless, this unused and useless warehouse was modified at a cost of **$400,000** even after it was clear that the building would never be needed.[6]

Back home, Veterans Affairs improperly, maybe even criminally, spent **$1.8 million** and just squandered **$40 million**. Let's start with the **$1.8 mil**. This is the sum the VA spent for salary increases and moving expenses for twenty-three senior Veterans Benefits Administration (VBA) executives who were reassigned in 2013–2015. Okay. Well, maybe they were really needed other than where they happened to be. But it is the *maybe* that's just the point. There is no way of knowing if these moves were really necessary, because VBA management never bothered to search for local applicants before moving everyone else all over the country. As the Office of the Inspector General (OIG) pointed out, "an agency cannot make a determination whether a position is difficult to fill [locally] if the agency does not actively search for or consider applicants for the position." In five of the twenty-three cases, vacancies were not even announced. It is exceptionally difficult to find employees if you keep the job openings a secret. When asked, one of the transferred executives frankly admitted that "salary increases and relocation incentives were a way to get around pay freezes and bans on performance bonuses."[7] Good answer.

Most voters would likely agree that banning performance bonuses isn't such a bad idea in the case of an agency notorious for scandals concerning ailing veterans literally dropping dead while waiting for care even as senior executives ordered subordinates to cover up data revealing the many delays that routinely clog the VA system.

Well, maybe more money would solve some of these problems. The undeclared wars of the 20th and 21st centuries have increased by 50% the number of veterans currently waiting to see doctors. The VA needs more staff—but has already spent beyond its budget and is threatening to lay off medical personnel and other employees to make up the shortfall. This, however, did not deter the VA in California from spending more than **$33.4 million** in 2015 on junkets sending staffers to conferences. The year before, 2014, the Palo Alto VA spent more than **$6 million** on artwork to adorn its facilities. Maybe it will give those sick vets something to look at while they wait for a doctor.[8]

BRIDGING THE PARTISAN DIVIDE

Remember that Aesop fable about the dog carrying a stolen bone in its mouth? He starts to cross a stream, looks down, and beholds his reflection in the water. Being possessed of nothing better than a dog's brain, he mistakes his reflection for another dog—one with a better bone. When Fido opens his mouth to bark, he drops his bone in the water.

You can be forgiven if this tale from the 6th century B.C. reminds you of the psychotically partisan U.S. Congress of today. Members glare at each other across the aisle and, instead of seeing a reflection of other public servants, see rivals with some bigger bones, open their mouths to bark, and lose in the process their sense of mission for the common good of the nation. But on a few things even the members of our canine Congress find room for bipartisan agreement. As Leon Wolf, writing in the conservative blog Red State, explains: "Here is a game that both parties play: when they attempt to persuade us angry taxpayers that there's no waste left to cut in the Federal budget, they discuss the budget in terms of 'non-defense spending.'" Military spending? Hands off! Liberals don't want to be accused of being soft on defense, and conservatives are vehement in their belief that "a strong military is one of the true legitimate functions of the Federal government." So, we taxpayers can pretty safely assume that both sides of the aisle unite in selling us on the proposition "that 'defense' spending is ipso facto, not wasteful." But then we learn that the "Department of Defense spent $43 million to build a gas station in Afghanistan that should have cost roughly $500,000"—a "discovery [that] came as part of a broader investigation into allegations of criminal activity within the DOD's ... program to kick-start the Afghan economy."[9]

And now, suddenly, both Democrats and Republicans begin questioning every aspect of military spending. In March 2015, Senate Armed Services Committee Chairman John McCain (R-Arizona) "blasted the Defense Department for wasting money on [a project] to study the bomb-sniffing capabilities of elephants." Senator McCain dutifully reported, "Thus far, they have found that, while elephants are more effective than dogs, using them is impractical," adding that "No bomb-sniffing elephants have been fielded."[10]

Speaking at the Center for Strategic and International Studies, McCain also mentioned the **$48 million** the Pentagon spends annually to ship "$25 million worth of food to U.S. military base grocery stores in Asia instead of using local producers" and the **$2.4 million** the National Guard spent in 2014 to advertise with professional sports interests, "including snowmobiling." McCain said that reducing waste was "urgent," even as he "vowed to continue his fight against budget caps that will slash defense spending by $500 billion over a decade." Now *this* is notable, since sequestration (which imposed those caps) is a 100% GOP plan. But maybe the senior senator from Arizona need not worry. Although the House had passed, a few days before he spoke, a defense budget that adhered to the cap of **$523 billion**, the budget also boosted a special "wartime spending account to $90 billion, nearly $40 billion above what the White House says it needs."[11]

Another Republican, Senator Tom Coburn of Oklahoma, singled out TALOS (the Tactical Assault Light Operator Suit, a/k/a the "Iron Man suit"), which is slated to cost **$80 million** to produce, but will (according to an industry source) likely climb to $1 billion. "Only someone with too much of someone else's money and not enough accountability for how it was being spent could come up with some of these projects," *Wastebook 2015* laments.[12] TALOS is a robotic exoskeleton that is supposed to be bulletproof, weaponized, monitor the wearer's vital signs, and, oh yes, give him or her superhuman strength and perception. We should know if TALOS finally works and what it finally costs around the year 2018.[13] We don't, however, have to wait until then for at least three **$1 billion** charges, to wit:

- **$1 billion** to destroy **$16 billion** worth of ammunition, "enough to pay a full year's salary for over 54,000 Army privates," according to Senator Coburn.
- **$1 billion** toward a ballistic missile defense system. Draw-

backs? First, it will stop just three out of ten incoming missiles. (Not cool.) Second, its total price tag is **$41 billion**. (Not cheap.)

- **$1.2 billion** to fund Department of Veterans Affairs disability compensation for sleep apnea. As of 2014, more than 149,000 veterans were drawing a 50% rating for the condition.

In addition, the year 2014 saw:

- **$9 million** in excess payments for helicopter parts. These were purchased under a sole-source noncompetitive contract with Bell Helicopter, which charged the American taxpayer sixteen times the going price. *It's priced at $297. For you? $2,356. Whadda deal!*
- **$468 million** spent for 20 planes around which the Afghan air force was supposed to be built. Before that could happen, however, they were all sold for scrap for a total return of **$32,000**.
- **$72,000** to distribute 9,500 copies of the U.S. Navy's *Currents* magazine. Among the topics covered was the Navy's use of "green" technologies—presumably including online publishing of documents to save paper and shipping costs.
- **$639,000** to enable the Air Force to send anthracite coal mined in Pennsylvania to Germany to heat U.S. bases there. In all fairness, this was not the Air Force's idea, but the result of an indelible earmark, which a Pennsylvania senator, intent on ensuring a future for Pennsylvania coal, superglued into the budget during the 1960s. The future is now.
- **$414,000** to develop America's Army, a "first-person shooter" video game available online. For free! Although it is intended as a recruiting tool, U.S. intelligence officials claim it also makes a handy terrorist training tool.
- **$21 million** spent on buildings in Afghanistan. Not built to international standards, however, they have a lamentable tendency to catch fire and burn to the ground.
- And, in the let's-add-injury-to-insult category—**$19 billion**

mostly to pay for administrative leave for Veterans Affairs employees who find themselves under investigation for alleged violations.[14]

ANECDOTES OF OUTRAGE

VERSUS BUSINESS AS USUAL

Former Senator Tom Coburn (R-Oklahoma) started publishing his *Wastebook* series in 2010, and Senator Jeff Flake (R-Arizona) has now taken it over. Available in hardcopy as well as online, the *Wastebooks* are humorous—well, better to call them tragicomic—yearbooks of irrational government spending. They are not journals of partisan opinion. That is, they don't contain programs and projects that one side of the aisle is likely to consider just great while the other side is sure to condemn. No, these are collections of fiscal missteps that practically everyone (except perhaps those receiving the money) will agree are idiotic. Too big to fail? These expenditures are too dumb to be believed—or would be, except that they are all too real.

So it is important that we know about them. Twenty-one million dollars spent to build firetrap buildings in Afghanistan, certain helicopter parts sold to everyone everywhere in the world for $297 apiece but retailed to the DoD for $2,356 per unit—these things are important to know about. Moreover, the fact that enough of these abominations happen every year to warrant inclusion in *annual* "worst of" collections proves that they are not mere aberrations but serious symptoms of a deeper disorder. They are examples—not of random error, isolated wrongdoing, and occasional incompetence, but of how the government does business.

Still, they *are* anecdotes, and in everything from understanding diseases and their cures to interpreting the online user reviews of the latest smartphone, we all learn to avoid doubling down on "anecdotal evidence." We need to trace the anecdotes to their systemic causes. We need to follow the money.

"The U.S. military is good at fighting wars, but it sucks at managing money," begins a *Fiscal Times* article titled "With $8.5 Trillion Unaccounted for, Why Should Congress Increase the Defense Budget?"[15] The sum mentioned in the title is the number of taxpayer dollars appropriated for military spending between 1996 and 2015 for which the DoD cannot give an accounting. It's hardly a fell-between-the-cracks, disappearance-between-the-sofa-cushions sort of thing. It's SOP: standard operating procedure.

Over the years, the DoD has developed a bookkeeping system so convoluted as to make one conclusion inescapable: Unlike conventional accounting, which aims for clarity, the DoD approach is deliberately designed to obscure and obfuscate. It is stealth technology brought from the battlefield and put into the hands of people with green visors. Back in 1996, Congress enacted legislation requiring an audit of the DoD. It was and is *the law*. But, somehow, the audit never happened. So, in 2009, Congress passed a new law that required the DoD to be "audit-ready"—by 2017! DoD responded by sinking billions of dollars into new accounting software that has, so far, consistently failed to do accounting.

The thing is, there seems to be method in the DoD's madness. More to the point, there is larceny in the DoD's incompetence. A Reuters story from November 18, 2013, could be a journalism school lesson on how *not* to bury the lead.[16] "Linda Woodford," it begins, "spent the last 15 years of her career inserting phony numbers in the U.S. Department of Defense's accounts."

Woodford explained to Reuters correspondent Scot Paltrow how, every month until she retired in 2011, a day would come when "the Navy would start dumping numbers on the Cleveland, Ohio, office of the Defense Finance and Accounting Service [DFAS], the Pentagon's main accounting agency." Woodford and her colleagues had the job of inputting the data into monthly reports that were supposed to reconcile the Navy's books with those of the U.S. Treasury. Every month, however, it was the same old set of problems: "Numbers were missing. Numbers were clearly wrong. Numbers came with no explanation of how the money had been spent or which congressional appropriation it came from." Some of the mysteries were solvable, but "many" were not, and when Woodford and her colleagues asked what to do about that, they were told to "take 'unsubstantiated change actions'—in other words, enter false numbers, commonly called 'plugs,' to make the Navy's totals match the Treasury's."

That adverb *commonly* in the last sentence demands some slack-jawed gawking, as does the very fact that the DoD actually has a term for made-up numbers: "plugs." It turns out that "plugs" are as common in DoD accounting as bullets are in infantrymen's rifles. Reuters calls their use "standard operating procedure" and the news agency's 2013 investigation "found that the Pentagon is largely incapable of keeping track of its vast stores of weapons, ammunition, and other supplies; thus, it continues to spend money on new supplies it doesn't need and on storing others long out of date."

> It has amassed a backlog of more than half a trillion dollars in unaudited contracts with outside vendors; how much of that money paid for actual goods and services delivered isn't known. And it repeatedly falls prey to fraud and theft that can go undiscovered for years, often eventually detected by external law enforcement agencies.
>
> The consequences aren't only financial; bad bookkeeping can affect the nation's defense. In one example of many, the Army lost track of $5.8 billion of supplies between 2003 and 2011 as it shuffled equipment between reserve and regular units. Affected units "may experience equipment shortages that could hinder their ability to train soldiers and respond to emergencies," the Pentagon inspector general said in a September 2012 report.[17]

Reuters found that between 2003 and 2013, the DoD "signed contracts for the provision of more than **$3 trillion** in goods and services. How much of that money is wasted in overpayments to contractors, or was never spent and never remitted to the Treasury, is a mystery. That's because of a massive backlog of 'close-outs'—audits meant to ensure that a contract was fulfilled and the money ended up in the right place." In fact, at "the end of fiscal 2011, the agency's backlog totaled 24,722 contracts worth $573.3 billion, according to DCAA [Defense Contract Audit Agency] figures. Some of them date as far back as 1996."[18]

Even though some units suffer shortages, Navy Vice Admiral Mark Harnitchek, who leads the Defense Logistics Agency (DLA), freely admits, "We have about $14 billion of inventory for lots of reasons, and probably half of that is excess to what we need"—in other words, as Reuters's Paltrow put it, it is "way too much stuff." More precisely, it is way too much stuff for which the DoD paid way too much money:

> Consider the "vehicular control arm," part of the front suspension on the military's ubiquitous High Mobility Multipurpose Vehicles, or Humvees. As of November 2008, the DLA had 15,000 of the parts in stock, equal to a 14-year supply, according to an April 2013 Pentagon inspector general's report.
>
> And yet, from 2010 through 2012, the agency bought 7,437 more of them—at prices considerably higher than it paid for the thousands sitting on its shelves. The DLA was making the new purchases as demand plunged by nearly half with the winding down of the Iraq and Afghanistan wars. The inspector general's report said the DLA's buyers hadn't checked current inventory when they signed a contract to acquire more.[19]

WILLFUL OBFUSCATION AND

SYSTEMIC DYSFUNCTION

For FY 2017, the military's **$632 billion** budget (projected outlay, **$604.452 billion**[20]) will claim 15% of a **$4.2 trillion** total federal budget. Add to this veterans' benefits—**$179 billion** or 4% of the federal budget—and you have total defense-related outlays of **$811 billion**, 19% of the federal budget.[21] The discretionary portion of the military budget (not including veterans' benefits) is **$622.6 billion**, or 54% of the total federal budget for *discretionary* spending—the spending Congress must legislate each and every year. Add the **$75.4 billion** in veterans' benefits that are part of the federal discretionary budget (7% of that budget), and you have discretionary defense-related spending of **$698 billion**—61% of the discretionary budget for FY 2017.[22] Step back for a global view, and you discover that this expenditure is 40% of all the military spending that takes place on planet Earth.[23]

Yet the fiscal culture and the management structure of the DoD, a combination of willful obfuscation and systemic dysfunction, treats it like pocket change. Nobody, for instance, even knows how many different accounting and business systems the DoD uses—"thousands and thousands of systems," according to former Deputy Secretary of Defense Gordon England. "I'm not sure anybody knows how many systems there are." In May 2011, then-Secretary of Defense Robert Gates admitted that he and his staff "learned that it was nearly impossible to get accurate information and answers to questions such as 'How much money did you spend?' and 'How many people do you have?'" In fact, "*Department* of Defense" may itself be a misnomer for what Gates more accurately called an "amalgam of fiefdoms."[24]

UNELECTED GOVERNMENT AND
ELECTED GOVERNMENT:
THE CAREER CONNECTION

Secretary Gates might have described the Department of Defense as an intensively "siloed" organization. Not long ago, *silo* was used exclusively as a noun that described a structure for storing material in bulk—most often grain or silage on a farm. The postwar era of nuclear and thermonuclear warfare introduced use of the term, still a noun, to describe the underground structures that house and launch intercontinental ballistic missiles (ICBMs). More recently, though, to *silo* has become a business buzz verb describing the act of isolating the components of an enterprise—departments, functions, systems, or processes—from one another, always to the detriment of the organization as a whole. A "siloed" organization is a) one in which the left hand never lets the right hand know what it's doing, and b) one with a whole lot of left and right hands.

Gates could have said "siloed," but he chose instead to describe the DoD as an "amalgam of fiefdoms." Words matter, and we can assume they matter quite a bit to Robert Gates, who is the author of at least three superb professional memoirs. Surely he knows that *silo* and *fiefdom* are two very different figures of speech. The first describes the isolation of components within an organization. The second describes an organization that resembles medieval feudal society, a social structure in which overlords parcel out their domains as fiefdoms or fiefs to vassals, who may rule their little piece of land as petty tyrants. The first is a description of a usually dysfunctional or at least suboptimal business organization. The second relates more to the leadership, management, governance, and priorities of such an organization. Fiefdoms are about power for the sake of power, however petty. Fiefdoms are about careerism.

One of the downsides of the unelected government we have called "the Administrative State" is its tendency to create fiefdoms. Like silos, these fragment an organization such that one department or function fails to communicate effectively with another. Even more importantly, however, each isolated department, division, or function tends to be ruled by an executive who sees his domain as more important than any other. The fief—not the job, not the larger organization, not the nation, and certainly not public service—becomes an end in itself. It is within the fief that a career is built, defended, and grown. In furtherance of individual careers, the particular welfare of the fief trumps the general welfare of the organization, let alone the nation. Moreover, a careerist can continue to aggrandize his fiefdom and thereby develop his career secure in the knowledge that the combination of civil service laws and civil service unions will protect him even if he never sees or thinks or even imagines beyond the confines and interests and benefits of his fiefdom.

Feudal societies were inherently limited. Vassals and their serfs could not see beyond the bounds of the fiefdom. They had no reason to entertain a vision any larger than this. No wonder the Middle Ages are so often called the Dark Ages. Allow a vast organization with a profound mission within a great nation that occupies a commanding place in a dangerous world to come to resemble a medieval realm, and you have a dramatic script with some comical content that is nevertheless the stuff of tragedy.

In terms of organization, it is apparent that the wasteful dysfunction of the American defense establishment is enabled by fragmentation not into mere managerial silos but into fiefdoms—an amalgam of them, at that. It is an example of Administrative State careerism at its most rampant.

When the unelected contingent of a government organization is allowed to shatter into fiefdoms, each with its own way of doing things, each bent to the service of whatever executive or executives hold sway over it, that organization is bound to be dysfunctional. This is bad enough, but there is even worse. For holding the purse strings of the organization is another organization, the Congress of the United States, which consists of the *elected contingent* of the government. Their function is to represent the people by crafting useful laws—in the case of the military, laws to provide for the common defense.

Such is the *function* of the members of the elected government. Their *career*, however, is politics.

In 2015, Tim Roemer (D-Indiana, 1991–2003), wrote a *Newsweek* opinion piece titled "Why Do Congressmen Spend Only Half Their Time Serving Us?" Roemer began by asking his readers to imagine ordering a pizza, opening the door, and being presented by the pizza guy with six of the twelve slices you paid for. "Imagine," Roemer continues, "paying a financial consultant to prepare your taxes and they complete half of your federal forms and still submit them to the IRS. Imagine going for your annual dental appointment and your dentist drills out your cavity but doesn't put in the filling." Then Roemer asks, "Are you feeling the pain?"[25]

Roemer reminds us that members of Congress are paid $174,000 a year for the job they are supposed to do full time for us but to which they actually devote only half of their time. The rest is spent "chasing money for their re-election campaigns." Bad enough that this time is robbed from the taxpayers, but, even worse, the 50% left to do the job for which they are paid comes to be at least partly owned by the people and special interests whom they have chased for campaign money. How much of each congressman's head, heart, and soul is left over for the business of the American people? To the degree that public service becomes a career, it is no longer a "career" in public service.

ALL POLITICS IS PORK BARREL

"All politics is local," the beloved 47th Speaker of the House of Representatives Tip O'Neill famously observed. It sounds innocent and wholesome enough. The idea is that elections are won not by ideological persuasion or by appealing to the nation, but by winning a constituency, solving local problems, bringing home to Peoria benefits from Washington. As a political formula, it is not very different from declaring all politics to be pork barrel politics.

Pork barrel is, after all, the ultimate in local politics. It is the advocacy by national legislators of local projects with local benefits. It is about appropriating federal funds to bring benefits to localized constituencies, and while it is not always bad by any means, pork barrel, measured against the standard of doing the greatest good for the greatest number, is prodigiously wasteful. Pork barrel politics in this sense is the subject of the chapters in Part IV. Doubtless, some representatives passionately love their home districts and therefore want to serve them first and foremost. Nevertheless, whatever moral or sentimental purpose pork barrel serves in a politician's career, it is at some level always a means of buying votes. It is at some level always less about public service than it is about defending, maintaining, and even growing one's career in politics.

MILITARY-GRADE PORK

A s discussed in Chapter 6, there is no field richer in pork barrel opportunity than defense-related expenditure. Not only are high-ticket, job-producing products, projects, and programs involved, but so are the economic prosperity and even economic survival of well-defined districts and powerful industrial companies. But what makes military-grade pork truly unique is the natural link between local and national politics, between the benefit some weapons system brings to the particular community or communities directly involved in its manufacture and the benefit the weapon system is perceived to bring to the nation as a whole. This is patriotic pork.

Indeed, military-grade pork is so valuable as a vote-buying currency that a mighty and enduring institution evolved as a result of World War II. It is none other than the military-industrial-Congressional complex. But "evolved" is actually a weak word for it, because it implies the gradual passage of time. In fact, the military-industrial-Congressional complex *exploded* into existence. *Evolution*? It was more like the Big Bang. The military-industrial-Congressional complex was forged by the urgent and dire demands of an all-engulfing war that, from the American perspective, began with a massive attack on U.S. Pacific territory on December 7, 1941. It was an unprecedented marshaling of national will, economy, and credit to build a dedicated arms industry where none had existed before. In big cities, existing factories were rapidly converted to war production, and employment surged. But even more was needed, and hitherto non-industrialized rural areas became the sites of brand-new dedicated defense plants, new military bases, and the major expansion of existing bases. Many such areas benefitted from augmented growth, and many more benefitted from the first real growth they had ever seen. The war transformed both the physical and fiscal landscape of rural America.

In previous wars, even America's two highly industrialized wars—the Civil War and World War I—all the weapons and materiel of war were produced in existing factories, which were retooled and expanded as necessary. No sooner were each of these wars ended than military production dramatically contracted. In all American wars prior to World War II, the outbreak brought crash programs of mobilization, including, in the Civil War and World War I, the mobilization of industry. The end of the war brought even faster demobilization, both of armies and of war industries. But industrial production was so integral to World War II—manufacturing was, for all belligerents, the ultimate weapon—that there could be no true demobilization. The military-industrial-Congressional complex not only survived V-E Day and V-J Day, but prospered and continued to grow. The Cold War environment that followed the end of World War II spawned a global community of nations caught between the poles of two great "superpowers." It gave rise to a fifty-year stretch of military history defined by an ongoing arms race between these superpowers. The arms race was an arms market; industry expanded to serve it, and members of Congress competed to ensure that this industry would expand in *their* districts.

THE *OTHER* TRIAD

"**O**utsider" presidential hopeful Donald Trump found himself a bit too far outside when he was stumped during a televised Republican Primary debate by the term "nuclear triad."[26] In fairness to him, there is that "other" military triad, which consists not of missiles, aircraft, and submarines, but of the elected government, industry, and the unelected government. The glue that holds this triad together is compounded of *career* and *profit*.

We have already discussed the motive the members of the elected government have to appropriate military pork: buying votes. Industry's motive, obviously, is financial profit. That leaves the unelected government. What *do* the bureaucrats want?

The more the federal government invests in the military, the bigger the Administrative State becomes. The bigger it becomes, the more secure the careers of those in the unelected government become. Moreover, the bigger each particular department or function—each fiefdom—becomes, the more salary managers and executives command. Growth of the military-industrial-Congressional complex builds and ensures government careers while also providing localized employment and prosperity in the districts of the relevant congressmen. The country at large does not necessarily gain a higher level of security. In fact, to the degree that current military spending is wasteful (which it is) and inefficient (which it is), the security of the nation is actually reduced (which it is). Nevertheless, the myth that defense spending should be immune from cost-cutting is incredibly durable, and, therefore, most weapons programs and defense initiatives make most Americans feel more secure, no matter the cost.

MERCENARY WARFARE AND PRIVATIZED PORK

The so-called War on Terror that followed the terrorist attacks of September 11, 2001, brought to the forefront of American popular consciousness what seemed like a new element in the U.S. military picture: the private military company (PMC). Of course, mercenaries—soldiers for hire—have been combatants since history's earliest wars. They were especially prominent in Europe during the Renaissance, and they experienced a kind of heyday in the 19th century with the rise of the French Foreign Legion. During the 1950s and 1960s, "soldiers of fortune" played a significant, colorful, controversial, and often disreputable role in the very violent wars for independence throughout Africa. But by the end of the 19th century, the majority of the world's states officially spurned the employment of mercenaries, and in 1989, UN resolution 44/34, which adopted the *International Convention against the Recruitment, Use, Financing, and Training of Mercenaries*, familiarly known since its entry into force on October 20, 2001, as the "UN Mercenary Convention," made it an offense under international law for any state, entity, or individual to employ a "mercenary."[27]

Nevertheless, despite the UN sanction and the general disdain for mercenaries, the profession of mercenary began to evolve a corporate image. The PMC, the private military company, emerged. Also known as private military firms (PMFs), PMCs have drawn much criticism from people who hold that a mercenary is a mercenary, driven by the motive of profit, not patriotism, liberty, altruism, idealism, or a struggle against oppression. And profit, the critics assert, is amoral if not immoral in the context of warfare. PMC proponents, on the other hand, concede that the companies do have a profit motive, but they argue that this is a good thing. As businesses, PMCs exist for profit rather than adventure, exhilaration, titillation, or the gratification of some psychopathological urge. Moreover, the soldiers who belong to modern state militaries also have a profit motive, especially in such all-volunteer forces (AVFs) as the contemporary U.S. military. Salaries in the U.S. AVF are competitive, and opportunities for advancement are significant. A service member who commits himself or herself to a career in the U.S. military has an excellent chance of rising through the ranks. If he or she excels and is promoted to the position of field-grade officer, salaries become comparable to senior managers in the private sector. Factor in provisions for living expenses, medical and insurance benefits, and pensions, and the U.S. military offers more than an opportunity to serve one's country. It provides a profitable living. Yet no one calls a U.S. soldier, marine, airman, or sailor a mercenary.

Second, there is the nature of corporate profit versus individual profit. PMCs profit openly. They are subject to taxation laws. If they are publicly traded, they answer to shareholders. They make deals with other companies. They may be subsidiaries of larger holding firms. They must show a considerable degree of transparency. Whereas individual mercenaries often operate on a black market, in the shadows, and deal only in cash, keeping their profit hidden from tax authorities and law enforcement officials, PMCs must be accountable to many agencies and stakeholders.

Third, there is the argument that PMCs actually recruit higher-quality military specialists than the national military does. PMC managers have a strong incentive to exercise due diligence and take great care in recruiting personnel with a high degree of specialized knowledge and professionalism. They recruit through a combination of public application processes, specialized data-bases of talent, and even corporate recruiters ("headhunters"); indeed, some of the larger PMCs have their own "head-hunting" staffs.

The greatest impetus to the acceptance of military privatiza-tion came during the Reagan Revolution. It was of a piece with the president's famous assertion, in his inaugural address, that "government is not the solution to our problem; government is the problem."[28] The Reagan Revolution touched off the nor-malization of privatization, the growing public acceptance of putting certain functions, traditionally the exclusive domain of the government, into private-sector hands. The U.S. movement toward privatization took place in the context of the privatiza-tion of state industries in the United Kingdom during the 1980s under Prime Minister Margaret Thatcher and the privatization of the truly massive state industries that followed the collapse of the Soviet Union early in the 1990s. Indeed, during this period, the trend toward privatization became a global phenomenon and, within the United States, affected not only the federal gov-ernment, but state and local governments as well. The rationale for this movement was that the private sector was more highly motivated than the public sector to deliver quality, efficiency, and value for money because the private sector operated according to the competitive pressures of the marketplace.

Still, it is one thing for a government to outsource, say, data processing or even tax collection, but quite another for it to make the leap to outsourcing its military functions. The bridge to acceptance in this area was the privatization, first, of certain domestic security functions. A variety of private-sector enter-prises have long employed private-sector security forces. Hotels, department stores, shopping malls, manufacturing plants, and colleges and universities are just a few examples. In many cases, private security personnel are not only fully armed, but are actually sworn peace officers, possessing much of the authority conferred on municipal or state police officials. Government agencies at the federal and state levels also extensively employ private security guards. Even some military bases and other facilities (including nuclear weapons facilities in South Carolina and Nevada) are patrolled by guards and specially trained SWAT response teams provided by the Wackenhut firm. In recent years, many states have privatized "corrections" and penal institutions, and many cities have privatized the assessment and collection of parking fines.

The proliferation of private-sector incursions into domestic functions that were traditionally the exclusive concern of government agencies has opened the pathway to acceptance of the privatization of military functions ranging from actual combat operations, to the formulation of tactical, strategic, and doctrinal policy, to the provision of logistics and training, to intelligence, and to risk assessment and security. The use of PMCs has steadily grown in the American military:[29]

WAR	CONTRACTORS	MILITARY	RATIO
World War I	85,000	2 million	1:24
World War II	734,000	5.4 million	1:7
Korean War	156,000	393,000	1:2.5
Vietnam War	70,000	359,000	1:5
Gulf War	9,000	500,000	1:56
Balkans	20,000	20,000	1:1
Iraq War	190,000	200,000	1:1

The Department of Defense spent approximately **$2.2 billion** on PMCs in the Balkans during a four-year period (1991–1995). In Iraq, during a four-year period (2003–2007), the PMC bill was **$85 billion**.[30] The base pay of an American soldier in Iraq or Afghanistan is **$19,000** per year. Private military contractors working in combat zones are paid between **$150,000** and **$250,000** per year.[31] Are private contractor soldiers, most of whom are former U.S. military personnel, really about ten times better than currently serving U.S. troops?[32] If the answer is yes, then we must conclude that the American soldier is a sorry specimen indeed.

But the answer isn't yes. The fact is that private contractors are very expensive, no better trained than regular national military personnel (often less well trained), and, to a large extent, operate outside of the regular chain of command and accountability. Just how expensive? The United States spent more than **$192.5 billion** on contracts and grants to PMCs and other private military-related contractors in Iraq and Afghanistan from FY 2002 through the first two quarters of FY 2011.[33] By the end of FY 2011, contract obligations were expected to reach **$206 billion**.[34]

In 2008, Congress created an independent, bipartisan Commission on Wartime Contracting in Iraq and Afghanistan to assess contingency contracting for reconstruction, logistics, and security functions and to examine the extent of waste, fraud, and abuse. The Commission filed interim reports to Congress in June 2009 and February 2011, in addition to five special reports. The final report came in August 2011. All of this is laudable, of course. Less worthy of praise and self-congratulation, however, is the fact that the final report came just four months before the official end of the Iraq War and well after some **$206 billion** had been lavished on contractors.

The August 2011 report concluded:[35]

1. Agencies over-rely on contractors for contingency and some mission-critical functions. It would seem that government is not the problem after all. At least when it comes to fighting wars, private contractors are the problem.
2. Standards in law, policy, and regulation that apply to government functions provide "insufficient guidance for contracting in contingencies." In other words, in matters of war, the government generally lacks the means to control the contractors it hires.

3. Government "inattention" leads to "massive waste, fraud, and abuse." The Commission concluded that "U.S. operations in Iraq and Afghanistan...entailed vast amounts of spending for little or no benefit. That is waste. The Commission's conservative estimate of waste and fraud ranges from **$31 billion** to **$60 billion** based on contract spending from FY 2002 projected through the end of FY 2011."

4. "But wait," as the TV pitchman says, "there's more!" A "particularly troubling" Commission finding was that "billions of dollars already spent, including spending on apparently well-designed projects and programs, will turn into waste if the host governments cannot or will not commit the funds, staff, and expertise to operate and maintain them. Money lost as a result of the inability to sustain projects could easily exceed the contract waste and fraud already incurred. Examples range from the **$35 billion** that Congress has appropriated since 2002 to train, equip, and support the Afghan National Security Forces, to scores of health-care centers in Iraq that far exceed the Ministry of Health's ability to maintain them."

5. Government agencies continue to "resist major reforms that would elevate the importance of contracting, commit additional resources to planning and managing contingency contracting, and institutionalize best practices within their organizations."

6. The "fiefdom" problem Secretary of Defense Robert Gates identified manifests itself in "structures and authorities [that] prevent effective interagency coordination," leading to "duplication of effort, gaps in continuity, improper phasing of operations, and waste."

7. "Agencies have failed to set and meet goals for [contractor] competition in Iraq and Afghanistan." They have "awarded task orders for excessive durations without adequate competition" and have "extended contracts and task orders past their specified expiration dates, increased ceilings on cost-type contracts, and modified task orders and contracts to add extensive new work." Most egregiously, the govern-

ment used (and still uses!) cost-plus contracting instead of fixed-price contracts. Cost-plus contracts[36] guarantee contractors full remittance on all costs incurred in their operations under the contract *and* guarantee at least 1% profit, scaling up to 9% based on the contractor's performance. Basically, the contractor cannot lose, and all the moral hazard is borne by the government (which means the taxpayer).

PRIVATIZATION AND CRONY CAPITALISM

The bigger the military contractor—or the deeper a firm's connections penetrate into a bigger corporate entity— the further removed it may appear from the world of the lone-wolf soldier of fortune. Generally, this is a good thing for the corporate identity of the PMC. But what happens when such firms appear *too* legitimate, when they are intimately connected with corporate concerns that are in turn intimately connected with the government or with government officials?

During the wars in Iraq and Afghanistan, more than a few eyebrows were raised concerning Vice President Dick Cheney's status as former Chairman and CEO of Halliburton (from 1995 to 2000), which made **$39.5 billion** on the Iraq War.[37] In an appearance on *The Tonight Show* (May 20, 2010), liberal journalist and MSNBC personality Chris Matthews told Jay Leno that "Cheney was head of Halliburton. When he got to be vice president, when he was signed for vice president [of the United States], the oil company [Halliburton] gave him a **$34 million** signing bonus to become vice president of the United States."[38] In analyzing this, PolitiFact commented that Matthews had taken "some artistic license with his comment," but, in fact, the news organization's research showed that Cheney did walk into the vice presidency with **$34 million** from the company he had just left. Similarly, former secretary of state (under George H. W. Bush) James Baker and former secretary of defense (under Ronald Reagan) Frank Carlucci served on the board of the Carlyle Group, an investment firm that owned BDM (Buildmax Limited), which in turn counted Vinnell Corporation among its subsidiaries.[39] In 2003, the DoD hired Vinnell to create the New Iraqi Army.[40]

PLAUSIBLE DENIABILITY

Crony capitalism, including the opportunity for highly placed government officials to profit from hiring certain PMCs, is one answer to why the federal government does not seem to think twice about lavishing riches on private contractors far beyond the point of unadulterated waste. But there is also another, more widely compelling reason. Call it "plausible deniability."

During the Reagan era, one traditional government function after another was outsourced to the private sector. For the most part, this movement was quite popular with the American public. At least one area, however, gave the public pause. The increasing outsourcing to the private sector of many of the functions of the national military created much controversy. For its part, the U.S. military leadership gave assurances that only "support" functions, not combat duties, were being privatized. Officials explained that logistics, food services, supply transport, air charter transportation of some personnel, maintenance, and certain aspects of facilities security could be more efficiently and inexpensively handled by private contractors than by service members. For the most part, officials demurred when it came to presenting an even more pressing case for privatization: The fact that the end of the military draft, suspended by Secretary of Defense Melvin P. Laird on January 27, 1973, with the creation of an all-volunteer force (AVF), meant that the national military had been reduced to numbers insufficient to fully staff many non-combat functions. There was no longer any choice; civilian contractors were now *necessary* to address the shortfall.

The government was even less willing to let the public in on yet another possible motive for privatization. In any major and prolonged deployment of forces, the "tail" (support, logistics, and other non-combat contingents) of the force deployed substantially outnumbers its "tooth," as the combat component is called. In the absence of private-sector outsourcing, a commander in chief who wanted to deploy, say, 40,000 combat troops to some global hotspot had to request 100,000, since the "tooth-to-tail ratio" required for such a deployment was about 4 to 6—four combat troops supported by six logistical troops. With privatization, that commander in chief had only to request 40,000, since the 60,000 support personnel, as civilian contractors, were not publicly reported in the deployment number. Presidents cherished the option to minimize the number of national troops they might have to request. The fewer the troops formally called for, the greater the president's latitude in the use of military power as an aspect of global diplomacy. Privatization enabled waging war in many situations for which the national AVF was either inadequate or at least widely perceived as inadequate. Expressed in positive terms, the use of private military contractors gave a commander in chief greater flexibility. Expressed more darkly, it tended more frequently to enable armed conflict as a viable choice in managing international relations. When it came to disclosing numbers of troops deployed, privatization furnished "plausible deniability"—an excuse to significantly underreport the numbers.

"A GOLDEN AGE FOR
PENTAGON WASTE"

"As the Pentagon prepares for the formal release of its budget next week," *U.S. News & World Report* reported on February 3, 2016, "there is much talk within the department that the **$600 billion-plus** that is likely to be proposed is inadequate. In fact, rooting out billions of dollars of waste in the Pentagon budget would leave more than enough to provide a robust defense of the country without increasing spending." The article puts a complex problem very simply, pointing out that all the Pentagon's wasteful-spending scandals going as far back as the 1960s are tied together by a single thread: "They all came on the heels of major military buildups. When there is too much money to go around and no one is minding the store, spending discipline goes out the window."[41]

Too simple? It looks that way, until one studies the problem, as the Commission on Wartime Contracting in Iraq and Afghanistan did. There can be little doubt that the members of the Commission would willingly subscribe to the conclusion the *U.S. News* reporter reached: "It's time for Congress, the president and the presidential candidates of both parties to speak out about Pentagon waste, and put forward concrete plans for reining it in. Otherwise, our era may have the dubious distinction of being the golden age of Pentagon waste."[42]

During the half-century of global cold war that followed the end of World War II, the two major thermonuclear superpowers, the United States and the Soviet Union, shared the same doctrine of nuclear deterrence. It was known by the acronym MAD, and it held that the use of atomic weapons by one side would ensure retaliation by the other, resulting in Mutually Assured Destruction. The time has come for a variant on MAD to describe the ultimate cost to the nation of Washington's military pork barrel culture. Call it PAD—Perpetually Assured Debt. We cannot sustain it.

SPENDING TOO MUCH AT THE CIVILIAN PORK BARREL

ONE MAN'S WASTE IS ANOTHER MAN'S DINNER

"Pork" or "pork barrel" is what most people first think of when they think of wasteful government spending. Actually, pork makes up only about 1% of the federal government's annual outlays. Some lawmakers and political scientists argue that this is a small price to pay for "greasing the wheels" of the legislative process. Then again, 1% of four or five trillion dollars is no small sum of money, especially when these dollars are collected from the entire nation to benefit a single district, part of a district, a town, an industry, or a company. This chapter defines pork barrel spending and the special form of pork called "earmarking"— as well as the new forms, "lettermarking" and "phonemarking." It details the origins of pork and the motives behind the practice, and explains just how the political pork sausages are made.

CHAPTER 10

FROM THE BOTTOM

OF THE BARREL:

GRINDING THE POLITICAL

PORK SAUSAGE

I t's a peculiar phrase, "pork barrel," and in December 1919 one Chester Collins Maxey, supervisor of the Training School for Public Services, New York Bureau of Municipal Research, set out to do the public a service by explaining it. He began by identifying May 20, 1826, as a "red-letter date in American political history." It was not the date of a decisive battle, he noted, or the birthday of a president, or the date of a significant speech. In fact, he demurred, "it is entirely devoid of dramatic interest; it merely marks the final enactment of the first omnibus appropriation measure for the improvement of rivers and harbors."

So what?

Chester Maxey had the answer: "That river bill was the forerunner of a system of financial legislation whose evil effects have been immeasurable and which still afflicts the financial processes of our national government like a terrible blight."[1]

A TERRIBLE BLIGHT

Prior to May 20, 1826, Mr. Maxey explained, every appropriation for improving rivers and harbors had to be put in its own separate bill or as part of a general appropriations bill. Although improving a river or harbor can have a national effect in that it improves commerce and navigation, the greatest advantage of such legislation is local. This fact reduces the chances of the bill's passage or the provision of a general bill surviving to reach a vote. Why, after all, should the resources of the entire nation be focused on providing a benefit for one particular locality? Yet every time a local improvement bill *was* passed, it "had the effect of arousing in all other localities a hunger for similar treatment regardless of the principle that national importance should afford the only justification for undertaking the improvement of a river or a harbor in any community." Soon, every jealous district pressured its representative for federal appropriations to make local improvements.[2]

At this point, Mr. Maxey felt obliged to introduce another colorful term. The "classic strategy of the legislator who is obliged to champion an intrinsically unmeritorious and indefensible proposition...has come to be called 'log-rolling,' after the picturesque custom of the early backwoods pioneers mutually exchanging help in the clearing of land and the erection of log buildings." Log-rolling is reciprocity. *You support my "unmeritorious and indefensible proposition," and I'll support yours.* The demand for national money to fund local river and harbor projects quickly became so intense, however, that old-fashioned log-rolling just couldn't keep up. The solution was to combine all proposed appropriations for rivers and harbors into a single bill, which was voted up or down. "The good items in such a bill would stand as apologists for the bad, and the bad could not be eliminated without losing the support of those who had procured their insertion and thus endangering the good, which would fail if the omnibus bill should be defeated. With the good and bad thus inextricably bound together in a bill often consisting of several hundred items ... about the only step necessary for the member seeking an appropriation for petty local purposes was to get his item into the omnibus bill." The first such omnibus bill—a bill bundling many appropriations measures into a single package—passed on May 20, 1826, and a new way of legislating was born.[3]

Chester Maxey's "summary analysis" of the resulting "pork barrel system" is as accurate today as it was in 1919. It goes like this:[4]

1. A committee or committees prepares an omnibus bill, each member taking care "to include all of their own pet items in the bill.... [V]ery few committeemen have the temerity to object to items desired by another member of the committee."
2. "Spurred by pride and ambition for political success, the committee desires to frame a bill that will ... pass by comfortable majorities." This requires ladling into the bill "enough items for the various states and congressional districts to enlist the enthusiasm and support of a majority, although not all of these items may be of the most commendable type."
3. Those members who, despite the ladling, can find no benefit to their constituents and therefore no benefit to themselves "lay siege to the committee with a combination of cajolery, imprecation, and fulmination that usually breaks the none too inflexible will of the committee." So more questionable provisions are added.
4. The bill proceeds through the House of Representatives "under the convoy of a steam-roller procedure controlled by the committee." This reduces the chances of debate and amendment. Should the bill falter, however, the solution is "simply to add to its items."
5. A conference committee smooths out any differences between what the House has poured into the bill and what the Senate wants.
6. This omnibus bill is passed and then rolls to the president's desk for signature.

Chester Maxey concluded:

> This system has acquired a name...as distinct and meaning-
> ful as "log-rolling." On the southern plantations in slavery
> days, there was a custom of periodically distributing rations
> of salt pork among the slaves. As the pork was usually packed
> in large barrels, the method of distribution was to knock the
> head out of the barrel and require each slave to come to the
> barrel and receive his portion. Oftentimes the eagerness
> of the slaves would result in a rush upon the pork barrel in
> which each would strive to grab as much as possible for him-
> self. Members of congress in the stampede to get their local
> appropriation items into the omnibus river and harbor bills
> behaved so much like negro [*sic*] slaves rushing to the pork
> barrel, that these bills were facetiously styled "pork-barrel
> bills," and the system which originated with them has thus
> become known as the "pork-barrel system."[5]

THE SEVEN DEADLY SINS OF

PORK BARREL POLITICS

Chester Maxey was neither an etymologist nor a philolo-
gist by profession, and the pork barrel, both as an artifact
and a phrase, was in use at least as early as the beginning
of the 18th century.[6] Nevertheless, the anecdote Maxey relates
concerning "pork barrel" is revealing in that it associates with
the obscenity of slavery the universal metaphor for the practice
of appropriating government funds in a manner intended to buy
local votes. Pork barrel legislation was a blight in the 19th century, a blight in 1919 when Chester Maxey presented his "little
history," and it remains a blight today.

In *The Pig Book: How Government Wastes Your Money*, Citizens
Against Government Waste (CAGW) lists seven criteria an item
of financial legislation must meet in order to be considered for
inclusion in the book. Let's call these "criteria" what they really

are: the Seven Deadly Sins of Pork Barrel Politics. An item of legislation is pork if it commits at least one of the following Deadlies (most pork appropriations commit at least two):

- Is requested by only one chamber of Congress
- Is not specifically authorized
- Is not competitively awarded
- Is not requested by the President
- Greatly exceeds the President's budget request or the previous year's funding
- Is not the subject of congressional hearings
- Serves only a local or special interest[7]

EARMARKS

Legislating at the national level to create strictly local benefits is bad enough, but the money-wasting effect of pork barrel politics is amplified—made even more wasteful, if you can believe it—by the log-rolling and potluck dimensions of the process. The quid pro quo of log-rolling ensures that Representative A's self-serving legislation will also sooner or later beget Representative B's self-serving legislation, because B supported A's bill on the understanding that A would support his when the time came. ("Some day, and that day may never come, I will call upon you to do a service for me," Don Vito Corleone tells the undertaker Amerigo Bonosera in *The Godfather*.[8]) As for the omnibus bills in which pork barrel appropriations are most often nested, they pass precisely because multiple representatives get to throw into the pot whatever is near and dear to their constituents. Pork barrel? More like a bottomless gumbo.

Chester Collins Maxey covered all this in 1919, and it was bad then. But he had no way of knowing that pork would get much worse. Classic pork barrel is federal spending for local or localized projects. While pork barrel legislation can be immoral, it is not unconstitutional. Closely related to pork barrel and often lumped in with it is earmarking. As the Office of Management and Budget

(OMB) defines them, "Earmarks are funds provided by the Congress for projects, programs, or grants where the purported congressional direction (whether in statutory text, report language, or other communication) circumvents otherwise applicable merit-based or competitive allocation processes, or specifies the location or recipient, or otherwise curtails the ability of the executive branch to manage its statutory and constitutional responsibilities pertaining to the funds allocation process."[9]

Quite a mouthful. Let's digest it.

Whereas ordinary pork consists of appropriations made for specific projects, earmarks *direct*—that is, order, demand, require—that a particular government department or agency use some portion of its congressionally appropriated budget for a specified purpose. For example, in 2009, Congress enacted 485 separate earmarks totaling **$301,692,000** within the budget of the Department of Agriculture alone. Each of these earmarks required specified portions of the department's budget to be spent on specified projects or programs legislators wanted to fund. This, the OMB correctly argues, violates the constitutional principle of separation of powers by projecting legislative authority onto the turf of the executive branch, curtailing the executive's ability "to manage its statutory and constitutional responsibilities pertaining to the funds allocation process." Whereas classic pork directly appropriates funds for geographically localized projects or provides benefits to some special interest group, earmarks hijack the budgets of executive departments and agencies to fund localized projects, serve some special interest group, or even funnel funding to some individual company or contractor—in the process, bypassing "merit-based or competitive allocation processes."

HIDING IN PLAIN SIGHT

Search the Internet for spasms of outrage over "pork barrel" and "earmarks." It is hardly a strenuous search, because the terms are commonly used interchangeably. This is unfortunate to the extent that failing to distinguish between the two loses the important distinction between spending that may be immoral but is constitutional (pork) and spending that may be immoral and, as a violation of separation of powers, is indeed unconstitutional (earmarks). Nevertheless, the indiscriminate use of the terms also demonstrates that they are more alike than they are different. Both pork barrel and earmarks rely heavily on stealth. The stealth warriors of feudal Japan known as ninjas were solitary figures who operated unseen. Pork and earmark appropriations, however, constitute vast ninja armies—who, despite their overwhelming numbers, still manage to operate unseen.

The 1826 invention of the omnibus appropriations bill for river and harbor improvements has proved remarkably durable. Despite recent efforts at reform, which I will discuss shortly, the omnibus spending bill remains the principal vehicle of pork barrel appropriations—so much so that political scientist Diana Evans, an expert on "distributive politics" (the academic, value-neutral phrase for "pork barrel politics"), has observed that the "scholarly literature on distributive politics focuses on omnibus pork barrel bills, legislation that consists of nothing but distributive [i.e., pork barrel] projects."[10]

The word *omnibus* was borrowed into English directly from Latin, where it means "for all." Just as anyone and everyone can purchase a seat on a city *bus*—the word is a shortened version of *omnibus*[11]—so any and every appropriation can "purchase" a niche in an omnibus bill. People on a bus cannot be said to hide there, but, in the aggregate, especially during rush hour, their numbers do make them anonymous, so that, intentionally or not, the riders hide in plain sight. And so it goes with the individual appropriations in omnibus spending bills, which Congress routinely uses to group together the annual budget appropriations for all departments. If Congress had enacted an individual bill titled The Swine Odor and Manure Management Act (SWOMM) of 2009, appropriating **$1.8 million** for research into this nationally non-urgent non-priority that almost nobody cares about, the media would have been all over it: "SWOMM Swamps Beltway Insiders," a typical headline might yawp. This appropriation is not a fictional example. It was actually made in

2009—but **$1.8 million** was not appropriated in a piece of stand-alone legislation. Had it been, the bill would never have made it to the House floor, let alone gained passage. No, this appropriation for research into swine odor and manure management, all **$1.8 million** of it, was just one of approximately 8,500 earmarks in the 2009 omnibus spending bill, and it rode that bus to passage and signing along with those 8,499 others, hidden in plain sight. For the morbidly curious, other Department of Agriculture earmarks in that 2009 bill—instances in which Congress (legislative branch) told the Department of Agriculture (executive branch) how to spend the budget Congress had appropriated for its use—included "$1.7 million for a honey bee laboratory in Weslaco, Tex.; $346,000 for research on apple fire blight in Michigan and New York; and $1.5 million for work on grapes and grape products, including wine," plus "$173,000 for research on asparagus production in Washington State; $206,000 for wool research in Montana, Texas and Wyoming; and $209,000 for efforts to improve blueberry production in Georgia," as well as "$208,000 to control a weed known as cogon grass in Mississippi; $1.2 million to control cormorants in Michigan, Mississippi, New York and Vermont; $1 million to control Mormon crickets in Utah; and $162,000 to control rodents in Hawaii."[12]

While most media, public, and even academic attention focuses on omnibus spending bills—which are vehicles expressly made to carry pork—the legislators themselves do not confine pork barrel politics to such bills. They also incorporate pork into specific items of so-called general interest legislation, legislation that affects the entire country or, at least, broad sections of it. As Diana Evans observes, such legislation "need not...fall evenly on all districts or individuals," nor does this category of bill imply that "general interest" is synonymous with "public interest." In fact, in these general interest bills, "Losers might well outnumber winners, or the total costs might be greater than the total benefits." Nevertheless, general interest legislation must provide some collective benefit beyond a single congressional district. The legislator prompting such a bill, for whatever reason, may fold into it narrowly focused pork barrel provisions as "'sweeteners' to buy the votes of enough members to create a majority coalition in favor of such bills."[13] In other words, the sponsor of a general interest, non-pork bill will, in a bid to gain passage, often bundle into it narrowly targeted pork sweeteners.

As with the creation of omnibus spending bills, the introduction of sweeteners into general interest legislation is routine— strictly standard operating procedure. This does not, however, mean that it is universally welcomed by all members of Congress. Whether out of sincere Mister-Smith-Goes-to-Washington reformist conviction or merely a desire to cultivate among their constituencies a distinctive "brand," some legislators vehemently oppose pork barrel politics, even to facilitate passage of a bill that might be 95% commendable and only 5% tooth-rottingly sweet pork. Typically, these objectors protest on ethical and moral grounds, but they may also argue that pork barrel politics is inefficient in the economic sense of the word ("inefficient" = scarce resources not being put to their best use) because *federal* funds funneled to a *localized* area cannot deliver sufficient benefit to sufficient numbers of national taxpayers to economically justify the cost to those taxpayers. In fact, quite often, pork is so narrowly targeted that the costs to taxpayers, even within the legislator's own district, outweigh the benefits to the district as a whole, let alone the nation.

Incredibly, the eminently rational inefficiency argument against pork gets precious little traction, even when the sponsors of pork themselves admit that, by strict cost-benefit accounting, direct benefits fail to justify direct costs. Pork barreling legislators argue that any cost spent *by* district residents is actually money spent *in* the district, and therefore creates an economic benefit to the district that is broader than the specific special interest, company, or individual who directly benefits. In the end, such heroic rhetorical and syllogistic contortions may be unnecessary. Since the costs of pork "are shared nationally by all taxpayers..., a legislator normally has little reason to care about the economic efficiency of his or her own project or of any bill that contains it." Add to this amoral, if not immoral, sentiment "the readiness with which federal agencies claim that a project's benefits equal or exceed its costs," and it becomes almost impossible to make "judgments about project efficiency in any case."[14]

Money, as the saying goes, isn't everything. Back in 1826 and thereabouts, pork barrel legislation funded physical "improvements," such as rivers, harbors, dams, canals, lighthouses, and roads. Although there was often a reasonable argument to be made that improving a *local* road or waterway or even harbor represented a de facto benefit to *national* commerce, there was remarkably little hypocrisy even concerning the actual legislative motive, which was first and last to secure the electoral support of the sponsor's constituency.

Yes, the benefits of any given project were distributed unequally. True, only in the town that got the harbor the nation paid for did benefits outweigh costs. Admittedly, everywhere else, costs exceeded benefits. But it's only money.

Pork facilitates the legislative process. It greases the wheels of Congress, and one greasy hand washes the other. To legislators, this benefit is priceless.

Besides, in the modern era, traditional "projects" such as dams, harbor dredging, and the construction of sanitary canals often create environmental impacts that reach far beyond the locality in which a project is built. Evans observes that "Congress has adapted" to this modern situation "with what has been called 'post-industrial' pork, which includes money for such things as environmental cleanup projects and university research, otherwise known as academic pork"[15] (yes, an actual term). So, let's get this straight. If a pork barrel dredging operation ($) creates a pollution problem downstream, a pork barrel environmental research study ($+1) and resulting project ($+2) will address this impact. You do the math. In the natural world, pigs beget pigs. In the world of modern American legislative politics, pork begets pork.

CUI BONO?

According to the great Roman orator and politician Cicero (107–43 B.C.), a celebrated judge named Lucius Cassius always weighed the evidence and arguments of a case by asking *Cui bono?*—"Who profits?"[16] Since then, cops, detectives, prosecutors, grand juries, and judges have been starting investigations and judicial proceedings by asking the very same question.

When it comes to pork, *cui bono?* Here's one answer, from a White House aide questioned by journalist Brian Kelly: "If you're a congressman and you want to get reelected—and you do because it's a pretty great job despite all the whining you hear from them—then you give things to the people who can vote for you. In return they keep electing you. The hell with what it means for the rest of the country."[17] Doubtless, this often seems to be the whole truth. Doubtless, it sometimes *is* the whole truth. But it is not *always* the whole truth. If it were, if the legislators were the only ones who profited from pork, pork barrel politics would not continue to be the enduring institution that it is.

The benefits—the profit—of pork may be either *concentrated* or *dispersed* within the constituency of a legislator.[18] When organized special interests or industry lobbyists provide support to a legislator or set of legislators, they do expect something in return. An asphalt company hires a lobbyist to lay siege to Congresswoman X, and, next thing you know, there is an earmark directing the Department of Transportation to spend some millions of its budget for a new highway section in the congresswoman's district. This is an example of the concentrated dispersion of pork.

1. Is the new section of highway of great benefit to the residents of this particular corner of Congresswoman X's district?
2. In making it easier to get to and from the nearest highway, does it even offer a benefit to the nation by connecting a group of district residents with the rest of the population of the contiguous forty-eight states?

3. Or does it benefit only the single asphalt contractor whose pockets are sufficiently deep to afford the services of a skilled lobbyist?

These are all legitimate questions to ask. Beyond question, however, the appropriation benefits Congresswoman X.

So much for *concentrated* benefits. Benefits are *dispersed* when a large and *unorganized* body of constituents enjoy them. In the case of Congresswoman X's appropriation, such dispersion of benefits would occur, say, if the towns in this part of his district really do desperately need a new highway.

Either way, concentrated or dispersed, the math is pretty easy to do. In the example above, in the case of concentration, a company profits, along with Congresswoman X. In the case of dispersion, a significant slice of the constituency profits, along with Congresswoman X. In both cases, Congresswoman X profits. While concentration *directly* yields fewer votes, it does generate a substantial campaign contribution (from the beneficiary company or other party)—which Congresswoman X can use to buy votes. Dispersion, on the other hand, will likely yield more constituent votes directly.

IN PORK WE TRUST:

THE SEMI-FAILED REFORMS OF 2010

John Adams inserted the phrase "a government of laws, and not of men" into the Massachusetts Constitution of 1780. This is a very good principle because laws endure, but men and their feelings change. Regrettably, Congress long ago abandoned Adams's principle to create instead "a government of pork, and not of men." Commenting on the omnibus spending bill of 2009, *The New York Times* observed that the pork-rich legislation "even includes earmarks requested by some lawmakers who have left Congress, like Senator Pete V. Domenici, Republican of New Mexico, and Representative William J. Jefferson, Democrat of Louisiana."[19]

"Chocolate Melts, Flowers Wilt, Diamonds Are Forever!" ran a 2014 Valentine's Day ad from the De Beers diamond cartel.[20] Substitute "Earmarks" for the third noun in the sentence, and you have an eloquent expression of how Congress had used earmarks from 1826 to 2010, the year the House of Representatives, with great fanfare, voted—holy smokes!—a "ban on earmarks."

On March 10, 2010, House Democrats, facing an election-year backlash over runaway spending—the 2009 omnibus bills gorged on **$19.6 billion** in pork—and ethics scandals, moved to address both spending and scandal by banning earmarks for private companies. This ban was intended to block no-bid federal grants to for-profit firms, which typically invested heavily in lobbyists who secured such lucrative earmarks. The measure, then-Speaker of the House Nancy Pelosi (D-California) declared, "ensures that for-profit companies no longer reap the rewards of congressional earmarks and limits the influence of lobbyists on members of Congress."[21]

The Democratic move immediately prompted House Republicans to up the ante by proposing a ban on *all* earmarks, including those to nonprofits, universities, and the like.[22] Republicans in the Senate applauded and, in November 2010, passed their own resolution—albeit non-binding—banning all earmarks in that chamber.[23]

Democrats held out until February 2011, when Senator Daniel Inouye (D-Hawaii), Democratic chairman of the Senate Appropriations Committee, finally waved the white flag. Announcing a two-year ban on all earmarks, he declared, "The handwriting is clearly on the wall. The president has stated unequivocally that he will veto any legislation containing earmarks, and the House will not pass any bills that contain them. Given the reality before us, it makes no sense to accept earmark requests that have no chance of being enacted into law."[24]

It sounded pretty final—and, for that matter, pretty momentous. Because most people use the terms "pork barrel" and "earmarks" interchangeably, many assumed that pork barrel politics had finally ended its 185-year run. Not quite. There would still be pork, just not the kind of pork that "earmarks" portions of each department's budget for specific programs, projects, or companies. Nevertheless, most pork comes in the form of earmarks, so banning them was still a big deal.

In theory.

"No one was more critical than Representative Mark Steven Kirk [R-Illinois] when President Obama and the Democratic majority in the Congress sought passage last year [2009] of a $787 billion spending bill intended to stimulate the economy," began a December 27, 2010 *New York Times* article. "And during his campaign for the Illinois Senate seat once held by Mr. Obama, Mr. Kirk, a Republican, boasted of his vote against 'Speaker Pelosi's trillion-dollar stimulus plan.'" Like other Republicans in 2009–2010, Kirk had "thundered against...lawmakers' practice of designating money for special projects through earmarks," but Kirk (like other lawmakers in both parties) did not shy away "from using a less-well-known process called *lettermarking* to try to direct money to projects" for his home district. On September 10, 2009, he sent a letter to the Department of Education asking it to "release money 'needed to support students and educational programs' in a local school district." Lo and behold, Woodland School District 50 subsequently "received about $1.1 million in stimulus money."[25]

Like lettermarking, *phonemarking* takes place outside of the regular legislative process but is nevertheless aimed at telling executive agencies how to spend some portion of their congressionally appropriated budget. As the name suggests, instead of using a letter as the vehicle of persuasion, a phone call does the job.

Both lettermarking and phonemarking are examples of "soft earmarks." In contrast to the "hard earmarks" that were enshrined in omnibus legislation and that had to be obeyed, soft earmarks are, shall we say, *suggestions* concerning spending. Why would agency officials yield to a letter or a call conveying such "suggestions"? For the same reason one legislator votes for another legislator's pork: to buy future support. A bureaucrat who wants his or her agency to get a generous portion of the fiscal pie in the next appropriations cycle treats key lawmakers well. Very well.

With non-earmark pork untouched and soft earmarks available to substitute for the banished hard stuff, the earmark ban was continued in 2011[26] and then renewed by House Republicans for the 113th Congress.[27] POLITICO's "Truth-O-Meter" gave the GOP high marks for sticking to the ban and successfully resisting the siren song of Representative Don Young (R-Alaska), who wanted to offer an amendment to the ban that would allow earmarks under certain circumstances. Young "eventually withdrew the amendment 'under pressure from Speaker John Boehner.'..."[28]

On January 10, 2013, two days after the laudatory Truth-O-Meter rating appeared, *Bloomberg Businessweek* published an article titled "Earmarks: The Reluctant Case for Ending the Ban" and subtitled: "Vilifying earmarks is easy. But they got the job done." The article cited a student of government spending, California political science professor Sean Kelly, who, based on "dozens of conversations with staffers and members of Congress," had concluded that the congressional appropriations process "has 'melted down'" since the earmark ban took effect. Six-term Oklahoma Republican representative Tom Cole told Professor Kelly, "There's a human element in lawmaking that is real. [Without earmarks], you're removing all incentive for people to vote for things that are tough."[29]

Cole went on to explain that banning earmarks hasn't reduced spending. It just moved the decision-making power Congress used to have to the executive branch. "You've still got earmarks. They're just getting done by unelected bureaucrats."[30]

The attentive reader must ask, *Isn't this "move" to the executive branch exactly what the Constitution mandates and specifies?*

No matter. As Kelly explains the position of Cole and other conservatives, *they* are the ones "who should love earmarks the most" because earmarks are all about decentralizing government by "making sure things are adapted to local conditions."[31]

Separation of powers? What's *that*?

In April 2013, *The Washington Post* went so far as to attribute to the earmark ban the failure of a 2013 bill to strengthen gun control by expanding background checks, a bill that had strong popular and political support after the tragic mass shooting at Sandy Hook Elementary School on December 14, 2012, in which 20 children and six school personnel were gunned down by a mentally ill assailant (who then took his own life).[32] "Washington used to be a place where lawmakers openly traded votes for both concrete and symbolic concessions from the executive branch.... But the press, watchdog groups and many politicians began demonizing this practice and now, appropriations bills are free of the so-called 'earmarks' that eased the passage of everything from the North American Free Trade Agreement under President Bill Clinton to prescription drug coverage for seniors under President George W. Bush."[33] In October, *USA Today* reported on lawmakers who were calling for an end to the earmark ban, to "revive the old-fashioned horse trading that used to help Congress get things done," that used to be "used to sweeten a bill to attract votes from reluctant lawmakers."[34]

Despite a significant clamor for a lifting of the earmark ban, the Republican-controlled House voted in November 2014 to renew the ban, even as Representative Mike Rogers (R-Alabama) put a more sharply partisan spin on the reason for lifting it: "I do not believe most people trust how President Obama spends our tax dollars." Restoring earmarks "would allow the conservative, Republican-controlled House to reassert its Constitutional authority over the Obama Administration and the spending decision it is currently making."[35] With this breathtaking rhetorical stroke, Rogers managed to invoke the Constitution to support the violation of the constitutional separation of powers. The lure of pork, as any bacon lover can attest, is intoxicating indeed.

"The practice of earmarking...might be officially banned in Congress," a January 2014 *Huffington Post* article began, "but within hours of the release of the 2,000-page omnibus budget bill Monday night, lawmakers from both parties were practically tripping over each other in a race to tell their constituents about the special funding they'd secured for projects in their home states."[36] Examples included "funds directed toward research facilities at local universities," the retention of arguably outmoded weapons systems,[37] a measure to reduce helicopter noise over Los Angeles, and a variety of provisions to address various local challenges to citrus crops and fisheries. While such projects walk, sound, and smell like earmarks, even Taxpayers for Common Sense claimed that the moratorium has been effective in reducing earmarks.[38] The trouble is that the purpose of a moratorium is complete *cessation* (at least for a time), not mere *reduction.*

So how have lawmakers succeeded in translating an absolute decree—"moratorium"—into a relative request—"reduction"?

> The difference between pet projects this year and those of the "Wild West" earmarking years of the early 2000s is that the directed spending of 2014 is cloaked in an aura of "worthy public purpose"—a term that earmark reformers, including President Barack Obama, have long held up as a litmus test for how government funds should be spent. And if a certain "worthy" project also helps a member of Congress get reelected by boosting incomes in his or her district? Well, that's just a bonus.[39]

When it comes to political pork these days, "the other white meat" is localized spending with a "worthy public purpose." *Worthy purpose*—it is just such phrases that have the power of transforming John Adams's idea of a "government of laws and not of men" into a "government of whatever men might agree to call something at a given time in a given place and under given circumstances." It is the essence of subjectivity "cloaked in an aura" of objective principle. One man's waste is another man's dinner.

PORK AND EARMARKS: THE SPEND

The *Pig Book,* published annually by Citizens Against Government Waste (CAGW), begins its 2016 edition with the observation that "Pork-barrel spending is alive and well in Washington, D.C., despite claims to the contrary. For the fourth time since Congress enacted an earmark moratorium that began in fiscal year (FY) 2011, Citizens Against Government Waste (CAGW) has unearthed earmarks in the appropriations bills." In fact, the 2016 edition exposes 123 earmarks, an increase of 17.1% from the 105 exposed in the 2015 edition. In terms of cost, earmarks vintage 2016 are worth **$5.1 billion**, an increase of 21.4% over the **$4.2 billion** in 2015. "While the increase in cost over one year is disconcerting, the two-year rise of 88.9% over the $2.7 billion in FY 2014 is downright disturbing."[40] The *Pig Book* compilers do note that the 2016 total comes nowhere near the record year of FY 2006, when earmarks reached **$29 billion**. "In order for earmarks to reach that level over the next decade, legislators would need to increase the cost of earmarks by $2.4 billion annually. Unfortunately, this is not out of the question given its growth over the past two years."[41]

The compilers note that all of the *Pig Books* published since the earmark moratorium was put in place do have fewer earmarks than before the moratorium; however, "far more money was spent on average for each earmark and no detailed description was provided. For instance, legislators added 15 earmarks costing $549.6 million for the FY 2016 Army Corps of Engineers in the Energy and Water Development and Related Agencies Appropriations Act. These earmarks correspond to 482 earmarks costing $541.7 million in FY 2010." Put another way, the average dollar amount per earmark in FY 2016 was **$36.6 million**, compared to **$1.1 million** in FY 2010.[42] What is more, whereas the pre-moratorium omnibus bill included the names of the members of Congress requesting each project and its location—as required by transparency rules in force at the time—"no such data" is included in the FY 2016 legislation, which "simply created a pool of money to be distributed at a later date without any specific information about the eventual recipients." In response to criticism of the abandonment of transparency, members of Congress "argue that their standards differ from the earmark criteria used in *The Pig Book,* and that the [post-moratorium] appropriations bills are earmark-free according to their definition."[43] As we say, one man's waste is another man's dinner.

So, according to CAGW, the FY 2016 spend on pork items—

YEAR	PORK ITEMS
FY 2015	$4.2 billion
FY 2014	$2.7 billion
FY 2013	$0 billion
FY 2012	$3.3 billion
FY 2011	$0 billion
FY 2010	$16.5 billion
FY 2009	$19.6 billion
FY 2008	$17.2 billion
FY 2007	$13.2 billion
FY 2006	$29.0 billion
FY 2005	$27.3 billion
FY 2004	$22.9 billion
FY 2003	$22.5 billion
FY 2002	$20.5 billion
FY 2001	$20.1 billion
FY 2000	$18.5 billion
FY 1999	$12.0 billion
FY 1998	$13.2 billion
FY 1997	$14.5 billion
FY 1996	$12.5 billion
FY 1995	$10.0 billion
FY 1994	$7.8 billion
FY 1993	$6.6 billion
FY 1992	$2.6 billion
FY 1991	$3.1 billion

The Pig Book identifies these as earmarks—was $5.1 billion. In previous years, it was[44]:

THE LITTLE ENGINE THAT COULD?

The sums listed in the table on page 297 are very large, especially if you consider that they represent *national* appropriations for *narrow* localities, specific industries, or individual companies. Most of the nation gets no direct benefit from each expenditure. In fact, in the case of most of the expenditures, the majority of the country gets no benefit whatsoever, direct or indirect, tangible or intangible. Nevertheless, as a percentage of the total federal outlay in any given year, pork barrel spending does not look huge. It averages about 1%.[45]

As some recent political scientists see it, 1% is a small price to pay for what *The New Republic* described in a 1998 article this way: "Even if every single pork barrel project really were a complete waste of federal money, pork still represents a very cheap way to keep our sputtering legislative process from grinding to a halt. In effect, pork is like putting oil in your car engine: it lubricates the parts and keeps friction to a minimum. This is particularly true when you are talking about controversial measures."[46] Such legislators as Oklahoma's Tom Cole say much the same thing, even arguing that pork is indispensable to the legislative process. As Diana Evans puts it in her aptly titled *Greasing the Wheels,* "pork barreling, despite its much maligned status, gets things done." To borrow from the phrasing in the subtitle of her book, it builds majority coalitions in Congress. "To be sure, it is a practice that succeeds at a cost, but it is a cost that many political leaders are willing to pay in order to enact the broader public policies that they favor."[47]

If, as a cost, 1% is little, can it be that pork barrel spending is not the mammoth villain of American political life, but its little hero? Is pork, in fact, the protagonist of the eponymous children's classic *The Little Engine That Could*? You remember it. A stranded train cannot pull its heavy load up the mountain track, and the only locomotive willing to take on that load is the little engine—maybe 1% of a full-sized engine—that huffs and puffs, chanting *I—think—I—can, I—think—I—can*. And, it turns out, it could. So should we therefore be praising our annual 1% slice of pork instead of condemning it?

No.

I come to bury wasteful government spending, not to praise it. Just because 1% is a small percentage does not change the fact that 1% of a **$4.2 trillion** budget is a great deal of money—and certainly too much to pay to furnish an incentive for elected public servants to do the jobs for which they were elected. Pork-barrel spending is wasteful spending. It is spending that creates suboptimization, benefitting at most a microconstituency at the expense of the nation. It is allocating funds to someone's or some group's particular welfare that should be allocated to the general welfare. One percent of **$4.2 trillion**? That is an outrageous price for a can of legislative grease. Whatever you call it, grease is made of dirty, slimy stuff. In the next chapter, we will examine its composition in detail.

Our government is addicted to wasteful spending. Some is the result of pork barrel politics, but some is the result of bad allocation choices, failure to prioritize (or even define) objectives, and, in some hardcore cases, a compulsion (it would seem) to waste for waste's sake. After introducing these categories of (mis)spending, this chapter moves to the place where pork intersects with the subject of lobbying. Together, the two topics naturally divide into five parts, corresponding to the five main "special interest" sectors that dominate the congressional appropriation process: agriculture, business, labor, energy, and the environment.

CHAPTER 11

LET THEM EAT PORK:

HOW

CONGRESS BUYS

VOTES

Between 2011 and 2014, the federal government, through the National Institutes of Health, spent **$5 million** on a program called HAH. Not *Hah!* But HAH, as in *Help A H*ipster—or, more fully, something called the Help A Hipster Commune. So now the government of the world's biggest capitalist democracy just spent **$5 million** to finance a commune.

But let's keep an open mind. Maybe it was worth it.

The San Diego Union-Tribune encapsulated the enterprise in a headline worthy of *Variety*: "Feds spend millions to split hipsters, cigs." And the lead went like this: "The federal government is paying hipsters to quit smoking." Per hipster smoker, the bounty was not stupendous: "up to" $100 per quitter. But that was just part of the $5 million price tag. Most of the money went to fabricating a "pseudo-underground effort to create an anti-smoking movement in San Diego, San Francisco, and Burlington, Vermont." The commune had a website (now defunct), which proclaimed, "we have rejected big corporations for a long time, like Big Music that hinders creative freedom and Big Fashion that runs sweatshops. Our stand against Big Tobacco is even more important, since the industry contributes to things like world hunger, deforestation, and neo conservative policies." (What about premature death? Well, you can't be expected to think of everything for **$5 million**.)

HAH threw parties (on the government dime) in bars and clubs with indie bands, DJs, beer (including free beer koozies, printed with the HAH logo), and other booze, all aimed at motivating hipsters to "take a stand against tobacco corporations" by quitting smoking. Since even hipsters can't party 24/7, HAH also suggested alternatives to smoking, such as "'styling your sweet mustache,' 'listening to your favorite band that no one has heard of,' or 'practicing your next Instagram pose.'"[2]

And when the parties proved an insufficient incentive to kick the smoking habit, HAH hit 'em with a bribe under the slogan, "Quit smoking, get cash." That's where the Benjamins came in.

How effective was *that*? "One of those who joined the 'commune quit group' is smoking again and admits, 'I did it for the money…I was wanting to not smoke as much, but knew I wasn't going to quit. Yeah, it's only $5 a week,' he said, but he was going to hang out at the Bluefoot [bar] anyway, so why not attend the group and make $5 each time?" Although this particular hipster said that he and his friends were "unaware that commune uses taxpayer funds, most of them said they didn't care as long as the movement continued throwing free parties and infusing money into the scene."[3]

WASTE FOR WASTE'S SAKE

Publications such as the annual *Wastebooks* are intended to provoke voters to anger and action. These are useful objectives, but achieving them does not necessarily dig to the roots of Washington's culture of wasteful spending. Pork barrel and earmark spending is waste with a purpose—at least from the perspective of congressional legislators. They use it to buy votes, either directly from their constituents or, indirectly, from special interests that provide campaign finance. Careerism drives pork barrel spending, and that's bad enough, but at least careerism is a rational source of spending. It's immoral, sure, but at least it makes sense. The *really* scary thing about our government's culture of waste is that careerism is far from being its sole driver. Waste often happens without any discernible pork barrel motive. Help A Hipster is just one example. Somebody at the National Institutes of Health decided HAH was an idea worth **$5 million**, and instead of stopping him or her or them, some other bureaucrat or collection of bureaucrats approved it.

The technical term for this is *foolishness.* And the foolishness began with the admission of the project leader, Pamela Ling, MD, MPH, that "Hipsters are hard to define, because being hard to define is part of their culture." This being the case, Ling and her team focused on what she admitted to be a momentary trend that "seems to bring a focus on flannel, facial hair, skinny jeans, and off-kilter-hats." So, to identify hipster targets, "government-paid researchers used photos of people in various modes of dress and style [and asked] young people to describe them. If a particular look screamed 'hipster' over and over, the researchers used that as a guide."[4]

Pork barrel waste begins with a legislator who at least knows who his or her constituents are. HAH spent money without even having this starting-line knowledge. Researchers began spending on a group defined not by residence within a congressional district, not by socioeconomic need, not by having some disease or disability, but by the wearing of a few articles of clothing and the assessment provided by "young people" the researchers asked.

Suboptimization happens when resources are allocated to gaining *particular* benefits—personal, political, or however the benefits are defined—without taking *overall* costs into account. In a classic pork barrel appropriation, exclusive focus on a localized constituency or a special interest creates suboptimization because the cost of appropriation fails to benefit the majority of taxpayers who paid that cost. Appropriating federal funds for a swimming pool in Podunk fails to benefit anyone and everyone who does not happen to live in Podunk. The desirable objective in appropriating federal funds is supposed to be the optimization of scarce resources, the allocation of scarce resources to provide the greatest good to the greatest number on a national basis. In the case of pork barrel spending, only a well-defined local constituency benefits. Sometimes, only a particular legislator benefits. Either way, we have waste. But when wasteful spending is divorced from pork, pretty much nobody benefits—except for a few hipsters in "off-kilter hats" who walk away with as much as **$100** for attending a party.

This kind of inherently reckless spending is like an irregularly shaped mole you suddenly notice as you glance at yourself in the mirror. You are tempted to ignore it, but, if you know what's good for you, you make an appointment with the dermatologist. Maybe, just maybe, it's a sign of something serious happening deep down—an existential threat to the whole system.

HAH is that telltale mole. It is a sign of a government spending for the sake of spending. You've heard of "Art for art's sake." Washington time and again lusts after "Waste for waste's sake."

AN ADMINISTRATIVE CULTURE OF
SUBOPTIMIZATION

pending without a well-defined purpose is by definition wasteful. Five million dollars devoted to HAH is a prime instance, and that's bad. But it gets even worse, because

HAH is also a symptom of the administrative culture that allowed it to happen.

Consider: The **$5 million** spent on the HAH quit-smoking endeavor was but the proverbial drop in the bucket compared to the combined **$230 million** the Centers for Disease Control and Prevention (CDC) spent on national antismoking ads during 2012–2014, and the additional $230 million the Food and Drug Administration (FDA) devoted to the two-year anti-smoking campaign it launched in 2014. So, on top of the **$5 million** tax-payer dollars for hipsters, there's **$460 million** heaped into the national effort against smoking. Since smoking is the nation's leading preventable cause of death and costs the federal government more than **$90 billion** a year for treating health problems, at least some of that **$460 million** is arguably money well spent. Until we step back and note that, in 2015, the same federal government (through the U.S. Department of Agriculture) injected **$119 million** into programs to support the tobacco industry in North Carolina and other states.[5]

Who knew that the words of Jesus in Matthew 6:3—"But when thou doest alms, let not thy left hand know what thy right hand doeth"—could be so thoroughly misapplied? Those members of our elected and unelected government who thrive in a culture of suboptimization, *that's* who.

BUT WAIT! THERE'S MORE!

When it comes to writing checks, the government often uses both hands, never letting the left hand know what the right hand is signing. For instance, quite prudently, the U.S. Department of State has issued a travel warning urging Americans "to avoid all travel to Lebanon because of ongoing safety and security concerns" related to terrorism. Yet the United States Agency for International Development (USAID)—an independent federal agency nevertheless subject to foreign policy guidance from the Secretary of State, among others—spent more than **$2 million** in 2015 to promote tourism to Lebanon through "two five-year programs—Lebanon Industry Value Chain Development (LIVCD) and Building Alliance for Local Advancement, Development, and Investment (BALADI)."[6]

— ★ —

And when those check-writing hands get going, they are hard to stop, even when there is literally no good reason to take out the checkbook in the first place. Consider: As any tailgater knows, the foam koozie plays a critical role in keeping a cold can of beer cold on a hot day. In 2013, the National Science Foundation spent a cool **$1.3 million** taxpayer dollars to find out just how it does this. Apart from the question *Do we really need to know?* is the admission by one of the University of Washington researchers who benefitted from the NSF grant that the underlying cooling mechanism is actually already well known. "The point of the exercise," it turns out, "wasn't really to break new ground in atmospheric physics (or in summertime beverage consumption), but 'to improve our intuition about the power of condensational heating,'" according to the researchers. Professor Dale Durran, one of beneficiaries of the NSF grant, explained that even though the findings were already "well-known," the researchers "want people to appreciate how powerful the effect is."[7] (Is the people's appreciation really worth **$1.3 million**?)

— ★ —

Or suppose there is a very, very good reason *not* to write a check. Is that sufficient to stay the government's busy hand?

Hell, no!

As we saw in Chapter 1, George Washington, in his farewell address, counseled his fellow Americans to shun the "common and continual mischiefs of the spirit of party." In 1789, Thomas Jefferson wrote to Francis Hopkinson, designer of the first official U.S. flag, "If I could not go to heaven but with a party, I would not go there at all."[8] Far more recently, it is clear that a growing number of Americans hold both major American political parties in very low esteem. A 2014 Gallup Poll reported that 43% of us identify ourselves as neither Democrat nor Republican, but as political independents, a new record.[9] Well, it seems that "Americans are not alone in their distaste for political parties." According to a report by the Office of the Inspector General (OIG) of the U.S. Agency for International Development (USAID), "Pakistanis distrust most parties, which they believe lack democratically developed policies and are driven by personal interests of an out-of-touch leadership."[10]

Point well taken, Mr. OIG! Did that stop USAID from providing "$21.5 million for a Political Party Development Program in Pakistan to help shape and build parties in the country"?

No, it did not.

Are you surprised to learn that the "program has been riddled by mismanagement and its resources have not been spent 'wisely'" and that it is "doubtful the program [will] achieve its objectives"?[11]

No, not surprised.

— ★ —

If paying for something nobody wants—and, in fact, hates—makes no sense, what about writing a *federal* check that comes awfully close to violating *federal* law?

Thanks to an **$853,000** grant from the National Science Foundation, Yakima Valley Community College was able to expand its Vineyard Technology and Winery programs to two other schools in Washington State. The three state colleges are using the grant, in part, to develop "articulation agreements creating pathways from high school through baccalaureate programs." Fortunately, students "don't have to fear a pop sobriety test," since Washington State allows underage minors 18 to 20 years old "to taste wine while they are enrolled in a community- or technical-college program teaching viticulture, enology, or culinary arts." The precise meaning of the word "taste" turns out to be relative, since Walla Walla Community College's viticulture program "requires students to try as many as 600 wines a year," which certainly sounds like more than a taste.[12] Bottoms up!

— ★ —

Another reason to put down that check-writing pen is when you're bankrupt and the check you're writing is going to pay for a lost cause. These imperatives to cap the pen nevertheless failed to stop the Federal Emergency Management Agency (FEMA) from paying out some **$1 million** through the bankrupt National Flood Insurance Program (NFIP)[13] to the owner of a seaside home in Scituate, Massachusetts, that FEMA has designated as a "severe repetitive loss" property. Homes so designated have received at least four payments from the NFIP.

The homeowner used the money NFIP payed him not only to raise the house a total of 8 feet, but then to convert what had been a modest vacation home into a four-bedroom, 3.5-bathroom "mansion." Apparently weary of continuing to live in a "severe repetitive loss property," that same owner subsequently sold the home for **$1 million** and moved to Florida in 2007.[14]

— ★ —

Yet another reason to think twice before writing a check is if you are spending on yourself money intended for others. This is what the Department of Housing and Urban Development (HUD) appears to have done in 2014 when it reserved **$5.5 million** to pay for temporary housing, travel, and other costs of its employees who may be relocated. The funds can be used "for everything from storage to airline tickets—and in some cases, the cost of home sales, which can be prohibitive in areas where many borrowers still owe more on their mortgages than their houses are worth." For instance, one HUD employee "received about **$102,000** in relocation expenses, including **$30,000** for the cost of offloading his property and **$18,000** for temporary housing."[15] As the 2015 *Wastebook* observes, "Creating 'quality affordable homes for all' is part of the stated mission of...HUD."[16]

— ★ —

Would you write a **$17,500** check to walk a mile in another person's shoes? The U.S. Department of Agriculture spent that sum to allow anyone with a hankering to walk a mile in another person's fat. The five-figure sum bought fabrication of a one-of-a-kind "'vest-like suit'...filled with 'gel material' and 'positioned around the body's midsection." The 20-pound fat suit is intended to be worn by participants in an "Empathy Exercise" for a minimum of twelve consecutive hours.[17]

As the 2015 *Wastebook* points out, the same "federal government [that] has stigmatized unhealthy eating is now trying to promote social acceptance of those who are overweight," even as it spent more "than $19 billion...to subsidize 'junk food ingredients' over the past 20 years, according to an analysis conducted by the U.S. Public Interest Research Group."[18]

— ★ —

Now let's rumble on to Kansas City, where, in 2014, one out of four major roads was reported to be in poor condition, the city having earned a non-coveted number-four position among cities with the worst pothole problems in the nation.[19] The Missouri Department of Transportation secured an **$86,000** grant from the U.S. Department of Transportation—good! To fix potholes?

Are you *serious*?

No, the city of Kansas City threw a block party for the purpose of encouraging neighborhoods to periodically close down sections of street so that families could bike, walk, jog, skate, and play. A group calling itself Citizens for Responsible Government complained that there were already too many block parties in KC and that it would be nice if the city would use grant money to fund basic services, like patching potholes to make the streets drivable when nobody is skating on them.[20]

IMPROPER PAYMENTS

The waste we've just sampled, as they say in some parts of the country, just ain't right. But there is also an entire category of wasteful spending that is just downright *improper.*

"Improper payments" occur when "funds go to the wrong recipient; the right recipient receives the incorrect amount of funds (including overpayments and underpayments); documentation is not available to support a payment; or the recipient uses funds in an improper manner."[21] According to the 2015 *Wastebook,* the federal government has made "nearly $1 trillion worth of erroneous payments...over the past decade [2005–2015].... [The] annual cost of improper payments has been near or above $100 billion every year since 2009, reaching a record high of $125 billion in 2014." Improper payments include the likes of "Bogus business tax benefits for corporations. Free lunches for the well-off. Student aid for prisoners and crime rings. Paying the same energy bills...twice. And billions of dollars in handouts for the dead.[22]

In 2014, the city of Baltimore approved more than **$6 million** "in questionable [U.S. Department of Health and Human Services] payments meant to help poor families pay their energy bills." The USDA's Food and Nutrition Service (FNS) paid nearly **$12.5 million** to provide free lunches and reduced-price meals for children whose families made far too much money to qualify for the program, and "a school food authority (SFA) in Florida spent **$207,763** intended for school lunches on 11 vehicles, including 4 sport utility vehicles (SUVs)."[23]

As for the dead on the federal dole, surely you recall the tagline from the 1999 film *The Sixth Sense*? "I see dead people," creepy little kid Cole Sear (Haley Joel Osment) confesses to his psychologist, Dr. Malcolm Crowe (Bruce Willis). Well, it turns out that the Social Security Administration is similarly afflicted. It sees about 6.5 million of them—folks "over the age of 111 in the U.S. who are not recorded as deceased." In the entire world, there just forty-two people known to be 111. That doesn't stop the SSA from issuing payments, which are eagerly accepted by family members of the deceased and professional fraudsters.[24]

Moving on to the IRS, it was reported in 2015 that this agency "erroneously paid corporations more than **$2.7 billion** in tax credits that had expired or for which the businesses did not even qualify." Earlier that year, the Government Accountability Office

(GAO) reported that the IRS had sent more than **$5.8 billion** in fraudulent refunds to identity thieves. Education tax credits were doled out to "more than a million Americans not enrolled in a school," as well as to prisoners and to children under the age of 14, who are too young to be attending a postsecondary educational institution. In short, some 3.8 million tax filers received "more than $5.6 billion in potentially erroneous education credits."

The Earned Income Tax Credit takes the prize for the highest improper payment rate of any federal program. The error rate here runs to 27.2%, translating into more than **$17 billion** in tax credits to persons who do not qualify for a benefit meant to aid low- and moderate-income workers. But vying with the IRS as the prey of choice among fraudsters is Medicaid. In March 2015, Brooklyn District Attorney Ken Thompson reported that "thousands of homeless people were 'lured' and 'recruited' from shelters and welfare offices and taken to medical clinics 'for unnecessary tests with the promise of free footwear such as sneakers, shoes, and boots.'" This "massive scheme" bilked Medicare in New York out of some **$7 million**, which, *Wastebook* comments, "represents just a small fraction of the cost of the mismanagement and fraud within [New York State's] health-care program for the poor." In fact, "nearly $1 billion, including $513 million in improper payments and missed revenue and $361 million in questionable transactions, has been identified by the New York Office of the State Comptroller (OSC) outlined in audit reports issued between January 2011 and February 2015."[25]

PORK BY THE SECTOR

Taken together, waste by poor judgment, waste by bureaucratic imbecility, waste by indifference and error, and waste by fraud are staggering in their dimensions. And it's not all about husbanding the taxpayers' money. Think about what a "found" trillion dollars could actually do for those with genuine, non-fraudulent need in the areas of basic food, clothing, shelter, health, and education. Yes, the nation is

being ripped off, but those the various Treasury and HHS entitlements and other programs are intended to serve, those with
actual needs, are being both robbed and assaulted.

Yet, whereas instances of "improper payments," including
fraud, ubiquitous though they are, are considered aberrations,
errors, or criminal acts, pork barrel and earmark spending is not
only institutionalized but systematized in American government.
It is suboptimization enshrined as political tradition. This category of wasteful spending may be divided into five main sectors:
agriculture, business, labor, energy, and environment.

AGRICULTURE SECTOR

The great toxic subprime mortgage meltdown of 2007–2008
taught us all a thing or two about moral hazard, which, as
explained in Chapter 7, is defined as a situation in which one
party takes more or greater risks because another party has
agreed to bear the burden of those risks. Banks sunk money
into mortgage-backed securities—massive bundles of individual
mortgages about whose true value they knew nothing. They got
burned. No matter. The American taxpayer assumed their moral
hazard and bailed them out.

Who came up with this idea? Today, we blame Wall Street and
the politicians in Wall Street's deep pockets, but the truth is that
the use of moral hazard in U.S. economic policy can be found
at least as far back as 1933 and the creation of the Agricultural
Adjustment Administration (AAA) as part of the Depression-era
New Deal. The AAA sought to both stabilize and raise belea-
guered agricultural prices through a combination of imposed
production limits and federal subsidies designed to raise agricultural prices to "parity." *Parity* with what? Why, parity with the
prices farmers enjoyed just prior to World War I, when domestic and global demand for agricultural commodities of all kinds
was at an unprecedented high. The taxpayer was put on the hook
for the farmer's moral hazard. As long as he obeyed the dictates
of the AAA, he received his subsidies to ensure parity. The
farmer is at the mercy of both weather and markets. These are

very powerful forces. But the AAA ambitiously sought to render both impotent when confronted with the full faith and credit of the United States. And so the AAA put the taxpayer in the position of fighting both markets and weather, spending the two into submission.

Writing in 1991, the acerbic political satirist P. J. O'Rourke explained that you could never really tell what each new congressional omnibus farm bill would actually cost because "if the weather's bad and we have lots of droughts and freezes, we'll have to give disaster aid and crop-insurance payments to farmers, and the farm bill will end up costing us more. On the other hand, if the weather's good and we have plentiful harvests, we'll have to buy up surplus commodities and pay farmers to cut down on planting, and the farm bill will end up costing us more." Now, to those who try to tamp down their outrage at this system of moral hazard in the agricultural sector by reasoning that, well, at least "millions and millions of farms across the nation" are benefitting from the provisions of an omnibus farm bill, the fact is that there are (O'Rourke figured in 1991) only about "314,000 full-time commercial farms in the U.S.," and it is only the "largest farms in America, those with gross receipts of more than $500,000, [that] receive 60% of all price-support money."[26]

Today (based on 2014 stats), some "600,000 farms, about 30% of the two million [farms in America], have any significant farm production, and about 120,000 farms, or 6% of the total, produce three-quarters of all U.S. farm output."[27] So go ahead. Get angry. You have no excuse not to, because the subsidy money—the big spend intended to defeat the weather itself—goes not to two million farm families, and not even to 30% of that two million, but to just 6%, 120,000 farm entities. Some are family owned and others are corporate owned. Either way, the farms in this 6% are big business—agribusiness. According to the American Farm Bureau Federation ("The Voice of Agriculture"), "Farm and ranch families comprise just 2% of the U.S. population."[28] So, 2% of the U.S. population of 322,762,018 comes to 6,455,240[29] people, and 6% of this is 387,314. The federal appropriations we all pay for and that benefit just 387,314 Americans are the pure product of pork barrel legislation.

On the one hand, these 387,314 are lucky. (Not to begrudge them their luck, but it comes at the expense of the rest of us.) They are the beneficiaries of something started in the Great Depression, eighty-three years ago, the Holy Grail of parity. O'Rourke marveled at the programs the USDA administered. There was (and still is) a Federal Wool and Mohair Program, a price-support program "'established...in 1954...to encourage domestic wool production in the interest of national security.' Really, it says that. I guess back in the fifties there was this military school of thought that held that in the event of a Soviet attack we could confuse and disorient the enemy by throwing blankets over their heads." O'Rourke cites scholarship noting that, between 1985 and 1989, "government spending on rice farms was equal to $1 million for every full-time rice farmer in America and that the annual subsidy for each American dairy cow is between $600 and $700—greater than the per capita income of half the world's population" in 1991. He also cites a George Mason University economics professor who pointed out that "since 1985 federally mandated attempts to boost citrus prices have resulted in the destruction (or use as cattle feed) of three billion oranges and two billion lemons (which explains why we so rarely hear about a cow with scurvy)." An article titled "Moscow on the Mississippi: America's Soviet-Style Farm Policy," by Conservative Texas Congressman Dick Armey, pointed out that "the 1985 farm bill paid farmers not to farm sixty-one million acres—an area equal to Ohio, Indiana, and half of Illinois—and that the amount we've spent on farm subsidies in the past ten years is enough to have bought the farms in thirty-three states."[30]

"If we applied the logic of parity to automobiles instead of feed and grain," P. J. O'Rourke explained in 1991, "a typical economy car would cost forty grand; $43,987.50 is what a Nash Rambler cost in 1990 dollars. And for that you got a car with thirty-four horsepower, no heat, no A/C, no tape deck or radio, and no windows. If farm parity were a guiding principle of human existence, we'd not only have lousy, high-priced economy cars, we'd have a total lack of civilization."[31]

So, agribusiness is lucky it still has the concept of parity and all the subsidies that go with it. But agribusiness does not rely on luck. It relies on lobbyists: 839 of them, on whom 375 reported clients spent in 2016 **$33,680,010**, which breaks down like this[32]:

> Agricultural services & products producers spent
> **$9,180,255**
> Food processing & sales producers spent **$7,406,482**
> Crop production & basic processing producers spent
> **$6,056,877**
> Tobacco producers spent **$4,346,463**
> Forestry & forest products producers spent **$3,767,157**
> Dairy producers spent **$1,727,480**
> Livestock producers spent **$718,296**
> Poultry & egg producers spent **$385,000**
> Miscellaneous producers spent **$92,000**

Most of the USDA budget is mandatory (established by existing law), not discretionary (appropriated annually by Congress). For FY 2017, President Obama requested **$130 billion** in mandatory funding and **$25 billion** in discretionary appropriations. The mandatory funding was **$8 billion** below the 2016 level, and the discretionary ask about **$1 billion** below 2016. It may surprise you to know that 71% of the proposed 2017 USDA outlays are dedicated to nutrition assistance programs. The remaining 29% of the budget goes to producers and others—7% to conservation and forestry, 16% to farm and commodity programs, and 6% to programs including Rural Development, Research, Food Safety, Marketing and Regulation, and Departmental Management.[33]

The FY 2017 Agriculture Appropriations Bill that was finally drawn up by the House Appropriations Committee appropriated **$2.3 billion** less than the total requested by President Obama. Subsidies remained intact—although you would never know it from the Committee on Appropriations press release[34]:

> • **$868 million** to help farmers, ranchers, and private forest landowners conserve and protect their land

- **$2.28 billion** for the rural development program, an increase of **$113 million** over 2016; funding includes:
    - **$920 million** in business and industry loans
    - **$1.25 billion** for rural infrastructure, in addition to **$6.94 billion** for rural electric and telephone infrastructure loans
    - **$24 billion** for rural housing and rental assistance
    - **$1.9 billion** for "overseas food aid and to promote U.S. agricultural exports"

The USDA distributes most of its farm and agribusiness largess through seven major categories of programs and numerous sub-programs:[35]

- Agricultural Research-Basic and Applied Research
- Agriculture and Food Research Initiative (AFRI)
- Appropriate Technology Transfer for Rural Areas
- Bioenergy Program for Advanced Biofuels
- Biomass Research and Development Initiative
- Competitive Grants Program
    - Business and Industry Loans
    - Export Guarantee Program
    - Food for Progress
    - Food for Progress-Section 416(b)
    - Grants for Agricultural Research-Competitive
- Research Grants
    - Grants for Agricultural Research-Special Research Grants
    - Market Access Program
    - Rural Development, Forestry, and Communities Grants
    - Small Business Innovation Research
    - Wood Utilization Assistance (also known as Forest Products Lab: Technology Marketing Unit)

On February 4, 2014, the Senate Committee on Agriculture, Nutrition, and Forestry issued a press release announcing what promised to be sharp cuts in farm subsidies that would save taxpayers $23.3 billion over the following ten years.[36] "Those projected savings, it turns out, were a mirage. According to new estimates for Farm Bill spending over the next few years released by the Congressional Budget Office, total aid to farmers will swell to $23.9 billion in 2017." Some observers were stunned. "What happened to the savings taxpayers were promised?" asked Colin O'Neil, representing an anti-subsidy organization called the Environmental Working Group. But Iowa State University agricultural economist Bruce Babcock remarked that "Cynics like me fully expected this to work out the way it has.... Farm policy isn't really about policy. It's about farmers getting their money. And the agricultural committees in Congress are there to make sure that farmers get their money."[37]

In the 2016 presidential primary race, agribusiness donated **$812,134** to Hillary Clinton (D) and **$464,200** to Bernie Sanders (D). Republican hopefuls received far more, the top fifteen receiving[38]:

CANDIDATE	RECEIVED
Marco Rubio	$6,300,755
Jeb Bush	$3,229,405
Mike Huckabee	$3,088,696
Rand Paul	$1,289,187
Ben Carson	$1,106,126
Ted Cruz	$1,082,857
John Kasich	$519,723
Chris Christie	$396,300
Rick Perry	$381,600
Scott Walker	$210,039
Carly Fiorina	$134,429
Lindsey Graham	$55,592
Bobby Jindal	$55,120
Donald Trump	$38,552
Rick Santorum	$20,468

In all election cycles from 1990 to 2016, the agriculture/agribusiness sector contributed a total of **$264,666,109** to the campaigns of House members (**$95,797,913** to Democrats, **$168,753,149** to Republicans, and **$115,047** to Independents). To Senate campaigns, 1990–2016 contributions totaled **$114,188,129** (**$43,177,581** to Democrats, **$70,670,298** to Republicans, and **$340,250** to Independents).[39]

BUSINESS SECTOR

Forbes, which used to advertise itself proudly as "Capitalist Tool," is not exactly a bastion of left-wing radicalism. But the headline of a story published in March 2014 did ask, "Where Is the Outrage over Corporate Welfare?" Author David Brunori begins with a reference to "Subsidizing the Corporate One Percent," by Philip Mattera, a "respected thought leader in our business. It says that three-quarters of all state economic subsidies went to just 965 corporations since...1976. The Fortune 500 corporations alone accounted for more than 16,000 subsidy awards, worth $63 billion—mostly in the form of tax breaks."[40]

"I don't blame the corporations," Brunori writes. "They act rationally. If someone gives you $1 billion, you take it." He goes on to blame the American electorate for a failure of outrage, "whether we are conservatives, liberals, or libertarians. And the outrage should be reflected in how we vote."[41]

True enough, but the corporations are not just *given* a billion dollars. They pay for it through deals arranged by lobbyists. In 2016, the top spenders on lobbyists in the business sector were[42]:

CORPORATION	SPENT
U.S. Chamber of Commerce	$22,925,000
National Association of Realtors	$11,999,165
American Medical Association	$6,810,000
Blue Cross/Blue Shield	$6,810,000
Pharmaceutical Research and Manufacturers of America	$5,982,500
American Hospital Association	$5,665,214
Dow Chemical	$4,840,982

CORPORATION	SPENT
Northrup Grumman	$4,740,000
National Association of Broadcasters	$4,738,000
AT&T Inc.	$4,480,000
Boeing Company	$4,480,000
Alphabet Inc.	$3,800,000
Comcast Corporation	$3,720,000
Verizon Communications	$3,680,000
Lockheed Martin	$3,672,737
Southern Company	$3,440,000
Pfizer, Inc.	$3,400,000
Exxon Mobil	$3,280,000
National Cable and Telecommunications Association	$3,280,000
Merck and Company	$3,260,000

"$6,000," begins an article on what corporate subsidies cost the average American family. "That's over and above our payments to the big companies for energy and food and housing and health care and all our tech devices. It's $6,000 that no family would have to pay if we truly lived in a competitive but well-regulated free-market economy." This figure is calculated on the basis of the **$100 billion** a year that the Cato Institute estimates the federal government spends on "corporate welfare," plus more than **$80 billion** from state, county, and city governments. Additional subsidies include **$83 billion** in interest rate subsidies to banks (3 cents per tax dollar), **$270 billion** in the excess cost of medications due to government-granted patent monopolies, more than **$100 billion** for corporate tax subsidies, and some **$141,588,000,000** for government revenue losses due to corporate tax havens.[43]

Between 2000 and 2015, the federal government provided **$68 billion** in direct grants and special tax credits to businesses. Two-thirds of this money went to large corporations. The top twenty beneficiaries during this period were[44]:

CORPORATION	SPENT
Iberdrola	$2,172,641,752
NextEra Energy	$1,938,811,949
NRG Energy	$1,730,060,410
Southern Company	$1,475,553,962
Summit Power	$1,441,936,555
SCS Energy	$1,254,154,000
Tenaska	$966,252,326
Duke Energy	$898,436,173
General Electric	$836,524,548
Exelon	$734,674,010
EDP-Energias de Portugal	$722,468,855
Leucadia National	$651,647,087
SunEdison	$649,564,635
General Atomics	$614,658,667
Abengoa	$605,128,646
Air Products & Chemicals	$604,170,312
Ameren	$594,809,786
E.ON	$576,149,728
AES	$566,920,950
Invenergy	$531,915,559

Numerous federal agencies have programs through which they distribute grants, loans, and subsidies to business, including most of the Cabinet-level departments, as well the Export-Import Bank of the United States, National Aeronautics and Space Administration (NASA), Overseas Private Investment Corporation, and the Small Business Administration.

Meantime, in Congress, among the leadership, business sector campaign contributions figure prominently:[45]

Top Five Sectors Contributing to Campaign Committees and Leadership PACs, as of June 12, 2016

HOUSE, 114TH CONGRESS, REPUBLICANS

Speaker Paul Ryan (Wisconsin)

Retired Persons[46]	$1,414,598
Securities & Investment	$1,109,022
Real Estate	$480,438
Insurance	$477,374
Health Professionals	$433,115

Majority Leader Kevin McCarthy (California)

Securities & Investment	$807,550
Real Estate	$572,100
Pharmaceuticals/Health Products	$409,850
Insurance	$408,100
Health Professionals	$372,935

Majority Whip Steve Scalise (Louisiana)

Oil & Gas	$254,000
Securities & Investment	$227,850
Insurance	$225,100
Health Professionals	$193,275
Real Estate	$166,032

Conference Chair Cathy McMorris Rodgers (Washington)

Securities & Investment	$186,450
Insurance	$144,660
Health Professionals	$135,175
Real Estate	$112,960
Retired Persons	$96,340

Policy Committee Chair Luke Messer (Indiana)

Insurance	$152,300
Securities & Investment	$88,400
Real Estate	$86,077
Commercial Banks	$43,400
Accountants	$39,000

(continues)

HOUSE, 114TH CONGRESS, DEMOCRATS	
Minority Leader Nancy Pelosi (California)	
Health Professionals	$152,350
Retired Persons	$126,896
Public Sector Unions	$106,000
Real Estate	$96,025
Securities & Investment	$76,135
Assistant Minority Leader James Clyburn (South Carolina)	
Electric Utilities	$147,500
Pharmaceuticals/Health Products	$113,962
Insurance	$97,750
Health Professionals	$90,940
Lawyers/Law Firms	$81,000
Minority Whip Steny Hoyer (Maryland)	
Electric Utilities	$293,700
Insurance	$260,500
Securities & Investment	$243,750
Health Professionals	$188,800
Real Estate	$172,742
Caucus Chair Xavier Becerra (California)	
Health Professionals	$115,240
Real Estate	$92,600
Securities & Investment	$86,526
Insurance	$71,000
Casinos/Gambling	$68,200
SENATE, 114TH CONGRESS, REPUBLICANS	
Majority Leader Mitch McConnell (Kentucky)	
Securities & Investment	$2,439,462
Retired Persons	$1,312,020
Oil & Gas	$1,048,058
Insurance	$1,124,250
Health Professionals	$1,097,995

Majority Whip John Cornyn (Texas)	
Securities & Investment	$1,335,693
Oil & Gas	$1,312,356
Health Professionals	$999,946
Lawyers/Law Firms	$758,602
Real Estate	$726,399
Conference Chair John Thune (South Dakota)	
Insurance	$618,000
Lobbyists	$536,735
Retired Persons	$525,510
Securities & Investment	$440,952
Real Estate	$396,234
Conference Vice Chair Roy Blunt (Missouri)	
Securities & Investment	$542,375
Leadership PACs	$485,246
Real Estate	$481,800
Lobbyists	$480,113
Health Professionals	$419,000
Retired Persons	$279,845
Policy Chair John Barasso (Wyoming)	
Health Professionals	$702,593
Oil & Gas	$560,466
Pharmaceuticals/Health Products	$449,500
Lobbyists	$365,594
Electric Utilities	$341,250
SENATE, 114TH CONGRESS, DEMOCRATS	
Minority Leader Harry Reid (Nevada)	
Lawyers/Law Firms	$581,533
Health Professionals	$539,450
Pharmaceuticals/Health Products	$516,400
Lobbyists	$501,944
Hospitals/Nursing Homes	$499,300

(continues)

Minority Whip Dick Durbin (Illinois)	
Lawyers/Law Firms	$1,715,312
Real Estate	$460,617
Securities & Investment	$408,250
Retired Persons	$374,981
Lobbyists	$290,789
Conference Secretary Patty Murray (Washington)	
Lawyers/Law Firms	$605,552
Pharmaceuticals/Health Products	$497,600
Retired Persons	$457,028
Lobbyists	$412,903
Health Professionals	$340,252
Policy Chair Charles Schumer (New York)	
Securities & Investment	$3,028,456
Lawyers/Law Firms	$1,959,373
Real Estate	$1,760,830
Insurance	$834,595
Retired Persons	$642,619

The presumptive Republican and Democratic nominees for president (plus Democrat Bernie Sanders, who had not suspended his campaign as of this writing, June 12, 2016) and two third-party candidates had received the following contributions (Campaign + Outside Groups) as of May 23, 2016:

AGRIBUSINESS[47]	
Hillary Clinton (D)	$864,343
Bernie Sanders (D)	$556,068
Donald Trump (R)	$44,118
Gary Johnson (Libertarian)	$3,200
Jill Stein (Green)	$600

COMMUNICATIONS/ELECTRONICS[48]	
Hillary Clinton (D)	$24,972,181
Bernie Sanders (D)	$5,014,890
Donald Trump (R)	$197,886
Jill Stein (Green)	$11,664
Gary Johnson (Libertarian)	$8,700
CONSTRUCTION[49]	
Hillary Clinton (D)	$2,879,047
Bernie Sanders (D)	$1,109,657
Donald Trump (R)	$107,619
Gary Johnson (Libertarian)	$4,250
Jill Stein (Green)	$1,292
DEFENSE[50]	
Bernie Sanders (D)	$323,467
Hillary Clinton (D)	$273,000
Donald Trump (R)	$17,818
Gary Johnson (Libertarian)	$3,483
Jill Stein (Green)	$35
ENERGY/NATURAL RESOURCES[51]	
Hillary Clinton (D)	$1,172,866
Bernie Sanders (D)	$355,905
Donald Trump (R)	$37,502
Gary Johnson (Libertarian)	$1,475
Jill Stein (Green)	$500
FINANCE/INSURANCE/REAL ESTATE[52]	
Hillary Clinton (D)	$46,950,038
Bernie Sanders (D)	$2,165,580
Donald Trump (R)	$571,032
Jill Stein (Green)	$7,575
Gary Johnson (Libertarian)	$3,000

(continues)

HEALTH[53]	
Hillary Clinton (D)	$9,852,510
Bernie Sanders (D)	$3,779,734
Donald Trump (R)	$149,662
Gary Johnson (Libertarian)	$6,900
Jill Stein (Green)	$3,575
TRANSPORTATION[54]	
Hillary Clinton (D)	$813,069
Bernie Sanders (D)	$592,898
Donald Trump (R)	$51,331
Jill Stein (Green)	$2,050
Gary Johnson (Libertarian)	$1,000

LABOR SECTOR

Once among the most powerful influencers in American political life, labor unions have been in sharp decline since their peak in the 1950s, when 35% of all American workers were unionized. By 2013, that number had fallen to 11.3% overall and, in the private sector, to just 6.6%.[55] Plenty of Americans said good riddance. They said that unions brought about their own demise with high-profile corruption—the reign of Jimmy Hoffa and other corrupt bosses who forged iron links between their unions and organized crime—and inflated salaries that made many American-made goods uncompetitive on the global market, prompted the shuttering of factories across the nation, and drove the transformation of the United States from net exporter to net importer. Consider: "During the 1970s the average family earned $24,000 a year while [union] steel workers were making $40,000."[56] And then there were the long-term strikes the unions financed with extortionary zeal, and the union's power to change work in ways that "limited production and increased costs,"[57] not only hitting consumers in the pocketbook, but further reducing

America's power to compete against offshore producers. True, labor unions were instrumental in creating the great American middle class of 1950s. As Nicholas Kristof observed, "The [union] abuses are real. But, as unions wane in American life, it's also increasingly clear that they were doing a of good in sustaining middle class life . . ."[58] Nevertheless, their excesses also played a role in the erosion of the middle class from the 1980s onward.

Mark Twain famously responded to a news story that he had died by remarking, drily and drolly, "the report of my death was an exaggeration."[59] In that vein, let us observe that while reports of the death of America's unions truly are exaggerations, the power of organized labor remains strong in the lobbies of federal, as well as state and local, government.

It is true that labor unions "are regularly outspent by other sectors when it comes to lobbying the federal government." In a 2011 snapshot, "interests within the health and finance sectors [were shown to] have each spent more than **$4.6 billion** on federal lobbying since 1998 [while] labor unions have spent just 10% of that sum. According to research by the Center for Responsive Politics, labor unions have spent $467 million on lobbying since 1998." Within this comparatively modest lobbying program, it has been the public sector unions, not the private sector unions, that have invested most heavily in federal lobbying. For instance, between January 2009 and June 2011, public sector unions spent **$35.6 million** on lobbying, compared to **$28.6 million** spent by transportation unions, **$21.6 million** by industrial unions, and **$9.6 million** by building trade unions.[60]

Despite labor's modest position among other lobbying interests, it "ranks as one of the largest contributors to Washington politicians every year." In 2010, *Mother Jones* crunched Open Secrets.org data and found that the labor sector was the top campaign backer of 159 House members (the same number as counted the finance, insurance, and real estate sectors as their top contributors). In the Senate, however, just two senators counted labor as their top supporter.[61]

Some of the biggest labor unions do not merely lobby, they

form political action committees (PACs). The AFL-CIO, Teamsters Union, and International Brotherhood of Electrical Workers (IBEW) are examples, and in 2010, the IBEW made a splash by donating some **$826,200** to federal candidates—more than any other labor lobbying group and more, even, than AT&T's mighty PAC.[62]

To bring the numbers up to date, in 2016, some 110 labor clients paid **$48,201,609** to 431 lobbyists. Public sector unions led the sector, spending **$13,780,450**. Transportation unions came next (**$11,135,616**), followed by industrial unions (**$10,696,614**), "miscellaneous unions" (**$7,623,929**), and building trade unions (**$4,965,000**).[63] During 2015–2016, the top twenty labor contributors to political campaigns were[64]:

Carpenters & Joiners Union	$7,200,033
Laborers Union	$6,928,378
National Nurses United	$4,332,409
AFL-CIO	$3,945,862
National Education Association	$3,466,862
International Brotherhood of Electrical Workers	$3,345,438
Communications Workers of America	$2,755,356
United Steelworkers	$2,402,224
Plumbers/Pipefitters Union	$2,280,309
American Federation of State/County/Municipal Employees	$1,904,003
American Federation of Teachers	$1,844,406
Operating Engineers Union	$1,558,138
Air Line Pilots Association	$1,530,190
Teamsters Union	$1,310,625
Service Employees International Union	$1,294,519
Machinists/Aerospace Workers Union	$1,194,601
National Air Traffic Controllers Association	$1,121,395
United Food & Commercial Workers Union	$1,121,395
Sheet Metal Workers Union	$1,048,050
United Auto Workers	$1,025,134

The overwhelming majority of contributions were made to Democrats and/or "Liberal Groups." Of the twenty top contributors, six made contributions exclusively to Democrats and/or "Liberal Groups." Only three unions, the Laborer's Union, IBEW, and the Operating Engineers Union, made any contributions to "Conservative Groups": **$250,000** out of **$6,928,378** total contributions, **$77,160** out of **$3,345,438**, and **$90,000** out of **$1,558,138**, respectively.

In all election cycles from 1990 to 2016, the labor sector contributed a total of **$448,821,244** to the campaigns of House members (**$394,198,411** to Democrats, **$53,440,544** to Republicans, and **$1,182,279** to Independents). To Senate campaigns, 1990–2016 contributions totaled **$71,310,924** (**$62,837,487** to Democrats, **$7,845,452** to Republicans, and **$627,985** to Independents).[65]

ENERGY SECTOR

In sharp contrast to the labor sector, the energy sector, led by the oil and gas industry, directed very nearly all of its political campaign funding gusher to Republicans and "Conservative Groups" in 2015–2016[66]:

Quantum Energy Partners	$10,093,550
Koch Industries	$4,613,209
Chevron Corporation	$3,932,346
Stewart & Stevenson	$3,074,200
Hunt Companies	$2,646,498
Western Refining	$2,606,860
Chief Oil & Gas	$2,456,293
Nextera Energy	$2,159,613
Energy Transfer Equity	$1,801,101
Edison Chouest Offshore	$1,751,239
Ariel Corporation	$1,578,300
Devon Energy	$1,452,776
National Rural Electric Cooperative Association	$1,434,477

Exelon Corporation	$1,431,364
Exxon Mobil	$1,239,554
Cumberland Development	$1,122,100
Kinder Morgan Inc.	$1,076,827
Boich Companies	$1,075,100
Otis Eastern	$1,015,848
Jasper Reserves, LLC	$1,000,000
Petrodome Energy	$1,000,000

Of the top twenty, only five made any contributions to Democrats: Nextera, **$196,243** out of **$2,159,613**; Chevron, **$100,640** out of **$3,932,346**; Exelon, **$437,862** out of **$1,431,364**; National Rural Electric Cooperative Association, **$374,902** out of **$1,434,477**; and Exxon Mobil, **$123,866** out of **$1,239,554**. The remaining fourteen top contributors contributed exclusively to Republicans and "Conservative Groups."

A reported 833 clients in the energy/natural resources sector spent **$332,821,621** on 1,943 lobbyists in 2016, with the oil and gas industry (**$129,836,004**) and electric utilities (**$117,735,016**) leading the way. "Miscellaneous energy" (**$51,962,839**), mining (**$21,742,082**), waste management (**$4,226,800**), environmental services/equipment (**$4,001,000**), and fisheries and wildlife (**$3,317,880**) followed.[67]

The sector's average contributions to members of the House of Representatives during 2010–2016 were[68]:

2010 $78,870 to Republicans; $49,090 to Democrats
2012 $123,430 to Republicans; $36,370 to Democrats
2014 $134,480 to Republicans; $36,450 to Democrats
2016 $68,377 to Republicans; $22,806 to Democrats

In the Senate during this same period[69]:

2010 $118,100 to Republicans; $101,900 to Democrats
2012 $134,470 to Republicans; $101,110 to Democrats

2014 $198,680 to Republicans; $105,950 to Democrats
2016 $176,117 to Republicans; $43,305 to Democrats

In the 2015–2016 presidential primary race, the top recipients were[70]:

Hillary Clinton (D)	$1,089,681
Jeb Bush (R)	$829,827
Marco Rubio (R)	$575,543
Bernie Sanders (D)	$356,055

In all election cycles from 1990 to 2016, the energy/natural resources sector contributed a total of **$273,645,117** to the campaigns of House members (**$85,293,786** to Democrats, **$188,292,631** to Republicans, and **$58,700** to Independents). To Senate campaigns, 1990–2016 contributions totaled **$140,179,647** (**$50,520,742** to Democrats, **$88,242,011** to Republicans, and **$1,179,647** to Independents).[71]

ENVIRONMENT SECTOR

During 2015–2016—and during the Obama administration generally—environmental groups were a significant lobbying presence in Washington, although the volume of their political contributions is significantly smaller than that of the industries they typically oppose. Nevertheless, the policies, legislation, and projects they promote have a profound impact on federal spending and the national economy. Eighteen of top twenty organizations contributed almost exclusively to Democrats and/or "Liberal Groups"[72]:

Environment America	$2,638,175
League of Conservation Voters	$1,090,379
ClearPath Foundation	$476,782
Nextgen Climate Action	$229,166
Global Green USA	$111,535
Natural Resources Defense Council	$68,258

Ocean Champions	$60,378
Trust for Public Land	$42,832
Sierra Club	$35,369
Nature Conservancy	$31,499
Center for Coastal Conservation	$29,250
Volunteer Environmental Activist	$29,200
Environmental Defense Fund	$24,268
Friends of the Earth	$20,950
Save the Everglades	$20,000
Earthworks	$16,200
Cool Globes Inc.	$16,200
Washington Forest Law Center	$13,632

Of the twenty, only three contributed to Republicans or Conservative Groups: ClearPath Foundation, **$476,782** out of **$476,782**; League of Conservation Voters, **$58,650** out of **$1,090,379**; and Center for Coastal Conservation, **$29,250** out of **$29,250**. The top lobbying clients among the environmental organizations in 2016 were the Natural Resources Defense Council, which spent **$239,076** on lobbyists; National Wildlife Federation, **$220,000**; Environmental Working Group, **$218,625**; Nature Conservancy, **$200,000**; and the Sierra Club, **$150,000**.

In 2015–2016, environmental organizations contributed to only one presidential candidate, Democrat Hillary Clinton (**$277,016**).[73]

Environmental groups contributed to both the House members and senators during 2010–2016. The average contributions were:[74]

House
2010 $10,595 to Democrats; $6,797 to Republicans
2012 $11,559 to Democrats; $4,478 to Republicans
2014 $15,156 to Democrats; $4,772 to Republicans
2016 $4,493 to Democrats; $5,901 to Republicans

Senate

2010	$24,647 to Democrats;	$4,783 to Republicans
2012	$25,941 to Democrats;	$5,268 to Republicans
2014	$72,138 to Democrats;	$11,037 to Republicans
2016	$27,163 to Democrats;	$5,942 to Republicans

MONEY AS FREE SPEECH

"Corporations are people, my friend," Republican presidential candidate Mitt Romney famously proclaimed on the stump at the Iowa State Fair on August 11, 2011.[75] The hapless Mitt was widely mocked for the comment, but the fact is that U.S. courts have consistently extended to corporations many of the constitutional protections afforded human beings. This has enhanced the legal theory of "corporate personhood," which holds that a corporation (sometimes referred to in a legal context as a "corporate person") has certain of the legal rights and certain of the legal responsibilities accorded to "natural persons" (that is, human beings).

The theory of corporate personhood was put to an extraordinary test in 2009–2010 when the case of *Citizens United v. Federal Election Commission* (08-205, 588 U.S. 310) was argued before the U.S. Supreme Court. In a decision handed down on January 21, 2010, the Court held (5–4) that the rights guaranteed to natural persons by the First Amendment—in this case, most pertinently, freedom of speech and the press—apply as well to corporations (as "corporate persons"). Independent political expenditures made by corporate persons were judged to constitute the equivalent of the expression of free speech in natural persons.[76] The decision originally applied to a nonprofit corporation, Citizens United, a conservative nonprofit organization, but the principles articulated in the decision have been extended to for-profit corporations and to labor unions and other associations. By equating independent political expenditures with freedom of speech, the decision allows unlimited election spending by individuals as well as corporations.

As Chris Cillizza observed in a 2014 article for *The Washington Post*, the Citizens United decision "drastically re-shaped the political landscape."[77] Independent political expenditures from corporations and individuals in the 2008 general election year were a bit over **$110 million**. In the midterm election year of 2010, the year of the Citizens United decision, they nearly doubled to just under **$220 million**. Two years later, in the general election year of 2012, independent expenditures were nearly **$1 billion** and constituted the vast majority of political expenditures. What is more, while campaign laws require political committees (PACs and super-PACS) to disclose their donor lists, they permit tax-exempt groups to withhold their lists from disclosure. Called 501(c)(4) groups—after the Internal Revenue Code (IRC) section that applies to them—these are nonprofit organizations "operated exclusively to promote social welfare," not particular political candidates.[78] In recent years, these groups have, in fact, promoted causes closely associated with certain candidates, and so they have become vehicles through which political contributors who wish to remain anonymous donate. With limits on contributions removed, unions, corporations, and individuals were able to make massive donations to and through 501(c)(4) groups, which could promote political advocacy of or opposition to candidates without having to identify the sources of their funding.

The post–Citizens United political landscape is indeed a strange new world in American politics. The theory of corporate personhood provided a legal platform for the Supreme Court's decision extending First Amendment protection to the right of individual and corporate donors to give candidates as much money as they desired. This greatly enhanced the practical power of wealthy donors—individual or corporate—to promote the election of their chosen candidates. To many Americans, this seems antithetical to democracy—a means by which the wealthy and the corporate could acquire pliable politicians and congenial laws. That posed a significant threat, many believed. Yet if candidates were compelled to disclose the identity of those who donated to their campaigns, at least voters could go to the polls in possession of valuable information about each candidate's likely biases and legislative mindset. A candidate whose major source of funding is the coal industry, for example, is not likely to support certain environmental legislation. But the combination of an unlimited legal capacity to fund a candidate *through* nonprofit organizations that are immune from disclosure requirements deprives voters of critical information about the candidate. As many see it, this compounds the challenge to democracy.

Or does it—really?

At the time of this writing, toward the end of the 2016 primary election cycle, many political surprises—*shocks* may be a more accurate word—have come and gone. The most potentially enduring of them, however, is neither the primary victory of one extreme "outsider" candidate, Donald J. Trump, running as a Republican, nor the extraordinary performance of a white-haired socialist Independent candidate running as a Democrat, Bernie Sanders. No. The most potentially epoch-making disruption of the political status quo is that the tsunami of corporate and special interest cash enabled by Citizens United has played a remarkably small role in the 2015–2016 political process so far.

Trump, a billionaire, has largely self-funded his rise to (at this writing) the presumptive GOP nominee, and Sanders, who has declined to take super-PAC (unlimited) contributions, has raised **$186 million**, mostly from individuals making small donations averaging **$27**. This is significant because only 0.25% of the U.S. population contributes **$200** or more to political candidates, and just 0.04% contributes $2,700 or more. Yet this tiny elite—0.29% combined—typically delivers 69.8% of campaign contributions.[79] Hillary Clinton, the "establishment" Democratic hopeful, raised **$186,735,031** as a result of her own campaign—essentially tying with Sanders. Unlike him, though, she has also accepted super-PAC funding, **$74,185,282**.[80] According to the Federal Election Commission, about 18% of Clinton's campaign funding has come from individual donations under **$200**, compared to 70% under **$200** for Sanders.[81]

On the GOP side, a huge field of seventeen major primary candidates—sixteen of whom availed themselves of post–Citizens United fundraising apparatuses, one of whom did not—fell by the wayside as the largely self-funded Trump, who spent comparatively little money, worked his way to the top. As of March 31, 2016, the top five Republican primary contenders (in terms of campaign receipts) were[82]:

Ted Cruz: $78,513,417 ($78,175,396 individual;
    $0 candidate; $79,922 PAC)
Ben Carson: $63,571,704 ($63,004,171 individual;
    $25,000 candidate; $5,588 PAC)
Donald Trump: $48,393,537 ($12,149,834 individual;
    $36,243,646 candidate; $0 PAC)
Marco Rubio: $44,380,162 ($44,079,383 individual;
    $0 candidate; $70,331 PAC)
Jeb Bush: $33,999,149 ($33,009,429 individual;
    $795,704 candidate; $194,017 PAC)

The Federal Election Commission data does not list super-PAC money because, unlike traditional PACs, super-PACs are prohibited from donating directly to candidates and their spending must not be coordinated with that of the candidates they benefit; however, they may raise unlimited contributions from corporations, unions, associations, and individuals. The top-contributing (over $100,000) super-PACs active during the 2016 presidential primary include[83]:

GROUP	SUPPORTS/ OPPOSES	INDEPENDENT EXPENDITURES	VIEWPOINT	TOTAL RAISED
Right to Rise USA	supports Bush	$86,817,138	Conservative	$121,141,408
Conservative Solutions PAC	supports Rubio	$55,443,483	Conservative	$60,564,219
America Leads	supports Christie	$18,578,852	Conservative	$20,291,894
Our Principles PAC	supports Clinton	$18,451,238	Conservative	$18,880,380
Priorities USA Action	supports Clinton	$16,346,173	Liberal	$75,983,220
Club for Growth Action		$12,412,554	Conservative	$13,493,218
New Day for America	supports Kasich	$11,168,205	Conservative	$15,245,068
Freedom Partners Action Fund		$9,895,341	Conservative	$12,841,612
Stand for Truth	supports Cruz	$9,523,814	Conservative	$11,143,185
Keep the Promise I	supports Cruz	$9,110,205	Conservative	$14,320,691
Senate Majority PAC		$7,638,267	Liberal	$16,804,516
Women Vote!		$5,015,959	Liberal	$7,606,171
Trusted Leadership PAC	supports Cruz	$4,881,851	Conservative	$8,408,923
National Nurses United		$4,750,353	Liberal	$4,355,934
New Day Independent Media Committee	supports Kasich	$4,487,799	Conservative	$2,380,813
2016 Committee	supports Carson	$4,164,705	Conservative	$12,315,174
Carly for America Committee	supports Fiorina	$3,837,155	Conservative	$14,296,380
Security Is Strength	supports Graham	$3,610,276	Conservative	$4,252,117
Pursuing America's Greatness	supports Huckabee	$3,510,323	Conservative	$4,964,562

(continues)

GROUP	SUPPORTS/ OPPOSES	INDEPENDENT EXPENDITURES	VIEWPOINT	TOTAL RAISED
Fighting for Ohio Fund	supports Portman	$3,316,867	Conservative	$3,082,820
Concerned American Voters	supports Paul	$2,971,831	Conservative	$5,348,349
Believe Again	supports Jindal	$2,634,870	Conservative	$4,472,589
Unintimidated PAC	supports Walker	$2,249,018	Conservative	$24,127,172
Ending Spending Action Fund		$2,171,311	Conservative	$2,674,489
Working for Us PAC		$2,125,450	Liberal	$1,100,000
National Association of Realtors		$1,937,837		$4,243,204
Planned Parenthood Votes		$1,869,236	Liberal	$6,619,205
Opportunity & Freedom PAC	supports Perry	$1,859,326	Conservative	$4,120,014
America's Liberty PAC	supports Paul	$1,673,394	Conservative	$4,561,405
Accountable Leadership	supports Sestak	$1,389,634	Liberal	$1,457,986
NextGen California Action Committee		$1,366,906		$325,000
Maryland USA	supports Hoeber	$1,363,958	Conservative	$2,101,000
Great America PAC	supports Trump	$1,322,008	Conservative	$1,066,587
Keep the Promise PAC	supports Cruz	$1,103,118	Conservative	$5,155,547
Defending Main Street		$871,021	Conservative	$2,093,646
Americans for Responsible Solutions		$834,278		$8,463,289
Arizona Grassroots Action		$826,877	Conservative	$1,192,261
New Leadership for Ohio	supports Sittenfeld	$788,104	Liberal	$1,016,001

GROUP	SUPPORTS/ OPPOSES	INDEPENDENT EXPENDITURES	VIEWPOINT	TOTAL RAISED
Americas PAC		$735,336	Conservative	$520,000
Future45		$731,509	Conservative	$1,368,648
Citizen SuperPAC	supports Shelby	$726,888	Conservative	$1,916,265
House Majority PAC		$699,970	Liberal	$12,864,017
Purple PAC		$671,624	Conservative	$1,180,000
New York Wins	opposes Heaney	$580,965		$500,000
Senate Leadership Fund		$533,664	Conservative	$17,905,600
American Opportunity PAC		$524,620	Liberal	$550,000
Indiana Jobs Now		$522,634		$500,000
Restoration PAC	opposes Clinton	$474,570	Conservative	$1,951,981
Citizens United Super PAC		$423,040	Conservative	$390,230
Let America Work	supports Johnson	$417,416	Conservative	$974,000
Senate Conservatives Action		$417,333	Conservative	$1,529,948
Generation Forward	supports O'Malley	$368,412	Liberal	$831,165
FreedomWorks for America		$340,843	Conservative	$466,740
Committee for Maryland's Progress	supports Van Hollen	$335,013		$606,005
The American Foundations Committee		$330,580	Conservative	$0
Grow the Economy PAC		$329,994		$0
American Working Families		$324,130	Liberal	$280,011
Courageous Conservatives PAC	supports Cruz	$311,403	Conservative	$359,108
Make DC Listen	supports Cruz	$307,959	Conservative	$1,307,646
Draft Biden 2016	supports Biden	$290,123	Liberal	$1,024,463

(continues)

GROUP	SUPPORTS/ OPPOSES	INDEPENDENT EXPENDITURES	VIEWPOINT	TOTAL RAISED
Tea Party Patriots Citizens Fund		$260,067	Conservative	$1,801,823
American Dental Association		$256,287		$93,000
American Unity PAC		$255,532	Conservative	$2,565,685
Illinois Voices Matter	supports Zopp	$242,000	Liberal	$273,375
Spirit of Democracy America		$241,571	Conservative	$114,800
NEA Advocacy Fund		$232,366	Liberal	$2,203,974
NeverTrump PAC	opposes Trump	$209,905		$305,858
Values Are Vital		$208,449	Conservative	$487,000
National Right to Life Victory Fund		$208,055	Conservative	$327,490
America Ascendant PAC		$180,093		$526,000
Congressional Leadership Fund		$175,924	Conservative	$2,124,113
Frugal Hoosiers		$171,428		$0
Working Again PAC	supports Santorum	$161,208	Conservative	$358,907
John Bolton Super PAC		$150,000	Conservative	$3,340,790
Tea Party Express Campaign Fund		$137,902	Conservative	$0
League of Conservation Voters		$136,702	Liberal	$965,335
American Crossroads		$135,378	Conservative	$3,949,049
Communications Workers of America		$131,450	Liberal	$1,595,849
We the People Foundation	opposes Trump	$130,882		$131,391
Americans United for Values		$126,900		$127,000

GROUP	SUPPORTS/ OPPOSES	INDEPENDENT EXPENDITURES	VIEWPOINT	TOTAL RAISED
Patriots for Trump	supports Trump	$122,463	Conservative	$131,622
Baby Got PAC	supports Rubio	$118,990	Conservative	$130,000
We the People, Not Washington	supports Pataki	$118,778	Conservative	$1,547,673
Americans for Concrete Solutions	supports Spurlino	$110,951	Conservative	$213,300
314 PAC		$108,276	Liberal	$89,380
USW Works		$101,059		$2,975,317
Cooperative of American Physicians		$100,346	Conservative	$1,946,230
Stand With America		$100,000	Conservative	$0
Americans for Accountability in Leadership		$94,682	Conservative	$95,200
Our Children's Future	supports Carson	$90,000	Conservative	$220,003
New Prosperity Foundation		$77,903	Conservative	$371,750
Our Voice Matters		$76,300		$80,000
Texans for Integrity		$73,000		$27,050
New York Jobs Council		$71,125	Liberal	$196,000
Conservative Texans		$63,079	Conservative	$85,020
Illinois Families First		$62,500		$78,000
Oregon Right to Life Victory PAC		$60,456	Conservative	$335,157
Grow NC Strong	supports Tillis	$60,000	Conservative	$98,777
Texas Tea Party Patriots PAC		$58,219	Conservative	$350,301
Texans for a Better Future		$57,676		$65,000
Republican Super PAC		$57,107	Conservative	$0
America Rising PAC		$54,683	Conservative	$883,256

(continues)

GROUP	SUPPORTS/ OPPOSES	INDEPENDENT EXPENDITURES	VIEWPOINT	TOTAL RAISED
Sierra Club Independent Action		$50,303	Liberal	$138,099
Wisconsin Right to Life Victory Fund		$49,838	Conservative	$92,500
A New Voice for Maryland	supports Rubin	$49,010	Liberal	$100,000
Victory 2016	supports Walker	$42,972	Conservative	$214,046
Florida Freedom PAC		$42,779	Liberal	$0
Unifying America PAC	opposes Donovan	$40,000	Liberal	$40,100
Future In America		$37,000		$57,050
Colorado Conservative PAC		$35,000	Conservative	$10,000
California's New Frontier		$34,489		$89,000
New Power PAC		$33,686	Liberal	$5,249
Restore American Freedom & Liberty		$32,000	Conservative	$215,693
Conservative Outsider PAC	opposes Banks	$28,078	Conservative	$0
Community Action Now	supports Lee	$27,898	Liberal	$354,999
Faith Family Freedom Fund		$27,239	Conservative	$63,614
Go Big Go Bold PAC	supports Walker	$26,633	Conservative	$209,906
21st Century Leaders		$26,580		$0
Jobs, Opportunity & Freedom PAC		$26,153	Conservative	$20,100
Middle Class Values Pac		$25,360		$0
Freethought Equality Super PAC	supports Raskin	$23,866	Liberal	$57,064
Blue America PAC IE Committee		$22,321	Liberal	$28,223

GROUP	SUPPORTS/ OPPOSES	INDEPENDENT EXPENDITURES	VIEWPOINT	TOTAL RAISED
Forward Philadelphia PAC		$19,865	Conservative	$11,100
Working for Maryland		$18,000		$0
State Conservative Reform Action PAC		$17,645	Conservative	$60,000
Fight for Tomorrow		$16,906	Conservative	$90,500
Watchdog PAC		$16,000		$162,030
Make America Awesome		$14,176		$38,668
Millennials Rising	supports Bush	$14,050	Conservative	$55,153
Rampart PAC	supports Stutzman	$13,650	Conservative	$28,530
RGA Right Direction		$13,376	Conservative	$6,356,720
Person to Person PAC		$13,088	Conservative	$24,655
Restore the Constitution Coalition		$11,500	Conservative	$56,868
Forever Free PAC	supports Paul	$11,380	Conservative	$55,412
Get Our Jobs Back		$10,166		$0
Mayday PAC		$8,675	Liberal	$303,297
Restoring Prosperity Fund		$8,535	Conservative	$8,835
Clean Slate Baltimore PAC		$8,443	Liberal	$474,064
Freedom and Liberty PAC		$6,350		$5,000
Do the Right Thing		$6,130		$15,010
Friends of Traditional Banking		$6,048	Conservative	$104,470
Keep Louisiana Working	opposes Landrieu	$5,685	Conservative	$0
America Speaks PAC		$5,000		$20,000
Tea Party Army		$4,893	Conservative	$19,052
Climate Hawks Vote		$4,719	Liberal	$38,525
Committee to Elect a Progressive Congress		$4,543	Liberal	$4,699
Veterans Against the Deal		$4,480		$0

(continues)

GROUP	SUPPORTS/ OPPOSES	INDEPENDENT EXPENDITURES	VIEWPOINT	TOTAL RAISED
Inland Empire Taxpayers Assn		$3,559	Conservative	$5
Women Speak Out PAC		$3,525	Conservative	$961,336
Progressive Kick	supports Sanders	$2,885	Liberal	$308,416
North Carolina Priorities		$2,875	Conservative	$7,315
Colorado Priorities		$2,867	Conservative	$7,907
Tarr, Donna Murphy Mrs.		$2,849		$0
Buffalo for Bernie Sanders	supports Sanders	$2,532	Liberal	$3,088
Iowa Priorities		$2,315	Conservative	$6,754
Brighter Future Fund		$2,195	Conservative	$0
Freedom Unincorporated		$2,086		$7,161
Louisiana Priorities		$2,067	Conservative	$9,034
New York Capital Region for Bringing Economic Revolution		$2,017		$6,832
Conservative Liberty Coalition		$2,000	Conservative	$54,935
Bluegrass Rural PAC	opposes McConnell	$1,658		$4,765
Montgomery County Tea Party		$1,628	Conservative	$28,326
Art of the Deal		$1,500	Conservative	$4,371
US Transportation Technology & Energy		$1,500		$4,000
All Citizens for Mississippi	supports Cochran	$1,259	Conservative	$0
Human Rights Campaign Equality Votes		$1,172	Liberal	$316,154
Broadhurst, Gerald Jack Jr.		$1,045		$0

GROUP	SUPPORTS/ OPPOSES	INDEPENDENT EXPENDITURES	VIEWPOINT	TOTAL RAISED
Freedom & Opportunity PAC		$1,010	Conservative	$10,087
Karen J Hay		$914		$0
Reclaim Chicago		$739	Liberal	$0
Sierra Club		$674	Liberal	$0
James E. Kaufman		$529		$0
Las Cruces for Bernie	supports Sanders	$510	Liberal	$5,248
Collective Actions PAC	supports Sanders	$443	Liberal	$8,795
Protecting Choice in California		$416	Liberal	$130,430
Kathy Yurista		$330		$0
We Vote—Nosotros Votamos		$316	Liberal	$3,510
Bring Back American Opportunity	supports Trump	$179	Conservative	$179
Human Action Super PAC	supports Paul	$150	Conservative	$7,035
Together We Thrive		$139		$180
Mission16		$114	Liberal	$1,847
Student Debt Reform PAC		$113	Liberal	$608
America's Teachers	supports Clinton	$109	Liberal	$1,828
Nicholas Thomas Rapak PAC		$80		$199
To Eliminate Doubt: Committee to Reveal the Unknown		$12		$12

While the super-PACs are major sources of funding, their influence in the 2015–2016 primary cycle has been surprisingly ineffective. As of May 2016, Hillary Clinton is the presumptive nominee of the Democratic Party, Bernie Sanders, who declined super-PAC money, remains a powerful influence with many supporters. On the Republican side, Donald Trump has become the presumptive nominee with little super-PAC support (two of the top contributors) and substantial super-PAC opposition (three of the top contributors). Ted Cruz, Trump's most determined primary rival, had the support of no less than seven super-PACs, but managed to win only two state primary contests.

An election year in which the outsiders have shaken the establishment candidates along with the established political parties threatens to disrupt the commonsense assumption that federal elections—and the legislation, regulations, preferences, and contracts that result from them—can be bought, provided the buyer has sufficiently deep pockets. The impact this will have on our elections going forward is still very much an open question. Even more speculative is the impact it will have on federal spending, the national debt, and the nation's economy. That there will an effect on elections, spending, the debt, and the economy is, however, certain.

WHAT TAXES COST US

TAX PLANS AND POLICY CHOICES

Within the 74,608 pages currently associated with the IRS code and federal tax regulations, anyone with sufficient resources can find a way to do almost anything to save millions or even make millions. Those without such resources, well, they're pretty much lost and abandoned.

The federal income tax became law in 1913. During its first twenty-six years, the volume of tax-related statutes, regulations, and case law grew modestly, from 400 to 504 pages. By 1984, it stood at 26,300 pages. Today, its length is about three times that. Such growth is no accident. It is deliberate policy, and this chapter explores how our tax policy had been hijacked for partisan purposes.

CHAPTER 12

ABANDON

ALL

HOPE?

According to the obituary that appeared in *The New York Times* on August 27, 1985, Leo Mattersdorf was an "Author and Tax Accountant," former secretary of the National Tax Association, and a director of the American Institute of Certified Public Accountants. He was also a former chairman of the Amateur Astronomers Association in New York and sufficiently avid in pursuit of this hobby to have written *Insight into Astronomy* (later published in paperback as *A Key to the Heavens*). "The book," the obituary proclaimed, "was proofread by Albert Einstein, who was an accounting client of Mr. Mattersdorf for many years."[1]

Twenty-seven years before his death, in February 1963, a letter by Mattersdorf was published in *Time Magazine*:

One year while I was at his Princeton home preparing his return, Mrs. Einstein, who was then still living, asked me to stay for lunch. During the course of the meal, the professor turned to me and with his inimitable chuckle said: "The hardest thing in the world to understand is income taxes." I replied: "There is one thing more difficult, and that is your theory of relativity." "Oh, no," he replied, "that is easy." To which Mrs. Einstein commented, "Yes, for you."[2]

Cute, huh? See, like even the smartest dude who ever lived had trouble doing his income tax. Feel better now?

But that's not really the point. The point is that Albert Einstein was not just making an idle joke for the benefit of his tax accountant and friend. He meant exactly what he said, and we need to take him at his word. The theory of relativity really *is* easy—at least compared to the 2,412,000-word-long Internal Revenue Code and the Federal Tax Regulations, which clocks in at 7,655,000 words. That is a total of 10,067,000 words, and it doesn't even count the incredibly voluminous, ever-growing body of tax-related case law on which much legal interpretation of the code and the regulations depends. The length of this is actually impossible to calculate.[3] If you figure an 8-by-5-inch page holds about 380 words (Times New Roman, 12 point, double-spaced), that's 26,492 pages.

So now we understand Einstein's comment, right? Federal tax regulations and law are just too high a data mountain for any mortal to climb. Actually, another way to measure the sheer volume of U.S. tax law is to look at the number of pages in *CCH Standard Federal Tax Reporter*, a reference published by CCH, a division of the Wolters Kluwer accounting group. This publication includes the IRS code, selected regulations, material on court cases, revenue rulings, and explanatory material. When Albert Einstein died in 1955, the page count of the *CCH Standard Federal Tax Reporter* was "just" 14,000 pages (this is the 1954 figure).[4]

That's still a lot to wade through, of course, but I don't think the volume of data alone was what Einstein found so daunting.

We get closer to the meaning of Einstein's remark if we look at the growth of the CCH publication rather its page count at any particular point in time[5]:

1913	400 pages
1939	504 pages
1945	8,200 pages
1954	14,000 pages
1969	16,500 pages
1974	19,500 pages
1984	26,300 pages
1995	40,500 pages
2004	60,044 pages
2007	67,204 pages
2010	71,684 pages
2011	72,536 pages
2012	73,608 pages
2013	73,954 pages
2015	74,608 pages

We think of figuring taxes as calculating a number. That is certainly the way Einstein thought of relativity. Conceptually, relativity theory is counterintuitive and therefore hard to understand. Nevertheless, it is ultimately capable of being expressed—*calculated*—mathematically by a very simple equation familiar to just about everyone: $E = mc^2$. As it turns out, calculating one's "correct" tax liability—expressing it with mathematical certainty and clarity—is far more difficult. In fact, for many, perhaps most, taxpayers, it is impossible or nearly so. Sure, you can come up with a number, maybe even a plausible number. But is it an accurate number? A real number? A valid value? To determine this, you may have to plow through more than ten million words, plus applicable case law, and then attempt to apply the relevant portions of this material to your particular instance. Even then, a range of possibly valid—or possibly criminal—possibilities may still exist.

In the case of most problems, additional knowledge and analysis lead to a form of simplification we call understanding. Relativity theory, which presents a level of complexity that quite literally defies common sense, can nevertheless be distilled into three mathematically unambiguous variables and an exponent. But when it comes to United States income tax policy, no matter how much accumulated knowledge and analysis we apply, the result is not the simplification called understanding, but a veritable metastasis of data, from 400 pages at the inception of the federal income tax in 1913 to 74,608 (and counting) today. If determining the valid mathematical value of one's tax obligation has become a needle in a haystack, U.S. tax policy has succeeded only in adding hay to the stack—bales of it, truckloads of it, seagoing cargo holds of it.

Einstein's relativity, it turns out, is an absolute. It has a correct answer, a valid value. In contrast, the relativity created by more than 10 million words, a legacy of case law, an army of accountants and attorneys, a legion of special interests, and fifty-two congresses since 1913 is without solution. It is pure relativity— genuinely *relative* relativity, a relativity capable of virtually infinite manipulation. Income taxes really *are* the "hardest thing in the world to understand." No joke!

WELL, THAT JUST AIN'T RIGHT

"The tax code is so confusing," political satirist P. J. O'Rourke observed, "that every time a federal appointment is made the appointee has to go before a congressional committee to explain how he got so confused that he didn't pay his taxes."[6]

Another joke? Not really. "Polls show that people consistently believe the federal tax burden to be significantly higher than it actually is, and few know that close to half of all tax filers either pay no federal income taxes at all or get a refund; that is, they have a negative tax rate."[7] The tax code, grown to quasi-infinite proportions, along with federal regulations and case law, is supposed to make income taxes efficient and fair. At the start of the 20th century, a majority of Americans actually clamored for a "progressive" tax on income and were overjoyed when the Sixteenth Amendment was ratified, making income taxes the law of the land. Now, at long last, people would be taxed according to their income. The poor, the middling, and the rich would all pay their fair share—not a penny less, not a penny more.

Ten-million-plus words later, this is anything but the case. Even worse, tax policy and the tax code have created an inefficient source of revenue for the nation. In 2015, federal income tax provided just 47% of federal tax revenue. Payroll taxes added another 33%. Payroll taxes are an old-fashioned, unfair "regressive" tax by which all but the wealthiest pay in tax the same percentage of their wages: 6.2%, with employers picking up another 6.2%, for a total tax of 12.4%. (The self-employed are stuck with paying the whole 12.4%.) The corporate income taxes paid by businesses yielded 11% of federal tax revenue in 2015, and, together, excise, estate, and "other taxes" (including profits on assets held by the Federal Reserve) chipped in enough to take care of 9%.

Now, if you have taken away nothing else from this book so far, you know very well that federal receipts, most of which come from all federal taxes, have for a very long time been insufficient to cover federal outlays. The result was a deficit of **$438.406 billion** for FY 2015 and an estimated **$615.805 billion** for FY 2016.[9] The shortfall in those two most recent years, as always, was covered with borrowed money, the interest on which added to the deficit and the debt.

If you are among the approximately 60% of U.S. taxpayers who, in 2015–2016, paid a "tax professional" to complete your return,[10] congratulations! You have surrendered to the ineluctable impenetrability of the tax code, just as Albert Einstein, the guy who explained the whole universe, did in the 1950s.

Well, that just ain't right.

Taxes should be, if not simple, at least transparent, comprehensible, and, *ultimately* absolute rather than subject to virtually infinite *relativity*—something even Einstein was unwilling to put up with. After all, the core purpose of any tax system is quite straightforward. It is "to raise the revenue needed to pay the government's bills," as tax historian, Reagan-era domestic adviser, and Treasury official under George H. W. Bush Bruce Bartlett puts it.[11] No more, no less.

Clearly, however, our government's tax system has failed to achieve this purpose in that:

- Many people who should be taxpayers pay no taxes (and some even manage to achieve a negative tax rate).
- Taxes are apportioned neither fairly nor even rationally.
- Most of all, the taxes collected unfairly and irrationally are not even sufficient to pay the government's bills.

GOOD LORD, HOW DID WE GET HERE?

To formulate a tax system that raises the revenues to pay the government's bills, Bruce Bartlett quite reasonably suggests that it is best to "start with a clear philosophy of what government should do and how much it should spend, and only then decide how to raise taxes."[12] This is not a conservative idea, a liberal idea, or a partisan idea. It is a very sensible idea. Too bad the makers of American tax policy have forgotten it, inadvertently ignore it, or deliberately reject it.

Let's go back to the beginning of the United States. The American Revolution was won in 1783. Two years earlier, in 1781, the embattled colonies drew up Articles of Confederation to facilitate governing, especially in a time of war. The Articles did not create a nation as we now typically think of a nation. Instead, they vaguely defined a "confederation" of states with a central "federal" government that was, by design, weak, so that the individual states would have most of the power to govern themselves. The greatest weakness of the federal government was its inability to tax anything or anyone. The federal government was totally dependent on the individual states to provide it with revenue to be used for the common good. The financial demands of the ongoing revolution were hard on the states, as was the economic climate that followed the revolution's successful conclusion. Hard-pressed, the states put paying the federal government very low on their list of priorities. As a result, the confederation was quickly swamped by financial crisis.

So, at the very beginning, America's seekers of independence failed to start with what Bruce Bartlett says is necessary to start with, namely "a clear philosophy of what government should do and how much it should spend." Fortunately, among the founders were exceptionally imaginative and innovative men who found a way to start fresh. They drew up a Constitution to replace the Articles of Confederation. Although one major function of the Constitution is to limit the power of the federal government, it did something the Articles avoided doing. It *created* a federal government made viable, largely, through possession of the power to levy and collect taxes independently of the states. As with much else in the Constitution, the parameters of the government's powers of taxation were left vague. They were outlines to be filled in. Potentially, however, the federal government was left with the option of taxing whatever it deemed taxable—except for exports and income.

The proscription against taxing exports is easy to understand and reflects a key aspect of the infant Republic's governing philosophy: to nurture exports and thereby build the national economy and dignity by giving the world a good reason to recognize, respect, and do business with the new country. Putting exports off-limits to taxation is perhaps the very first example of a tax preference in federal tax policy. Here was a category of income declared immune to taxation. This constitutional provision may be seen as the prototype of how tax law can be used to encourage aspects of economic and political development.

The second limitation, the bar on "direct taxation"—that is, taxing the income or profits of the person who pays the tax rather than taxing goods or services—is even more important. Some tax reformers argue that the framers of the Constitution considered the notion of taxing income and profit so abhorrent that they specified it as one of the only two forbidden categories of taxation. These reformers go on to argue that the Sixteenth Amendment, adopted to overcome this proscription, was nothing more or less than a very bad idea. In fact, this interpretation may offer some valid insight into the framers' state of mind; however, their more immediate reason for including the bar on "direct taxes" was the desire of the slaveholding southern states to prevent the federal government from taxing slaves. Such taxation would not only be costly in itself, but could be wielded as an economic-political instrument to ultimately force the abolition of slavery by making it too expensive. In any case, income tax would not debut in the United States until the unprecedented financial demands of the Civil War sent the Lincoln administration on a frenzied treasure hunt for additional revenue.

As it was, the two constitutional limits on federal taxing power were not enough to stave off some passionate, even violent, resistance to federal taxation. The federal excise tax on whiskey provoked an armed rebellion during 1791–1794, mostly among farmers in western Pennsylvania. The so-called Whiskey Rebellion prompted President George Washington to federalize the militias of New Jersey, Maryland, Virginia, and Pennsylvania, creating a force of nearly 13,000 troops, to suppress the insurrection. Deftly, Washington's secretary of the treasury, Alexander Hamilton, acting in the wake of the Whiskey Rebellion, moved for federal assumption of the debts states had incurred during the American Revolution. This prompted the rapid reduction of state taxes and, in the process, won widespread acceptance of the principle of federal taxes.

Excise taxes such as that on whiskey (among other goods) were not the primary revenue source of the federal government in the early days of the Republic. Prior to the Civil War, import tariffs produced some 90% of all federal revenue. Tariffs offered two benefits in addition to revenue. First, they were a kind of socially fair progressive tax. Since only the wealthy could afford to regularly purchase imported goods, the tariff burdened them more than it did less affluent citizens. Second, by adding cost to imported goods, tariffs encouraged the development and growth of domestic manufacturing enterprises by protecting them from foreign competition. The downside of this was that tariffs favored the North, which was far more industrialized than the South. The predominantly agricultural economy of the South depended heavily on exporting cotton, lumber, and other agricultural produce in exchange for manufactured goods from abroad. Because the South took in more imports than the North did, the cost of the tariffs hit the South disproportionately, whereas the North disproportionately enjoyed the benefits of the tariffs. The tariffs were as much a cornerstone of the northern economy as slavery was key to the southern economy. This put the federal government at odds with the agricultural, slaveholding South. Indeed, we could reasonably argue that federal tax policy played an essential role in causing the Civil War.

Up to the Civil War, federal taxation was simple and efficient. What is more, it paid the bills! It paid them year after year, so that the American people became accustomed to a government that, for the most part, spent no more than it took in. And if it did need to borrow, the resulting debt was discharged as quickly as possible. This principle in itself—pay for what you spend, and when you borrow, pay it back right away—implied the existence of that "clear philosophy" of government Bartlett wrote of. Americans wanted a government that, whatever else it did, lived within its means.

A bolt from the blue and the gray, the Civil War disrupted all of this. It brought an urgent and spectacular need for revenue. Some of it could—and would—be borrowed, but Lincoln and his cabinet understood that it would be ruinous to try to borrow it all. For this reason, in August 1861 a 3% tax was levied on annual incomes over $800. The Lincoln administration gambled that the war emergency would check any legal challenge that might be based on the constitutional prohibition against direct taxes. The first law was soon repealed and replaced the next year with a 3% tax on incomes between **$600** and **$10,000**. Incomes higher than this were taxed at 5%, and, in 1864, the law was amended to raise the rate to 5% on incomes between **$600** and **$5,000**, 7.5% on incomes in the **$5,000–$10,000** range, and 10% on everything higher.

By 1866, the year after the Civil War ended, income taxes brought in 55% of federal revenues, but the law was so unpopular that it was allowed to expire in 1872.[13] It was replaced by an expansion in excise taxes on alcohol and tobacco, which, by the end of the century, accounted for 43% of federal revenue, with import tariffs raising an additional 41%. Seeking to reduce the tariffs that were working a hardship on the agricultural South and West, Democrats, in 1894, sponsored and passed a 2% flat-rate tax on incomes over **$4,000** (approximately **$105,000** in today's money). The Supreme Court found the tax unconstitutional (*Pollock v. Farmers' Loan and Trust Co.* [1895]),[14] but popular agitation for a *progressive* income tax grew and, in 1909, Republican president William Howard Taft supported a constitutional amendment to permit the tax. Taft was no champion of the social merits of progressive taxation, but he did want to mollify those who were clamoring for tariff cuts, which would hurt the Republicans' strong base in the domestic manufacturing sector.

The proposed Sixteenth Amendment slowly worked its way to ratification, which came in 1913, virtually on the eve of the inauguration of Democrat Woodrow Wilson, who acted quickly in coaxing Congress not only to legislate a permanent income tax, but also to cut tariffs. (Taft be damned.) At its debut, the new income tax imposed a 1% rate on earners with incomes greater than the personal exemption of **$3,000** (equivalent to about **$72,500** in today's money).[15] The top rate was 7% on incomes above **$500,000** (over **$12 million** in today's currency). These rates did not last for long, however. When the Great War (World War I) broke out in Europe in 1914, the United States firmly asserted its absolute neutrality—yet Congress raised the rates that year in anticipation of eventual U.S. entry into the war. In 1916, the rates were hiked again for the same reason. In 1917, after the United States entered the war in April, another rise was instituted, so that, by 1918, the last year of the war, the lowest rate was 6% on incomes above **$1,000** (about **$24,000** today), with the top rate soaring to a virtually confiscatory 77% on incomes over **$1 million** (**$24 million**, more or less, in today's money). The rates were reduced after the war, but never came close to their prewar levels. The lowest rate was 4%, the highest 73%. The brackets were the same as during the war, but substantial postwar inflation actually lowered the real income levels at which the rates became effective.

Groaning under the weight of the new income tax levels, the electorate agitated for tax cuts, the promise of which helped to propel Republican Warren G. Harding to a landslide victory against the Democratic ticket of James M. Cox and Franklin D. Roosevelt in 1920. Under his Treasury secretary Andrew Mellon (who also served Harding's successor, Calvin Coolidge), income tax rates plummeted to 0.375% at the low end and 24% at the top—the threshold for which, however, was significantly lowered to **$100,000** (some **$1.336 million** today).

People were generally happy about their government and the economy. Except for a brief recession, the 1920s not only saw a reduction in the income tax rates, but also substantial reductions in the national debt, both under Harding and his successor, Calvin Coolidge. The stock market crash of 1929, however, kicked off the Great Depression, which cut federal revenues by 50% between 1930 and 1932. Historical mythology paints Herbert Hoover as obtusely refusing to commit federal funds to relief measures. As discussed in Chapter 2, he certainly had reservations about doling out federal funds to individuals, but he nevertheless authorized emergency relief programs that elevated spending by 40% in four years and increased the federal debt by 33%. Anxious to increase federal revenue, Hoover secured hikes in the income tax. The new rate jumped back to 4% at the bottom and settled at 63% on incomes above **$100,000** (**$1.574 million** today). This was bitter medicine during a time of high unemployment and reduced wages, but far worse was his insistence on levying a laundry list of excise taxes. The budget was balanced, but the

Depression deepened, and the stage was set for a disruption to the American economy—and American tax policy—even bigger than that wrought by World War I.

THROWN TO THE WOLVES

After defeating Hoover by a landslide in November 1932, Democrat Franklin D. Roosevelt launched the emergency relief and "New Deal" programs discussed in Chapter 2. The new president also made radical changes in the income tax rates. In 1935, he persuaded Congress to raise the top rate to 79%. On the face of it, this looked like confiscatory redistribution of wealth—and, to this day, some of FDR's detractors accuse him of precisely this sin. In fact, 1935's hike to 79% was accompanied by a sharp rise in the threshold income at which this would kick in: **$5 million**, which is equivalent to **$87.321 million** today. Reportedly, only a single person in all of the United States was a candidate for the top rate, John D. Rockefeller Jr.

Roosevelt never expected to raise sufficient revenue by soaking the rich. Yet he *would* soak the rich. He explained why to E. D. Coblentz, an "emissary" from publishing titan William Randolph Hearst:

> I am fighting Communism, Huey Longism, . . . I want to save our system, the capitalist system; to save it is to give some heed to the world thought of today, I want to equalize the distribution of wealth. [Louisiana senator] Huey Long says that 92% of the wealth in this country is controlled by 8% of the population. He would change this situation by giving a five-thousand-dollar home to each head of a family, twenty-five hundred dollars a year, etc. To combat this and similar crackpot ideas, it may be necessary to throw to the wolves the forty-six men who are reported to have incomes in excess of one million dollars a year. This can be accomplished through taxation.[16]

Clearly, Roosevelt did not expect that these forty-six million-aires would yield sufficient revenue to bring about a general redistribution of wealth, no matter how hard he squeezed them. Their sacrifice, however, would serve a symbolic purpose per-haps sufficient to check the "crackpot" threats against America's Depression-beleaguered democratic capitalism. As he said in a message to Congress on June 19, 1935, "People know that vast personal incomes come not only through the effort or ability or luck of those who receive them, but also because of the opportu-nities for advantage which government itself contributes. There-fore, the duty rests upon the government to restrict such incomes by very high taxes."[17]

Wielding tax policy to restrict the highest incomes and thereby defend democracy was a radical new use for the tax system and a sharp shift from simply raising "the revenue needed to pay the government's bills."

Restricting top incomes—radical? Yes. Rational? Maybe not so much.

And we should, while we're at it, question the rationality of another form of taxation instituted two years later. We think of Social Security as a government *benefit*, but it is also a *tax*—a radical and regressive tax on payroll itself. It was first collected in 1937 at the flat rate of 2%, regardless of the size of the paycheck. Its purpose was to finance post-retirement Social Security pay-ments, but in the "short" term (that is, until the worker retired, which, in the case of a young worker, could be a very long time), Social Security was a substantial tax increase on the working population—the very people among whom Roosevelt aimed to redistribute some of the top-end wealth. Indeed, many of these workers earned too little to pay income taxes, so that the payroll tax represented for them a tax hike of 100%.

The entry of the United States into World War II in 1941 threw all taxpayers to the wolves—albeit as a matter of national sur-vival. For those with incomes above **$200,000 ($3.255 million** today), the rate was 94%. For those at the bottom, making more than **$500** a year (**$8,138** in today's money), the rate vaulted from 4% to 23%. This was a shock, surely, but people not only accepted it, they contributed even more to the war effort through the purchase of war stamps and bonds. The problem is that, as with the "emergency" measures enacted during the Great Depression, the emergency that was World War II never quite lifted. After the war, tax rates were reduced, but they settled well above their prewar levels: The top rate inched down to 82.1%, and the bottom rate to 16.6%. The Cold War, with its two major hot wars—in Korea (1950–1953) and in Vietnam (1955–1975)—kept military spending high, while President Eisenhower's well-founded fear of deficit spending blocked tax cuts for eight years.

THE INCOME TAX ELIXIR

Many Americans old enough to have grown up in the 1950s remember the Eisenhower years with nostalgia. Business, by and large, was booming, and, for an unprecedented number of families, the American dream was a reality. Yet as a new decade brought a new, young president, John F. Kennedy, there was a widespread feeling that the economy was slipping into the doldrums and needed a boost. JFK's Keynesian advisers wanted a program of federal spending to stimulate growth. Despite the contrast between Eisenhower, who left office a benign old man, and Kennedy, who entered office on the premise, as he put it in his inaugural address, that the "torch had been passed to a new generation," JFK leaned toward conservative economic policies. He resisted the call to increase spending, but heeded the recommendation that tax policy be used instead of spending to provide an economic stimulus. Cut the tax rate substantially, and both supply and demand would receive a shot in the arm, he believed.

Kennedy asked Congress to lower the top income tax rate from 91% to 65% and the bottom rate to 14% from 20%. Despite initial trepidation, Wall Street endorsed the move—but Kennedy fell to an assassin's bullet before Congress passed the legislation. Lyndon Johnson picked up where JFK had left off—but asked that the top rate be reduced to 70% rather than 65%. At first, the results were highly encouraging, as the economy heated up nicely. By the end of the 1960s, however, it became too hot, with most economists and most voters in agreement that inflation had become America's number-one economic problem.

The Kennedy and Johnson administrations had used taxes not merely to raise revenue in order to pay the government's bill, but also as an elixir to energize a sluggish economy. This set a precedent. What is more, when the manipulation of tax policy resulted in runaway inflation, tax policy was yet again chosen as the key economic lever. In 1968, LBJ levied a regressive 10% surtax on *everyone's* income taxes, regardless of bracket. This induced a moderate recession, which certainly did lower the rate of inflation.

Asa we saw in Chapter 3, the administration of John F. Kennedy elevated to a position of great influence the Council of Economic Advisers (CEA), a group of esteemed academic economists who believe that enlightened manipulation of any and all available economic levers was an enlightened way to manage the economy. Tax policy, which had been exclusively a matter of generating revenue to run the government, was now just another lever waiting to be pushed or pulled. The takeaway from the Kennedy-Johnson experiment in experimental economic policy, however, was that all those levers were interconnected—often in ways invisible to those who decided which ones to pull, which ones to push, and which ones to leave alone. The interconnection produced any number of unintended consequences, including, in the case of inflation that was either generated or exacerbated by tax rate cuts, an amplification of the damage. Inflation raises both prices and wages. While a higher wage enables workers to pay those higher prices, it also pushes workers into a higher tax bracket, so that they are taxed at a higher rate. The net result for a given family may be a *reduction* in purchasing power and in savings—a decline caused by the toxic combination of a higher wage coupled with a higher tax bracket.

The perfect storm of spending created by the combination of

LBJ's "guns and butter" economy (Chapter 3) created deficits and debt that his successor, Richard Nixon, sought to address in part by abandoning the gold standard and floating the U.S. dollar (Chapter 3). This created an especially nasty witch's brew known as stagflation, which poisoned both the Ford and Carter years. The solution that presidential candidate Ronald Reagan proposed was a new tax cut in the spirit of JFK: a rate reduction across all brackets. Rates fell from 70% to 50% at the top and 14% to 11% at the bottom. Five years later, the Tax Reform Act of 1986 raised the bottom rate to 15% even as it lowered the top rate to 28% in line with the "supply-side"/"trickle-down" notion that reducing the tax burden on "job creators" would lift the whole economy. George H. W. Bush, who succeeded Reagan on a promise of no new taxes ("read my lips"), raised the top rate to 31%. To liberal and moderate voters, this seemed at least a baby step toward restoring fairness in tax policy, but it lost the G. H. W. Bush conservative support and, of greater consequence, according to Bruce Bartlett, it "poisoned the well for future tax reforms."[18] All that non-conservatives noted (with disdain) in the 1986 bill was the reduction in the top income tax rate. If they had looked closer, they would have seen that the cut was made in exchange for reforms that closed loopholes (tax preferences) that favored the wealthiest taxpayers. When the senior Bush raised the top rate in 1990, he did not restore the preferences. To conservatives, this seemed to demonstrate that G. H. W. Bush's tax reform was wealth distribution in disguise.

Loss of conservative enthusiasm for George H. W. Bush in 1992 helped send Bill Clinton to the White House. He prevailed on Congress to raise the top rate to 39.6% the year he took office. At the same time, however, he pushed the threshold for that rate up from **$86,500** to **$250,000** (about **$415,000** today) for individuals, and **$500,000** (about **$828,000** today) for couples. This moderated a tax increase that nevertheless produced a reduction in the deficit as well as in spending. Contrary to all Republican expectation, the "New Democrat" Clinton introduced a level of fiscal conservatism that had not been seen since before the Great Depression.

WE DON'T GET NO SATISFACTION

Bill Clinton left office with a surplus rather than a deficit. Politics can do strange things to what most people under most circumstances agree on as reality. In his 2000 campaign, Republican presidential candidate George W. Bush argued that we should get no satisfaction from the Clinton surplus. Although it represented 2.4% of GDP, he asserted that this was far from being a good thing and was, in fact, a dangerous thing—for the simple reason that Congress would probably spend it. He pledged instead to use the surplus as a predicate for cutting taxes, which he did. The surplus duly vanished, and the presidency of the junior Bush ended with a deficit representing 3.2% of GDP—a total reversal of 5.6%.

To Bush's credit, he believed that cutting taxes would stimulate the economy. So powerful had the belief become that tax policy is not merely about paying the government's bills, but is also a formula for concocting elixirs to work magic on the national economy, Bush continued to cut taxes even after two costly wars got underway following 9/11, one in Afghanistan, the other in Iraq. A great deal of money was borrowed, the tax cut elixir failed to do its stuff, and the economy all but imploded in 2007–2008. As for Bush's successor, Barack Obama, he announced as his policy that the Bush tax cuts would be allowed to expire as scheduled at the end of 2010, but then, in the eleventh hour, he agreed to a two-year extension of the cuts—which, as it turned out, endured throughout the Obama presidency. In tax policy, "temporary" measures have a way of becoming permanent. This has been true since the Civil War.

"IT DEPENDS UPON WHAT

THE MEANING OF THE WORD 'IS' IS"

Perhaps you recall when President Bill Clinton, testifying before a grand jury on the truthfulness of his denial of a sexual relationship with White House intern Monica Lewinsky, questioned the meaning of the word *is*? "If...'is' means is and never has been...that is one thing. If it means there is none, [what I said] was a completely true statement."[19] Blithely disputing so basic a verb hardly cast the president in a rosy light. How much gloomier, then, is the light that shines upon the makers of American income tax policy when we discover that they have yet to define, in law, the meaning of *income*.[20]

That's right. In more than 10 million words of tax code and regulation, the IRS has been able to come up with only these measly seven words to define *income*: "means all income from whatever source derived."[21] There has been endless dispute over counting as income capital gains, savings, rent, dividends, and interest. Some economists define income as what one takes out of the economy. Others define income to include what one *could* take out if one wanted to—for instance, *unrealized* capital gains. Prior to passage of the Mortgage Forgiveness Debt Relief Act of 2007, the IRS could consider the cancellation of mortgage debt due to foreclosure on one's primary residence as taxable income. Chew on this: The bank clawed back your house when you couldn't pay your mortgage on it. You were then potentially liable for taxes on the amount of the loan cancelled or forgiven.[22] Prior to the 2007 legislation, as far as the IRS was concerned, your financial downfall was a financial windfall in disguise. You lucky devil.

Because *income* is so vaguely defined, there is a fundamental disconnect between the income people actually take home and the distribution tables the Treasury Department and the congressional Joint Committee on Taxation use to evaluate, rationalize, and justify the economic and individual impact of each proposed tax bill. The tables are built on data that never shows up on income tax returns for the simple reason that the IRS never asks for it. This data includes unreported and underreported income, pension contributions, nontaxable transfer payments, employer-provided fringe benefits, and other non-taxable forms of income. "Much of the complexity of the tax code results because a [given] tax bill was being tweaked to make the distribution tables come out right."[23]

Other aspects of "income" also remain open issues. For instance:[24]

- *The "tax unit."* As originally conceived, income tax was a tax on individual income. This seemed straightforward enough until the U.S. Supreme Court ruled in *Poe v. Seaborn* (1930)[25] that married couples living in community property states (which divide household income 50/50 between spouses) could be taxed as if the husband and wife each earned half the couple's total income. In 1930, when very few couples consisted of two income earners, this gave an unlegislated tax advantage to couples living in community property states. Filing as individuals, as if each "earned" half the income reported, single-earner couples in community property states paid less income tax than single-earner couples living in non-community property states. Very soon, vote-hungry legislators in non-community states fell all over one another to give their constituents a tax break by passing community property laws. Faced with the prospect of significantly reduced tax revenue, Congress revised the tax code to tax individuals and married couples differently. This sometimes resulted in two-earner families paying more on their combined income than if they filed separately. More laws were passed, but, thanks to progressive tax rates that are subject to legislative change, the problem has yet to be fully solved.
- *The time period.* Also never perfectly resolved is what would seem the self-evident question of the time period over which to tax people. We file returns on a yearly basis, and for many

of us, this works out just fine. We are taxed on our salary for the calendar year. But not everyone earns a regular salary. Some people take home a large chunk one year and little or nothing in some others. You may be taxed like a millionaire in a good year, even though, on average, you are barely getting by.

MADNESS AND METHOD

Ten million words—yet certitude remains as elusive as Bill Clinton's understanding of "is" or the government's definition of *income*. Once a nation decides to tax more than property and goods, their importation and their consumption, and turns as well to taxing income, the enterprise of creating a tax system that is both efficient and fair as well as an instrument of broader political, social, and economic policy becomes the mother of all games of Jenga.

You know Jenga—that block-stacking game in which players take turns removing one block at a time from a block tower, then try to balance each removed block on top of the tower—without, of course, knocking over the increasingly unstable edifice. To address one fault or inequity in the tax code often creates other faults and inequities, which then have to be addressed. Fixing these affects other aspects of code, often creating additional problems. Sooner than you think, you have compiled millions of words and tens of thousands of pages. If the tax code is a giant Jenga tower, its entrance should be graced with the words of Dante: "Abandon hope, all ye who enter here."

But—and this is important—we should also add Shakespeare's Polonius: "Though this be madness, yet there is method in't." The voluminous complexity of the tax code and tax regulations is not exclusively the incidental and unfortunate side effect of tweaking a very complex, intensively dynamic system. The complexity is also purposeful and deliberate. It enables individuals, corporations, and political interests to invest their assets and talents in reshaping, distorting, exploiting, and even altogether escaping one of the only two things Ben Franklin pronounced "certain"—taxes. Given a sufficiently shrewd and rapacious will, taxes can be transformed into subsidies and preferences that create secret social safety-net programs, middle- and upper-end entitlements, and the boundless bounty of corporate welfare. These things are the subjects of the next chapter.

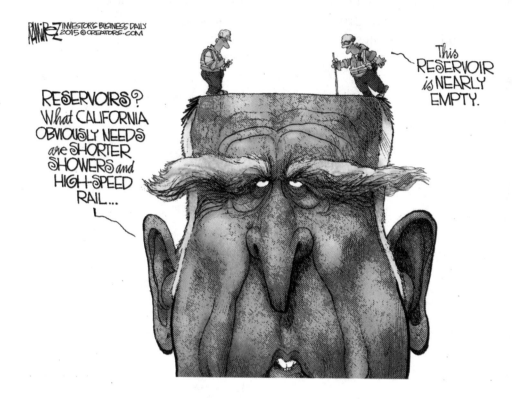

The fantastic complexity of our federal tax code and regulations is the ideal platform on which to build an inherently deceptive tax policy, which labels spending as tax cuts, exemptions, deductions, and credits. These constitute secret social safety-net programs, middle- and upper-end entitlements, and the boundless bounty of corporate welfare. Far from being a one-way means of collecting revenue, our federal tax code creates the equivalent of stealth subsidies and covert preferences that make intelligent, reality-based budget decisions nearly impossible.

CHAPTER 13

WHEN

SUBSIDIES AND

PREFERENCES

PASS FOR TAXES

The odds are pretty good that you've seen it. Maybe you've even been conned by it. Three-card monte has been around since at least the 15th century, and it's played on any horizontal surface—often atop a cardboard box—set up on a New York City street corner, an alley in Jaffa, Israel, a public square in Warsaw. You name the place, three-card monte's likely been there.

It looks like gambling, but it's really a shell game, with cards instead of shells. It looks like gambling, but you cannot win. It's actually a confidence game concocted of illusion—shills make it look legit—and sleight of hand. In theory, it couldn't be simpler. The dealer, also called a thrower, lays three cards face down. He flips one face up—a red card, usually, often the queen of hearts, the "lady"—and then the other two. He turns them all face down again, then picks up all three cards, one in one hand, two in the other. He turns his hands toward you, and you see that the queen is the bottom card in the hand that holds two cards. You *see* this. He then throws the cards face down in a row, one after the other, and you clearly see that the queen is the first card thrown. Then he moves the cards around. His hands fly, but it's easy to follow the lady card. When the thrower stops, you lay your twenty-dollar bill on what you *know* to be the queen. The thrower flips your card face up.

It's the jack of spades. You lose. The queen of hearts is elsewhere.

But the thrower feels really bad. Just terrible. (He admits this to you.) And so he offers you a chance to recoup your money.

"Can I bet *more* than twenty?"

"Oh…well…okay…I guess."

In 1994, American magician John Lenahan appeared on a BBC TV show called *How Do They Do That?* and revealed to the world just how three-card monte works, how the thrower holds the two cards so that the top card, not the queen at the bottom, actually gets thrown down first. The queen, it turns out, was never where you thought it was. For this public service, by the way, John Lenahan became the first member to be drummed out of the London-based Magic Circle for violating its motto: *Indocilis private loqui* ("Not apt to disclose secrets").

FROM THREE CARDS TO 10 MILLION WORDS

If one con man can always take your money using just three playing cards, think of what of 535 legislators can do with the 10-million-plus words of IRS code and federal tax regulations. Either way, it's a combination of sleight of hand, some well-placed shills, your natural assumptions, and your willingness to believe in the full faith and credit of the United States.

You—we, all of us—assume and believe that "taxes" are the money government collects from us, whereas "spending" is the use to which the government puts out "taxes." Just like the location of the red queen among three cards, nothing could be clearer.

Taxes are taxes, spending is spending, and never the twain shall meet.

But consider, just for instance, the mortgage interest deduction—the tax "loophole" most familiar to us. With ratification of the Sixteenth Amendment in 1913, income tax became legal in a constitution that had forbidden direct taxes. Carried over from the 1894 attempt at income tax—which the Supreme Court correctly declared unconstitutional—was a provision allowing a deduction for all interest expenses, including mortgage interest. People believe that the origin of the deduction for mortgage interest expense was the attempt of a benevolent Congress to encourage and facilitate home ownership. In fact, both in 1894 and 1913, there was no incentive to encourage home owner-ship—whether in general or through tax policy. The original 1913 income tax automatically excluded the first **$3,000** of income (**$4,000** for married couples) at a time when less than 1% of the nation's taxpayers earned more than this—**$3,000** being equiv-alent to **$72,503.33** today.[1] Moreover, early in the century, rel-atively few homeowners had mortgages. People either owned their homes outright or they rented. It was in the post–World War II era, the late 1940s and 1950s, as millions of GIs returned from military service, that mortgages became the key to buy-ing a home. The ability to deduct the mortgage interest expense was now really important, and when income taxes underwent a major reform under President Reagan in 1986, the deduction for general interest expenses was eliminated, but the deduction for mortgage interest remained. Congress said that it wanted to encourage home ownership.[2]

The federal government forgoes, forsakes, forswears, gives up, loses about **$100 billion** in tax revenue because of the mortgage interest deduction. Add to this another **$35 billion** sacrificed because most home sales are exempted from capital gains taxes. For that matter, because property taxes on one's home are also deductible, another **$25 billion** is forgone.[3] Collectively, then, Americans are exempted from **$160 billion** in federal income taxes just because they own a home. This is very unusual among the world's developed nations. Only the Netherlands and Switzerland allow an income tax deduction similar to that of the United States. Tax law in Canada, France, India, Norway, Belgium, Sweden, and Ireland provides very severely limited deductions for mortgage interest expense, but all other nations allow none at all.

Okay, so we're different. So what? Hey, it's American exceptionalism! In any case (you point out), a deduction or an exemption is a tax thing, not a spending thing. Income tax authority Bruce Bartlett (one of the architects of the last major American attempt at tax reform, the Tax Reform Act of 1986) calls this distinction—between *tax* deductions, exemptions, and preferences (items legally omitted to reduce taxable income) on the one hand, and government *spending* on the other—"budget semantics." By way of illustrating budget semantics in operation, Bartlett cites a hypothetical instance posed by the economist David Bradford:

> Suppose the Defense Department decided to pay for a new bomber by giving the contractor a tradable, refundable tax credit instead of just writing a check. The contractor would save an amount of taxes exactly equal to what it would otherwise charge DOD, and if its tax liability wasn't large enough, it could simply sell the tax credit to another company. In this example, government spending will be lower by the cost of the bomber, and taxes will also be lower by the amount of the tax credit. Superficially it would appear that we have achieved a magical way of cutting the size of government costlessly. But it is just sleight of hand.[5]

It is sleight of hand achieved through budget semantics. Returning to the matter of the deductions and exemptions specifically available to homeowners, ask yourself what the difference is between the **$160 billion** in revenue the government *never receives* versus **$160 billion** the government *spends*? Go ahead. Do the math. The answer is 0. There is 0 difference—to the economy and to conditions in the real world. In the world of accounting, however, that **$160 billion** never received never shows up as spending, for the simple reason that the word *spending* is never attached to it.

TAX EXPENDITURES: CAN SUCH THINGS BE?

Shakespeare's power-at-any-cost Macbeth commands the murder of his loyal pal Banquo, whose ghost later haunts him right in the middle of a celebratory feast. Talk about awkward.

"Can such things be...?" a terrified Macbeth blurts out among his guests, who, non-haunted, are oblivious.[6]

Can such things be? We should ask this very same question about the total absence of difference between federal spending and tax revenue declared uncollectible. The answer is *Yes, such things can be.*

Unfortunately, most of the people we the electorate have put in high places avoid the question. Take Senator Orrin Hatch (R-Utah), Chairman on Finance. He declared in a statement on July 12, 2011: "The federal government cannot spend money that it never touched and never possessed." He was explaining "tax expenditures," which he defined as something that "let[s] taxpayers keep more of their own money."[7] The term and the concept of tax expenditures were coined in 1967 by Stanley S. Surrey, a Harvard law professor and tax law scholar who had been assistant secretary of the Treasury for tax policy under President Kennedy. In a 1976 scholarly article[8] and a 1985 book,[9] Surrey bluntly defined tax expenditures as the product of the government's decision to "grant monetary assistance to an activity or group." Pursuant to such a decision, the government may make a "direct... grant or subsidy" or a "government loan... perhaps at a special interest rate." It may also guarantee a private loan. Alternatively, however, the government "may use the income tax system and reduce the tax otherwise applicable, by adopting a special exclusion, deduction or the like.... These tax reductions, in effect, represent monetary assistance by the government." The 1976 article was in response to the Congressional Budget Act of 1974, "the most concrete recognition taken by any country that tax subsidies constitute a form of government spending and thus are essentially linked to the methods of government spending traditionally covered in budget documents."

Thus, the man who invented the term *tax expenditures* explained that they are a form of spending. *Can such things be?* Unlike the chairman of the Senate Finance Committee, the late Mr. Surrey unhesitatingly answered yes. This puts Senator Hatch in the unfortunate position of trying to divorce "government spending" from an aspect of tax policy, "tax expenditures," which is defined precisely as "a form of government spending." As Bruce Bartlett remarks, this position "is complete nonsense."[10]

Senator Hatch was at pains to define "tax expenditures" as tax cuts and therefore as a de facto reduction in the size of government, but, as Bartlett contends, it is "sophistry to think that all tax cuts reduce the role of government in the economy."[11] The point is this: When the government decides to "grant monetary assistance to an activity or group," it does not matter whether the government directly spends the taxpayers' money to do so or accomplishes the same thing by forgoing revenues through tax deductions or exclusions. In either case, funds that might have been used for some broader public purpose are no longer available. It makes no economic difference in the real world, but it makes a world of difference on the government's ledger book. What would have been "traditionally covered in budget documents" as *spending* can now, by sleight of semantics, be labeled, quite misleadingly, as a *tax cut*.

WOULD YOU BELIEVE "NEGATIVE SPENDING"?

Another sleight of semantics is *negative spending,* also called "offsets," "offsetting receipts," or "offsetting collections." This is money the government collects but instead of counting as revenue, nets it against outlays, so that, in effect, the sum appears to reduce spending rather than raise revenue. The premiums the government collects for Medicare Part B (**$61 billion** collected in 2010) are, for example, counted as negative spending. Classing some receipts as negative spending makes the government's impact on the economy appear smaller than it actually is—in 2010, **$600 billion** smaller.[12] It provides a fiction of smaller government, a fantasy that mollifies some conservatives.

LOOPHOLE NATION

Negative spending is an example of revenue masquerading as reduced spending. Even more common is spending that is disguised as tax cutting, as in the mortgage interest deduction. Those of us who take or have taken advantage of this deduction—and our numbers are legion—call it a "right" or a "law" or "one of government's few good ideas." What we hardly ever call it is what it really is: yet another tax loophole.

Well, *loophole* is an ugly word, after all. Merriam-Webster defines it as "an error in the way a law, rule, or contract is written that makes it possible for some people to legally avoid obeying it." The *Oxford English Dictionary* is a trifle more generous, calling a loophole an "ambiguity or omission in a statute, etc., which affords an opportunity for evading its intention." None of us wants to be classed with "some people" who habitually exploit an *error, ambiguity*, or *omission* to *avoid* or *evade* the intention of a *contract* or, God forbid, the *law*. But the 10-million-plus words of our taxation scriptures have transformed the United States into a nation of loopholes and have converted Americans into a population of avoiders and evaders, arguably unpatriotic but unarguably unprosecutable.

Do any of us feel guilty or ashamed when we deduct our mortgage interest and real estate taxes? Of course not. There's even a line for it on your 1040. That's an invitation you cannot turn down! In fact, many of us are impressed by those who go far beyond the mortgage interest expense deduction and venture into the tangled terra incognita of the tax code itself to find the most obscure loopholes. "It's as if the concept of taxation as theft—rather than as a shared burden that all should contribute toward as the cost of maintaining a civil society—is now so widely shared that many people applaud those who have figured out how to game the system and pay less than their fair share rather than condemn them as social parasites who claim society's benefits without paying for them."[13] As Walt Kelly's Pogo declared in a daily strip of the same name published on Earth Day 1971, "Yep, son, we have met the enemy and he is us."[14]

In 2010, the Tax Policy Center published a research report titled "Variation in Effective Tax Rates." Before we dip into this report, let's admit that all of us are subject to different tax rates. There is our *statutory tax rate,* which is a percentage imposed by law. And there is our *effective tax rate,* which is the percentage of our income we *actually* pay in taxes. The effective rate is always lower than the statutory rate because of the array of deductions, exemptions, credits, exclusions, and other sleights of hand the IRS code and federal tax regulations allow. So, with this crucial distinction in mind, let's dip in.

The thesis of the 2010 report is this: "The expansion of refundable tax credits and the proliferation of specialized tax breaks means that households with similar incomes can face wildly different effective federal tax rates. For example, among middle-income households, the median effective income tax rate is 3%, but 10% of those households face effective rates exceeding 9% and another 10% receive a net government subsidy greater than 4% of their cash income."[15] The mortgage interest expense deduction is an example of a *specialized tax break,* and we'll look at *refundable tax credits* in a moment, but the salient point of the 2010 report breaks down this way:

1. The subject is a tax on *income.*
2. People with similar (or even identical) incomes nevertheless "face wildly different effective federal tax rates" on that income.
3. This is the result of loopholes and knowing how to squeeze through them.

And the *wildly* in "wildly different" applies not just to middle-income households, but much more wildly to the top 1%—and not even in the way you probably think it does. As reported in 2010, those in the *bottom* 10% of the *top* 1% had an effective tax rate of just 2.6%, whereas the effective rate for those in *top* 10% of the *top* 1% was 23.9%: ten times greater![16] Forty-four states plus the District of Columbia, Puerto Rico, and the U.S. Virgin Islands conduct lotteries. You know how they work. You play a set of numbers. If these numbers are drawn in a lottery, you win—big. Thanks to the complexity of the U.S. tax law and tax policy, federal taxes are startlingly similar to these state and territorial lotteries. If you hit the numbers that propel you, say, to the bottom of the top 1% of income earners, you win big when it comes to taxes. Your rate is just 2.6%. But thanks to those same laws and that same policy, U.S. income taxes also take a perverse detour from the lottery model. The best that can happen in a lottery is that you win a lot of money. The worst is that you lose the modest price of a lottery ticket—without incurring further penalty. The case of taxes can be very different. If you hit the "wrong" numbers in the tax code lottery and end up, say, at the top of the top 1% bracket, you are effectively taxed at 26.9% (as reported in 2010). Compared to the 2.6% rate for your slightly less wealthy fellow 1-percenters, that comes across not as a failure to win some money, but as a confiscatory penalty—money the government has picked out of your pocket.

So, has taxation in the United States become a matter of luck, like winning or losing the lottery? Shouldn't this make us angry? Outraged? Flabbergasted? Appalled? *Something?*

"People used to be incensed when the rich paid tax rates lower than those barely in the middle class," but today it "appears... that taxpayers no longer feel that one taxpayer's exploitation of tax loopholes comes at their expense."[17] Our era talks a lot about "feelings." Most of us agree that it is right to *feel* outrage against those who break the law, especially when the law is clearly designed to protect innocent people or society as a whole. Few of us, however, *feel* outraged by the profusion of loopholes in tax law and tax policy. Few of us *feel* outrage when one taxpayer legally exploits a loophole. After all, do we get angry at the winner of a lottery? His or her good luck has no impact on us. But in the case of taxes, the preferential treatment created by the existence and exploitation of a loophole comes at the expense of all taxpayers.

It's as if the lottery winner did not collect from the state lottery fund, but sent each of us an invoice, payable on receipt.

THE REFUNDABLE TAX CREDIT LOOPHOLE

So let's at least attach the correct ugly word—*loophole*—to all instances in which tax policy transforms taxation into spending. We have just glanced at injustice among the 1-percenters. Now let's drop down to the lower half—or, to be precise, to the lower 45%.[18] This, in 2015, was the fraction of Americans who paid no federal income tax. They are not breaking the law. In 2016, 77.5 million American households that filed their returns for 2015 had no federal individual income tax liability. Many even received tax credits—in effect, a refund on taxes they did not pay. This means they had a *negative* tax rate. Our Uncle Sam owed *them*.

The reason for most of this is the Earned Income Tax Credit (EITC). Its origin was a **$400** child credit enacted in 1997 (but by a Republican Congress during the Democratic Clinton administration), which was subsequently raised under President George W. Bush to **$1,000** per child. It was then taken in a new direction by Democrats, under President Obama, to provide a refundable tax credit for first-time home buyers and a sort of all-purpose refundable credit known as the Making Work Pay Credit, designed to get people off welfare and into whatever low-paying jobs might be available. Today, in addition to these refundable tax credit programs, there are credits for adoption and health insurance as well as some others. Altogether, these credits have exempted 45% from paying income tax—but the EITC alone is responsible for the lion's share of the exemptions, including those that result in a negative tax rate. Like a nonrefundable credit, a refundable credit is subtracted from your income tax liability; but, whereas a nonrefundable credit is subtracted up to the amount you owe (so that $0 liability is possible), a refundable credit can reduce your liability beyond zero, which means you get a refund on taxes you did not pay. You have a negative tax rate.

Before we go on to probe the EITC further, note that some (typically right-leaning) sources stop right here, by noting the high percentage of those who pay no income tax or who actually have a negative tax rate. In fact, in 2015, 73.1% of all "tax units" (individuals and married couples filing jointly)—not just roughly 55%—did pay *either* federal income tax, federal payroll taxes, or both. Payroll taxes are flat and regressive—a 6.2% tax each for the employee and employer, regardless of income level; the self-employed pay the total tax, 12.4%.[19] For tax year 2016, out of a total of 166.0 million tax units, an estimated 23.8 million tax units—just 14%—had a zero or negative income tax rate *and* also paid zero payroll tax.[20] Thus, most earners who pay no income tax are still on the hook for the flat tax on payroll. Despite this, the impact of the EITC and other credits is significant, especially because it is a sleight of semantics—welfare spending labeled as a tax cut.

Here are the EITC income limits as specified by the IRS for tax year 2016[21]:

Earned income and adjusted gross income (AGI) must each be less than:

IF FILING...	QUALIFYING CHILDREN CLAIMED			
	Zero	One	Two	Three or more
Single, Head of Household or Widowed	$14,880	$39,296	$44,648	$47,955
Married Filing Jointly	$20,430	$44,846	$50,198	$53,505

The maximum credit amounts payable are:

$6,269 with three or more qualifying children
$5,572 with two qualifying children
$3,373 with one qualifying child
$506 with no qualifying children

The growth of EITC tax expenditures has been dramatic. The number of recipients in 1990 was 12.5 million, which expanded to 28 million in 2015. The dollar amount in credits grew (in 2015 dollars) from **$14 billion** in 1990 to **$45 billion** in 2000 to an estimated **$69 billion** in 2015.[22] Folks can argue about the morality, cost, and benefit of paying subsidies to low-income families.[23] But that is not the point at issue here. What is at issue is the fundamental and fundamentally destructive practice of using the term and concept of "tax expenditures" to disguise as *tax cuts* what is actually *spending* for a welfare program that the administration, the legislature, or both want to keep out of the budget. Whether labeled as direct spending or deceptively labeled as a tax expenditure, the **$69 billion** is no longer available to pay the government's bills. How can a government and the people who elect it make informed decisions when a significant portion of the budget is rendered invisible? As Bruce Bartlett puts it:

> When one properly accounts for tax expenditures, the American welfare state is far larger than most people imagine. They tend to look at taxes and spending as a share of GDP, see that those percentages are much lower in the United States than in countries in Europe that have long embraced "big government," and conclude that we are fundamentally different. But it's more a difference of semantics than substance, economists increasingly conclude.[24]

As a citizen, taxpayer, and voter, you may well decide that the cost of the American welfare state is worth paying, or you may decide the expenditure should be less or far higher. But unless we all know the true size of the American welfare state, our decisions, no matter what they are, will be flawed to the extent that our knowledge is incomplete and distorted.

THE HEALTH-CARE LOOPHOLE

Although debate over "Obamacare" in 2009 briefly brought into question the wisdom of continuing to make employer-provided health insurance the cornerstone of the American health-care system, this feature was finally carried over into the Patient Protection and Affordable Care Act as signed into law on March 23, 2010. And thus was born a loophole that is by far the single largest of our tax expenditures.

Because health insurance is largely provided by employers, it is deductible as a business expense for employers and is not taxable to employees. The insurance is, in fact, excluded from the tax base and not reported on individual tax returns. Not only is the insurance benefit exempted from income tax, it is also excluded from payroll taxes. Additionally:

- Individuals pay no taxes on Medicare benefits received over and above their contributions.
- Individuals may deduct unreimbursed medical costs that exceed 10% of adjusted gross income.
- Health-care savings accounts may be established, allowing individuals to make tax-deductible contributions to pay non-reimbursed medical expenses.

What the government calls employee-sponsored insurance (ESI) costs the federal government an estimated **$250 billion** in income and payroll taxes in 2015, well over twice the second-largest tax expenditure, the mortgage interest expense deduction, which we have already discussed.[25] Like the mortgage deduction, the health-care deductions are classed as a tax cut rather than government spending, and they are accounted for as such.

But make no mistake, we all pay for the massive unavailability of a quarter-trillion dollars in federal revenue. And we pay in another way as well. When Congress codified the exemption of ESI benefits from individual income taxes in 1954, health insurance coverage grew rapidly. Because it was a "free" (or mostly "free") "fringe benefit" provided by employers, consumers purchased insurance coverage that paid for just about everything—not just major, high-ticket medical expenses (surgery, long-term care, etc.), but routine doctors' visits, prescription drugs, and so on:

> Overbuying health insurance and the declining amount of medical care paid out of pocket led to a vast increase in demand for such services and raised their cost. Medical cost inflation drove up health insurance premiums, which consumed a rising share of employee compensation. This is a key reason cash wages have stagnated since the 1970s. Productivity gains have largely been channeled into increasingly expensive benefits rather than paychecks. In 1970 pension and health benefits constituted just 4.5% of total employee compensation; by 2010 that figure had almost doubled to 8.5%—more than $1 trillion.[26]

Over the long term, therefore, "free" employer-provided health insurance, enabled and incentivized by U.S. tax policy, has proven to be extremely expensive.

CHARITY BEGINS IN THE LOOPHOLE

Uncle Sam may not always seem like a generous soul, but nobody gives more to charity than he. Of course, you'd never know it if you combed through the annual U.S. budget in search of the line labeled "Charitable contributions." Our uncle disguises his giving as a tax cut he calls a tax expenditure. We do know that in 2012, the tax expenditure for charitable contributions was **$53 billion** and individuals in the top tax bracket saved 35 cents for every charitable dollar they donated.[27]

If you think trotting out the "Uncle Sam" personification is a cheap shot because the federal government is in real life nobody's uncle and doesn't actually care what charities you give to, allow me to defend my use of the avuncular terminology. Because the tax saving for charitable deductions is greater the higher one's tax bracket, Uncle Sam's tax policy actually *does* affect giving by providing the wealthy with a greater incentive to contribute; therefore, causes and organizations that appeal to the wealthy tend to receive more charitable donations than causes and organizations that do not. Sixty-six percent of contributions by those with incomes below **$100,000** go to religious institutions, and only 7% go to organizations in the fields of education or the arts. Those with incomes over **$1 million** contribute 66% to health, education, or the arts—and just 17% to religious organizations.[28]

It is very possible—highly likely, in fact—that, via tax expenditures (that is, revenue lost), the federal government is contributing to charities that support causes you either do not care about or of which you actually, perhaps even passionately, disapprove. Attempts to correct this injustice inevitably run up against a formidable phalanx of nonprofit lobbyists. If the amount of the allowed deduction is decreased, they protest, or (heaven forbid!) eliminated, charitable giving will decline. But even when tax reformers propose lowering the marginal tax rate at the top, those same lobbyists protest—and do so for the same reason: Giving will decline because the size of the deduction will be reduced. Thus the very charities that depend most on the amply incentivized generosity of wealthy givers "reward" those givers by doing all they can to block any lowering in their tax rate.

While we're on the subject of justice and fairness, we should note that only those taxpayers who itemize their deductions can take advantage of the deduction for charitable contributions. If your income is such that it makes economic sense to take nothing more than the standard deduction, Uncle Sam becomes Uncle Scrooge and rewards your charitable spirit not at all. (Bah, humbug!)

Finally, charitable deduction is an area ripe for outright fraud at worst and artful spin at best. Individual taxpayers may inflate the value of items or services they contribute to charitable organizations in lieu of cash. They may also simply invent contributions on the mostly justifiable assumption that no auditor will ever question them. As for many charitable organizations, they have long ago discovered that engaging in charity does not necessarily mean paying key staff a pauper's wage. This is especially true of political, social, and other nonprofit think tanks that qualify for deductible donations yet pay their top executives salaries comparable to those of CEOs in major for-profit corporations.

TAXES SHOULD BE AS CERTAIN AS DEATH

The total of all tax expenditures in FY 2015 comes to **$1.3 trillion**, with **$131 billion** in corporate expenditures and **$1.2 trillion** in individual expenditures.[29] None of this is budgeted as government spending. Legislators tout much of it as tax cuts. By whatever name, they all constitute revenue unavailable to the government and, variously, to the governed.

Cloaked as tax cuts, preferences, deductions, exclusions, and exemptions, these financial contributions in the form of revenue forgone, credits granted, and refunds made become de facto instances of stealth spending. More often than not, they are not so much deliberate attempts to deceive voters, taxpayers, and even legislators as they are symptoms of an unwillingness to confront the realities of government spending and how **$1.3 trillion** even in a single year, let alone some such amount year after year, adds to the national debt.

"Nothing is certain but death and taxes," Ben Franklin said. Were he to reappear among us today, those words might stick in his throat. Taxes have become uncertain. Taxes have sometimes become deductions, exemptions, and refundable credits. Taxes have become expenditures. Quite often, taxes have become spending. Worst of all, taxes, like regulations, are currently used to bestow economic benefits on some and not upon others. As a nation with a government of, by, and for the people, we need taxes to be as certain as death. And so it is high time we avoided they guy on the corner offering his game of three-card monte. It is not a wager or a gamble. It is a con: 100% rigged. You cannot win because there is no winning. In the case of calling reality by unreal names, nobody wins. Not even the dealer.

SOLUTIONS

ASKING THE RIGHT QUESTIONS

And they SLEPT and SLEPT and SLEPT through ALL the SCANDALS...

As a nation, we perch together on the tipping point of the national debt crisis. It's a particularly sharp tipping point. It hurts. Yet, perplexed and frustrated, we can't seem to climb off this thing—even though we are dangerously near to falling off.

This chapter is a guide for the frustrated and the perplexed. It is about evaluating—at first hand and for ourselves—the multifarious and vexing issues of spending and taxes. It is about making decisions instead of struggling to live with those made by others. It is a guide to getting skeptical and staying curious.

CHAPTER 14

HOW MUCH LONGER

DO WE HAVE TO PERCH

ON THIS PAINFUL

TIPPING POINT?

Drawing near to the end of this book, dear reader, my hope is that you have the uncomfortable sense of arrival at a tipping point, a point at which decisions have to be made concerning what kind of economic future we will, together, share. Actually, we have been at this tipping point for some time now. Somehow, through a combination of denial, inertia, partisan ideologies too often oblivious to fact, and a paucity of leadership married to a plethora of careerism, we have been perched, uncomfortably yet complacently, atop this tipping point. It's finally starting to really hurt. My hope is that you—we—can feel the pain together, recognize its source, and prepare to make the decisions that will tip us at long last in a more sustainable direction.

As discussed in the introduction to this book, the tipping point on which we find ourselves is not just a figure of speech. It is an actual figure. As you may recall, the economic historians Carmen M. Reinhart and Kenneth S. Rogoff found that, throughout some 800 years of history, advanced economies that allow the ratio of debt to GDP to exceed 90% are rare—for the simple reason that they do not survive.[1] That debt-to-GDP ratio, 90%, is an actual, not a figurative, tipping point. And the thing is, as of the first quarter of 2016, the United States' national debt stands at 105.72874% of GDP.[2]

As discussed in the introduction, although some economists have questioned the reliability of the 90% ratio as a portent of economic disaster,[3] Reinhart and Rogoff do present us with *800 years* of what had happened when nations exceed a 90% debt-to-GDP ratio. Even if there is reason to question the degree of validity of the 90% ratio, at nearly sixteen points beyond it, our situation, based on 800 years of data, still looks pretty urgent.

MOMENT OF DECISION

If we are perched on a tipping point—or even approaching one—it is high time to decide which way we should tip. We need to take charge of our nation's economic inclination. There are, to begin with, two essential decisions to make.

Number one, accept the proposition that a government should raise sufficient revenue to pay for its proper and legitimate functions. This seems self-evident—a no-brainer, in fact. Yet we as a nation have not been able to pay for our government's functions. We've borrowed, year after year after year.

This is partly because we have not yet, as a nation, made decision number two: Decide what the proper and legitimate functions of government are.

This tipping point is not getting any less pointed. We need to get off it. But, at the risk of dulling our sense of urgency in this matter, we are obliged to make a third decision before we can go back and decide on the second.

Decision number three is deciding whether it is too late to

make decision number two. As we saw in Chapter 5, the founding fathers who framed the Articles of Confederation in 1777 (and ratified them in 1781) started the country without having made the number two decision. They never inventoried the proper and legitimate functions of government. The result of this omission was a kind of faux government that bumbled through the American Revolution, never had enough money to fight it properly, and ended up independent but broke. Fortunately, the United States was very young, young enough to start over with a Constitution that not only decided on the proper and legitimate functions of government, but also erected the limits within which those functions were to be executed for the people of the United States.

The Constitution was ratified in 1788—at this writing, 228 years ago. The country is no longer the infant it was in 1777–1781. After more than two and a quarter centuries of government and the results of government, change is not nearly as easy as it was back then. So formidable an edifice! So many stakeholders so deeply vested!

True: Factually speaking, it is too late to start from scratch or, as was done in 1788, even to start from close to scratch. "Scratch" is a place long faded from our national rearview mirror.

But how much of the past 228 years can and should we jettison? And how much can we revise or even reinvent? History—and each of our very own lives—is full of reinvention. If 800 years of history shows us the need for action to reduce the ratio of debt to GDP, far more of history shows us both the need for and possibility of reinvention.

Within our current major laws, any reinvention on which we decide to embark is limited by one hard stop. The federal budget, you'll recall, is divided into two broad categories: mandatory spending and discretionary spending. The adjectives are self-explanatory, and it is the mandatory category that constitutes the hard stop on reinvention. Social Security and Medicare are the two largest items in the mandatory category. While paying the interest on the national debt is not contained in the mandatory budget, the consequences of failing to pay it are so dire that we cannot bring ourselves to call it, let alone think of it, as discretionary. Spending on the mandatory items is effectively automatic, dictated by existing law, not by an annual congressional appropriation. The only way to legally change mandatory spending is by repealing major laws or enacting new ones, something that would have serious consequences in the case of entitlements financed by payroll taxes. In the case of interest payments, they are backed by the "full faith and credit" of the United States. Fail to pay, and we sacrifice our nation's financial credibility.

None of this means that mandatory spending is unchanging. Quite the contrary. Mandatory spending grows as the number of retirees eligible for Social Security and Medicare benefits grows. The Congressional Budget Office (CBO) projects that Social Security outlays, which stood at 4.9% of GDP in FY 2015, will hit 5.3% in 2021 and 6.1% in 2035.[4] Mandatory spending for major health-care programs, including Medicare, were 5.2% of GDP in 2015, projected to reach 6.1% in 2025, and then 8.0% in 2040. "Mainly because of the aging of the population and rising health-care costs, the extended baseline projections show revenues that fall well short of spending over the long term, producing a substantial imbalance in the federal budget. As a result, budget deficits are projected to rise steadily and, by 2040, to raise federal debt held by the public to a percentage of GDP seen at only one previous time in U.S. history—the final year of World War II and the following year."[5] The ratio was 114.9% in 1945 and 118.9% in 1946.[6]

If we do nothing, mandatory spending will push the national debt well beyond 100% of GDP (we're already at 105.72874%), which means that the nation cannot simply grow its way out of debt since, at this level, the long-term real interest rate is about equal to the long-term rate of real economic growth. The interest on the debt will continue to push the debt-to-GDP ratio higher. Default looms.

In the category of discretionary spending, a greater range of action is of course possible. But two obstacles stand in the way. To begin with, the mandatory spending budget, plus interest on the debt, is now two-thirds of the total budget. This means that Congress has, through annual appropriations, meaningful control over only about a third of the total budget. The second obstacle is *political will*, something that may be measured in what spending for what items legislators, special interests, and the people in general are willing or unwilling to compromise on or give up entirely. The discretionary budget requires answering many questions about what we want and what we want to spend to get it. Among the push and pull of a multiplicity of interests and motives, the prospect of arriving at a set of consensus answers is daunting.

THE CONSEQUENCES OF INDECISION

Measuring the debt-to-GDP ratio is an indicator of economic health, but according to Morgan Stanley economist Arnaud Marès, "Whatever the size of a government's liabilities, what matters ultimately is how they compare to the resources available to service them." Marès weighs the "debt against the maximum level of revenues that governments can realistically obtain from using their tax-raising power to the full. This is, inter alia, a function of the people's tolerance for taxation and government interference." As the International Monetary Fund's Simon Johnson put it, the "key to debt sustainability" is "whether a country has the political will to raise taxes or cut spending when under pressure from the financial markets."[7]

A government may be deficient either in revenue resources, the political will to raise taxes and cut spending, or both. Writing in 2012, income tax authority Bruce Bartlett cited as an example of the effect of the failure of will the possibility that the Bush tax cuts[8] would not be allowed to expire as scheduled at the end of the year: "[A]ll that is necessary for the revenue rise to take effect is do nothing and let the law take effect as written. According to CBO, permitting the Bush tax cuts to expire would allow revenues to rise to 20.8% of GDP in 2021 and 23.2% in 2035. Almost by itself, that is enough to stabilize the debt/GDP ratio."[9] Congress wanted to renew the cuts, while President Obama favored their expiration. In the end, a compromise bill, the American

Taxpayer Relief Act of 2012, was passed on January 1, 2013, which made permanent the lower rate of much of the Bush tax cuts, but retained the higher rate at upper income levels. The effect, according to a CBO estimate, was a revenue loss of **$279.840 million** in 2013 and total losses of **$3.639 billion** from 2013 through 2022, for a total increase in deficits for that period of **$3.971 billion**.[10]

The 2012 act was not a total failure of political will in that it did not *kick* the can down the road, as simply continuing the cuts would have. But it did *roll* it down that road. What would it take to sufficiently stiffen political will to resist both kicking and rolling? Bartlett suggests that a significant rise in the inflation rate, a rise faster than the CBO projected, would do it. Now, inflation can be a kind of backdoor alternative to outright default, provided the debt in question has a fixed maturity of long duration, since "higher inflation will erode the real value of the debt to some degree. This is essentially how the nation paid off the debts accumulated during World War II."[11] But we are no longer in the war bond era, and a great deal of today's debt consists of relatively short-duration Treasury bills. So inflation is no longer the ally of an indebted government, but yet another enemy adding to the cost of the debt. If interest rates are 1% higher than projected over the ten years from 2012 to 2022, **$1 trillion** will be added to the national debt.

And it gets even worse.

Whereas the debt after World War II was domestic, overwhelmingly owned by Americans, today 50% or more is owned by foreign interests, including the Chinese and Japanese. A sharp rise in U.S. inflation would cause the exchange value of the dollar to fall. If it fell sufficiently, foreign investors would be motivated not to roll over their American investments unless they were issued in favorable foreign currencies. Should this come to pass, it would be another crucial tipping point. So far, U.S. debt continues to be denominated entirely in U.S. currency, which remains the world's reserve currency, the chief medium of international exchange. But if our currency significantly weakens, default will indeed become a real possibility.[12]

In 2011, the United States approached the so-called debt ceiling, which is the statutory maximum amount of money the U.S. Treasury is permitted to borrow. This was not a novel occurrence. In fact, it was so common that raising the debt ceiling, which requires congressional authorization, had become virtually pro forma. In 2011, however, Republican representatives, led by the Tea Party coalition of staunch fiscal conservatives, decided to force spending cuts by refusing to rubber-stamp yet another increase in the debt ceiling. Democrats objected, pointing out that the debt ceiling does not limit spending levels, but simply enables the government to pay for spending to which Congress has already committed the nation. In effect, they argued, it enables government to pay its bills. They pointed to the dire consequences of sovereign default: Either suspend payment to bondholders or curtail payments to companies, contractors, and others to whom the government owed money but had not yet paid. There was talk of a credit downgrade.[13]

Some Republicans countered that the specter of sovereign default was already implicit in yet another increase in an already unsustainable debt. They argued that raising the debt ceiling yet again merely enabled continuance along an unsustainable course.

In fact, during the so-called debt ceiling crisis, the Dow Jones Industrial Average (DJIA) lost 2,000 points during July–August, including a one-day drop of 635 points, and on August 5, the major credit rating agency (CRA) Standard & Poor's (S&P) downgraded the government's credit rating from AAA (outstanding) to AA+ (excellent). For all this, critics blamed those who stood firm in refusing to raise the debt ceiling.[14] But it is important to note that the stand forced a deal for future spending cuts, and Republican hardliners agreed on July 31 to raise the debt ceiling in exchange for that deal. The agreement came nearly a week before the S&P downgrade, and the authorization was voted up on August 2, four days before the downgrade. That the downgrade took place and the market volatility continued after the debt ceiling was raised suggests that these were not (as many Democrats insisted) the result of a trumped-up "self-inflicted" crisis,[15] but, rather, responses to the very real budget and spending crisis that underlay the very need for lifting the debt ceiling. The timing suggests that S&P and the markets were responding to the message and not to the messenger—the messenger at whom Democrats and even many "moderate" Republicans were trying very hard to shoot. The volatility and the downgrade were not responses to any "self-inflicted" debt ceiling crisis, but to urgent fears of recession brought on by long-term debt.

"I think some of our members may have thought the default issue was a hostage you might take a chance at shooting," Senate Majority Leader Mitch McConnell (R-Kentucky) observed after the crisis was resolved. "Most of us didn't think that." Had McConnell stopped here, his statement would have been a simple criticism of the most fiscally conservative wing of his own party. But McConnell continued: "What we did learn is this—it's a hostage that's worth ransoming. And it focuses the Congress on something that must be done."[16]

GIVEN THE WILL, WHAT ARE THE OPTIONS?

Still, it appears that the prospective impact of inflation (with runaway interest rates) and of default are among the very few things on earth that most politicians, political leaders, and citizens find more distasteful than the prospect of spending cuts or higher taxes, or even both together. Fail to act to reduce the growth of the national debt, and you invite inflation, double-digit interest rates, and even default. These plagues, if they seem likely enough (as they did during the debt ceiling crisis), can move political will.

There are really just three approaches to reducing the deficit and the debt:

1. Cut spending.
2. Increase revenue.
3. Cut spending and increase revenue.

Conservatives gravitate toward option 1—or at least say they do.

The problem is, how do you do it? Remember, about two-thirds of the budget is mandatory—incapable of being cut without major changes in the law or making the choice to default. Congress certainly has the power to change the laws governing Social Security and Medicare. It could craft and pass legislation that would, presumably over a gradual phase-in period, transform Social Security and Medicare from regressive universal entitlements to progressive needs-tested programs. Instead of continuing to exist as increasingly costly and untenable programs inextricably woven into the fabric of American economic life, they would become the basis of a discrete social safety net to protect those below a certain level of income and wealth—those, in other words, with a demonstrated need for the programs.

This prospect, of course, raises questions of political will. Traditionally, entitlement reform has been a third rail in American politics: untouchable. Will Republicans and Democrats now collaborate on the transformation of Social Security and Medicare at a time when the segment of the electorate receiving benefits has never been larger? In 2000, 12.4% of the U.S. population was age 65 or older. By 2050, the fraction will be 20.7%. The steepest, fastest growth in this cohort is taking place between 2010 and 2030.[17] The eligible cohort is not diminishing, it is growing—and will continue to grow for a long time. This will not only create increased demand for benefits, regardless of financial need, it will create an expanding voting bloc favoring the benefits. The need for change has never been greater and will only become greater still. Yet the prospects for change are not bright.

So what? To be sure, it is difficult to give up what we have been told we are "entitled" to. It is especially difficult when we define the "general welfare," which the Constitution charges the government to "promote," strictly in terms of the existing entitlements. But the Constitution itself does not define the "general welfare" in such terms. The urgent truth is that we must now look beyond entitlements precisely in order to promote the general welfare. The non-partisan Congressional Budget Office projects federal spending to rise from 21,1% of GDP in 2016 to 23.1% by 2026 if current law governing (among other things) mandatory spending remains unchanged. The CBO further projects tax revenues to remain essentially flat, at about 18.2% of GDP.[18] Responding to these projections, Chris Edwards, Director of Tax Policy Studies at the Cato Institute, a Libertarian think tank, concludes that "Policymakers should change course. They should cut spending and eliminate deficits," and he presents a plan to reduce spending to 17.7% of GDP by 2026, nearly a quarter less than what the CBO currently projects for that year.[19]

The Edwards plan is certainly not the only approach to reducing and ultimately eliminating our unsustainable national debt. But the plan is worth detailing here if only to demonstrate the existence of real alternatives to complacency, ignorance, neglect, and the continued policy of holding the general welfare of the nation hostage to a menu of manifestly unsustainable entitlements. In the areas of health care and social security, Edwards proposes the following:

AGENCY AND ACTIVITY	ANNUAL SAVINGS $BILLIONS, 2026
Health Care	
Repeal ACA exchange subsidies	103
Repeal ACA Medicaid expansion	122
Block grant Medicaid and grow at 2%	128
Increase Medicare premiums	63
Increase Medicare cost sharing	20
Cut Medicare improper payments by 50%	78
Cut HHS non-Medicaid state grants by 50%	47
Total cuts	561
Social Security Administration	
Price index initial Social Security benefits	39
Raise the normal retirement age for Social Security	10
Cut Social Security Disability Insurance by 25%	54
Cut Supplemental Security Income by 25%	18
Total cuts	122
Total annual spending cuts in 2026	$683

Edwards's figures for the impact of cuts in health care and Social Security show estimated annual savings by 2026. Note that he does not specify how the cuts are to be made. Transitioning to a needs-tested regime is perhaps the most obvious and viable option. It is also the fairest. Indeed, the savings realized by transitioning from having to fund a universal entitlement to a needs-tested set of programs would likely exceed the magnitude of the cuts suggested here. The extra savings could be applied to those whose need is greatest, and thus the general welfare served more efficiently and more humanely.

Alas, as we exit the Libertarian think tank and enter the chambers of Congress today, we see little evidence of this degree of political courage. At present, the only benefit reduction the major parties are openly contemplating is a phased-in rise in the retirement age. Fortunately, in contrast to mandatory spending, discretionary spending lends itself to more, and more immediate, cutting. These expenditures are matters of annual appropriation, not established law. In the area of discretionary spending, Edwards proposes[20]:

AGENCY AND ACTIVITY	ANNUAL SAVINGS $BILLIONS, 2016
Department of Agriculture	
End farm subsidies	29.3
Cut food subsidies by 50%	53.5
End rural subsidies	6.5
Total cuts	89.3
Department of Commerce	
End telecom subsidies	0.6
End economic development subsidies	0.4
Total cuts	1.0
Department of Defense	
End overseas contingency operations	59.0
Total cuts	59.0

(continues)

AGENCY AND ACTIVITY	ANNUAL SAVINGS $BILLIONS, 2016
Department of Education	
End K–12 education grants	25.3
End all other programs	53.8
Total cuts (terminate the department)	79.1
Department of Energy	
End subsidies for renewables	2.2
End fossil/nuclear/electricity subsidies	1.9
Privatize power marketing administrations	0.8
Total cuts	4.9
Department of Homeland Security	
Privatize TSA airport screening	4.9
Devolve FEMA activities to the states	16.6
Total cuts	21.5
Department of Housing and Urban Development	
End rental assistance	30.5
End community development subsidies	11.0
End public housing subsidies	5.8
Total cuts (terminate the department)	47.3
Department of the Interior	
Reduce net outlays by 50% through spending cuts, privatization, and user charges	7.0
Department of Justice	
End state/local grants	6.7
Department of Labor	
End employment and training services	3.6
End Job Corps	1.6
End trade adjustment assistance	0.8
End Community Service for Seniors	0.4
Total cuts	6.4

AGENCY AND ACTIVITY	ANNUAL SAVINGS $BILLIONS, 2016
Department of Transportation	
Cut highway/transit grants to balance trust fund	12.0
Privatize air traffic control (federal fund savings)	2.1
Privatize Amtrak and end rail subsidies	3.6
Total cuts	17.7
Department of the Treasury	
Cut earned income tax credit by 50%	30.7
End refundable part of child tax credit	21.6
End refundable part of AOTC	4.4
Total cuts	56.7
Other Savings	
Cut foreign aid by 50%	8.0
Cut federal civilian compensation costs by 10%	32.9
Privatize the Corps of Engineers (Civil Works)	6.7
Privatize the Tennessee Valley Authority	0.5
Repeal Davis-Bacon labor rules	9.0
End EPA state/local grants	4.1
Total cuts	61.2
Total annual spending cuts	$457.8

The savings here are valued in 2016, but Edwards assumes they would be phased in one-tenth each year over the decade 2016–2026.

WHAT IF WE CAN'T CUT ENOUGH?

Mathematically, it is easy to balance the budget. Politically, it is hard. To promote the general welfare, it is necessary. To be sure, there are certain cuts everyone can agree on, such as acting to reduce improper payments and fraud in Medicare. In July 2015, for example, the General

Accounting Office (GAO) uncovered **$60 billion** in "improperly paid" Medicare benefits. Sixty billion dollars was 10% of Medicare's total 2015 budget. The fraud unmasked was hardly subtle: "They are supposed to be doctor's offices, clinics, or hospitals, not hamburger stands, vacant lots, and mailbox shops, but that's what some of the 23,400 potentially fake or bad addresses on Medicare's list of health-care providers are, according to" the GAO report.[21] But even if consensus could be reached on a large number of cuts not only in health and Social Security but across numerous departments, taxation experts such as Bruce Bartlett and budget experts such as David Stockman do not believe reducing the debt-to-GDP ratio to a reasonable level, let alone reducing deficits sufficiently to produce a balanced budget, can be achieved through spending cuts alone. In April 2011, Stockman criticized Representative Paul Ryan's (R-Wisconsin) budget plan for its exclusive dependence on spending cuts. "It doesn't address in any serious or courageous way the issue of the near and medium-term deficit," he said. "I think the biggest problem is revenues. It is simply unrealistic to say that raising revenue isn't part of the solution. It's a measure of how far off the deep end Republicans have gone with this religious catechism about taxes."[22]

It is necessary for taxpayers and politicians in both parties to ask: *What could possibly be worse than higher taxes?* The answer is simple. The consequences of insufficient revenue can be far worse—runaway inflation, double-digit interest rates (and difficulty securing any credit at all), slow or negative economic growth, and a reign of financial repression. (*Financial repression* is "a term used to describe measures sometimes used by governments to boost their coffers and/or reduce debt. These measures include the deliberate attempt to hold down interest rates to below inflation, representing a tax on savers and a transfer of benefits from lenders to borrowers.... [W]estern governments were being accused of financial repression following the 2008/2009 financial crisis as they embarked on measures including quantitative easing, capping interest rates, and creating more domestic demand for their own bonds."[23]) A 2011 of polls compiled by

Bruce Bartlett revealed that, contrary to conservative ideology and no-tax-raise pledges among Republican legislators, "to get the deficit under control the American people support some increase in taxation versus cutting spending alone by a 2-to-1 margin."[24] In any event, it may be necessary neither to introduce new taxes nor to persuade the electorate to accept them. Tax reform that targets tax expenditures (see Chapter 13) for curtailment will, in and of itself, add considerable revenue.

TAX REFORM AS AN ALTERNATIVE
TO HIGHER TAXES

Given our position not just on the economic tipping point, but actually already tipping the wrong way—with the debt-to-GDP ratio now greater than 100%—the most effective decision is to both increase revenue *and* make cuts in spending. As just suggested, revenue can be increased through tax reform rather than heavy-handedly raising rates. What is also true is that tax reform can be used as a means of motivating spending cuts. If reforms remove deductions, exemptions, and preferences that affect specific groups and special interests, many motives for spending simply vanish.

"Starve the beast" has long been a provocative mantra among some conservatives. It describes the political tactic of cutting taxes in order to reduce revenue and thereby forcing the federal government to reduce spending. Thoughtful tax reform does not starve the beast, but it does put it on a diet. Essential to this type of reform is the concept of *tax neutrality.*

As politically divisive as the subject of tax reform gets, everyone at least says they agree on the principle that the goal of tax reform is tax neutrality. This means that reforms should create a tax system that makes economic sense—that promote rather than interfere with the "natural" flow of capital toward productive uses. Despite what everyone says they agree on, however, the concept of tax neutrality actually runs contrary to what our tax policy has become, namely a means of subsidizing one or another set of people in order to encourage them to do something or to do one thing instead of another. Think, for instance, of the familiar deduction for the mortgage interest expense. This provision is the product of the very opposite of a tax-neutral policy. It uses the tax code not to ensure an economically viable system of taxation, but to encourage, goad, or bribe the taxpayer to buy a home. Or consider employer-provided health insurance. Current tax policy exempts this benefit from employee income taxes *and* it allows employers to deduct their costs for providing it. The result is that each dollar of employer-provided health insurance is worth much more than each dollar of cash wages. That tax expenditure has a huge cost for taxpayers in the form of massive tax revenues that are no longer available for other purposes. Moreover, it creates the unintended consequence of greatly increasing the costs of health care due to excessive demand for a product and service paid for by what seems like other people's money. This, too, is as far from tax neutrality as you can get.

On the face of it, tax reform—especially curtailing tax expenditures—should be easier to achieve than simply raising tax rates; however, our tax system has grown so far from neutrality and has been so tightly bound up with political motives and objectives for so long that any changes are doomed to meet with objections and resistance from one faction or another or many. In fact, committed political ideologues may refuse to make any distinction between an increase in tax rates and the closing of loopholes, labeling both equally as tax increases and therefore barring their passage *on principle*. Delivering the keynote address to the Columbia Law and Business Schools Cross Border Securities Market Mergers Conference on December 19, 2007, Security and Exchange Commission chairman Christopher Cox quoted the Columbia alumnus and historian Jacques Barzun, "In any assembly, the simplest way to stop the transacting of business and split the ranks is to appeal to a principle."[25]

Our recent politics have become so polarized by "principles" that, while most Republicans demand cuts in spending, when spending cuts alone prove inadequate to significantly reduce the deficit, they shift onto the Democrats the onus of finding additional revenue, leaving members of that party to propose rate hikes or loophole closures, which, either way, the Republicans portray as tax increases—to which they, on principle, are unalterably opposed. "The political trap is obvious," writes Bruce Bartlett. "Any reform that would increase revenue will be attacked by Republicans as a tax increase. They will send out fundraising letters to the affected group or industry requesting campaign donations to prevent the Democrats from increasing its taxes. They will not mention that the reforms would be coupled with tax rate reductions in a revenue-neutral[26] manner that neither raises nor lowers net tax revenue in the aggregate. Unfortunately this strategy will doom any hope of tax reform."[27]

Bartlett's formulation of the relentless politicization of what should be tax-neutral—that is, politics-free—tax reform may itself sound like a highly partisan condemnation of Republican legislators. Yet Bartlett served in both the Reagan and George H. W. Bush administrations and was one of the architects of the Reagan-era Tax Reform Act of 1986. He most recently counts himself as neither a Republican nor a Democrat, but an Independent, explaining, "I still consider myself to be a Reaganite. But I don't see any others anywhere in the GOP these days, which is why I consider myself to be an independent." In the end, it is not so much the Republican Party that Bartlett criticizes, but "mindless partisanship."[28]

Caught in a "political trap," both major parties are locked in stalemate. The need for reform is urgent. We are no longer precariously balancing on the tipping point, but actually tipping. Yet the political inaction is stunning:

> In principle, everyone favors tax reform—as long as it doesn't take away a person's own favorite deduction or credit or raise his or her taxes in any way. In principle, everyone favors tax simplification, base broadening, and lower rates. And in principle, everyone favors reducing the deficit, and a solid majority even support increasing taxes—as long as it's not their own taxes. Action before the election is unlikely

because both parties will want to campaign on tax reform, hoping that the election results will strengthen their hand.[29]

THE PRESIDENTIAL CONTENDERS

IN ALPHABETICAL ORDER

As this book nears completion, the 2016 general election is just six months away. At this moment, there are four significant contenders for the presidency. Here they are, in politically neutral alphabetical order, together with what we currently know about their proposed tax policies.

HILLARY CLINTON, DEMOCRAT

Clinton proposes few changes in current tax policy. Her reforms raise taxes modestly and are estimated to increase revenues by **$500 billion** to **$1.1 trillion** over a decade. She proposes:[30]

- a 4% surcharge on incomes over **$5 million**.
- a 30% minimum rate on adjusted gross incomes above **$1 million**.
- limiting itemized deduction benefits to 28%.
- raising rates on medium-term capital gains to between 27.8% and 47.4%.
- increasing the top estate tax rate to 45% while lowering the taxation threshold to **$3.5 million**.
- limiting the value of tax-deferred retirement accounts.
- creating a caregiver tax credit of up to **$1,200**.

Except for the very highest income earners, the tax increases will have little impact on the vast majority of Americans.

GARY JOHNSON, LIBERTARIAN

Johnson advocates:[31]

- eliminating tax subsidies.
- eliminating the "double taxation embodied in business income taxes."
- replacing "all income and payroll taxes with a single consumption tax that will allow every American and every business to determine their tax burden by making their own spending decisions.
- "prebating" (rebating in advance) taxes on "purchases for basic necessities . . . with all other purchases taxed equally regardless of income, status, or purpose."

In his presidential campaign of 2012, Johnson advocated the Fair-Tax, which would replace all federal taxes on income, including payroll, gift taxes, and estate taxes, with a national retail sales tax on new goods and services.

BERNIE SANDERS, INDEPENDENT (RUNNING AS DEMOCRAT)

The Sanders tax plan is intended to finance an array of programs, including free college education (at public institutions), universal health care, and extensive infrastructure rebuilding. The tax increases Sanders proposes would add **$10–15 trillion** in revenues over the coming decade—although probably not enough to finance all of the candidate's programs. He proposes:[32]

- replacing the top three income brackets with four, beginning at the **$250,000+** income level: 37%, 43%, 48%, and 52%.
- a 2.2% health-care premium tax for households and a 6.2% payroll tax for employers to fund single-payer universal health care.
- a 0.2% payroll tax on employers to fund paid family leave.
- a tax on Wall Street speculation to fund free college tuition.
- four estate tax brackets to replace the current top bracket of

20%; estates worth more than **$3.5 million** would be taxed at 45%, 50%, 55%, and 65%.
- taxing capital gains and dividends as ordinary income for households earning more than **$250,000.**
- eliminating the alternative minimum tax and payroll tax cap for incomes over $250,000 to fund expansion of Social Security.

The top 1% of taxpayers would pay (on average) **$525,000** more in taxes, while middle-income households would pay about **$4,700** more. Sanders argues that most Americans would save money due to universal health care.

DONALD TRUMP, REPUBLICAN

Trump promises major tax cuts—which will reduce revenues by about **$10 trillion** over a decade, a shortfall that will have to be made up by unprecedented spending cuts and/or increased federal borrowing. As of this writing, candidate Trump has provided no details addressing the gap. He proposes:[33]

- consolidating the seven current income brackets (10% to 39.6%) into just three—10%, 20%, and 25%.
- increasing the standard deduction from **$6,300** to **$25,000** for single filers and from **$12,600** to **$50,000** for joint filers.
- phasing out most itemized deductions, except for charitable giving and mortgage interest.
- eliminating the estate tax, the alternative minimum tax, the Affordable Care Act taxes (ACA to be repealed), and the marriage penalty.

Thirty-seven percent of Trump's proposed cuts benefit the top 1% of earners. On average, the wealthy would enjoy a **$275,000** tax reduction, while middle-income households would save **$2,700,** and 110 million lower-income households would pay no taxes (up from the current 77 million).

IS TAX NEUTRALITY POSSIBLE?

Nobody ever said a word against unicorns. Nobody's ever actually seen one, either. Much the same is true of tax neutrality. No one denounces it, but no one has ever seen it. Unlike unicorns, however, it is possible to create tax plans that are neutral. It is a matter of accounting and planning exclusively in economic terms. Once such plans leave the accountant's desk, however, they are instantly contaminated by political, social, and business interests. They cease to be tax neutral. Alas, the unicorn is dead on arrival.

Unless voters demand that all proposed *tax* plans succeed as *economic* plans, there never will be a plan that embodies tax neutrality. Since many, probably most, voters want taxes to promote certain political, social, and business issues—home ownership, for instance, or employer-funded health insurance—it is not likely that voters, living under current tax law, will ever go to the mat for tax neutrality.

There are alternatives to the current income tax system that, in theory at least, promote tax neutrality:

1. The true flat income tax—in which one tax rate is applied to all personal income without any deductions. This is the tax system that may be reduced to the size of a postcard.
2. The Hall-Rabushka flat tax—in which a flat tax (without deductions, exclusions, or credits) would be levied on individual cash wages and on business receipts, less purchases from other businesses for supplies, etc. Exemption allowances are assigned to fixed levels for single filers, joint filers, and heads of households.[34]

These two flat income taxes rely on their flatness (nothing geared to income levels and no deductions) to achieve tax neutrality. Another approach is taxing consumption instead of income:

1. The FairTax (also spelled *FAIRtax*) is a proposed national retail sales tax, such as that advocated (in 2012) by Libertarian presidential candidate Gary Johnson. There would be

no federal taxes on income, and only a single 23% retail sales tax.[35]

2. The Value-Added Tax (VAT), used in every major country except for the United States, taxes consumption in a different way from sales taxes.[36] Instead of levying a single tax at the point of the final retail sale of a good or service, the VAT levies a tax at each stage of production or distribution, giving credit for taxes previously paid, so that there is never double taxation. Here is a nutshell illustration of the VAT:

The farmer grows wheat, and a tax is assessed when it is sold to the miller to make flour. When the miller sells the flour to the baker to make bread, the tax is assessed again, but the miller gets credit for the taxes he paid when he bought the wheat. When the baker sells the bread to the grocer, the tax is assessed again, with the baker getting credit for the taxes paid by both the farmer and the miller. When the grocer sells the bread to a consumer, the tax is assessed once again, but the grocer gets credit for all of the previous taxes paid by the farmer, the miller, and the baker. In practice the consumer pays all the tax.[37]

The chief objection raised to the flat income tax is that is regressive, taxing the poor, the middling, and the wealthy at the same rate. In the case of taxes on consumption, it may be argued that the wealthy, who consume more than the middling and the poor, are actually taxed more heavily; therefore, a consumption tax is inherently progressive. On the other hand, even the poor must consume, and the flat VAT exacts, per item consumed, a heavier burden on the poor person than it does on those who are financially better off. In this sense, it is still a regressive tax. The VAT is widely used throughout the world and may well someday be adopted in the United States—more probably as a supplement to a reduced and simplified income tax than as a replacement for the income tax.

So, back to our question: *Is tax neutrality possible?*

The problem is that a nation committed to justice and basic

fairness is unlikely to swallow—whole—a regressive taxation system. This being the case, the answer to the question is not yes. But it is also not no. It is something like: *A degree of tax neutrality is possible.*

And that, at least, would be a step in the right direction. Who will move it that way? We voters have to do the pushing and pulling. No politician is likely to *lead* us toward it. It is incumbent on each of us to educate ourselves about taxes and spending. Having done this, we need to press our elected representatives and those who aspire to elective office to create tax policy and economic plans that move ever closer to working efficiently on an exclusively economic level, not as a tool to achieve some political or social purpose, most of which are ultimately aimed at propelling an individual or a party into office or keeping them there.

We need to know enough to evaluate plans in economic terms. We need to demand detailed answers to our questions about taxes and spending—not only from our elected officials and candidates aspiring to election, but also from the so-called mainstream media, which too often indulges partisan biases instead of acting in good faith as public educators. Most of all, we need to reject any plan that is based on ideology or ideological dogma. We must refuse to accept any response from politicians that is based on ideology—liberal, conservative, libertarian, Democratic, Republican, Socialist. The source of meaningful reform will never be found in dogmatic adherence to ideology. The source will be found in the values of democratic capitalism, with equal weight given to the adjective *democratic* and the noun *capitalism*. Having found the source, we must all, as the citizens and financiers of a democracy, get skeptical and stay curious. The final chapter will help with that.

Cutting expenses, downsizing government, and saving our Republic is not impossible—mathematically. Politically, it can be a lot harder. This book has invited readers to ask questions. This chapter shares some answers to a few of them. Even more important, it suggests some specific questions to ask—both of ourselves and our political representatives. Finally, it presents a guide to sources of data, analysis, and opinion to aid every American stakeholder in being heard and taking action.

CHAPTER 15

STAY CURIOUS,

GET SKEPTICAL:

RESOURCES, REFERENCES,

AND POLICY CHOICES

Whenthe dyspeptic Victorian historian and essayist Thomas Carlyle gave the study of economics the nickname by which it is still known—the "dismal science"—it wasn't just his notorious indigestion talking.[1] The core assumption of economics is scarcity. The field of economics exists to address a problem, scarcity, it assumes is inevitable and unavoidable. In other words, economics sets out to solve an insoluble problem. And *that*, ladies and gentlemen, is dismal indeed.

In our still-unfolding era of digital revolution and ever-ramifying interconnectivity, a new economy has emerged alongside the old. It is the information economy, and its core assumption is as bright as the other is dismal, for it assumes that, thanks to technology, all information is available to everybody everywhere.

Scarcity? *What* scarcity?

The new economy of abundant information will not replace the old economy of scarce resources, but it can make it less dismal. For one thing, the information economy is not strictly divided into producers and consumers. In contrast to one-way broadcast mass media—the earlier technology that it is supplanting—the new technology of the information economy is interactive. It is at minimum two-way and, more often, multi-way. It is about the creation of information by many people as much as it is about the consumption of information by many people. In the information economy, everyone is both a producer and a consumer of information.

It is fitting and proper that the Internet, the core technology of the information economy, was invented in the United States, the wellspring of modern democracy, and, as Abraham Lincoln for that reason called it, the "last best hope of earth."[2] Digital technology, the Internet, the information economy—all of these are inherently democratic. Larry Diamond, a senior fellow at the Hoover Institution, a public policy think tank based at Stanford University, coined the term "liberation technology" as a label for what he calls "a striking ability of the Internet . . . to empower individuals, facilitate independent communication and mobilization, and strengthen an emergent civil society." In a 2010 paper titled "Liberation Technology," Diamond explained: "Liberation technology enables citizens to report news, expose wrongdoing, express opinions, mobilize protest, monitor elections, scrutinize government, deepen participation, and expand the horizons of freedom."[3]

As the liberation technology of our information economy is the product of democracy, so it is an enabler and multiplier of democracy. This is a good thing for the old economy, the still-necessary economy of scarce resources, because the best possible economic systems have always developed in democracies. But as we have seen in this book, those good old economies get into serious trouble to the degree that the naturally democratic shape they take is deformed by the unintended consequences of non-democratic, inorganic, unnatural interventions from central planners in government—people, by the way, who are usually moved by the best of intentions. To the degree that well-meaning government meddling has made a democratic economy undemocratic, the remedy for this condition is a fresh dose of democracy. And if a little democracy is good, more democracy is even better.

Our information economy contains democracy in abundance, and this final chapter guides you to some of it in the form of—well—information. This chapter concludes by listing many of the sources used to create this book—and even more. It includes the key sources of information that will help us make the decisions necessary to steer our economy back to democratic health. As democracy is government of, by, and for the people, so must its economy be of, by, and for them. Getting there takes information. A little is good. More is better.

QUESTIONS

ARE MORE IMPORTANT THAN ANSWERS,

BUT HERE ARE SOME ANSWERS

The sources of information at the end of this chapter help us all to ask productive questions of our elected and unelected representatives, administrators, and leaders. The questions are more important than the answers for the simple reason that answers tend to stop the further flow of questions. And we should never stop questioning. But because our information economy is interactive, both inviting and requiring us to do more than ask questions and consume answers, let me produce a few answers of my own. What follows is a handful of economic solutions to some of the major issues raised in this book.[4]

OUR CLIMATE OF MORAL HAZARD:
FROM NEW DEAL TO RAW DEAL (CHAPTER 7)

Most of the solutions I want to share concern the elements of our current economic policy that put us all on the hook for the consequences of choices made by others. This situation, you'll recall, is the very definition of moral hazard. Here are several suggestions for curbing the production of moral hazard.

1. It is time for us to stop insuring the bank deposits of other people. National banks should continue to be chartered and examined by federal regulators to ensure that they meet high standards of banking. But interest-bearing deposits of any kind represent a risk, which should, like the risk of any investment, be borne individually. If the people of the United States want a "perfectly" safe place to park their money, they may ask their legislators to emulate the practice in many countries by creating a postal savings system, which would provide a low interest rate (below that of the national banks, which will be uninsured) but also backing by the full faith and credit of the United States.

2. It is time to bring back the absolute separation of deposit banking from investment banking—Glass-Steagall[5] with Teeth. Deposit banks cannot be permitted to jeopardize ordinary depositors on account of the risks taken by investors. If banks are not stopped from doing so, the government will always be tempted, in time of catastrophe (and there will be catastrophe), to bail out all parties concerned, thereby creating moral hazard for all taxpayers. Investment banks must be made aware that they are sailing on their own, out in the open sea, without the possibility of being thrown a lifeline. Compelled to own their own risk, they will no longer be in position to create moral hazard for the rest of us.

3. The government needs to get out of the insurance business. Payroll-financed entitlements, including Social Security, and all tax expenditure-subsidized employer-provided health insurance should be phased out and replaced by

private-sector products and services at competitive prices offered in the free market. Social Security is not actual insurance, and it is based on an unsustainable actuarial model. As for health insurance lavishly but inefficiently subsidized by tax expenditures, it has had the unintended consequence of creating massive inflation of health-care costs. As the government eases itself out of the health insurance business, the health-care market will be forced to adjust, costs will decline, and, quite likely, the quality of health care will improve. This process of exiting all government insurance programs will have to be gradual to avoid undue social shock, hardship, and damage, but if a democracy cannot believe in its most democratic institution, which is the free market, then it cannot continue as a democracy. As already stated in #2 above, government's exit from the insurance business is also to include the FDIC insurance provided to depositors and, by implication, to investors.

4. To the extent possible, reduce the role of government to two major functions: *military* defense and means-tested *social* defense. We'll get to the subject of military defense momentarily, but we can define government's responsibility for means-tested social defense here. The government must get out of the insurance business, but it must enthusiastically embrace the business of weaving an effective and efficient social safety net. The high form of civilization we call democracy is not obliged to ensure economic equality for everyone. It is, however, obliged to enhance and to save people's lives by devoting adequate resources only to those individuals and families that demonstrably do not possess the means to do without government financial aid. This is not insurance or (like Social Security) the fiction of insurance. It is vital help to those in legally demonstrable need. A civilized democracy throws no one away, and it does not dilute available resources by indiscriminately giving them away regardless of need.

THE UNINTENDED CONSEQUENCES OF
UNELECTED GOVERNMENT (CHAPTER 6)

5. Curb careerism. Our founders never intended government work to be a career. It was conceived as public service—a moral necessity and, in most cases, a financial sacrifice for the individuals involved. In the case of the unelected government (the "Administrative State"), clear rules and regulation can help to curb careerism. In the case of the elected government, however, incumbency must simply cease to be a goal by ceasing to be a possibility. Term limits should be imposed for all federal elective offices, the length of political campaigns should be limited by statute, and the financing of campaigns should be by public funds.

IN GOVERNMENT WE TRUST (CHAPTER 5)

6. Chapter 5 began with an American paradox. Most people say they've lost faith in government and yet most, perhaps yielding to force of habit, actually put great and unquestioning faith in government. It is not a bad thing to believe in government; however, as President Ronald Reagan said of establishing a basis of good faith in U.S.-Soviet relations, "Trust but verify."[6] When it comes to the management of the nation's taxes and spending, the most effective means of verification is a law—or constitutional amendment—requiring that each Congress balance the federal budget over the course of its two-year term. (Exceptions would be made for congressionally declared war and other extreme emergencies.)

THE PENTAGON AND PORK CHOP HILL (CHAPTER 9)

7. Dismantle what University of Washington political scientist Rebecca Thorpe calls the American Warfare State[7] and institute in its place a significantly reduced defensive apparatus that is adequate to prevent and retaliate against existential threats to the nation (for example, nuclear attack), but that

is insufficient as a standing army to support a routine policy of global military intervention. Distinguish between terrorist threats to homeland security and genuinely existential military threats. Deploy resources accordingly. Break up the military-industrial-Congressional complex.

WHEN SUBSIDIES AND PREFERENCES PASS FOR TAXES (CHAPTER 13)

8. Demand tax neutrality. Stop using tax policy (tax expenditures, deductions, credits, and exemptions) as the covert means of spending on favored political programs, social initiatives, and interest groups. Return to the pure purpose of taxation, which is to fund the proper business of the government. This means that tax policy must be crafted to generate revenues in ways that are most efficient in economic terms. As a practical matter, it may prove impossible (certainly, it is very difficult) to achieve an adequate level of tax neutrality in a system of taxation based mainly on taxing income. We the people should study and consider taxes based instead on consumption, such as some adaptation of the value-added tax (VAT) that is levied in most nations of the world.

DON'T LEAVE WITHOUT ASKING QUESTIONS—

HERE ARE A FEW

Understandably, most of us rate the value of a discussion—especially the prolonged discussion that is a book—by how many questions it answers. Maybe an even more useful criterion is how many questions it raises. In making political and economic choices, consider asking at least some of the following:

• Are the rules for government debt different from the rules for personal debt, the rules to which we all are subject?

Should they be different?

- Does government spend more under liberal presidents or conservative presidents, Democrats or Republicans? (See the "national debt by presidential administration" boxes in the introduction and reexamine chapters 1–4.)
- How reliable are the information sources we regularly use? Answering this question requires asking these: Who advertises via major media, big business or small? Which receives the greater benefits from big government—big business or small? (Take a second look at the discussion of "corporate welfare" in Chapter 11.)
- This book weighs the benefits against the liabilities of big government. Big government, we have seen, delivers an array of subsidies and tax preferences to big business. We can conclude that big government has an affinity for big business. What are the benefits and liabilities of big business? (See Chapter 13.)
- This book has considered the cost of fraud, waste, and abuse in government programs. What is the cost of fraud, waste, and abuse in the private economy?
- Consider that, as small businesses cannot afford waste and fraud for nearly as long as big business can, would it be reasonable to conclude that small government would not be nearly as tolerant of waste and fraud as big government is?

Think about these last two questions in particular. Please.

In the last eight years, $10 trillion dollars or more has been spent by the government, in *our* name, and guaranteed by *our* full faith and credit. Moral hazard has become real hazard as real money is sent in prodigious yet unproductive quantities to somebody or somebodies. And we and our children and their children are expected to pay for it.

No one person or group or political interest group can possibly be responsible for a scam of such magnitude. Waste in the form of "improper payments" and outright criminal fraud is institutionalized and enshrined within our political and administrative systems. When a political leader, a political candidate, a whistle-blowing bureaucrat (they *do* exist), or even your next-door neighbor offers news that threatens the institution and the shrine, it is difficult to resist the impulse nurtured and encouraged by a majority of our politicians and by the politically connected, politically dependent big business we call the mainstream media. It is difficult to resist the impulse to shoot the messenger.

Don't shoot the messenger. Instead, evaluate what he or she tells you.

To the degree that we fail to listen and fail to evaluate, we become enablers of waste, either through ignorance or because of our decision to go along in order to get along with those people and institutions that benefit from a status quo built on prodigal spending.

Let us think about it. The status quo produces unsustainable debt and is therefore itself unsustainable. Even so, there is compelling incentive to keep the money flowing, to keep the system going just as it is. No incentive is more compelling than self-interest. Clearly, a number of influential and powerful people, both within the government and outside it, have their hands on the spigot that continues spewing unearned dollars. They dedicate their efforts to convincing the rest of us that letting our dollars flow to others, to them, is somehow in our own interest as well. It's fiction at best and a lie at worst, and, from time to time, somebody offers the truth.

Don't shoot that messenger.

The politics of personal and professional destruction, which dominates political campaigns at every level these days, is a device to distract us from the all-too-real damage being done to our national and individual finances. The name calling and scandal mongering are the equivalent of the perpetual patter that accompanies the three-card monte dealer's scam. It is meant to misdirect our attention from the policies and processes that misappropriate funds, that send money to people and entities unknown and unaccountable, or that appropriate funds to finance unexamined purposes. Even in the perfectly aligned columns of an annual budget, there is somehow ample space for "improper payments."

Improper payments. These are the proverbial tip of the fiscal iceberg, of course. The phrase is meant to describe government payments made either in error or by fraud. But in a national fiscal status quo that relies on very few people questioning very many expenditures, improper payments are not just occasional mistakes and criminal acts. They are the very products of government as usual.

Why do we keep purchasing these products? We the people—and our children and their children—are now on the hook for trillions and counting, trillions of dollars with precious little value to show for them. But we keep on buying.

It is unimaginable. But it is a fact.

Isn't it time that we, as individuals and as stakeholders in our nation, stop buying absolutely everything the government sells us? No one, not even the wealthiest among us, can afford such a shopping spree.

We need to stop. We need to evaluate what the federal government has done for us and what it is doing for us with *our* money. Each of us has to decide what parts and pieces of the government's value proposition are worth the cost—to us, as individuals and as a society. What's worth our money? What's not? Each of us has to decide.

There is no doubt that *some* good will be purchased with the **$4.5 trillion** that is in the budget for FY 2017. But do we really need to spend all **$4.5 trillion** to achieve what we need to achieve?

The answer to this question must come from selfishness informed by data. At stake is our money. That's the motive for selfishness, because it is, after all, *our* money. We must demand from the legislators who appropriate *our* money absolutely compelling reasons for spending it as they propose to. We have a right to truth in spending. To get at that truth, we must demand that our legislators make a fact-based, data-based case for that spending. We don't need a partisan response, since partisan responses are built almost exclusively on the politics of personal and professional destruction—a politics that is empty of value to *us*. We need the facts.

One fact is that our nation is an enterprise that loses $400 billion to $1 trillion annually. We have to assume that some people somewhere benefit from these losses while some others pay for them. Are you benefitting? You are certainly paying.

When political leaders ask to fund social change, they typically admit the high cost but claim that the benefits are impossible to quantify and therefore must be accepted on faith. We have a right and a responsibility to demand more. When a charitable enterprise solicits our donation for a social good, our impulse may be to give.

"It's the right thing to do," we say.

But, no. The *right* thing to do is to ask the management of the charity how much is going to fund its advertised projects and programs and how much is devoted to "overhead." The *right* thing to do is to get the answers to those questions, evaluate them, and then make an informed donation or an informed refusal to donate. If the charity in question will not or cannot give you clear and credible answers, the right thing to do is find another that is capable of giving you the answers you need.

To demand that the government provide the level of data and clarity you expect from a charity is hardly setting the bar unreasonably high. Good management is the mark of a good charity as well as a good government. We should demand it from both. But when it comes to government, we rarely do. Maybe it's because we have become accustomed to incompetent, faithless, and unresponsive management in government.

To the degree that we do not learn enough to relentlessly demand accountability, our government will continue to take our money and then leave us undisturbed until it needs more. That's the bargain of the uninformed.

Change is difficult, scary, and uncertain. Yet change also offers promise and the opportunity to grow and improve. But organizations built on the incumbency of the status quo respond to change the way antibodies respond to infection. They try to engulf it, smother it, devour it. In 1990s, Bill Clinton and Al Gore offered change that was rejected by their own Democratic Party. More recently, Ted Cruz was personally demonized by *his* own

Republican Party. Neither party readily accepts discussion or debate over fiscal responsibility—*especially* when it is instigated by one of their own. The monte dealer goes right on collecting the dollars of those who do not question why the money card is never where it ought to be.

KEY INFORMATION RESOURCES

The only way to change the resistant reality of the status quo is by understanding that reality, evaluating it, and learning about alternatives. What follows is a guide to sources of information that are key to understanding the national economy, the national debt, and the federal budget. These resources are divided into three broad categories: First, sources of raw data, unfiltered, without opinion or spin. Second are a small, select group of polls and rankings on economic issues. Third are selected sources of analysis and plans for action. The list is by no means exhaustive. It is intended to start conversations, not put a stop to them. The value of these resources may be measured by the degree to which they provoke more questions than they answer.

UNFILTERED DATA

There is an abundance of data available on the U.S. economy, budget, and debt. This information is unfiltered and tells its own story, before others get to it and spin it.

BUREAU OF LABOR STATISTICS (BLS)

The BLS, a bureau of the U.S. Department of Labor, has online data tables in the areas of Inflation and Prices, Employment, Unemployment, Pay and Benefits, Spending and Time Use,

Productivity, and so on. Go to www.bls.gov/data/ to access. To inform your view of decisions concerning budgets and taxes, you will find the following BLS databases and tools most useful:

CPI Inflation Calculator, www.bls.gov/data/inflation_calculator. htm. Calculate the changing value of the dollar from 1913 to 2016.

Labor Force Statistics from the Current Population Survey, www. bls.gov/cps/tables.htm. A detailed snapshot of American workers, who are, after all, at the heart of the American economy and all the issues that it involves.

Unemployment Rate, http://data.bls.gov/timeseries/LNS 14000000. Detailed current and historical information on unemployment in the United States.

CONGRESSIONAL BUDGET OFFICE (CBO)

The CBO is tasked with producing independent (that is, non-partisan) analyses of budgetary and economic issues. Perhaps it tries to. Perhaps it actually does so. Nevertheless, we should be aware of the probable influence of whatever party controls Congress at a particular time. For instance, in 2015, the Republican-controlled Congress directed the CBO to use "dynamic scoring" for the first time in history to evaluate the economic impact of legislative proposals. Dynamic scoring seeks to estimate how much a proposal would expand the economy to the tax base as a result of changes in labor supply or investment. It also seeks to calculate how these changes in the economy would affect the federal budget. Democrats protest that dynamic scoring skews analysis to favor tax-cutting legislative proposals.[8] Nevertheless, the CBO remains a key resource—albeit when taken with a grain of salt. Go to. www.cbo.gov. The most useful resources are:

Budget and Economic Outlook and Updates, https://www.cbo. gov/about/products/RecurringReports#1. Informed projections of economic and budget outcomes.

Analysis of the President's Budget, https://www.cbo.gov/about/products/RecurringReports#3. A non-partisan estimate of the impact of the president's proposed annual budget.

Budget Options, https://www.cbo.gov/about/products/RecurringReports#4. Examines options for reducing budget deficits.

Long-Term Budget Outlook, https://www.cbo.gov/about/products/RecurringReports#2. The budget through a 10-year window.

Long-Term Projections for Social Security, https://www.cbo.gov/about/products/RecurringReports#5. Non-partisan, data-driven projections for the future of Social Security.

FEDERAL RESERVE BANK OF ST. LOUIS, ECONOMIC RESEARCH (FRED)

Federal Reserve Bank of St. Louis, Economic Research, https://research.stlouisfed.org. A trove of economic data and research. The most frequently consulted include:

Consumer Price Index for All Urban Consumers, https://research.stlouisfed.org/fred2/series/CPIAUCSL. A reliable way to track prices from 1947 to the present.

Real Gross Domestic Product, https://research.stlouisfed.org/fred2/series/GDPC1. Track US GDP from 1947 to the present.

Total Public Debt as percent of GDP, https://research.stlouisfed.org/fred2/series/GFDEGDQ188S. Most (but not all) economists believe the ratio of debt to GDP is a crucial indicator of a nation's economic health.

INFLATION CALCULATOR

The U.S. Inflation Calculator at www.usinflationcalculator.com/inflation/historical-inflation-rates/ is a complete historical representation of inflation from 1914 to the present, including data as well as news and explanatory material.

NATIONAL DEBT DATA
FROM NON-GOVERNMENT SOURCES

Here are private-sector sources of data—current, historical, and projected—on the national debt:

National Priorities Project. "United States National Debt," https://www.nationalpriorities.org/campaigns/us-federal-debt-who/. A pie chart approach that makes the current debt visual.

Polidiotic. "US National Debt by Year," www.polidiotic.com/by-the-numbers/us-national-debt-by-year/. A clear and to-the-point historical survey by presidential administration.

United States Debt Clock. U.S. Debt Clock.org, www.usdebt clock.org/current-rates.html. This spectacular website provides up-to-the second data on the growth of the debt and other major indicators—a masterpiece of dynamic data presentation.

OFFICE OF MANAGEMENT AND BUDGET (OMB)

The OMB is instrumental in assembling the annual budget request the president sends to Congress. The OMB compiles and maintains a great deal of data, the most important of which relate to the current budget, budgets through history, and budget projections. Be sure to see Historical Tables, "Summary of Receipts, Outlays, and Surpluses or Deficits: 1789–2021," https://www.whitehouse.gov/omb/budget/Historicals. As with the Congressional Budget Office (CBO), the OMB is supposed to be independent and non-partisan. It is nevertheless important to bear in mind that it functions within the executive branch to serve the needs of the president and those who work for the president. Reader beware.

OPENSECRETS.ORG

The website (https://www.opensecrets.org) of the Center for Responsive Politics, Open Secrets presents interactive data on politicians, elections, influence, and lobbying. The data used for Chapter 11 of this book draws heavily on the website, which details the contributions of organizations, PACs, business sectors, and individual corporations to members of Congress and presidential candidates.

PAYMENT ACCURACY

An official U.S. government website, https://paymentaccu racy.gov/ provides tables and graphs on "improper payments" by Social Security, Medicare, Medicaid, and other entitlement and social welfare programs. This is a must for understanding the scope of waste, inefficiency, and fraud in American government.

TAX EXPENDITURES

These three resources are indispensable for understanding tax expenditures—the vehicle Congress uses when it wants to disguise spending as tax cuts:

Joint Committee on Taxation. "Estimates of Federal Tax Expenditures for Fiscal Years 2014–2018" (August 5, 2014), https://www.jct.gov/publications.html?func=startdown&id=4663.

U.S. Congress Joint Committee on Taxation. "Estimates of Federal Tax Expenditures for Fiscal Years 2014–2018" (August 5, 2014), https://www.jct.gov/publications.html?func=startdown&id=4663.

U.S. Treasury. "Tax Expenditures 2014–2024," https://www.treasury.gov/resource-center/tax-policy/Documents/Tax-Expenditures-FY2016.pdf.

TREASURYDIRECT

A website maintained by the Department of the Treasury, https://www.treasurydirect.gov is rich in reports, among the most interesting of which are "Interest Expense on the Debt Outstanding" (https://www.treasurydirect.gov/govt/reports/ir/ir_ expense.htm) and "Charts and Analysis" (https://www.treasury direct.gov/govt/charts/charts.htm), with attractive graphic realizations of public debt data and other economic data. Great for those of us who respond better to pictures than to numbers.

U.S. CENSUS BUREAU

Along with the Bureau of Labor Statistics, the Census Bureau (www.census.gov) compiles data on all aspects of the U.S. population. The most unique statistics are those relating to income and poverty, www.census.gov/topics/income-poverty/data.html.

"Income, Poverty, and Health Insurance Coverage in the United States: 2008" (September 2009), table A1, www.census.gov/ prod/2009pubs/p60–236.pdf.

US GOVERNMENT SPENDING

At www.usgovernmentspending.com, this independent website draws on a wide variety of government sources to create current and historical views of budgeting, borrowing, and spending. Highly interactive, the website allows users to assemble their own datasets, graphs, and Excel spreadsheets. Historical data goes back to 1792. The interface takes some getting used to, but the site provides access to a huge amount of data.

POLLS AND RANKINGS

FIVETHIRTYEIGHT

A website (www.fivethirtyeight.com) that averages the data in many national polls from different polling organizations to create composite snapshots of opinion in many fields, with special emphasis on politics and economics.

GALLUP

Long the gold standard of political polling, Gallup is especially valuable for its "Presidential Approval Ratings—Gallup Historical Statistics and Trends" (www.gallup.com/poll/116677/Presidential-Approval-Ratings-Gallup-Historical-Statistics-Trends.aspx) and economics-related polls (www.gallup.com/topic/economy.aspx).

The following three Gallup polls on confidence in government are especially revealing:

Justin McCarthy. "Americans Losing Confidence in All Branches of U.S. Gov't." Gallup (June 30, 2014), www.gallup.com/poll/171992/americans-losing-confidence-branches-gov.aspx.

Justin McCarthy. "Confidence in U.S. Branches of Government Remains Low." Gallup (June 15, 2015), www.gallup.com/poll/183605/confidence-branches-government-remains-low.aspx.

Lydia Saad. "Americans Call for Term Limits, End to Electoral College." Gallup (January 18, 2013), www.gallup.com/poll/159881/americans-call-term-limits-end-electoral-college.aspx. Related to the issue of diminishing confidence in American government is the increasing volume of calls for term limits for all elected officials. Here are recent poll results.

PEW RESEARCH CENTER

Pew (www.pewresearch.org/) is another reliable source of public opinion data, especially in the realm of politics (www.people-press.org/), where its researchers' questions go beyond the typical *who-are-you-voting-for-and-why?* variety. See in particular:

Pew Research Center. "Beyond Distrust: How Americans View Their Government" (November 23, 2015), www.people-press.org/2015/11/23/beyond-distrust-how-americans-view-their-government/.

Pew Research Center. "Public Trust in Government: 1958–2015" (November 23, 2015), www.people-press.org/2015/11/23/public-trust-in-government-1958-2015/.

ABOUT USING STATISTICS AND

OTHER NUMERICAL DATA

Accessing and understanding unfiltered data is essential to making informed political and economic decisions. Yet it is very easy to drown in numbers. A remarkable book by Trevor Hastie, Robert Tibshirani, and Jerome Friedman, *The Elements of Statistical Learning*, 2nd ed. (New York: Springer, 2009), can help us all make the most of the data we encounter. The book is available online free of charge at http://statweb.stanford.edu/~tibs/ElemStatLearn/download.html.

ANALYSIS AND ACTION PLANS

Access to unfiltered data on our economy, its performance, budgets, spending, waste, fraud, and tax policy and proposals is vital, but so are the opinions of economists, political leaders, and thought leaders. What follows are some of the clearest and most provocative views of our economic life. It may feel good to read only those views you know you will agree with, but it is far better to find others that challenge your beliefs.

BUDGETS, SPENDING, AND THE DEBT

William Bonner and Addison Wiggin. *The New Empire of Debt*, 2nd Ed. Hoboken, NJ: John Wiley & Sons, 2009. In this exuberantly snarky but deeply researched book, the authors trace the history of runaway spending, greedy consumerism, and military adventurism that has transformed the United States into what they term an "empire of debt." This is a fascinating, intensely absorbing analysis. Just be advised that it provides no exit plan.

Todd G. Buckholz. *The Price of Prosperity: Why Rich Nations Fail and How to Renew Them.* New York: HarperCollins, 2016. A former White House director of economic policy explores the economic vulnerabilities of wealthy nations and how to transform these weaknesses into strengths.

Cato Institute, www.cato.org. A distinguished conservative public policy think tank, Cato conducts independent, nonpartisan research on a range of policy issues, with special emphasis on the economy.

Coalition for Fiscal and National Security, www.pgpf.org/pgpf-programs-and-projects/coalition-for-fiscal-and-national-security. Formed under the auspices of the Peter G. Peterson Foundation, the coalition is a bipartisan think tank for leaders in defense, economic, and national security policy.

Senator Tom A. Coburn. *The Debt Bomb: A Bold Plan to Stop Washington from Bankrupting America.* Nashville: Thomas Nelson, 2012. Former Senator Coburn (R-Oklahoma) makes the case for the explosive impact of America's accumulating national debt and outlines a plan to reform spending in ways that strengthen the social safety net while reducing waste and paying down the debt.

Club for Growth, www.clubforgrowth.org/. A national network advocating free enterprise and limited government.

Committee for a Responsible Federal Budget, crfb.org. A nonpartisan, deliberately objective organization, the CRFB promotes "fiscal responsibility" in federal government.

Competitive Enterprise Institute, https://cei.org. This libertarian think tank focuses on fighting excessive government regulation in order to promote free enterprise and innovation.

Senator Pete Domenici and Dr. Alice Rivlin. *Domenici-Rivlin Debt Reduction Task Force Plan 2.0,* http://bipartisanpolicy.

org/wp-content/uploads/sites/default/files/D-R%20Plan%20 2.0%20FINAL.pdf. This is the latest version of a bipartisan plan (first proposed in 2010) to reduce the national debt to a sustainable level.

The Concord Coalition, www.concordcoalition.org/. This nationwide, non-partisan, grassroots organization advocates "generationally responsible fiscal policy."

Chris Edwards. "A Plan to Cut Federal Spending." *Downsizing the Federal Government* (April 4, 2016), www.downsizing government.org/plan-to-cut-federal-spending.

Heritage Action for America, heritageaction.com. A conservative policy advocacy organization, Heritage Action advocates fiscal conservatism and has been called "the most influential lobby group among Congressional Republicans."

Glenn Hubbard and Tim Kane, *Balance: The Economics of Great Powers from Ancient Rome to Modern America.* New York: Simon and Schuster, 2013. The dean of Columbia University's Graduate School of Business and the chief economist of the Hudson Institute present a comprehensive history of economic imbalance and how it can—and has—caused civic collapse.

Mattea Kramer. *A People's Guide to the Federal Budget.* Northampton, Mass.: Interlink Books, 2012. This is a non-partisan, straightforward introduction to the federal budget—its history, the processes by which it is built, and its current status. Call it a guide for the perplexed.

Arnaud Marès. "Ask Not Whether Governments Will Default, but How." InvestorsInsight.com (September 20, 2010), www. investorsinsight.com/blogs/john_mauldins_outside_the_box/ archive/2010/09/20/sovereign-subjects-ask-not-whether-gov ernments-will-default-but-how.aspx. Available online, this article by a senior vice president in Moody's Investor Services gets to the heart of what it means when a government defaults on its national debt. An eye-opener.

Peter G. Peterson. *Running on Empty: How the Democratic and Republican Parties Are Bankrupting Our Future and What Americans Can Do About It.* New York: Farrar, Straus and Giroux, 2004. The focus here is on steps to take now in order to secure our children's economic security.

Peter G. Petersen Foundation. Established in 2008 by the secretary of Commerce in the Cabinet of Richard M. Nixon, the Petersen Foundation addresses what it calls "sustainability challenges that threaten America's future." Click on www.pgpf.org/ and navigate to "Finding Solutions." Here you will find a variety of proposals, from all segments of the political spectrum, for tax reform, health-care reform, retirement solutions, and national security solutions, in addition to comprehensive economic solutions and approaches to simply understanding the budget and budgeting process. The foundation website also features a Resource Library, which contains raw data, research data, and polling results based mostly on original Petersen Foundation studies. Consider making the Resource Library a first stop on your exploration of the national budget and the national debt.

Carmen M. Reinhart and Kenneth S. Rogoff. *This Time Is Different: Eight Centuries of Financial Folly.* Princeton and Oxford: Princeton University Press, 2009. This remarkable work of economic history—800 years of it—explores the significance of the ratio of a nation's debt to its gross domestic product (GDP). This sounds more academic and technical than it is. The question the authors explore is actually quite basic: What is the tipping point at which debt (what the government and its people owe) overpowers GDP (the monetary measure of the value of all goods and services a nation's people produce)? The findings are sobering.

State Policy Network, https://spn.org/. Founded in 1992, SPN is a nationwide network of state-focused policy think tanks.

David Stockman. *The Great Deformation: The Corruption of Capitalism in America.* New York: Public Affairs, 2013. At 770 pages, this is not casual beach reading—but it is both lively and illuminating. Stockman is best remembered as Ronald Reagan's director of the Office of Management and Budget. He is also a student of American economic history, and he presents a revisionist view that will make both conservatives and liberals acutely uncomfortable. *The Great Deformation* should be called "The Great Untangling," because to read this book is to untangle the complex story of how the United States reached the critical point it now uneasily occupies in its economic history.

THE PROPER ROLE OF GOVERNMENT

Stephen Breyer. *Breaking the Vicious Circle: Toward Effective Risk Regulation.* Cambridge, MA: Harvard University Press, 1995. Although this volume by an Associate Justice of the Supreme Court is more than twenty years old, it is still important reading for anyone who wants to understand the regulatory process and fix it instead of complaining about it or simply chucking it.

Congressional Budget Office. "Economic Effects of Policies Contributing to Fiscal Tightening in 2013" (November 2012), www. cbo.gov/sites/default/files/cbofiles/attachments/11-08-12-Fis calTightening.pdf. Government shutdown—which happens when Congress creates a funding gap by choosing not to enact legislation to fund government operations—has been used by legislators to force changes in tax and spending policies aimed at reducing the federal budget deficit. The prospect of shutdown triggers hysteria from both the right and the left. The CBO produced this study to predict the actual effects of fiscal tightening. Instead of arguing and trading threats, look at the numbers.

Congressional Budget Office. "Estimated Impact of the American Recovery and Reinvestment Act on Employment and Economic Output from October 2011 to December 2011," www.cbo. gov/sites/default/files/cbofiles/attachments/02-22-ARRA.pdf. The "stimulus package" passed in 2009 by the 111th Congress in response to the economic crisis of 2008 was extremely expensive and created bitter controversy. Here is the CBO's attempt at a non-partisan analysis of its actual impact. Also see Douglas Elmendorf, below.

Steven Conn, ed. *To Promote the General Welfare: The Case for Big Government*. New York: Oxford University Press, 2012. The subtitle of this collection of essays explains just what this book sets out to do—make the case for the value of "big government." Read it in conjunction with Walter E. Williams's *American Contempt for Liberty* (see below), which makes the case for small government.

Clyde Wayne Crews Jr. "Congress Better Fix 'Regulatory Dark Matter.'" Forbes (July 12, 2015), www.forbes.com/sites/wayne crews/2015/07/12/congress-better-fix-regulatory-dark-mat ter/. "Dark Matter" is what astronomers call the fraction of mass and energy in the universe that is essentially invisible yet there. Crews, policy director of the Competitive Enterprise Institute, uses the term to describe the mass of government regulation that is likewise essentially invisible but there, impacting costs while creating little if any benefit. Indeed, the exact cost of federal regulations is difficult to determine, which makes calculating the benefits of much regulation downright impossible.

Clyde Wayne Crews Jr. "Nobody Knows How Many Federal Agencies Exist." Competitive Enterprise Institute, https://cei. org/blog/nobody-knows-how-many-federal-agencies-exist. What Crews calls "regulatory dark matter" is created by a bureaucracy, or Administrative State, made up of federal agencies so obscure that nobody knows their number. Seriously. Nobody knows.

Clyde Wayne Crews Jr. "Ten Thousand Commandments," Competitive Enterprise Institute, https://cei.org/10KC. Here is the place to download the latest edition of "Ten Thousand Commandments," which is the Competitive Enterprise Institute's annual survey of the "federal regulatory state that (the author argues) imposes "enormous burdens on American consumers, businesses, and the economy" through "[u]nnecessary and meddlesome overregulation and intervention."

Susan E. Dudley. "Is There a Constituency for OIRA? Lessons Learned, Challenges Ahead." Regulation (Summer 2009), http://object.cato.org/sites/cato.org/files/serials/files/regu lation/2009/6/v32n2-1.pdf. The original impetus behind government regulation was to "promote the general welfare" by protecting consumers and others from faulty products, fraudulent advertising, and so on. OIRA (Office of Information and Regulatory Affairs) is a government oversight agency intended to regulate the regulators. This article, by OIRA's former administrator, tells you how that's been going.

Susan E. Dudley and Jerry Brito. *Regulation: A Primer.* Arlington, VA, and Washington, DC: George Mason University and George Washington University, 2012. This modest book is just what its title proclaims, a primer on government regulation. It is neither an argument for nor against regulation, but a straightforward explanation of how it works. Understanding the "regulatory state" is essential to understanding modern American government.

Douglas Elmendorf, Congressional Budget Office. "Policies for Increasing Economic Growth and Employment in 2012 and 2013." Testimony to the Senate Budget Committee (November 15, 2011), www.cbo.gov/sites/default/files/cbofiles/attach ments/11-15-Outlook_Stimulus_Testimony.pdf. Testimony from the director of the CBO concerning the impact of the massive stimulus program enacted in response to the economic meltdown of 2008. This is an important case study focusing on a major instance of government intervention. Also see Congressional Budget Office, "Estimated Impact of the American Recovery and Reinvestment Act on Employment and Economic Output from October 2011 to December 2011," above.

Mike Lofgren. *The Deep State: The Fall of the Constitution and the Rise of a Shadow Government.* New York: Viking, 2016. A former senior analyst on both the House and Senate budget committees, Lofgren penetrates Beltway politics to expose the activities of a "shadow government" of administrators, regulators, and special interests that collectively circumvent constitutional government.

Paul Moreno. *The American State from the Civil War to the New Deal: The Twilight of Constitutionalism and the Triumph of Progressivism*. Cambridge, UK, and New York: Cambridge University Press, 2013. If you want to know how Progressivism came to overtake Constitutionalism, here is the story. Today's argument between conservatives and liberals is rooted in the period between the Civil War and the Depression-era New Deal.

National Association of Manufacturers. "The Cost of Federal Regulation to the U.S. Economy, Manufacturing and Small Business (Executive Summary)," www.nam.org/Data-and-Reports/ Cost-of-Federal-Regulations/Federal-Regulation-Executive-Summary.pdf. An accounting of regulatory costs—not rendered by the government, but by the manufacturing sector.

Jay Sekulow. *Undemocratic: How Unelected, Unaccountable Bureaucrats Are Stealing Your Liberty and Freedom*. New York: Howard Books, 2015. Attorney Jay Sekulow lashed out at America's unelected government, the "Administrative State," as essentially undemocratic and therefore dangerous.

Dwight Waldo. *The Administrative State: A Study of the Political Theory of American Public Administration, 2nd ed.* New York: Holmes & Meier, 1984. This is a classic study of U.S. "public administration"—the administrative bureaucracy—and how it differs from both elected government and private sector administration.

Walter E. Williams. *American Contempt for Liberty*. Stanford University, Stanford, CA: Hoover Institution Press, 2015. This collection of articles by a Libertarian economist who is Distinguished Professor of Economics at George Mason University makes the case for small (as in minimal) government as envisioned (Williams argues) by the framers of the Constitution. It takes the opposite position of Steven Conn's *To Promote the General Welfare: The Case for Big Government* (see above).

James Q. Wilson. *Bureaucracy: What Government Agencies Do and Why They Do It*. New York: Basic Books, 1989. A dated but still informative study of American bureaucracy.

MORAL HAZARD AND THE U.S. ECONOMY

Laurence J. Kotlikoff. "America's Fiscal Insolvency and its Generational Consequences." Testimony to the Senate Budget Committee (February 25, 2015), www.budget.senate.gov/republican/public/index.cfm?a=Files.Serve&File_id=5e791473-386f-4149-8db0-00e50fdcdbf8. The Warren Fairfield Professor of Economics at Boston University, Kotlikoff delivered stunning testimony to the Senate Budget Committee in 2015, arguing that the way the government accounts for the national debt is inaccurate and profoundly misleading. In his view, the national debt is more than ten times than is currently reported. This is a must-read.

Mark R. Levin. *Plunder and Deceit: Big Government's Exploitation of Young People and the Future.* New York: Threshold Editions, 2015. Like Kotlikoff (above), conservative commentator Levin advocates a generational accounting approach to decisions about budgets, borrowing, and spending, arguing that the spending and borrowing of the present generation is creating an intolerable financial burden for rising generations.

WASTE, PORK BARREL SPENDING, FRAUD, AND INEFFICIENCY

David Brunori. "Where Is the Outrage over Corporate Welfare?" *Forbes* (March 14, 2014), www.forbes.com/sites/taxanalysts/2014/03/14/where-is-the-outrage-over-corporate-welfare/#22cd52dd6881. Published in *Forbes,* hardly a bastion of leftwing political thought, this article highlights the volume and scope of subsidies and tax preferences the federal government lavishes on big corporations in contravention of free market capitalism.

Paul Buchheit. "Average American Family Pays $6K a Year in Big Business Subsidies." Moyers & Company (September 24, 2013), http://billmoyers.com/2013/09/24/average-american-family-pays-6k-a-year-in-subsidies-to-big-business/. This article deals with the personal impact of big corporate subsidies.

Charles Dan Charles. "Farm Subsidies Persist and Grow, Despite Talk of Reform." NPR (February 1, 2016), www.npr.org/sec tions/thesalt/2016/02/01/465132866/farm-subsidies-persist-and-grow-despite-talk-of-reform. Beginning early in the 20th century, agribusiness has been a beneficiary of massive government subsidies, which deform the functioning of free markets.

Citizens Against Government Waste, www.cagw.org/. A private, nonpartisan nonprofit organization, CAGW works to document and eliminate waste, fraud, abuse, and mismanagement in government through research and public education initiatives.

Citizens Against Government Waste. *2016 Congressional Pig Book Summary.* Washington, DC: CAGW, 2016. Citizens Against Government Waste (CAGW) at www.cagw.org/ is a pork barrel/earmark watchdog that may be best known through its annual *Pig Book,* a rogue's gallery of pork barrel projects and spending. The first installment came out in 2005 (see next entry).

Citizens Against Government Waste. *The Pig Book: How Government Wastes Your Money.* New York: Thomas Dunne Books, 2005. The inaugural volume of this annual catalog of pork barrel politics.

Diana Evans. *Greasing the Wheels: Using Pork Projects to Build Majority Coalitions in Congress.* Cambridge and New York: Cambridge University Press, 2004. Here is an alternative view of pork barrel politics—not as inherently wasteful spending, but as the necessary cost of building majority legislative coalitions.

Senator Jeff Flake. *Wastebook: The Farce Awakens* (December 2015), www.flake.senate.gov/public/_cache/files/03714fa3-e01d-46a1-9c19-299533056741/wastebook-the-farce-awakens.pdf. The latest in an annual series begun by former Senator Tom Coburn, the *Wastebook* is a compilation of particularly egregious instances of wasteful government spending. The value of the *Wastebook* series is as a series of snapshots of some of the more mind-boggling things our legislators and the administrators of our unelected government are funding with our money.

Brian Kelly. *Adventures in Porkland: How Washington Wastes Your Money and Why They Won't Stop*. New York: Villard, 1992. A classic exposé on the world of pork barrel politics.

Hunter Lewis. *Crony Capitalism in America 2008–2012*. Edinburg, VA: AC² Books, 2013. When relations between business and government become so close that business success depends on individuals in business developing close relationships with individuals in government, the result is crony capitalism. This volume is a careful study of the phenomenon following the economic meltdown of 2008.

Philip Mattera and Kasia Tarczynska. "Uncle Sam's Favorite Corporations: Identifying the Large Companies that Dominate Federal Subsidies." Good Jobs First (March 2015), www.goodjobsfirst.org/sites/default/files/docs/pdf/Uncle SamsFavoriteCorporations.pdf. Published by Good Jobs First (www.goodjobsfirst.org/), a website that tracks subsidies and promotes accountability in economic development, this publication reveals the large corporations that have received two-thirds of the **$68 billion** in grants and special tax credits the U.S. government bestowed on businesses. Call it corporate welfare.

Philip Mattera. "Subsidizing the Corporate One Percent: Subsidy Tracker 2.0 Reveals Big-Business Dominance of State and Local Development Incentives." Good Jobs First (February 2014), www.goodjobsfirst.org/sites/default/files/docs/pdf/ subsidizing thecorporateonepercent.pdf. This subsidy tracker focuses on state and local development incentives, which, like federal subsidies and special tax credits, mostly go to the nation's largest corporations.

Chester Collins Maxey. "A Little History of Pork." *National Municipal Review*, vol. 8, no. 10 (December 1919), 691. http:// onlinelibrary.wiley.com/doi/10.1002/ncr.4110081006/abstract. Yes, this was published one year after World War I, but it remains the best explanation of how pork barrel politics came into being and then became a permanent part of the way we govern.

Office of Management and Budget. "Payment Accuracy: The Problem," https://paymentaccuracy.gov/about-improper-pay ments. Even the government knows it has a huge problem with "improper payments." This document explains what they are, what's behind them, and how much they cost.

Scot Paltrow. "How the Pentagon Cooks the Books to Hide Massive Waste." *The Fiscal Times* (November 18, 2013), www. thefiscaltimes.com/Articles/2013/11/18/How-Pentagon-Cooks-Books-Hide-Massive-Waste. Politicians too often view defense appropriations as sacrosanct. That is why this revealing look at waste in military spending is important reading.

Tim Roemer. "Why Do Congressmen Spend Only Half Their Time Serving Us?" *Newsweek* (July 29, 2015), www.newsweek. com/why-do-congressmen-spend-only-half-their-time-serv ing-us-357995. This article highlights the damage careerism is doing to American government. We elect representatives to rep- resent us in making laws. They spend half the time we are paying for not in crafting laws but in promoting their own reelection.

Rebecca Thorpe. *The American Warfare State: The Domestic Pol- itics of Military Spending.* Chicago: University of Chicago Press, 2014. Why does the United States spend so much on its mili- tary? Because a broad swath of the private sector profits from that spending. Here is a serious, historically based study of what Dwight Eisenhower originally called the military-industrial- Congressional complex.

United States Office of Government Ethics, https://www.oge. gov/. This government office oversees the executive branch eth- ics program with the objective of preventing conflicts of inter- est within the branch, especially conflicts that give rise to waste, fraud, and other abuses. This is the place to locate laws and regu- lations relating to conflict of interest.

TAXES AND TAX REFORM

Americans for Tax Reform, www.aft.org. Founded in 1985 by Grover Norquist at the request of President Ronald Reagan, AFT has a single mission: to oppose all tax increases as a matter of principle. The AFT advocates "simpler, flatter, more visible, and lower taxes."

Bruce Bartlett. *The Benefit and the Burden: Tax Reform—Why We Need It and What It Will Take.* New York: Simon and Schuster, 2012. Currently a columnist for *The Fiscal Times,* Bartlett served on the staffs of Congressmen Ron Paul and Jack Kemp as well as that of Senator Roger Jepson. He was executive director of the Joint Economic Committee of Congress, senior policy analyst under Ronald Reagan, and deputy assistant secretary of economic policy in the Treasury under George H. W. Bush. This is his remarkably clear and thoughtful prescription for tax reform. Bartlett argues the need for reform eloquently, and he outlines the options both in and out of the mainstream.

James M. Bickley. *Tax Reform: An Overview of Proposals in the 112th Congress.* Washington, D.C.: Congressional Research Service, 2011. An objective summary of the recent major proposals for tax reform—none of which (as of this writing) have been acted upon.

Center on Budget and Policy Priorities. "Policy Basics: Where Do Federal Tax Revenues Come From?" (Updated March 4, 2016), www.cbpp.org/research/policy-basics-where-do-federal-tax-revenues-come-from. If you want to know where the government gets the money it uses to run the country, look no further.

Alan Cole. "Corporate and Individual Tax Expenditures." Tax Foundation (August 3, 2015), http://taxfoundation.org/article/corporate-and-individual-tax-expenditures. Everything you always wanted to know about tax expenditures but didn't know you wanted to know.

Chris Edwards and Veronique de Rugy. "Earned Income Tax Credit: Small Benefits, Large Costs." CATO Institute (October 14, 2015), www.cato.org/publications/tax-budget-bulletin/earned-income-tax-credit-small-benefits-large-costs. The earned income tax credit (EITC) is intended as a cost-efficient means of helping the working poor. But does it work? This study concludes that the costs outweigh the benefits.

FAIRtax, "How FAIRtax Works," https://fairtax.org/about/how-fairtax-works?gclid=CjoKEQjw-Mm6BRDTpaLgj6Ko4KsBEi QA5f2oE8vyNTC-S17LiiCjZeuVLskk61gTVF4iorfkcUeXm_YaAsix8P8HAQ. An alternative to income tax you may not have heard of.

Scott Greenberg. "Federal Tax Laws and Regulations Are Now Over 10 Million Words Long." The Tax Policy Blog (October 8, 2015), http://taxfoundation.org/blog/federal-tax-laws-and-regulations-are-now-over-10-million-words-long. The reasons behind the incredible complexity and sheer density of our nation's tax laws and regulations.

Catey Hill. "45% of Americans pay no federal income tax." *Market Watch* (April 18, 2016), www.marketwatch.com/story/45-of-americans-pay-no-federal-income-tax-2016-02-24. Why so many Americans pay no federal income tax—and the impact of these "lost" taxes on revenue.

National Commission of Fiscal Responsibility and Reform, https://www.fiscalcommission.gov/. Created by President Obama, the commission is responsible for "identifying policies to improve the fiscal situation in the medium term and to achieve fiscal sustainability over the long term." The website is open to ideas from the public and invites submissions.

Peter G. Peterson Foundation. "Ask the Candidates," www.pgpf.org/askforaplan. The Peterson Foundation provides you with a convenient way to ask all candidates for federal office how they plan to "address the national debt and secure our future."

Peter G. Peterson Foundation. "Tax Reform," www.pgpf.org/finding-solutions/tax-reform. I discussed the Peterson Foundation above. Here is a link that focuses specifically on options for tax reform. It is a very thorough summary of current ideas.

Stanley S. Surrey and Paul R. McDaniel. "The Tax Expenditure Concept and the Budget Reform Act of 1974." *Boston College Industrial and Commercial Law Review*, vol. 17, no. 5 (June 1976); available online at http://lawdigitalcommons.bc.edu/cgi/view content.cgi?article=1529&context=bclr. Surrey invented the term "tax expenditure" and was its chief scholar until his death in 1984.

Stanley S. Surrey and Paul R. McDaniel. *Tax Expenditures.* Cambridge, Mass.: Harvard University Press, 1985. This is the classic treatment of tax expenditures, the remarkable device by which Congress clothes spending in garments tailored to look like tax cuts.

Tax Foundation, http://taxfoundation.org/. Since 1937, the organization has been conducting independent, nonpartisan research and analysis of tax policy at the federal, state, and local levels. This website is its repository of extensive, original, and freely available research.

Tax Policy Center, www.taxpolicycenter.org/. Under the auspices of the Brookings Institute, the TPC provides independent analyses of current and longer-term tax issues. Though criticized for a liberal bias, it is nevertheless a valuable resource.

Tax Policy Center. *Briefing Book*: "How does the tax exclusion for employer-sponsored health insurance work?" www.tax policycenter.org/briefing-book/how-does-tax-exclusion-em ployer-sponsored-health-insurance-work. Ever wondered what impact employer-sponsored health insurance has on the economy? Read this.

The Wall Street Journal editors. "Should the U.S. Adopt a Value-Added Tax?" *The Wall Street Journal* (February 18, 2016), www.wsj.com/articles/should-the-u-s-adopt-a-value-added-tax-1456715703. The United States is one of the few developed nations that does not have a value-added tax (VAT). This article asks if it is time that we did.

NOTES

INTRODUCTION

1 Pollingreport.com, www.pollingreport.com/prioriti.htm.

2 U.S. Debt Clock.org, www.usdebtclock.org/current-rates.html. President Obama's budget request for FY 2017 reports the gross federal debt as $20.149 trillion (The White House, Office of Management and Budget, *Budget of the U.S. Government: Fiscal Year 2017*, Table S-13, 165, https://www.whitehouse.gov/sites/default/files/omb/budget/fy2017/assets/budget.pdf). TreasuryDirect offers "The Debt to the Penny and Who Holds It," at www.treasurydirect.gov/govt/reports/pd/pd_debttothepenny.htm. On June 23, 2016, the Treasury reported the total debt at $19,252,431,295,170.04.

3 Michael Pearson and John Zarrella, "A Loud Crash, Then Nothing: Sinkhole Swallows Florida Man," CNN (March 5, 2013), www.cnn.com/2013/03/01/us/florida-sinkhole/.

4 The White House, Office of Management and Budget, *Budget of the U.S. Government: Fiscal Year 2017*, Table S-13, 165, https://www.whitehouse.gov/sites/default/files/omb/budget/fy2017/assets/budget.pdf.

5 The White House, Office of Management and Budget, *Budget of the U.S. Government: Fiscal Year 2017*, Table S-1, 115, https://www.whitehouse.gov/sites/default/files/omb/budget/fy2017/assets/budget.pdf.

6 U.S. Treasury, "Interest Expense on the Debt Outstanding," https://www.treasurydirect.gov/govt/reports/ir/ir_expense.htm.

7 Josh Zumbrun, "The Legacy of Debt: Interest Costs Poised to Surpass Defense and Nondefense Discretionary Spending," *The Wall Street Journal* (February 3, 2015), http://blogs.wsj.com/economics/2015/02/03/the-legacy-of-debt-interest-costs-poised-to-surpass-defense-and-nondefense-discretionary-spending/.

8 See "Full Faith and Credit," Investopedia, www.investopedia.com/terms/f/full-faith-credit.asp.

9 Adapted by Alan Axelrod and John Olivieri from historical data at US Government Spending, www.usgovernmentspending.com/.

10 John Maynard Keynes, *A Tract on Monetary Reform* (London: Macmillan, 1923), 80.

11 William Bonner and Addison Wiggin, *The New Empire of Debt*, 2nd ed. (Hoboken, NJ: John Wiley & Sons, 2009), 274.

12 Bonner and Wiggin, 275.

13 The White House, Office of Management and Budget, *Budget of the U.S. Government: Fiscal Year 2017*, Table S-4, 120, https://www.whitehouse.gov/sites/default/files/omb/budget/fy2017/assets/budget.pdf.

14 The White House, Office of Management and Budget, *Budget of the U.S. Government: Fiscal Year 2017*, Table S-13, 165, https://www.whitehouse.gov/sites/default/files/omb/budget/fy2017/assets/budget.pdf.

15 National Priorities Project, "United States National Debt," https://www.national priorities.org/campaigns/us-federal-debt-who/.

16 The Congressional Research Service reported $6.118 trillion in foreign-held public debt as of December 2015. See Marc Labonte and Jared C. Nagel, "Foreign Holdings of Federal Debt," Congressional Research Service (March 28, 2016), 1, https://www.fas.org/sgp/crs/misc/RS22331.pdf.

17 Labonte and Nagel, 2.

18 Labonte and Nagel, 2.

19 Senator Tom A. Coburn, M.D., *The Debt Bomb: A Bold Plan to Stop Washington from Bankrupting America* (Nashville: Thomas Nelson, 2012), 3-10.

20 Carmen M. Reinhart and Kenneth S. Rogoff, *This Time Is Different: Eight Centuries of Financial Folly* (Princeton and Oxford: Princeton University Press, 2009), Kindle ed.; chapter 7.

21 Federal Reserve Bank of St. Louis, Economic Research, "Federal Debt: Total Public Debt as% of Gross Domestic Product," 2016Q1, https://research.stlouisfed.org/fred2/series/GFDEGDQ188S.

22 Thomas Herndon, Michael Ash, and Robert Pollin, "Does High Public Debt Consistently Stifle Economic Growth? A Critique of Reinhart and Rogoff," *Political Economy Research Institute Working Paper Series*, no, 322 (April 2013), 1-25, www.peri.umass.edu/fileadmin/pdf/working_papers/working_papers_301-350/WP322.pdf.

23 Jacob Davidson, "How Much Does America's Huge National Debt Actually Matter?" *Time* (February 11, 2016), http://time.com/4214269/us-national-debt/?iid=sr-link1; Free exchange, "The 90% question," *The Economist* (April 20, 2013), www.economist.com/news/finance-and-economics/21576362-seminal-analysis-relationship-between-debt-and-growth-comes-under.

24 Peter Schiff, *The Real Crash: How to Save Yourself and Your Country, Revised and Updated* (New York: St. Martin's, 2014), 21.

25 International Monetary Fund, "Press Release: IMF's Executive Board Completes Review of SDR Basket, Includes Chinese Renminbi," November 30, 2015, Schiff, 28.

26 www.imf.org/external/np/sec/pr/2015/pr15540.htm and International Monetary Find, "Press Release: IMF Executive Board Completes the 2015 Review of SDR Valuation," December 1, 2015, www.imf.org/external/np/sec/pr/2015/pr15543.htm.

27 International Monetary Fund, "Enhancing International Monetary Stability--A Role for the SDR?" January 7, 2011, www.imf.org/external/np/pp/eng/2011/010711.pdf.

28 Zhou Xiaochuan, "Reform the International Monetary System," March 23, 2009, www.bis.org/review/r090402c.pdf and International Monetary Fund, "Enhancing International Monetary Stability--A Role for the SDR?" January 7, 2011, https://www.imf.org/external/np/pp/eng/2011/010711.pdf.

29 Ronald Reagan, Inaugural Address (January 20, 1981), The American Presidency Project, www.presidency.ucsb.edu/ws/?pid=43130.

30 Reagan, www.presidency.ucsb.edu/ws/?pid=43130.

31 Bureau of Labor Statistics, "Current Employment Statistics-CES (National), www. bls.gov/web/empsit/ceseeb1a.htm.

32 See, for instance, www.heritage.org/research/reports/2007/11/the-birth-of-the-administrative-state-where-it-came-from-and-what-it-means-for-limited-government or www.usatoday.com/story/opinion/2016/01/18/glenn-reynolds-constitution-amendments-convention-greg-abbott-column/78933518/.

33 Dwight Waldo, PhD, *The Administrative State: A Study of the Political Theory of American Public Administration*, 2nd ed. (New York: Holmes & Meier, 1984).

34 Peter T, Kilborn, "U.S. Turns into Debtor Nation," *The New York Times* (September 16, 1985), www.nytimes.com/1985/09/17/business/us-turns-into-debtor-nation.html.

35 Marcus Tullius Cicero, "Pro Roscio Amerino," http://thelatinlibrary.com/cicero/sex.rosc.shtml.

36 Abraham Lincoln, The Gettysburg Address, November 19, 1863, www.abrahamlincolnonline.org/lincoln/speeches/gettysburg.htm.

37 Matthew Frankel, "The 10 Richest Counties in the United States," The Motley Fool (September 20, 2015), www.fool.com/investing/general/2015/09/20/the-top-10-richest-counties-in-the-united-states.aspx. Number 1 is Loudon County, Virginia (median household income, $117,680); #2 Fairfax County, Virginia ($110,658), #3 Howard County, Maryland ($108,503), #6 Arlington County, Virginia ($101,533), and #8 Montgomery County, Maryland ($97,873).

CHAPTER 1

1 Addison Wiggin and William Bonner, *The New Empire of Debt: The Rise and Fall of an Epic Financial Bubble*, 2nd ed. (Hoboken, NJ: Wiley, 2009); 1-2; Kindle ed.

2 Jared Sparks, *The Writings of George Washington...* (Boston: Russell, Shattuck, and Williams, 1836), 10: 69.

3 Doris Kearns Goodwin, *Team of Rivals: The Political Genius of Abraham Lincoln* (New York: Simon & Schuster, 2005).

4 George Washington, Farewell Address, 1796, at The Avalon Project, http://avalon.law.yale.edu/18th_century/washing.asp.

5 "Combined—Control of the U.S. House of Representatives-Control of the U.S. Senate.png," https://commons.wikimedia.org/wiki/File:Combined--Control_of_the_U.S._House_of_Representatives_-_Control_of_the_U.S._Senate.png.

6 I. D. Spencer, *The Victor and the Spoils: A Life of William L. Marcy* (Providence, RI: Brown University Press, 1959), 59-60.

7 Alexis de Tocqueville, *Democracy in America* (Adelaide, South Australia: eBooks@ Adelaide, 2010), Book I, Chapter 18, Part IX; Kindle ed.

8 Harry S. Truman, "Do-nothing Presidents—Taylor, Fillmore, Pierce, and Buchanan," in Margaret Truman, ed., *Where the Buck Stops: The Personal and Private Writings of Harry S. Truman* (New York: Warner Books, 1989), 19-27.

9 Addison Wiggin and William Bonner, *The New Empire of Debt: The Rise and Fall of an Epic Financial Bubble*, 2nd ed. (Hoboken, NJ: Wiley, 2009), 90-91; Kindle ed.

10 Quoted in John Avlon, *Wingnuts: Extremism in the Age of Obama* (New York: Beast Books, 2014), 11.

11 "Military-industrial Complex Speech, Dwight D. Eisenhower, 1961," http://coursesa.matrix.msu.edu/~hst306/documents/indust.html.

12 John Steele Gordon, "The High Cost of War," *Barron's* (April 9, 2011), www.barrons.com/articles/SB50001424052970203990104576191061207786514.

13 Christopher R. Gabel, *Railroad Generalship: Foundations of Civil War Strategy* (Ft. Leavenworth, KS: U.S. Army Command and General Staff College, 1977), 13. Although the USMRR was authorized to control all railroads, in practice it seized only those lines captured in the South.

14 "Proclamation of Thanksgiving," Abraham Lincoln Online: Speeches & Writings, www.abrahamlincolnonline.org/lincoln/speeches/thanks.htm.

15 Competitive Enterprise Institute, "Ten Thousand Commandments 2015: A Fact Sheet," https://cei.org/sites/default/files/Ten%20Thousand%20Commandments%20-%20Fact%20Sheet%20-%202015%20Edition%20%20-%2005-12-15.pdf.

16 Editorial Board, "Mr. Ryan's Plan to Revert, Regress and Deregulate," New York Times (June 18, 2016), www.nytimes.com/2016/06/19/opinion/sunday/mr-ryans-plan-to-revert-regress-and-deregulate.html?_r=1, and Glenn Kessler, "The claim that American households have a $15,000 regulatory 'burden,'" *The Washington Post* (January 14, 2015), https://www.washingtonpost.com/news/fact-checker/wp/2015/01/14/the-claim-that-american-households-have-a-15000-regulatory-burden/. By law, the OMB prepares an annual cost/benefit analysis of federal regulations. The 2015 report shows a net benefit of regulations from October 1, 2004 to September 30, 2014. See 2015 Draft Report to Congress on the Benefits and Costs of Federal Regulations and Agency Compliance with the Unfunded Mandates Reform Act (Washington, D.C.: Office of Management and Budget, 2015), 1–2.

CHAPTER 2

1 Woodrow Wilson, Address to Congress Asking for a Declaration of War, April 2, 1917.

2 John F. Kennedy, Inaugural Address, January 20, 1961.

3 John F. Kennedy, Inaugural Address, January 20, 1961.

4 Alan Axelrod, *Selling the Great War: The Making of American Propaganda* (New York: Palgrave Macmillan, 2009), 77-96.

5 U.S. Espionage Act, June 15, 1917, www.firstworldwar.com/source/espionageact.htm.

6 Peter Finn and Sari Horwitz, "U.S. Charges Snowden with Espionage," *The Washington Post* (June 21, 2013), https://www.washingtonpost.com/world/national-security/us-charges-snowden-with-espionage/2013/06/21/507497d8-dab1-11e2-a016-92547bf094cc_story.html.

7 Homeland Security, https://www.dhs.gov/about-dhs.

8 Homeland Security, *Budget-in-Brief: Fiscal Year 2017,* https://www.dhs.gov/sites/default/files/publications/FY2017_BIB-MASTER.pdf.

9 Franklin D. Roosevelt, Address Accepting the Presidential Nomination at the Democratic National Convention in Chicago, July 2, 1932, The American Presidency Project, www.presidency.ucsb.edu/ws/?pid=75174.

10 David Stockman, *The Great Deformation: The Corruption of Capitalism in America* (New York: Public Affairs, 2013), 165.

11 Stockman, 147-148.

12 Stockman, 137.

13 Stockman, 166.

14 Clyde Wayne Crews Jr., "Nobody Knows How Many Federal Agencies Exist," Competitive Enterprise Institute, https://cei.org/blog/nobody-knows-how-many-federal-agencies-exist; Grassley estimate, "Prepared Statement of Senator Chuck Grassley of Iowa...Hearing on 'Examining the Federal Regulatory System to Improve Accountability, Transparency and Integrity, June 10, 2015, www.judiciary.senate.gov/imo/media/doc/06-10-15%20Grassley%20Statement.pdf.

15 Clyde Wayne Crews Jr., "Congress Better Fix 'Regulatory Dark Matter,'" *Forbes* (July 12, 2015), www.forbes.com/sites/waynecrews/2015/07/12/congress-better-fix-regulatory-dark-matter.

16 *United States v. Curtiss-Wright Export Corporation*, FindLaw, http://caselaw.findlaw.com/us-supreme-court/299/304.html.

17 Lend-Lease Act, www.ourdocuments.gov/doc.php?flash=true&doc=71.

18 Transcript of Executive Order 9066: Resulting in the Relocation of Japanese (1942), www.ourdocuments.gov/doc.php?doc=74&page=transcript.

19 *Toyosaburo Korematsu v. United States*, FindLaw, http://caselaw.findlaw.com/us-supreme-court/323/214.html.

20 Brandon Rottinghaus and Justin Vaughan, "New Ranking of U.S. Presidents Puts Lincoln at No. 1. Obama at 18; Kennedy Judged Most Overrated," *The Washington Post* (February 16, 2015), https://www.washingtonpost.com/blogs/monkey-cage/wp/2015/02/16/new-ranking-of-u-s-presidents-puts-lincoln-1-obama-18-kennedy-judged-most-over-rated/.

21 Nick Tomboulides, "Myth-busting 101: Are Term Limits Anti-Democratic?" *U.S. Term Limits* (July 3, 2014), https://www.termlimits.org/myth-busting-101-term-limits-anti-democratic/.

22 Lydia Saad, "Americans Call for Term Limits, End to Electoral College," Gallup (January 18, 2013), www.gallup.com/poll/159881/americans-call-term-limits-end-electoral-college.aspx.

CHAPTER 3

1 Environmental legislation included the Clean Air Act of 1963, Wilderness Act of 1964, Water Quality Act of 1965, Land and Water Conservation Fund Act of 1965, Solid Waste Disposal Act of 1965, Motor Vehicle Air Pollution Control Act of 1965, Endangered Species Preservation Act of 1966, National Historic Preservation Act of 1966, National Trails System Act of 1968, Wild and Scenic Rivers Act of 1968, Aircraft Noise Abatement Act of 1968, and the National Environmental Policy Act of 1969.

2 Robert Higgs, "The Economics of the Great Society: Theory, Policies, and Consequences" (Independent Institute, February 1, 2011), www.independent.org/issues/article.asp?id=3157.

3 "Did the United States lose the war on poverty?" Digital History, www.digitalhistory.uh.edu/topic_display.cfm?tcid=111.

4 Carmen DeNavas-Walt and Bernadette D. Proctor, "Income and Poverty in the United States: 2014," U.S. Census Bureau (September 2015), https://www.census.

gov/content/dam/Census/library/publications/2015/demo/p60-252.pdf; Gillian
B. White, "America's Poverty Problem Hasn't Changed," *The Atlantic* (September
16, 2015), www.theatlantic.com/business/archive/2015/09/americas-poverty-
problem/405700/.

5 The Washington Times, "Editorial: The not-so-Great Society turns a rickety 50,"
The Washington Times (May 21, 2014), www.washingtontimes.com/news/2014/
may/21/editorial-the-not-so-great-society/.

6 Table 1.1, "Summary of Receipts, Outlays, and Surpluses or Deficits," Office of Management and Budget, https://www.whitehouse.gov/omb/budget/Historicals.

7 David A. Stockman, *The Great Deformation: The Corruption of Capitalism in America*
(New York: Public Affairs, 2013), 247.

8 Stockman, 246.

9 Stockman, 249.

10 Reported in Stockman, 249.

11 "Tonkin Gulf Resolution" (1964), www.ourdocuments.gov/doc.
php?flash=true&doc=98.

12 David Frum, *How We Got Here: The '70s* (New York: Basic Books, 2000), 298.

13 U.S. Bureau of Labor Statistics (November 13, 2012), www.google.com/
publicdata/explore?ds=z1ebjpgk2654c1_&ctype=l&strail=false&bcs=d&
nselm=h&met_y=unemployment_rate&fdim_y=seasonality, and Tim McMahon,
"Historical Inflation Rate," InflationData.com, http://inflationdata.com/inflation/
Inflation_Rate/HistoricalInflation.aspx?dsInflation_currentPage=3.

14 Paul Krugman, "The Gold Bug Variations," www.pkarchive.org/cranks/goldbug.
html.

15 Paul Krugman, "The Gold Bug Variations," www.pkarchive.org/cranks/goldbug.
html.

16 Paul Krugman, "The Gold Bug Variations," www.pkarchive.org/cranks/goldbug.
html.

17 Paul Krugman, "The Gold Bug Variations," www.pkarchive.org/cranks/goldbug.
html.

18 Stockman, 289.

19 U.S. Bureau of Labor Statistics, "Labor Force Statistics from the Current Population
Survey," 01/70-01/75, http://data.bls.gov/timeseries/LNS14000000.

20 US Inflation, "Historical Inflation Rate: 1914-2016," www.usinflation
calculator.com/inflation/historical-inflation-rates/.

21 US Inflation, "Historical Inflation Rate: 1914-2016," www.usinflation
calculator.com/inflation/historical-inflation-rates/.

22 "Ronald Reagan TV Ad: 'It's morning in America again,'" https://www.youtube.
com/watch?v=EU-IBF8nwSY.

23 Ronald Reagan, Inaugural Address, January 20, 1981, The American Presidency
Project, www.presidency.ucsb.edu/ws/?pid=43130.

24 Jeanne Sahadi, "Taxes: What people forget about Reagan," CNN Money (September 12, 2010), http://money.cnn.com/2010/09/08/news/economy/reagan_
years_taxes/.

25 Martin Feldstein, "The tax reform evidence from 1986, American Enterprise Institute" (December 24, 2011), www.aei.org/publication/the-tax-
reform-evidence-from-1986/.

26 Bruce Bartlett, "Reagan's Tax Increases," *Stan Collender's Capital Gains and Games* (April 6, 2010), http://capitalgainsandgames.com/blog/bruce-bartlett/1632/reagans-tax-increases.

27 Office of Management and Budget, Fiscal Year 2013 Historical Tables, Budget of the U.S. Government, Table 6.1, https://www.whitehouse.gov/sites/default/files/omb/budget/fy2013/assets/hist.pdf.

28 US Federal Deficit as percentage of GDP by Year, www.multpl.com/u-s-federal-deficit-percent/table.

29 US Federal Deficit as percentage of GDP by Year, www.multpl.com/u-s-federal-deficit-percent/table.

30 Adjusted for inflation to 2009 dollars, this is $2.1 trillion at the end of the Carter years to $4.2 trillion at the end of the Reagan administration.

31 Jonathan Weisman, "Reagan Policies Gave Green Light to Red Ink," *The Washington Post* (June 9, 2004), www.washingtonpost.com/wp-dyn/articles/A26402-2004Jun8.html.

32 Addison Wiggin and William Bonner, *The New Empire of Debt: The Rise and Fall of an Epic Financial Bubble* (Hoboken, NJ: Wiley, 2009), 191-192; Kindle ed.

33 BBC News, "Reaganomics or 'voodoo economics'?" BBC News (June 5, 2004), http://news.bbc.co.uk/2/hi/americas/270292.stm.

34 Wiggin and Bonner, 196.

CHAPTER 4

1 Robert Ajemian, "Where Is the Real George Bush? The Vice President must now step out from Reagan's Shadow," *Time* (January 26, 1987), http://content.time.com/time/magazine/article/0,9171,963342-2,00.html.

2 Joe Weisenthal, "This Is What the Economy Did the Last Time a President Didn't Win Reelection," *Business Insider* (July 8, 2012), www.businessinsider.com/the-economy-under-george-hw-bush-2012-7.

3 "S&P Historical Prices by Year," www.multpl.com/s-p-500-historical-prices/table/by-year; Bureau of Labor Statistics, "Labor Force Statistics from the Current Population Survey," 1989-1993, http://data.bls.gov/timeseries/LNS14000000.

4 "The Somalia Mission; Clinton's Words on Somalia: 'The Responsibilities of American Leadership,'" *The New York Times* (October 8, 1993), www.nytimes.com/1993/10/08/world/somalia-mission-clinton-s-words-somalia-responsibilities-american-leadership.html?pagewanted=all.

5 *New York Times,* Opinion, "Mr. Clinton's Economic Scorecard," *The New York Times* (April 29, 1996), www.nytimes.com/1996/04/29/opinion/mr-clinton-s-economic-scorecard.html.

6 Congressional Budget Office, "The Economic and Budget Outlook: Fiscal Years 1996-2000 (January 1995), Summary Table 3," https://www.cbo.gov/sites/default/files/104th-congress-1995-1996/reports/doc07-entire.pdf.

7 Gallup, "Presidential Approval Ratings—Gallup Historical Statistics and Trends," www.gallup.com/poll/116677/Presidential-Approval-Ratings-Gallup-Historical-Statistics-Trends.aspx.

8 Adapted from US Government Spending, www.usgovernmentspending.com/, and adjusted for inflation to 2009 dollars.

9 Adjusted for inflation to 2009 dollars, the deficit is $290 billion and the surplus $155 billion.

10 Josh Gerstein, "Candid Bush Calls Presidential Win 'Amazing,'" *ABC News* (June 14, 2001), http://abcnews.go.com/Politics/story?id=121564.

11 Office of Management and Budget, Historical Tables, "Summary of Receipts, Outlays, and Surpluses or Deficits: 1789-2021," https://www.whitehouse.gov/omb/budget/Historicals.

12 Congressional Budget Office, Historical Budget Data, https://www.cbo.gov/about/products/budget_economic_data#2.

13 CBS News, *Face the Nation* (July 10, 2011), www.cbsnews.com/htdocs/pdf/FTN_071011.pdf?tag=contentMain;contentBody.

14 Dylan Matthews, "CBO: Letting upper-income tax cuts expire would barely hurt economy," *The Washington Post* (November 8, 2012), https://www.washingtonpost.com/blogs/ezra-klein/wp/2012/11/08/cbo-letting-upper-income-tax-cuts-expire-would-barely-hurt-economy/; Congressional Budget Office, "Economic Effects of Policies Contributing to Fiscal Tightening in 2013" (November 2012), www.cbo.gov/sites/default/files/cbofiles/attachments/11-08-12-Fiscal Tightening.pdf.

15 Mark Thoma, "The Bush Era Tax Cuts Didn't Create the Wealth They Were Supposed To," *Business Insider* (December 5, 2012), www.businessinsider.com/bush-era-tax-cuts-didnt-fix-economy-2012-12.

16 U.S. Census Bureau, "Income, Poverty, and Health Insurance Coverage in the United States: 2008" (September 2009), see Table A1, www.census.gov/prod/2009pubs/p60-236.pdf.

17 Douglas Elmendorf, Director, Congressional Budget Office, "Policies for Increasing Economic Growth and Employment in 2012 and 2013," Testimony to the Senate Budget Committee, November 15, 2011, at p. 34, www.cbo.gov/sites/default/files/cbofiles/attachments/11-15-Outlook_Stimulus_Testimony.pdf.

18 See, for example, "Myth #5" in Brian M. Riedl, "Ten Myths about the Bush Tax Cuts" (January 29, 2007), www.heritage.org/research/reports/2007/01/ten-myths-about-the-bush-tax-cuts.

19 National Priorities Project, "Wars Costs to Date," https://www.nationalpriorities.org/cost-of/resources/notes-and-sources/.

20 Office of Management and Budget, Historical Tables, Table 1.2, https://www.whitehouse.gov/omb/budget/Historicals.

21 "Bush departs with lousy stock stats in his wake," *Market Watch* (January 20, 2009), www.marketwatch.com/story/obama-inherits-battered-market-dow-dips-below-8000.

22 Floyd Norris, "Ranking the President's by G.D.P.," *The New York Times* (July 29, 2011), http://economix.blogs.nytimes.com/2011/07/29/ranking-the-presidents-by-g-d-p/?_r=0. In July 2011, when the article was written, Obama fared worse than Bush, having achieved only 1.2% GDP growth; however, as of July 20, 2015, this number had risen to 2.3% (Editorial, "Obama's Economic Growth Gap Now Tops $2 Trillion," *Investor's Business Daily* [July 30, 2015], www.investors.com/politics/editorials/tepid-gdp-growth-leaves-economy-even-further-behind-the-pace/).

23 The White House, "Setting the Record Straight: Six Years of Unheeded Warnings for GSE Reform" (October 2008), https://georgewbush-whitehouse.archives.gov/news/releases/2008/10/20081009-10.html.

24 Jo Becker, Sheryl Gay Stolberg, and Stephen Labaton, "Bush drive for home ownership fueled housing bubble," *The New York Times* (December 21, 2008), www.nytimes.com/2008/12/21/business/worldbusiness/21iht-admin.4.18853088.html.

25 Full Text: Bush's Speech, *The Guardian* (March 17, 2003), www.theguardian.com/world/2003/mar/18/usa.iraq.

26 Text of Bush Speech, CBS Video, www.cbsnews.com/news/text-of-bush-speech-01-05-2003/.

27 National Priorities Project, "Wars Costs to Date," https://www.nationalpriorities.org/cost-of/resources/notes-and-sources/.

28 Congressional Budget Office, "Monthly budget review: FY 2008 deficit of $438 billion" (October 7, 2008), https://www.cbo.gov/publication/24843; Michael B. Kelley and Geoffrey Ingersoll, "The Staggering Cost of the Last Decade's US War in Iraq—In Numbers," *Business Insider* (June 20, 2014), www.businessinsider.com/the-iraq-war-by-numbers-2014-6.

29 Congressional Budget Office, "The Budget and Economic Outlook: An Update" (September 2008), https://www.cbo.gov/sites/default/files/110th-congress-2007-2008/reports/09-08-update.pdf.

30 James Rosen, "Early transition? Obama takes the lead in economic crisis," *McClatchyDC* (November 23, 2008), www.mcclatchydc.com/news/politics-government/article24511822.html.

31 The incident is very well covered in "Northwest Airlines Flight 253," Wikipedia, https://en.wikipedia.org/wiki/Northwest_Airlines_Flight_253.

32 Brian Montopoli, "White House: Obama Can Walk and Chew Gum," CBS News (January 4, 2010), www.cbsnews.com/news/white-house-obama-can-walk-and-chew-gum/.

33 Pew Research Center, "Well Known: Twitter; Little Known: John Roberts," July 15, 2010, www.people-press.org/2010/07/15/well-known-twitter-little-known-john-roberts/.

34 Congressional Budget Office, "Estimated Impact of the American Recovery and Reinvestment Act on Employment and Economic Output from October 2011 to December 2011," www.cbo.gov/sites/default/files/cbofiles/attachments/02-22-ARRA.pdf; IFM Forum, "Economic Stimulus" (February 15, 2012), www.igmchicago.org/igm-economic-experts-panel/poll-results?SurveyID=SV_cw5O9LNJL10z4Xi; IFM Forum, "Economic Stimulus (revisited)" (July 29, 2014), www.igmchicago.org/igm-economic-experts-panel/poll-results?SurveyID=SV_5bfARfqluG9VYrP.

35 Knowledge@Wharton, "Nobel Laureate Paul Krugman: Too Little Stimulus in Stimulus Plan" (February 19, 2009), http://knowledge.wharton.upenn.edu/article/nobel-laureate-paul-krugman-too-little-stimulus-in-stimulus-plan/.

36 U.S. Debt Clock, www.usdebtclock.org/.

CHAPTER 5

1 Justin McCarthy, "Confidence in U.S. Branches of Government Remains Low," Gallup (June 15, 2015), www.gallup.com/poll/183605/confidence-branches-government-remains-low.aspx; Justin McCarthy, "Americans Losing Confidence in

All Branches of U.S. Gov't," Gallup (June 30, 2014), www.gallup.com/poll/171992/americans-losing-confidence-branches-gov.aspx.

2 Pew Research Center, "Beyond Distrust: How Americans View Their Government" (November 23, 2015), www.people-press.org/2015/11/23/beyond-distrust-how-americans-view-their-government/.

3 McCarthy, www.gallup.com/poll/183605/confidence-branches-government-remains-low.aspx.

4 Pew Research Center, "Public Trust in Government: 1958-2015" (November 23, 2015), www.people-press.org/2015/11/23/public-trust-in-government-1958-2015/.

5 Pew Research Center, "Beyond Distrust: How Americans View Their Government" (November 23, 2015), www.people-press.org/2015/11/23/beyond-distrust-how-americans-view-their-government/overview-1/.

6 Bob Cesca, "Keep Your Goddamn Government Hands Off My Medicare!," Huffpost Politics (May 25, 2011), www.huffingtonpost.com/bob-cesca/get-your-goddamn-governme_b_252326.html.

7 IMDb, "*The Verdict*: Quotes," www.imdb.com/title/tt0084855/quotes.

8 Adherents.com, "Major Religions of the World Ranked by Number of Adherents," www.adherents.com/Religions_By_Adherents.html.

9 Constitution of Massachusetts, 1780, Part the First, Article XXX.

10 John Adams, letter to Roger Sherman, July 18, 1789.

11 John Adams, letter to Thomas Jefferson, October 9, 1787.

12 Thomas Jefferson, letter to James Madison, December 20, 1787. Source: American History from Revolution to Reconstruction and Beyond, www.let.rug.nl/usa/presidents/thomas-jefferson/letters-of-thomas-jefferson/jefl66.php.

13 Jefferson to Madison, October 9, 1787.

14 Thomas Jefferson to James Madison, January 30, 1787.

15 Jefferson to Madison, October 9, 1787.

16 Henry David Thoreau, *The Writings of Henry David Thoreau* (Boston: Houghton Mifflin and Company, 1906), vol. 3, 356.

17 Office of Personnel Management, "Historical Federal Workforce Tables," https://www.opm.gov/policy-data-oversight/data-analysis-documentation/federal-employment-reports/historical-tables/total-government-employment-since-1962/.

18 White House, *Federal Budget FY 2017*, Table S-1, 115, https://www.whitehouse.gov/sites/default/files/omb/budget/fy2017/assets/tables.pdf.

19 Adapted from National Priorities Project, "President Obama Proposes 2017 Budget," https://www.nationalpriorities.org/analysis/2016/president-obamas-2017-budget/.

20 Adapted from National Priorities Project, "President Obama Proposes 2017 Budget," https://www.nationalpriorities.org/analysis/2016/president-obamas-2017-budget/.

21 A Glossary of Political Economy Terms, "Entitlement program," www.auburn.edu/~johnspm/gloss/entitlement_program.

22 Steven Conn, ed., *To Promote the General Welfare: The Case for Big Government* (New York: Oxford University Press, 2012), Preface; Kindle ed.

23 James Madison, "Veto of federal public works bill," March 3, 1817, www.constitution.org/jm/18170303_veto.htm.

24 Walter E. Williams, *American Contempt for Liberty* (Stanford University, Stanford, CA: Hoover Institution Press, 2015), 5-6.

25 See Matthew Frankel, "The 10 Richest Counties in the United States," The Motley Fool (September 20, 2015), www.fool.com/investing/general/2015/09/20/the-top-10-richest-counties-in-the-united-states.aspx. Number 1 is Loudon County, Virginia (median household income, $117,680); #2 Fairfax County, Virginia ($110,658); #3 Howard County, Maryland ($108,503); #6 Arlington County, Virginia ($101,533); and #8 Montgomery County, Maryland ($97,873).

26 David Mickelson, "Did Willie Sutton give his reason for robbing banks as 'That's where the money is'?" Snopes.com, www.snopes.com/quotes/sutton.asp.

27 Jason L. Riley, "Bernie Sanders and the Soak-the-Rich Myth," *Wall Street Journal* (October 20, 2015), www.wsj.com/articles/bernie-sanders-and-the-soak-the-rich-myth-1445379556.

28 William G. Gale, Melissa S. Kearney, and Peter R. Orszag, "Would a significant increase in the top income tax rate substantially alter income inequality" *Economic Studies at Brookings* (September 2015), www.brookings.edu/~/media/research/files/papers/2015/09/28-taxes-inequality/would-top-income-tax-alter-income-inequality.pdf.

29 Kenneth Quinnell, "Executive PayWatch 2015: CEO Pay Continues to Skyrocket," AFL-CIO Now (May 13, 2015), www.aflcio.org/Blog/Corporate-Greed/Executive-PayWatch-2015-CEO-Pay-Continues-to-Skyrocket.

30 Mark J. Perry, "Lots of problems with AFL-CIO's 'CEO-to-worker pay' analysis including small sample size and using part-time worker pay," *AEIdeas* (May 16, 2015), https://www.aei.org/publication/lots-of-problems-with-the-afl-cios-ceo-to-worker-pay-analysis-including-using-part-time-worker-pay/.

31 Robert Schlesinger, "The Size of the U.S. and the World in 2016," *U.S. News & World Report* (January 5, 2016), www.usnews.com/opinion/blogs/robert-schlesinger/articles/2016-01-05/us-population-in-2016-according-to-census-estimates-322-762-018.

32 Bureau of Labor Statistics, "Current Employment Statistics – CES (National)," www.bls.gov/web/empsit/ceseeb1a.htm.

33 Federal Reserve Bank of St. Louis, "Federal Net Outlays as Percent of Gross Domestic Product," https://research.stlouisfed.org/fred2/series/FYONGDA188S.

34 U.S. Government Spending, "US Federal Government Spending Breakdown in% GDP," www.usgovernmentspending.com/breakdown_2016USpf_17ps5n.

35 Chris Edwards, "Federal Government Pay Exceeds Most Industries" (October 5, 2015), www.cato.org/blog/federal-government-pay-exceeds-most-industries.

36 Andrew G. Biggs, "How Generous Are Federal Employee Pensions?" (September 30, 2011), https://www.aei.org/publication/how-generous-are-federal-employee-pensions/.

CHAPTER 6

1 It should be noted that a Zombie Zin (Zinfandel) is currently available (www.chateaud.com), as are wines from the "Zombie Wine Collector's Series": The UnDead Apocalyptic Red, Cadaver Cabernet Sauvignon, Still Alive by way of The

Antidote, and The Zinfection Blight Zinfandel (https://www.personalwine.com/walking-dead).

2 Jason Pye, "19 Ridiculous Federal Criminal Laws and Regulations," Freedom-Works (January 14, 2016), www.freedomworks.org/content/19-ridiculous-federal-criminal-laws-and-regulations.

3 The following discussion of the relationship between the regulatory agencies of the Administrative State and the three constitutional branches of government is based on Susan E. Dudley and Jerry Brito, *Regulation: A Primer* (Arlington, VA, and Washington, DC: George Mason University and George Washington University, 2012), chapter 3.

4 The most important recent regulatory review laws are the Regulatory Flexibility Act of 1980 (aimed at assessing the impact of a regulation on small businesses); Paperwork Reduction Act of 1980 (under which OICRA was created); Unfunded Mandates Act of 1995 (to assess burdens of federal regulations on state, local, and tribal governments); Small Business Regulatory Fairness Act of 1996 (another law relating to the impact of regulation on small businesses); Congressional Review Act of 1996 (requires documentation to be submitted for congressional review); Omnibus Consolidated and Emergency Supplemental Appropriations Act of 1999 (requires the OMB to make yearly reports to Congress on the costs and benefits of regulations and to make recommendations for reform); Truth in Regulating Act of 2000 (allows Congress to request a General Accounting Office [GAO] evaluation of economically significant regulations prior to implementation); and Information Quality Act of 2000 (requires OMB standards to ensure quality of data used in rule-making). See Oyez, Chevron U.S.A. v. Natural Resources Defense Council, Inc. (467 US 837 [1984]), https://www.oyez.org/cases/1983/82-1005; and Rep. John Ratcliffe, "Taking Back Powers Usurped by Unelected Bureaucrats," RedState (July 11, 2016), www.redstate.com/diary/johnratcliffe/2016/07/11/rep.-john-ratcliffe-restoring-constitutional-balance-government/.

5 Michael Snyder, "12 Ridiculous Government Regulations That Are Almost Too Bizarre To Believe," *Business Insider* (November 12, 2010), www.businessinsider.com/ridiculous-regulations-big-government-2010-11?op=1.

6 Institute for Justice, "Texas Computer Repair," http://ij.org/case/rife-v-texas-private-security-board-economic-liberty/.

7 Julianne Pepitone, "Hey bloggers! Philly wants you to buy a license," *CNN Money* (August 24, 2010), http://money.cnn.com/2010/08/24/technology/philadelphia_blogger_tax/index.htm.

8 Jason Adkins, "Regulations show courts have duty to protect economic liberty," *Wisconsin Law Journal* (November 3, 2010), http://wislawjournal.com/2010/11/03/regulations-show-courts-have-duty-to-protect-economic-liberty/.

9 *New State Ice Co. v. Liebmann*, 285 US 262-Supreme Court 1932, "Mr. Justice Brandeis dissenting," https://scholar.google.com/scholar_case?case=14454584999299199739&q=new+state+ice+co.+v.+liebmann&hl=en&as_sdt=80006&as_vis=1.

10 "*Wickard v. Filburn*, 317 U.S. 111 (1942) 317 U.S. 111," http://law2.umkc.edu/faculty/projects/ftrials/conlaw/wickard.html.

11 Dudley and Brito, 1-4.

12 Upton Sinclair, *The Jungle* (New York: Doubleday, Jabber & Company, 1906).

13 Albert Beveridge quoted in Paul Moreno, *The American State from the Civil War to the New Deal: The Twilight of Constitutionalism and the Triumph of Progressivism* (Cambridge, UK, and New York: Cambridge University Press, 2013), 92.

14 Lewis L. Gould, *America in the Progressive Era 1890–1914* (London and New York: Routledge, 2013), 45; also see Robert W. Cherny, "The Jungle and the Progressive Era," *History Now: The Journal of the Gilder Lehrman Institute of American History*, https://www.gilderlehrman.org/history-by-era/politics-reform/essays/jungle-and-progressive-era.

15 Clyde Wayne Crews, *Ten Thousand Commandments 2015*, CEI Publications, https://cei.org/10kc2015.

16 Clyde Wayne Crews, *Ten Thousand Commandments 2015*, CEI Publications, https://cei.org/10kc2015. As noted in Chapter 1, the $1.9 trillion figure is disputed by some, and the OMB shows a net benefit of the 2014 regulatory regime. See Chapter 1, note 15.

17 National Association of Manufacturers, *The Cost of Federal Regulation to the U.S. Economy, Manufacturing and Small Business* (Executive Summary), www.nam.org/Data-and-Reports/Cost-of-Federal-Regulations/Federal-Regulation-Executive-Summary.pdf. Commissioned by the Association, the analysis was compiled by economists Nicole V. Crain and W. Mark Crain, who based it on "previous analyses [they] conducted...for the U.S. Small Business Administration's Office of Advocacy.

18 Clyde Wayne Crews, *Ten Thousand Commandments 2015*, CEI Publications, https://cei.org/10kc2015.

19 Dudley and Brito, 105.

20 Philip Bump, "The 113th Congress is historically good at not passing bills," *The Washington Post* (July 9, 2014), https://www.washingtonpost.com/news/the-fix/wp/2014/07/09/the-113th-congress-is-historically-good-at-not-passing-bills/.

21 Clyde Wayne Crews, *Ten Thousand Commandments 2015*, CEI Publications, https://cei.org/10kc2015.

22 Bureau of Labor Statistics, "Current Employment Statistics-CES (National), www.bls.gov/web/empsit/ceseeb1a.htm.

23 Dudley and Brito, 57.

24 Josh Zumbrun, "The Federal Government Now Employs the Fewest People Since 1966, *The Wall Street Journal* (November 7, 2014), http://blogs.wsj.com/economics/2014/11/07/the-federal-government-now-employs-the-fewest-people-since-1966/.

25 Dudley and Brito, 57, 105.

26 Dudley and Brito, 106, and U.S. Department of Homeland Security, "Budget in Brief: Fiscal Year 2017," https://www.dhs.gov/sites/default/files/publications/FY2017_BIB-MASTER.pdf.

27 Dudley and Brito, 106, and Morrison & Foerster, "The Dodd-Frank Act: A Cheat Sheet," http://media.mofo.com/files/uploads/images/summarydoddfrankact.pdf.

28 James Q. Wilson, *Bureaucracy: What Government Agencies Do and Why They Do It* (New York: Basic Books, 1989).

29 Stephen Breyer, *Breaking the Vicious Circle: Toward Effective Risk Regulation* (Cambridge, MA: Harvard University Press, 1995), 11.

30 Susan E. Dudley, "Is There a Constituency for OIRA? Lessons Learned, Challenges Ahead," *Regulation* (Summer 2009), http://object.cato.org/sites/cato.org/files/serials/files/regulation/2009/6/v32n2-1.pdf.

31 Dudley, http://object.cato.org/sites/cato.org/files/serials/files/regulation/2009/6/v32n2-1.pdf.

32 Dudley, http://object.cato.org/sites/cato.org/files/serials/files/regulation/2009/6/v32n2-1.pdf.

33 Dudley, http://object.cato.org/sites/cato.org/files/serials/files/regulation/2009/6/v32n2-1.pdf.

34 Dudley, http://object.cato.org/sites/cato.org/files/serials/files/regulation/2009/6/v32n2-1.pdf.

35 The following draws on Tibor R. Machan, "Government Regulation of Business: The Moral Arguments," presented at the Southwestern University School of Law, Los Angeles, March 1988, and reproduced by the Foundation for Economic Education (FEE), http://fee.org/articles/government-regulation-of-business-the-moral-arguments/.

36 Clyde Wayne Crews, *Ten Thousand Commandments 2015*, CEI Publications, https://cei.org/10kc2015.

CHAPTER 7

1 Estimate interpolated from Federal Interagency Forum on Aging-Related Statistics, *Older Americans 2012: Key Indicators of Well-Being* (Washington, D.C.: U.S. Government Printing Office, June 2012), 82, www.agingstats.gov/agingstatsdotnet/Main_Site/Data/2012_Documents/Docs/EntireChartbook.pdf.

2 History.com. "The Great Depression," www.history.com/topics/great-depression.

3 Office of Management and Budget, Historical Tables, Table 1.2 and Table 1.1, https://www.whitehouse.gov/omb/budget/Historicals.

4 United States History, "Unemployment Statistics during the Great Depression," www.u-s-history.com/pages/h1528.html.

5 PBS.org, *The First Measured Century,* "Measurements and Myths of the Great Depression," www.pbs.org/fmc/segments/progseg6.htm.

6 PBS.org, *The First Measured Century,* "Measurements and Myths of the Great Depression," www.pbs.org/fmc/segments/progseg6.htm.

7 PBS.org, *The First Measured Century,* "George Gallup and the Scientific Opinion Poll," www.pbs.org/fmc/segments/progseg7.htm.

8 Jodie T. Allen, "How a Different America Responded to the Great Depression." Pew Research Center (December 14, 2010), www.pewresearch.org/2010/12/14/how-a-different-america-responded-to-the-great-depression/.

9 It is true that some 12,000 banks failed during 1920–1933, "but 10,000 of these were tiny rural banks located in places of less than 2,500 population." Their failure was "largely irrelevant to the nation's overall GDP." See David A. Stockman, *The Great Deformation: The Corruption of Capitalism in America* (New York: Public Affairs, 2013), 151.

10 Trevor Hastie, Robert Tibshirani, and Jerome Friedman, *The Elements of Statistical Learning*, 2nd ed. (New York: Springer, 2009), vii, http://statweb.stanford.edu/~tibs/ElemStatLearn/download.html.

11 Office of Management and Budget, Historical Tables, Table 1.2, https://www.whitehouse.gov/omb/budget/Historicals.

12 Adapted from United States History, "Unemployment Statistics during the Great Depression," www.u-s-history.com/pages/h1528.html.

13 See Ben S. Bernanke, *Essays on the Great Depression* (Princeton, NJ: Princeton University Press, 2004). Even Bernanke agrees with the consensus that the New Deal itself did not end the Great Depression; he argues, however, that it cleared the way for a "natural" recovery.

14 Stockman, 139.

15 Stockman, 145-146.

16 Yaron Brook and Don Watkins, "Why the Glass-Steagall Myth Persists," *Forbes* (November 12, 2012), www.forbes.com/sites/objectivist/2012/11/12/why-the-glass-steagall-myth-persists.

17 Brook and Watkins, www.forbes.com/sites/objectivist/2012/11/12/why-the-glass-steagall-myth-persists; italics added.

18 Brook and Watkins, www.forbes.com/sites/objectivist/2012/11/12/why-the-glass-steagall-myth-persists.

19 See Stockman, "The Myth of New Deal Keynesian Reflation" in *The Great Deformation,* 163-164.

20 Office of Management and Budget, Historical Tables, Table 1.2, https://www.whitehouse.gov/omb/budget/Historicals.

21 Office of Management and Budget, Historical Tables, Tables 1.1 and 1.2, https://www.whitehouse.gov/omb/budget/Historicals.

22 Stockman, 172.

23 Mark R. Levin, *Plunder and Deceit: Big Government's Exploitation of Young People and the Future* (New York: Threshold Editions, 2015), 5.

24 Stockman, 172.

25 Laurence J. Kotlikoff, "44 Social Security 'Secrets' All Baby Boomers and Millions of Current Recipients Need to Know—Revised!" *Forbes* (July 3, 2012), www.forbes.com/sites/kotlikoff/2012/07/03/44-social-security-secrets-all-baby-boomers-and-millions-of-current-recipients-need-to-know/#3314b5a650b9. Kotlikoff goes on to point out that the Social Security Administration's Program Operating Manual System (POMS) "has thousands upon thousands of explanations of those [2,728] rules," explanations intended as guidance on implementing them. "Talk about a user's nightmare!"

26 Stockman, 172.

27 Social Security, "Agency History," Research Note #19, https://www.ssa.gov/history/percent.html.

28 Center on Budget and Policy Priorities, "Policy Basics: Where Do Our Federal Tax Dollars Go?" (updated March 4, 2016), www.cbpp.org/research/federal-budget/policy-basics-where-do-our-federal-tax-dollars-go?fa=view&id=1258.

29 Center on Budget and Policy Priorities, "Policy Basics: Where Do Our Federal Tax Dollars Go?" (updated March 4, 2016), www.cbpp.org/research/federal-budget/policy-basics-where-do-our-federal-tax-dollars-go?fa=view&id=1258.

30 Herbert Stein, "Herb Stein's Unfamiliar Quotations," *Slate* (May 16, 1997), www.slate.com/articles/business/it_seems_to_me/1997/05/herb_steins_unfamiliar_quotations.single.html.

31 Social Security and Medicare Boards of Trustees, "Status of the Social Security and Medicare Programs: A Summary of the 2015 Annual Reports," https://www.ssa.gov/oact/trsum/; italics added.

32 Social Security and Medicare Boards of Trustees, "Status of the Social Security and Medicare Programs: A Summary of the 2015 Annual Reports," https://www.ssa.gov/oact/trsum/.

33 Social Security and Medicare Boards of Trustees, "Status of the Social Security and Medicare Programs: A Summary of the 2015 Annual Reports," https://www.ssa.gov/oact/trsum/.

34 2015 OASDI Trustees Report, "D. Projections of Future Financial Status," Figure II.D6.—Cumulative Scheduled OASDI Income Less Cost, From Program Inception Through Years 2014-89, https://www.ssa.gov/oact/tr/2015/II_D_project.html#105057.

35 Laurence J. Kotlikoff, "America's Fiscal Insolvency and its Generational Consequences," Testimony to the Senate Budget Committee (February 25, 2015), 5, www.kotlikoff.net/sites/default/files/Kotlikoffbudgetcom2-25-2015.pdf.

36 Levin, 41-42.

37 U.S. Government Accountability Office. (2012, June 14). Testimony. National Medicaid Audit Program. CMS Should Improve Reporting and Focus on Audit Collaboration with States (p. 1), www.gao.gov/assets/600/591601.pdf.

38 Payment Accuracy, "Improper Payment Amounts (FYs 2004–2015)," https://paymentaccuracy.gov/improper-payment-amounts; "High-Error Programs," https://paymentaccuracy.gov/high-priority-programs.

39 Levin, 43.

40 Social Security and Medicare Boards of Trustees, "Status of the Social Security and Medicare Programs: A Summary of the 2015 Annual Reports," https://www.ssa.gov/oact/trsum/.

41 Social Security Administration, "Social Security and Medicare Tax Rates," https://www.ssa.gov/oact/ProgData/taxRates.html.

42 New York State Office of the State Comptroller, "New York City Securities Industry Bonus Pool" (March 7, 2016), www.osc.state.ny.us/press/releases/mar16/nyc_security_bonus_pool.pdf.

43 Renae Merle, "Why $146,200 is a terrible bonus for Wall Street," *The Washington Post* (March 7, 2016), https://www.washingtonpost.com/news/business/wp/2016/03/07/why-146200-is-a-terrible-bonus-for-wall-street/.

44 U.S. Commodity Futures Trading Commission, "Clearing Organizations," www.cftc.gov/IndustryOversight/ClearingOrganizations/index.htm.

45 David M. Herszenhorn, Carl Hulse, and Sheryl Gay Stolberg, "Talks Implode During a Day of Chaos; Fate of Bailout Plan Remains Unresolved," *The New York Times* (September 25, 2008), www.nytimes.com/2008/09/26/business/26bailout.html?_r=2&hp=&oref=slogin&pagewanted=all.

46 David Goldman, "The $8 trillion bailout," *CNN Money* (January 6, 2009), http://money.cnn.com/2009/01/06/news/economy/where_stimulus_fits_in/.

47 Barack Obama, Address to Joint Session of Congress. February 24, 2009, https://www.whitehouse.gov/the-press-office/remarks-president-barack-obama-address-joint-session-congress.

48 Veronique de Rugy and Jakina Debnam, "Does Government Spending Stimulate Economies?" *Mercatus on Policy*, no. 77 (July 2010),1-2, http://mercatus.org/sites/default/files/publication/MOP77_SBI_Spending%20Multiplier_web%20(2).pdf.

49 De Rugy and Debnam, 2.

50 Christina D. Romer and David H. Romer, "The Macroeconomic Effects of Tax Changes: Estimates Based on a New Measure of Fiscal Shocks" (working paper, University of California–Berkeley, March 2007), http://eml.berkeley.edu/~dromer/papers/RomerandRomerAERJune2010.pdf.

51 De Rugy and Debnam, 4.

52 Kotlikoff, 2, www.kotlikoff.net/sites/default/files/Kotlikoffbudgetcom2-25-2015.pdf.

53 Kotlikoff, 3-4.

54 Kotlikoff, 4.

55 The Nobel laureate economist Paul Krugman concisely argues the counterpoint to Kotlikoff in a *New York Times* op ed, "The Conscience of a Liberal," *New York Times* (August 2, 2014), http://krugman.blogs.nytimes.com/2014/08/02/quadrillions-and-quadrillions/?_r=0, and even Kotlikoff himself has pointed out the potential for abusing infinite horizon budget accounting to promote a political agenda: Center for Economic and Policy Research, "Larry Kotlikoff Tells Us Why We Should Not Use Infinite Horizon Budget Accounting," *CEPR Beat the Press* (July 31, 2014), http://cepr.net/blogs/beat-the-press/larry-kotlikoff-tells-us-why-we-should-not-use-infinite-horizon-budget-accounting.

56 Ben Austen, "The Post-Post-Apocalyptic Detroit," *The New York Times Magazine* (July 11, 2013), www.nytimes.com/2014/07/13/magazine/the-post-post-apocalyptic-detroit.html?_r=0.

57 Kotlikoff, 7. The source of the data are calculations by Laurence Kotlikoff based on CBO Alternative Fiscal Scenario Projections.

58 Kotlikoff, 10.

CHAPTER 8

1 Washington's Farewell Address, 1796, Yale Law School Lillian Goldman Law Library, The Avalon Project, http://avalon.law.yale.edu/18th_century/washing.asp.

2 Dwight D. Eisenhower, Farewell Address (January 17, 1961), http://mcadams.posc.mu.edu/ike.htm. All quotations from the speech are from this source.

3 Italics added.

4 WashingtonsBlog, "What Eisenhower REALLY Said About the 'Military Industrial Complex,'" WashingtonsBlog(October10,2015),www.washingtonsblog.com/2015/10/what-eisenhower-really-said-about-the-military-indutrial-complex.html.

5 "US Defense Spending History," www.usgovernmentspending.com/defense_spending.

6 U.S. Government Publishing Office, Historical Tables, Table 3.1-Outlays—by Superfunction and Function, 1940-2021, https://www.whitehouse.gov/omb/budget/Historicals.

7 John Esterbrook, "Rumsfeld: It Would Be a Short War," CBS News (November 15, 2002), www.cbsnews.com/news/rumsfeld-it-would-be-a-short-war/.

8 "US Defense Spending History," www.usgovernmentspending.com/defense_spending.

9 Daniel Trotta (Reuters), "Iraq War Cost U.S. More than $2 Trillion, Could Grow to $6 Trillion, Says Watson Institute Study," *The Huffington Post* (May 14, 2013), www.huffingtonpost.com/2013/03/14/iraq-war-cost-more-than-2-trillion_n_2875493.html.

10 U.S. Government Publishing Office, Historical Tables, Table 3.1-Outlays—by Superfunction and Function, 1940-2021, https://www.whitehouse.gov/omb/budget/Historicals.

11 U.S. Government Publishing Office, Historical Tables, Table 5.3—Budget Authority by Function and Subfunction, 1976-2019, https://www.gpo.gov/fdsys/search/pagedetails.action?granuleId=BUDGET-2015-TAB-5-1&packageId=BUDGET-2015-TAB&fromBrowse=true.

12 The precedent for the 2013 BCA sequesters was the Gramm-Rudman-Hollings Balanced Budget Act of 1985, which introduced the sequester mechanism as automatic budget cuts that would be triggered if the federal deficit exceeded a set of fixed deficit targets.

13 Congressional Budget Office, "The Budget and Economic Outlook: Fiscal Years 2013 to 2023" (February 2013), https://www.cbo.gov/publication/43907.

14 U.S. Government Publishing Office, Historical Tables, Table 5.1, https://www.gpo.gov/fdsys/search/pagedetails.action?granuleId=BUDGET-2015-TAB-5-1&packageId=BUDGET-2015-TAB&fromBrowse=true.

15 U.S. Government Publishing Office, Historical Tables, Table 5.3, https://www.gpo.gov/fdsys/search/pagedetails.action?granuleId=BUDGET-2015-TAB-5-1&packageId=BUDGET-2015-TAB&fromBrowse=true.

16 Calculated from U.S. Government Publishing Office, Historical Tables, Tables 5.1 and 5.3, https://www.gpo.gov/fdsys/search/pagedetails.action?granuleId=BUDGET-2015-TAB-5-1&packageId=BUDGET-2015-TAB&fromBrowse=true.

17 See Chapter 5 and Laurence J. Kotlikoff, "America's Fiscal Insolvency and its Generational Consequences," Testimony to the Senate Budget Committee (February 25, 2015), 2, www.budget.senate.gov/republican/public/index.cfm?a=Files.Serve&File_id=5e791473-386f-4149-8db0-00e50fdcdbf8.

18 See Lauren Carroll, "Retired general says al-Qaida has grown 'fourfold' in last 5 years," Punditfact (February 1, 2015), www.politifact.com/punditfact/statements/2015/feb/01/jack-keane/retired-general-says-al-qaida-has-grown-fourfold-l/.

19 Rebecca Thorpe, *The American Warfare State: The Domestic Politics of Military Spending* (Chicago: University of Chicago Press, 2014), Introduction; Kindle ed.

20 Thorpe, Introduction; Kindle ed.

21 Thorpe, Introduction; Kindle ed.

22 Thorpe, Introduction; Kindle ed.

23 Duncan Campbell, "Bush talks of first war of 21st century," *The Guardian* (September 14, 2001), https://www.theguardian.com/world/2001/sep/14/september11.usa8.

24 Thorpe, Introduction; Kindle ed.

25 Thorpe, Introduction; Kindle ed.

26 Thorpe, Introduction; Kindle ed.

27 See Non GMO Project, "GMO Facts," FAQs, www.nongmoproject.org/learn-more/.

28 David A. Stockman, *The Great Deformation: The Corruption of Capitalism in America* (New York: Public Affairs, 2013).

CHAPTER 9

1 Senator Jeff Flake, *Wastebook: The Farce Awakens* (December 2015), 4, www.flake. senate.gov/public/_cache/files/03714fa3-e01d-46a1-9c19-299533056741/waste-book---the-farce-awakens.pdf.

2 Flake, 49.

3 Flake, 91-92.

4 Flake, 103.

5 Flake, 112.

6 Flake, 146.

7 Flake, 72. See also David Boyer, "Philly VA director got $288K 'relocation' bonus," *The Washington Times* (March 25, 2015), www.washingtontimes.com/news/2015/mar/25/philly-va-director-got-288k-relocation-bonus/.

8 Flake, 139-140.

9 Leon H. Wolf, "'Defense Spending' Can Be Wasteful, Too," *Red State* (November 2, 2015), www.redstate.com/leon_h_wolf/2015/11/02/defense-spending-can-wasteful/.

10 Kristina Wong, "McCain: Pentagon Wasting Money Studying 'Bomb-Sniffing Elephants," *The Hill* (March 26, 2015), http://thehill.com/policy/defense/budget-appropriations/237044-mccain-vows-to-fight-sequestration-wasteful-defense. Details of the South African study, which is funded by the U.S. Army Research Office, can be found in Christopher Torchia, "Bomb-Sniffing Elephants? Not So Nutty, U.S. Army Says," *USA Today* (March 11, 2015), www.usatoday.com/story/news/world/2015/03/11/bomb-sniffing-elephants/70149110/.

11 Wong, http://thehill.com/policy/defense/budget-appropriations/237044-mccain-vows-to-fight-sequestration-wasteful-defense.

12 Bryant Jordan, "Senator Takes Aim at Military Programs for Wasteful Spending," *Military.com* (October 22, 2014), www.military.com/daily-news/2014/10/22/senator-takes-aim-at-military-programs-for-wasteful-spending.html.

13 Stew Magnuson, "SOCOM's 'Iron Man' Suit Faces Major Technological Hurdles," *National Defense* (January 28, 2015), www.nationaldefensemagazine.org/blog/lists/posts/post.aspx?ID=1725.

14 Jordan, www.military.com/daily-news/2014/10/22/senator-takes-aim-at-military-programs-for-wasteful-spending.html.

15 Jacqueline Leo and Brianna Ehley, "With $8.5 Trillion Unaccounted for, Why Should Congress Increase the Defense Budget?" *The Fiscal Times* (March 19, 2015), www.thefiscaltimes.com/2015/03/19/85-Trillion-Unaccounted-Should-Congress-Increase-Defense-Budget.

16 Scot Paltrow, "How the Pentagon Cooks the Books to Hide Massive Waste," *The Fiscal Times* (November 18, 2013), www.thefiscaltimes.com/Articles/2013/11/18/How-Pentagon-Cooks-Books-Hide-Massive-Waste.

17 Paltrow, www.thefiscaltimes.com/Articles/2013/11/18/How-Pentagon-Cooks-Books-Hide-Massive-Waste.

18 Paltrow, www.thefiscaltimes.com/Articles/2013/11/18/How-Pentagon-Cooks-Books-Hide-Massive-Waste.

19 Paltrow, www.thefiscaltimes.com/Articles/2013/11/18/How-Pentagon-Cooks-Books-Hide-Massive-Waste.

20 U.S. Government Publishing Office, Historical Tables, Table 3.1-Outlays—by Super-function and Function, 1940-2021, https://www.whitehouse.gov/omb/budget/Historicals.

21 "President Obama Proposes 2017 Budget," National Priorities Project, https://www.nationalpriorities.org/analysis/2016/president-obamas-2017-budget/.

22 National Priorities Project, "The President's 2017 Budget Proposal in Pictures," https://www.nationalpriorities.org/analysis/2016/presidents-2017-budget-in-pictures/.

23 Genevive LaFranc, "Defense spending is wasteful, and it might actually make the US less safe", *Business Insider* (July 24, 2015), https://www.nationalpriorities.org/pressroom/articles/2015/07/24/defense-spending-wasteful-unsafe/.

24 Paltrow, www.thefiscaltimes.com/Articles/2013/11/18/How-Pentagon-Cooks-Books-Hide-Massive-Waste.

25 Tim Roemer, "Why Do Congressmen Spend Only Half Their Time Serving Us?" *Newsweek* (July 29, 2015), www.newsweek.com/why-do-congressmen-spend-only-half-their-time-serving-us-357995.

26 CNN Politics, "Trump appears stumped by question on nuclear triad" (December 17, 2015), www.cnn.com/videos/politics/2015/12/17/what-is-nuclear-triad-debate-sot.cnn. The nuclear triad is, of course, the three weapons systems capable of delivering nuclear or thermonuclear ordnance against an enemy: ICBM missiles, long-range bomber aircraft, and missile-launching nuclear submarines.

27 United Nations General Assembly, "44/34. International Convention against the Recruitment, Use, Financing, and Training of Mercenaries" (December 4, 1989), www.un.org/documents/ga/res/44/a44r034.htm.

28 Ronald Reagan, Inaugural Address (January 20, 1981), www.presidency.ucsb.edu/ws/?pid=43130.

29 Jimmie I. Wise, *Outsourcing Wars: Comparing Risk, Benefits and Motivation of Contractors and Military Personnel in Iraq and Afghanistan (2009-2011)* (Monterey, CA: Naval Postgraduate School, 2012), 3.

30 Wise, 2-3.

31 John W. Whitehead, "Privatizing the War on Terror: America's Military Contractors," The Rutherford Institute (January 16, 2012), https://www.rutherford.org/publications_resources/john_whiteheads_commentary/privatizing_the_war_on_terror_americas_military_contractors.

32 It is important to note that most contractors are logistical and support personnel, who are paid much less than these combat wages—but, typically, still more than U.S. military basic pay.

33 Commission on Wartime Contracting in Iraq and Afghanistan, *Transforming Wartime Contracting: Controlling Costs, Reducing Risks,* Final Report to Congress (August 2011), http://cybercemetery.unt.edu/archive/cwc/20110929213922/http://www.wartimecontracting.gov/docs/CWC_FinalReport-highres.pdf, 22, Table 2. The figure includes $166.6 billion in DoD contracts, $12.2 billion in Department of State contracts, and $8.4 billion in USAID contracts, in addition to a total of $5.3 billion in State and USAID grants.

34 Commission on Wartime Contracting in Iraq and Afghanistan, 22.

35 Commission on Wartime Contracting in Iraq and Afghanistan, 2-12.

36 Information on cost-plus PMC contracting from Alan Axelrod, *Mercenaries: A Guide to Private Armies and Private Military Companies* (Los Angeles: SAGE Reference/CQ Press, 2014), 281.

37 Angelo Young, "Cheney's Halliburton Made $39.5 Billion on Iraq War," *International Business Times* (March 20, 2013), http://readersupportednews.org/news-section2/308-12/16561-focus-cheneys-halliburton-made-395-billion-on-iraq-war. From 1995 to 2007, KBR was a wholly owned subsidiary of Halliburton. The Commission on Wartime Contracting in Iraq and Afghanistan lists KBR as the #1 contingency contractor in Iraq and Afghanistan during FY 2002–FY 2011. U.S. contract obligations to the company totaled $40.8 billion (*Transforming Wartime Contracting: Controlling Costs, Reducing Risks*, 25, http://cybercemetery.unt.edu/archive/cwc/20110929213922/www.wartimecontracting.gov/docs/CWC_FinalReport-highres.pdf).

38 Louis Jacobson, "Chris Matthews says Cheney got $34 million payday from Halliburton," PolitiFact (May 24, 2010), www.politifact.com/truth-o-meter/statements/2010/may/24/chris-matthews/chris-matthews-says-cheney-got-34-million-payday-h/.

39 Axelrod, *Mercenaries*, 190.

40 Axelrod, *Mercenaries*, 305-306.

41 William D. Hartung, "A Golden Age for Pentagon Waste: Ridiculous Pentagon spending may be reaching historic levels," *U.S. News & World Report* (February 3, 2016), www.usnews.com/opinion/blogs/world-report/articles/2016-02-03/the-pentagon-could-reach-a-historic-level-of-wasteful-spending.

42 Hartung, www.usnews.com/opinion/blogs/world-report/articles/2016-02-03/the-pentagon-could-reach-a-historic-level-of-wasteful-spending.

CHAPTER 10

1 Chester Collins Maxey, "A Little History of Pork," *National Municipal Review*, vol. 8, no. 10 (December 1919), 691.

2 Maxey, 691.

3 Maxey, 692-693.

4 Maxey, 693.

5 Maxey, 693.

6 Patricia T. O'Connor and Stewart Kellerman, "The pork in 'pork barrel,'" *Grammarphobia* (February 11, 2014), www.grammarphobia.com/blog/2014/02/pork-barrel.html.

7 Citizens Against Government Waste, *The Pig Book: How Government Wastes Your Money* (New York: Thomas Dunne Books, 2005), xvi.

8 IMDb, "Quotes for Don Vito Corleone from *The Godfather* (1972), www.imdb.com/character/ch0000791/quotes.

9 Office of Management and Budget, "What Is an Earmark?" https://earmarks.omb.gov/earmarks-public/.

10 Diana Evans, *Greasing the Wheels: Using Pork Projects to Build Majority Coalitions in Congress* (Cambridge and New York: Cambridge University Press, 2004), Introduction; Kindle ed.

11 And also the root of the pun in the title of political satirist P. J. O'Rourke's retrospective collection of essays, *Thrown Under the Omnibus: A Reader* (New York: Atlantic Monthly, 2015). "Agricultural Policy," in that collection (pp. 175-185), is a satirical (as in 100% accurate) discussion of how agricultural pork works.

12 Robert Pear, "House Passes Spending Bill, and Critics Are Quick to Point Out Pork," *The New York Times* (February 25, 2009), www.nytimes.com/2009/02/26/us/politics/26spend.html?_r=0.

13 Evans, Introduction; Kindle ed.

14 Evans, Introduction; Kindle ed.

15 Evans, Introduction; Kindle ed.

16 Marcus Tullius Cicero, "Pro Roscio Amerino," http://thelatinlibrary.com/cicero/sex.rosc.shtml.

17 Brian Kelly, *Adventures in Porkland: How Washington Wastes Your Money and Why They Won't Stop* (New York: Villard, 1992), 6.

18 This discussion is based on Evans, Introduction; Kindle ed.

19 Pear, www.nytimes.com/2009/02/26/us/politics/26spend.html?_r=0.

20 J. Courtney Sullivan, "Why 'A Diamond Is Forever' Has Lasted So Long," *The Washington Post* (February 7, 2014), https://www.washingtonpost.com/opinions/why-a-diamond-is-forever-has-lasted-so-long/2014/02/07/f6adf3f4-8eae-11e3-84e1-27626c5ef5fb_story.html.

21 Paul Kane, "House bans earmarks to for-profit companies," *The Washington Post* (March 11, 2010), www.washingtonpost.com/wp-dyn/content/article/2010/03/10/AR2010031002084.html.

22 Jordan Fabian and Molly K. Hooper, "House GOP votes to ball all earmarks, *The Hill* (March 11, 2010), http://thehill.com/blogs/blog-briefing-room/news/86203-house-gop-approves-conference-wide-earmark-ban.

23 Devin Dwyer and Matthew Jaffe, "Senate Republicans Ban Earmarks; Will Democrats Follow?" ABC News (November 16, 2010), http://abcnews.go.com/Politics/earmark-moratorium-republicans-poised-ban-pork-barrel-spending/story?id=12155964.

24 Lisa Mascaro, "Ban on earmark spending ends political battle," *Los Angeles Times* (February 1, 2011), http://articles.latimes.com/2011/feb/01/news/la-pn-earmark-ban-20110201.

25 Ron Nixon, "Lawmakers Finance Pet Projects Without Earmarks," *The New York Times* (December 27, 2010), www.nytimes.com/2010/12/28/us/politics/28earmarks.html?_r=4&src=twt&twt=nytimespolitics.

26 General Memorandum 11-017 (February 4, 2011), "Earmark Ban Approved by House and Senate," www.npaihb.org/images/resources_docs/weeklymailout/2011/february/week2/GM_11-017_EarmarkBanFY2011CR.pdf.

27 Paul Ryan, Speaker of the House, "House Republicans Renew Earmark Ban for 113th Congress" (November 16, 2012), www.speaker.gov/general/house-republicans-renew-earmark-ban-113th-congress.

28 Louis Jacobson, "GOP approved earmark ban for 112th Congress and re-upped for 113th," *PolitiFact* (January 8, 2013), www.politifact.com/truth-o-meter/

promises/gop-pledge-o-meter/promise/685/refuse-to-consider-house-legislation-that-includes/.

29 Brendan Greeley, "Earmarks: The Reluctant Case for Ending the Ban," *Bloomberg Businessweek* (January 10, 2013), www.bloomberg.com/news/articles/2013-01-10/earmarks-the-reluctant-case-for-ending-the-ban.

30 Greeley, www.bloomberg.com/news/articles/2013-01-10/earmarks-the-reluctant-case-for-ending-the-ban.

31 Greeley, www.bloomberg.com/news/articles/2013-01-10/earmarks-the-reluctant-case-for-ending-the-ban.

32 CNN, "Sandy Hook shooting: What happened?" www.cnn.com/interactive/2012/12/us/sandy-hook-timeline/.

33 Juliet Eilperin and Sean Sullivan, "How the ban on earmarks killed the gun bill," *The Washington Post* (April 19, 2013), https://www.washingtonpost.com/news/the-fix/wp/2013/04/19/how-the-ban-on-earmarks-killed-the-gun-bill/.

34 Erin Kelly, "Some want earmarks back to help Congress pass bills," *USA Today* (October 29, 2013), www.usatoday.com/story/news/politics/2013/10/29/congress-earmarks-legislation-spending/3295509/.

35 "Posted by streiff," "House Continues Ban On Earmarks," *Red State* (November 13, 2014), www.redstate.com/streiff/2014/11/15/house-continues-ban-earmarks/.

36 Paul Blumenthal and Christina Wilkie, "Omnibus Budget Proves That Earmarks Will Never Die In Congress," *Huffington Politics* (January 25, 2014), www.huffingtonpost.com/2014/01/15/omnibus-budget-earmarks_n_4603141.html.

37 See Senator John Hoeven, "Omnibus Appropriations Bill Includes North Dakota Priorities for Global Hawk, Missile Silos" (January 14, 2014), https://www.hoeven.senate.gov/news/news-releases/omnibus-appropriations-bill-includes-north-dakota-priorities-for-global-hawk-missile-silos. The U.S. Air Force wanted to retire its Northrop Grumman RQ-4 Global Hawk vintage 1998 obsolescent drones and dismantle some of its aging ICBM missile silos. These moves threatened the eventual closure of North Dakota's two U.S. Air Force bases, which provide much-needed employment in the state.

38 Taxpayers for Common Sense cited in Blumenthal and Wilkie, www.huffingtonpost.com/2014/01/15/omnibus-budget-earmarks_n_4603141.html.

39 Blumenthal and Wilkie, www.huffingtonpost.com/2014/01/15/omnibus-budget-earmarks_n_4603141.html.

40 Citizens Against Government Waste, *2016 Congressional Pig Book Summary* (Washington, D.C.: CAGW, 2016), 1.

41 Citizens Against Government Waste, 1.

42 Citizens Against Government Waste, 1.

43 Citizens Against Government Waste, 1-2.

44 Adapted from Citizens Against Government Waste, "Earmark Spending, 1991-2016," http://cagw.org/reporting/pig-book. The "$0 billion" amounts reported for 2011 and 2013 presumably mean that the CAGW researchers found in these years either no spending (or no significant spending) that was classifiable as "earmarks."

45 See, for example, FactCheck.Org, "Pork-barrel Spending," www.factcheck.org/2007/12/pork-barrel-spending/.

46 Jonathan S. Cohn, "Roll Out the Barrel," *The New Republic* 218 (April 20, 1998), 23.

47 Evans, Introduction; Kindle ed.

CHAPTER 11

1 Morgan Cook, "Feds spend millions to split hipsters, cigs," *The San Diego Union-Tribune* (March 21, 2015), www.sandiegouniontribune.com/news/2015/mar/21/millions-spent-to-separate-hipsters-from-their/; Senator Jeff Flake, comp., "Hipster Parties," *Wastebook: The Farce Awakens* (December 2015), 11, www.flake.senate.gov/public/_cache/files/03714fa3-e01d-46a1-9c19-299533056741/wastebook---the-farce-awakens.pdf.

2 Flake, 12.

3 Cook, www.sandiegouniontribune.com/news/2015/mar/21/millions-spent-to-separate-hipsters-from-their/.

4 Cook, www.sandiegouniontribune.com/news/2015/mar/21/millions-spent-to-separate-hipsters-from-their/.

5 Flake, 30-32.

6 Flake, 9.

7 NBC News, "Cosmic Log," "Scientists show how a hot, steamy afternoon kills the chill on a beer can" (April 26, 2013), http://cosmiclog.nbcnews.com/_news/2013/04/26/17934333-scientists-show-how-a-hot-steamy-afternoon-kills-the-chill-on-a-beer-can, and Flake, 15-16.

8 "Thomas Jefferson to Francis Hopkinson, March 13, 1789," Founders Online, National Archives, *The Papers of Thomas Jefferson*, volume 14, October 8, 1788–March 26, 1789 (Princeton: Princeton University Press, 1958, 649-651. Retrieved from http://founders.archives.gov/documents/Jefferson/01-14-02-0402.

9 Jeffrey M. Jones, "In U.S., New Record 43% Are Political Independents," Gallup (January 7, 2015), www.gallup.com/poll/180440/new-record-political-independents.aspx.

10 Flake, 43.

11 U.S. Agency for International Development Office of Inspector General, "Audit of USAID/Pakistan's Political Party Development Program" (October 26, 2015), https://oig.usaid.gov/sites/default/files/audit-reports/g-391-16-001-p.pdf, and Flake, 42-43.

12 Flake, 44-45.

13 U.S. Government Accountability Office (GAO), "GAO High Risk List: National Flood Insurance Program" (2015), www.gao.gov/highrisk/national_flood_insurance/why_did_study.

14 Flake, 64-66.

15 Jon Prior, "HUD aid for its own workers includes $100k move," *POLITICO* (June 15, 2015), www.politico.com/story/2015/06/hud-aid-for-its-own-workers-includes-100k-move-118957.html.

16 Flake, 73.

17 Flake, 74.

18 Flake, 75.

19 "Missouri Transportation by the Numbers: Meeting the State's Need for Safe and Efficient Mobility," *TRIP* (April 2015), http://tripnet.org/docs/MO_Transportation_by_the_Numbers_TRIP_Report_April_2015.pdf, and John Pepitone, "Kansas City among the worst cities with pothole problems," FOX News 4 (April 9, 2014), http://fox4kc.com/2014/04/09/kansas-city-among-the-worst-cities-with-pothole-problems/.

20 Flake, 99-101.

21 Office of Management and Budget, "Payment Accuracy: The Problem," https:// paymentaccuracy.gov/about-improper-payments.

22 Flake, 105.

23 Flake, 106.

24 Flake, 107.

25 Flake, 105-106.

26 P. J. O'Rourke, "Agricultural Policy," in *Thrown Under the Omnibus: A Reader* (New York: Atlantic Monthly Press, 2015), 176-177.

27 Daniel A. Sumner, "American Farms Keep Growing: Size, Productivity, and Policy, *Journal of Economic Perspectives*, 28, no. 1 (Winter 2014), 147, http://pubs.aeaweb. org/doi/pdfplus/10.1257/jep.28.1.147.

28 American Farm Bureau Federation, "Fast Facts about Agriculture," www.fb.org/ newsroom/fastfacts/.

29 Robert Schlesinger, "The Size of the U.S. and the World in 2016," *U.S. News & World Report* (January 5, 2016), www.usnews.com/opinion/blogs/ robert-schlesinger/articles/2016-01-05/us-population-in-2016-according-to-census-estimates-322-762-018.

30 O'Rourke, "Agricultural Policy," 177-178.

31 O'Rourke, "Agricultural Policy," 179.

32 Open Secrets.Org, "Agribusiness Sector Profile, 2016," https://www.opensecrets. org/lobby/indus.php?id=A.

33 United States Department of Agriculture, "FY 2017 Budget Summary," 1-2, www. obpa.usda.gov/budsum/fy17budsum.pdf.

34 Committee on Appropriations Press Releases, "Appropriations Committee Releases the Fiscal Year 2017 Agriculture Appropriations Bill" (April 12, 2016), http://appro-priations.house.gov/news/documentsingle.aspx?DocumentID=394490.

35 Philip Mattera and Kasia Tarczynska, "Uncle Sam's Favorite Corporations: Iden-tifying the Large Companies that Dominate Federal Subsidies," Good Jobs First (March 2015), Appendix A, 14, www.goodjobsfirst.org/sites/default/files/docs/ pdf/UncleSamsFavoriteCorporations.pdf.

36 U.S. Senate Committee on Agriculture, Nutrition, and Forestry, "Senate Approves 2014 Farm Bill, Legislation Heads to the President…Legislation Makes Landmark Reforms in Agriculture Policy, Saves $23 Billion," *Minority News* (February 4, 2014), www.agriculture.senate.gov/newsroom/press/release/ senate-approves-2014-farm-bill-legislation-heads-to-the-president.

37 Dan Charles, "Farm Subsidies Persist and Grow, Despite Talk of Reform," NPR (February 1, 2016), www.npr.org/sections/thesalt/2016/02/01/465132866/ farm-subsidies-persist-and-grow-despite-talk-of-reform.

38 OpenSecrets.org, "Agribusiness Sector Totals to Candidates," https://www. opensecrets.org/pres16/select-sectors.php. Data released April 21, 2016.

39 OpenSecrets.org, "Agribusiness: Money to Congress," https://www.opensecrets. org/industries/summary.php?ind=A&recipdetail=A&sortorder=U&cycle=All. Data released on April 16, 2016.

40 David Brunori, "Where Is the Outrage over Corporate Welfare?" *Forbes* (March 14, 2014), www.forbes.com/sites/taxanalysts/2014/03/14/where-is-the-outrage-over-corporate-welfare; Philip Mattera, "Subsidizing the Corporate One Percent: Subsidy Tracker 2.0 Reveals Big-Business Dominance of State and Local Develop-

ment Incentives," Good Jobs First (February 2014), www.goodjobsfirst.org/sites/
default/files/docs/pdf/subsidizingthecorporateonepercent.pdf.

41 Brunori, www.forbes.com/sites/taxanalysts/2014/03/14/where-is-the-
outrage-over-corporate-welfare.

42 OpenSecrets.org, "Lobbying: Top Spenders," https://www.opensecrets.org/
lobby/top.php?showYear=2016&indexType=s.

43 Paul Buchheit, "Average American Family Pays $6K a Year in Big Business Subsidies,"
Moyers & Company (September 24, 2013), http://billmoyers.com/2013/09/24/
average-american-family-pays-6k-a-year-in-subsidies-to-big-business/.

44 Matera and Tarczynska, Appendix B, 17, www.goodjobsfirst.org/sites/default/files/
docs/pdf/UncleSamsFavoriteCorporations.pdf.

45 OpenSecrets.org, "Congress," https://www.opensecrets.org/politicians/; data
accessed on June 12, 2016.

46 Retired persons do not constitute an industry, but they are among the top contributors to politicians and political campaigns. See "Retire: Background," OpenSecrets.
org, https://www.opensecrets.org/industries/background.php?ind=W06.

47 OpenSecrets.org, "Agribusiness," https://www.opensecrets.org/pres16/select-
sectors.php?sector=A.

48 OpenSecrets.org, "Communications/Electronics," https://www.opensecrets.org/
pres16/select-sectors.php?sector=B.

49 OpenSecrets.org, "Construction," https://www.opensecrets.org/pres16/select-
sectors.php?sector=C.

50 OpenSecrets.org, "Defense," https://www.opensecrets.org/pres16/select-sectors.
php?sector=D.

51 OpenSecrets.org, "Energy/Natural Resources," https://www.opensecrets.org/
pres16/select-sectors.php?sector=E.

52 OpenSecrets.org, "Finance/Real Estate," https://www.opensecrets.org/pres16/
select-sectors.php?sector=F.

53 OpenSecrets.org, "Health," https://www.opensecrets.org/pres16/select-sectors.
php?sector=H.

54 OpenSecrets.org, "Transportation," https://www.opensecrets.org/pres16/select-
sectors.php?sector=M.

55 Mike Collins, "The Decline of Unions Is a Middle Class Problem," Forbes (May 19,
2015), www.forbes.com/sites/mikecollins/2015/03/19/the-decline-of-
unions-is-a-middle-class-problem.

56 Collins, www.forbes.com/sites/mikecollins/2015/03/19/the-decline-of-
unions-is-a-middle-class-problem/#566a153518be, and Kristof, www.nytimes.
com/2015/02/19/opinion/nicholas-kristof-the-cost-of-a-decline-in-unions.
html?_r=1.

57 Collins, www.forbes.com/sites/mikecollins/2015/03/19/the-decline-of-
unions-is-a-middle-class-problem/#566a153518be.

58 Nicholas Kristof, "The Cost of a Decline in Unions," The New York Times (February
19, 2015), www.nytimes.com/2015/02/19/opinion/nicholas-kristof-the-cost-of-a-
decline-in-unions.html?_r=1.

59 The entire quotation is "James Ross Clemens, a cousin of mine, was seriously ill two
or three weeks ago in London, but is well now. The report of my illness grew out of
his illness; the report of my death was an exaggeration" and come from a note Mark
Twain wrote from London on May 31, 1897 to reporter Frank Marshall White. See

Shelley Fisher Fishkin, *Lighting Out For the Territory: Reflections on Mark Twain and American Culture* (New York: Oxford University Press, 1996), 134.

60 Michael Beckel and Seth Cline, "Labor Lobbying, Union PAC Contributions and More in Capital Eye Opener: Sept. 5," OpenSecrets.org (September 5, 2011), www.opensecrets.org/news/2011/09/labor-lobbying-union-pac-money/.

61 Dave Gilson, "Who Owns Congress? A Campaign Cash Seating Chart," *Mother Jones* (September/October 2010), www.motherjones.com/politics/2010/09/congress-corporate-sponsors.

62 Beckel and Cline, www.opensecrets.org/news/2011/09/labor-lobbying-union-pac-money/.

63 OpenSecrets.org, "Labor Sector Profile, 2016," https://www.opensecrets.org/lobby/indus.php?id=P.

64 OpenSecrets.org, "Labor: Top Contributors, 2015–2016," https://www.opensecrets.org/industries/indus.php?ind=P. Data released on May 16, 2016.

65 OpenSecrets.org, "Labor: Money to Congress," https://www.opensecrets.org/industries/summary.php?ind=P&recipdetail=A&sortorder=U&cycle=All. Data released May 16, 2016.

66 OpenSecrets.org, "Energy/Natural Resources: Top Contributors, 2015–2016," https://www.opensecrets.org/industries/indus.php?ind=E. Data released May 16, 2016.

67 OpenSecrets.org, "Energy/Natural Resources Sector Profile, 2016," https://www.opensecrets.org/lobby/indus.php?id=E. Data released April 25, 2016.

68 OpenSecrets.org, "Energy/Natural Resources Sector: Average Contributions to Members of Congress," https://www.opensecrets.org/lobby/indus.php?id=E. Data released April 25, 2016.

69 OpenSecrets.org, "Energy/Natural Resources Sector: Average Contributions to Members of Congress," https://www.opensecrets.org/lobby/indus.php?id=E. Data released April 25, 2016.

70 OpenSecrets.org, "Energy/Natural Resources Sector: Average Contributions to Members of Congress," https://www.opensecrets.org/lobby/indus.php?id=E. Data released April 25, 2016.

71 OpenSecrets.org, "Energy/Natural Resources: Money to Congress," https://www.opensecrets.org/industries/summary.php?ind=E&recipdetail=A&sortorder=U-&cycle=All. Data released May 16, 2016.

72 OpenSecrets.org, "Environment Sector, Top Contributors, 2015–2016," www.opensecrets.org/industries/indus.php?ind=q11. Data released May 16, 2016.

73 OpenSecrets.org, "Environment Sector, Top Contributors, 2015–2016," www.opensecrets.org/industries/indus.php?ind=q11. Data released May 16, 2016.

74 OpenSecrets.org, "Environment Sector, Top Contributors, 2015–2016," www.opensecrets.org/industries/indus.php?ind=q11. Data released May 16, 2016.

75 "Romney: Corporations Are People, My Friend, August 11, 2011," YouTube, https://www.youtube.com/watch?v=KlPQkd_AA6c.

76 U.S. Supreme Court, *Citizens United v. Federal Election Comm'n*, 558 U.S.___ (2010), https://supreme.justia.com/cases/federal/us/558/08-205/.

77 Chris Cillizza, "How Citizens United changed politics, in 7 charts," *The Washington Post* (January 22, 2014), https://www.washingtonpost.com/news/the-fix/wp/2014/01/21/how-citizens-united-changed-politics-in-6-charts/.

78 IRS, "Social Welfare Organizations," https://www.irs.gov/Charities-&-Non-Profits/ Other-Non-Profits/Social-Welfare-Organizations.

79 OpenSecrets.org, "Donor Demographics, 2016," https://www.opensecrets.org/ overview/donordemographics.php.

80 Inside Gov, "Campaign Committees," http://presidential-candidates.insidegov. com/compare/35-40/Bernie-Sanders-vs-Hillary-Clinton.

81 Zoe Thomas, "US election 2016: Who's funding Trump, Sanders and the rest?" *BBC News* (March 17, 2016), www.bbc.com/news/election-us-2016-35713168.

82 Federal Election Commission, "2016 Presidential Campaign Finance," www.fec. gov/disclosurep/PCandList.do.

83 OpenSecrets.org, "Super PACs," https://www.opensecrets.org/pacs/superpacs. php. Data released June 12, 2016.

CHAPTER 12

1 "Leo Mattersdorf, 81, Author And Tax Consultant, Is Dead," *The New York Times* (August 27, 1985), www.nytimes.com/1985/08/27/nyregion/leo-mattersdorf-81-author-and-tax-consultant-is-dead.html.

2 "The Hardest Thing in the World to Understand is Income Taxes," *Quote Investigator: Exploring the Origins of Quotations*," http://quoteinvestigator.com/2011/03/07/ einstein-income-taxes/. Among those Mattersdorf acknowledges in his *Insight into Astronomy*, Albert Einstein figures prominently "for his kindness in reading the manuscript and, then, sitting down with me and offering many helpful suggestions" (Leo Mattersdorf, *Insight into Astronomy* [New York: Lantern Press, 1952], 11).

3 Scott Greenberg, "Federal Tax Laws and Regulations Are Now Over 10 Million Words Long," The Tax Policy Blog (October 8, 2015), http://taxfoundation.org/ blog/federal-tax-laws-and-regulations-are-now-over-10-million-words-long; Jason Russell, "Look at how many pages are in the federal tax code," *Washington Examiner* (April 15, 2016), www.washingtonexaminer.com/look-at-how-many-pages-are-in-the-federal-tax-code/article/2563032.

4 Wolters Kluwer CCH, "Federal Tax Law Keeps Piling Up," www.cch.com/TaxLaw-PileUp.pdf. Note that these figures are often mistaken for the page count of the "IRS code" or the "federal tax code." For a discussion of how some politicians inflate the volume of the nation's tax code, see C. Eugene Emery Jr., "U.S. Senate candidate Barry Hinckley says the nation's tax code is 80,000 pages," PolitiFact (December 27, 2011), www.politifact.com/rhode-island/statements/2011/dec/27/barry-hinckley/ us-senate-candidate-barry-hinckley-says-nations-ta/.

5 Wolters Kluwer CCH, "Federal Tax Law Keeps Piling Up," www.cch.com/TaxLaw-PileUp.pdf.

6 P. J. O'Rourke, "Taxes," in P. J. O'Rourke, *Thrown Under the Omnibus: A Reader* (New York: Atlantic Monthly, 2015), 743.

7 Bruce Bartlett, *The Benefit and The Burden: Tax Reform—Why We Need It and What It Will Take* (New York: Simon and Schuster, 2012), Introduction; Kindle ed.

8 Center on Budget and Policy Priorities, "Policy Basics: Where Do Federal Tax Revenues Come From?" (Updated March 4, 2016), www.cbpp.org/research/ policy-basics-where-do-federal-tax-revenues-come-from.

9 Office of Management and Budget, Historical Tables, "Table 1.1. Summary of Receipts, Outlays, and Surpluses or Deficits (-), 1789–2021," https://www.white-house.gov/omb/budget/Historicals.

10 Susan Johnston Taylor, "12 Times When It Makes Sense to Hire a Tax Preparer," *U.S. News & World Report* (March 2, 2016), http://money.usnews.com/money/personal-finance/articles/2016-03-02/12-times-when-it-makes-sense-to-hire-a-tax-preparer.

11 Bartlett, Introduction; Kindle ed.

12 Bartlett, Introduction; Kindle ed.

13 Except where noted, statistics here and in the following paragraphs are from Bartlett, chapter 1; Kindle ed.

14 *Pollock v. Farmers' Loan & Trust Co.* 157 U.S. 429 (1895), JUSTIA: US Supreme Court, https://supreme.justia.com/cases/federal/us/157/429/.

15 This and the calculations of current value that follow are based on Bureau of Labor Statistics, CPI Inflation Calculator, www.bls.gov/data/inflation_calculator.htm.

16 Quoted in Mark Leff, *The New Deal and Taxation, 1933–1939* (Cambridge, UK, and New York: Cambridge University Press, 1984), 149.

17 Franklin D. Roosevelt, "93 - Message to Congress on Tax Revision, June 19, 1935," The American Presidency Project, www.presidency.ucsb.edu/ws/?pid=15088.

18 Bartlett, Chapter 1; Kindle ed.

19 "H.Doc. 105-211-Appendices to the Referral to the United States House of Representatives Pursuant to Title 28, United States Code, Section 595(c) Submitted by the Office of the Independent Counsel," Volume III...William J. Clinton Statements," U.S. Government Publishing Office, https://www.gpo.gov/fdsys/pkg/GPO-CDOC-105hdoc311/content-detail.html#N_1091_.

20 For a discussion of the quest for a definition of *income* in the context of income taxes, see Bartlett, Chapter 3; Kindle ed.

21 Bartlett, Chapter 3; Kindle ed.

22 IRS, "Home Foreclosure and Debt Cancellation," https://www.irs.gov/uac/home-foreclosure-and-debt-cancellation.

23 Bartlett, Chapter 3; Kindle ed.

24 Bartlett, Chapter 3; Kindle ed.

25 *Poe v. Seaborn* 282 U.S. 101 (1930), JUSTIA: US Supreme Court, https://supreme.justia.com/cases/federal/us/282/101/.

CHAPTER 13

1 Bureau of Labor Statistics, CPI Inflation Calculator, www.bls.gov/data/inflation_calculator.htm.

2 Roger Lowenstein, "Who Needs the Mortgage-Interest Deduction?" *The New York Times* (March 5, 2006), www.nytimes.com/2006/03/05/magazine/305deduction.1.html?pagewanted=1&_r=2.

3 Bruce Bartlett, *The Benefit and The Burden: Tax Reform—Why We Need It and What It Will Take* (New York: Simon and Schuster, 2012), chapter 10; Kelly Phillips Erb, "9 Tax-Related Myths about Selling Your Home," *Forbes* (October 10, 2012), www.forbes.com/sites/kellyphillipserb/2012/10/10/9-tax-related-myths-about-selling-your-home.

4 Wikipedia, "Home mortgage interest deduction," https://en.wikipedia.org/wiki/Home_mortgage_interest_deduction.

5 Bartlett, Chapter 10; Kindle ed.

6 William Shakespeare, *Macbeth*, Act 3, Scene 4, lines 114-120.

7 Orrin Hatch quoted in Bartlett, Chapter 10; Kindle ed.

8 Stanley S. Surrey and Paul R. McDaniel, "The Tax Expenditure Concept and the Budget Reform Act of 1974," *Boston College Industrial and Commercial Law Review*, vol. 17, no. 5 (June 1976), http://lawdigitalcommons.bc.edu/cgi/viewcontent.cgi?article=1529&context=bclr.

9 Stanley S. Surrey and Paul R. McDaniel, *Tax Expenditures* (Cambridge, Mass.: Harvard University Press, 1985).

10 Bartlett, Chapter 10; Kindle ed.

11 Bartlett, Chapter 10; Kindle ed.

12 Bartlett, Chapter 10; Kindle ed.

13 Bartlett, Chapter 10; Kindle ed.

14 Reproduced in Wikipedia, "*Pogo* (comic strip), https://en.wikipedia.org/wiki/Pogo_(comic_strip).

15 Katherine Lim and Jeffrey Rohaly, "Variation in Effective Tax Rates," Abstract, *Tax Policy Center* (February 22, 2010), www.taxpolicycenter.org/publications/variation-effective-tax-rates.

16 Katherine Lim and Jeffrey Rohaly, "Variation in Effective Tax Rates," Full Report, *Tax Policy Center* (February 22, 2010), www.taxpolicycenter.org/publications/variation-effective-tax-rates/full; also see Bartlett, Chapter 10; Kindle ed.

17 Bartlett, Chapter 10; Kindle ed.

18 Catey Hill, "45% of Americans pay no federal income tax," *Market Watch* (April 18, 2016), www.marketwatch.com/story/45-of-americans-pay-no-federal-income-tax-2016-02-24.

19 IRS, Publication 15, Circular E, https://www.irs.gov/pub/irs-pdf/p15.pdf. Also see Ryan McMaken, "Myth: Half of Americans Don't Pay Federal Taxes," Mises Institute (March 7, 2016), https://mises.org/blog/myth-half-americans-dont-pay-federal-taxes.

20 Tax Policy Center, "T09-0333-Tax Units with Zero or Negative Tax Liability, 2009-2019" (July 1, 2009), www.taxpolicycenter.org/model-estimates/tax-units-zero-or-negative-tax-liability/tax-units-zero-or-negative-tax-liability.

21 IRS, "2016 EITC Income Limits, Maximum Credit Amounts and Tax Law Updates," https://www.irs.gov/credits-deductions/individuals/earned-income-tax-credit/eitc-income-limits-maximum-credit-amounts-next-year.

22 Chris Edwards and Veronique de Rugy, "Earned Income Tax Credit: Small Benefits, Large Costs," Cato Institute (October 14, 2015), www.cato.org/publications/tax-budget-bulletin/earned-income-tax-credit-small-benefits-large-costs.

23 For a critical cost-benefit discussion of EITC, see Edwards and de Rugy: "The EITC was designed to counter the anti-work effects of welfare programs and the federal payroll tax. But as we have seen, the EITC creates a range of problems of its own, including errors and fraud, disincentives to increase earnings in the phase-out range, and deadweight losses caused by extracting taxes to pay for it." An argument in support of EITC is Chuck Marr, Chye-Ching Huang, Arloc Sherman, and Brandon Debot, "EITC and Child Tax Credit Promote Work, Reduce Poverty, and Support Children's Development, Research Finds," Center on Budget and

Policy Priorities (Updated October 1, 2015), www.cbpp.org/research/federal-tax/eitc-and-child-tax-credit-promote-work-reduce-poverty-and-support-childrens: "Recent ground-breaking research suggests that the EITC and CTC help families at virtually every stage of life. In addition to the credits' well-established benefits of encouraging work and reducing poverty, recent research suggests that starting from infancy—when higher tax credits are linked to more prenatal care, less maternal stress, and signs of better infant health—children who benefit from tax credit expansions have been found to do better throughout childhood and have higher odds of finishing high school and thus going on to college. The education and skill gains associated with the CTC and EITC likely keep paying off for many years through higher earnings and employment, researchers say. This growing body of research highlights the positive long-term benefits of the working-family tax credits for millions of families."

24 Bartlett, Chapter 10; Kindle ed.

25 Tax Policy Center, *Briefing Book*: "How does the tax exclusion for employer-sponsored health insurance work?" www.taxpolicycenter.org/briefing-book/how-does-tax-exclusion-employer-sponsored-health-insurance-work; Joint Committee on Taxation, "Estimates of Federal Tax Expenditures for Fiscal Years 2014-2018" (August 5, 2014), https://www.jct.gov/publications.html?func=startdown&id=4663.

26 Bartlett, Chapter 11; Kindle ed.

27 Bartlett, Chapter 14; Kindle ed.

28 Bartlett, Chapter 14; Kindle ed.

29 Alan Cole, "Corporate and Individual Tax Expenditures," Tax Foundation (August 3, 2015), http://taxfoundation.org/article/corporate-and-individual-tax-expenditures. Also see U.S. Treasury, "Tax Expenditures [2014-2024], https://www.treasury.gov/resource-center/tax-policy/Documents/Tax-Expenditures-FY2016.pdf; and Joint Committee on Taxation, "Estimates of Federal Tax Expenditures for Fiscal Years 2014-2018" (August 5, 2014), https://www.jct.gov/publications.html?func=startdown&id=4663.

CHAPTER 14

1 Carmen M. Reinhart and Kenneth S. Rogoff, *This Time Is Different: Eight Centuries of Financial Folly* (Princeton and Oxford: Princeton University Press, 2009), Kindle ed.; Chapter 7.

2 Federal Reserve Bank of St. Louis, Economic Research, "Federal Debt: Total Public Debt as% of Gross Domestic Product," 2016Q1, https://research.stlouisfed.org/fred2/series/GFDEGDQ188S.

3 For critiques of Reinhart and Rogoff, see Thomas Herndon, Michael Ash, and Robert Pollin, "Does High Public Debt Consistently Stifle Economic Growth? A Critique of Reinhart and Rogoff," *Political Economy Research Institute Working Paper Series*, no, 322 (April 2013), 1-25, www.peri.umass.edu/fileadmin/pdf/working_papers/working_papers_301-350/WP322.pdf; Jacob Davidson, "How Much Does America's Huge National Debt Actually Matter?" *Time* (February 11, 2016), http://time.com/4214269/us-national-debt/?iid=sr-link1; and Free exchange, "The 90% question," *The Economist* (April 20, 2013), www.economist.com/news/finance-and-

economics/21576362-seminal-analysis-relationship-between-debt-and-growth-comes-under.

4 Congressional Budget Office, "CBO's 2015 Long-Term Projections for Social Security," https://www.cbo.gov/sites/default/files/114th-congress-2015-2016/reports/51047-SSUpdate-2.pdf.

5 Congressional Budget Office, "Key Projections Under CBO's Extended Baseline," *The 2015 Long-Term Budget Outlook,* June 2015, 3 and 2, www.cbo.gov/sites/default/files/114th-congress-2015-2016/reports/50250-LongTermBudget Outlook-3.pdf.

6 Office of Management and Budget, Historical Tables, Table 7.1—"Federal Debt at the End of the Year: 1940-2021," https://www.whitehouse.gov/omb/budget/Historicals.

7 Arnaud Marès, "Ask Not Whether Governments Will Default, but How," InvestorsInsight.com, September 20, 2010, www.investorsinsight.com/blogs/john_mauldins_outside_the_box/archive/2010/09/20/sovereign-subjects-ask-not-whether-governments-will-default-but-how.aspx; Bruce Bartlett, *The Benefit and The Burden: Tax Reform—Why We Need It and What It Will Take* (New York: Simon and Schuster, 2012), Chapter 20; Kindle ed.

8 The Bush tax cuts included the Economic Growth and Tax Relief Reconciliation Act of 2001, the Jobs and Growth Tax Relief Reconciliation Act of 2003, and (during the Obama administration) the Tax Relief, Unemployment Insurance Reauthorization, and Job Creation Act of 2010 as well as the American Taxpayer Relief Act of 2012. The 2010 legislation extended the cuts two years beyond their original sunset deadline. The 2012 act partially extended the cuts further.

9 Bartlett, Chapter 20; Kindle ed.

10 Congressional Budget Office, "Estimate of the Budgetary Effects of H.R. 8, the American Taxpayer Relief Act of 2012, as passed by the Senate on January 1, 2013," January 1, 2013, https://www.cbo.gov/sites/default/files/112th-congress-2011-2012/costestimate/american-taxpayer-relief-acto.pdf.

11 Bartlett, Chapter 20; Kindle ed.

12 Bartlett, Chapter 20; Kindle ed.

13 U.S. Department of the Treasury, "Get the Facts: Raising the Debt Limit," https://www.treasury.gov/initiatives/Pages/debtlimit.aspx.

14 Rebecca Hyam, Ben Atherton, and Michael Janda, "Market dives to two-year low on recession fears," ABC News (August 5, 2011), www.abc.net.au/news/2011-08-05/market-falls-on-opening/2825954; Binyamin Appelbaum and Eric Dash, "S&P Downgrades Debt Rating of U.S. for the First Time," *The New York Times* (August 5, 2011), www.nytimes.com/2011/08/06/business/us-debt-downgraded-by-sp.html?_r=0.

15 Jack M. Balkin, "The Not-So-Happy Anniversary of the Debt-Ceiling Crisis," *The Atlantic* (July 31, 2012), www.theatlantic.com/politics/archive/2012/07/the-not-so-happy-anniversary-of-the-debt-ceiling-crisis/260458/.

16 David A. Fahrenthold, Lori Montgomery, and Paul Kane, "In debt deal, the triumph of the old Washington," *The Washington Post* (August 3, 2011), https://www.washingtonpost.com/politics/in-debt-deal-the-triumph-of-the-old-washington/2011/08/02/gIQARSFfqI_story.html.

17 U.S. Census Bureau, "Working Beyond Retirement-Age" (August 2, 2008), https://www.census.gov/people/laborforce/publications/Working-Beyond-Retirement-Age.pdf.

18 Congressional Budget Office, "Updated Budget Projections: 2016 to 2026," https://www.cbo.gov/publication/51384.

19 Chris Edwards, "A Plan to Cut Federal Spending," *Downsizing the Federal Government* (April 4, 2016), www.downsizinggovernment.org/plan-to-cut-federal-spending.

20 Edwards, www.downsizinggovernment.org/plan-to-cut-federal-spending.

21 Jim Avila, Serena Marshall, and Gitika Kaul, "Medicare Funds Totaling $60 Billion Improperly Paid, Report Finds," ABC News (July 23, 2015), http://abcnews.go.com/Politics/medicare-funds-totaling-60-billion-improperly-paid-report/story?id=32604330.

22 Bartlett, Chapter 20; Kindle ed.; Stockman quoted in Eric Schroeck, "Fox Adopts GOP Talking Point That Deficit Is a 'Spending Problem, Not a Revenue Problem,'" Media Matters for America (April 18, 2011), http://mediamatters.org/research/2011/04/18/fox-adopts-gop-talking-point-that-deficit-is-a/178776.

23 Financial Times, ft.com/lexicon, "Definition of financial repression," http://lexicon.ft.com/Term?term=financial-repression. "Quantitative easing" is a term of art (or perhaps an outright euphemism) for introducing new money into the money supply by a central bank—as when the Fed authorizes the printing of more currency. See R. A., "What is quantitative easing?" *The Economist* (March 9, 2015), www.economist.com/blogs/economist-explains/2015/03/economist-explains-5.

24 Bartlett, Chapter 20; Kindle ed.

25 Christopher Cox, "Keynote Address to the Columbia Law and Business Schools Cross Border Securities Market Mergers Conference" (December 19, 2007), https://www.sec.gov/news/speech/2007/spch121907cc.htm.

26 "Revenue neutrality" is an approach to taxation that allows the government to change tax law without changing the amount of revenue it receives. The change may raise taxes for one group and lower them for another, but the total revenue remains unchanged. This is not to be confused with "tax neutrality," which refers to tax provisions that are consistent with economically efficient, effective, or ideal objectives rather than to achieve political or social purposes.

27 Bartlett, Chapter 20; Kindle ed.

28 Bruce Bartlett interviewed in "Where is the GOP of yesteryear?" *The Economist* (September 2, 2009), www.economist.com/blogs/democracyinamerica/2009/09/where_is_the_gop_of_yesteryear.

29 Bartlett, "Conclusion"; Kindle ed.

30 "Economy: A plan to raise American incomes," https://www.hillaryclinton.com/issues/plan-raise-american-incomes/; About Money, "Hillary Clinton 2016 Economic Plan," http://useconomy.about.com/od/fiscalpolicy/p/Hillary_Economy.htm; Trent Gillies, "Tax Foundation rates tax plans: Who comes out on top?" CNBC (March 13, 2016), www.cnbc.com/2016/03/11/tax-foundation-rates-tax-plans-who-comes-out-on-top.html; Linda Qiu, "PolitiFact's guide to the 2016 presidential candidate tax plans" (April 7, 2016), www.politifact.com/truth-o-meter/article/2016/apr/07/politifacts-guide-2016-candidates-tax-plans/; Tax Foundation, "Comparing the 2016 Presidential Tax Reform Proposals," http://taxfoundation.org/comparing-2016-presidential-tax-reform-proposals.

31 Gary Johnson 2016, "Issues: Government Spending," https://garyjohnson2016. com/issues/; Libertarian, "Issues: Taxes," https://www.lp.org/issues/taxes; On the Issues, "Libertarian Party on Budget & Economy: Party Platform," www.ontheis- sues.org/Celeb/Libertarian_Party_Budget_+_Economy.htm.

32 Bernie 2016, "How Bernie pays for his proposals," https://berniesanders.com/ issues/how-bernie-pays-for-his-proposals/; Jackie Calmes, "Left-Leaning Econ- omists Question Cost of Bernie Sanders's Plans," *The New York Times* (February 15, 2016); Trent Gillies, "Tax Foundation rates tax plans: Who comes out on top?" CNBC (March 13, 2016), www.cnbc.com/2016/03/11/tax-foundation-rates- tax-plans-who-comes-out-on-top.html; Laura Meckler, "Price Tag of Ber- nie Sanders's Proposals: $18 Trillion," *The Wall Street Journal* (September 14, 2015), www.wsj.com/articles/price-tag-of-bernie-sanders-proposals-18- trillion-1442271511; Linda Qiu, "PolitiFact's guide to the 2016 presidential candi- date tax plans" (April 7, 2016), www.politifact.com/truth-o-meter/article/2016/ apr/07/politifacts-guide-2016-candidates-tax-plans/; Tax Foundation, "Comparing the 2016 Presidential Tax Reform Proposals," http://taxfoundation.org/compar- ing-2016-presidential-tax-reform-proposals; Paul Waldman, "No, Bernie Sanders is not going to bankrupt America to the tune of $18 trillion," *The Washington Post* (September 15, 2015), https://www.washingtonpost.com/blogs/plum-line/ wp/2015/09/15/no-bernie-sanders-is-not-going-to-bankrupt-america-to-the- tune-of-18-trillion/.

33 James C. Capretta, "The Trump Plan: Big Tax Hikes or Big Deficits," *National Review* (March 25, 2016), www.nationalreview.com/article/433249/donald- trumps-budget-tax-hikes-or-deficits; Trent Gillies, "Tax Foundation rates tax plans: Who comes out on top?" CNBC (March 13, 2016), www.cnbc.com/2016/03/11/tax- foundation-rates-tax-plans-who-comes-out-on-top.html; Ruth Marcus, "Donald Trump's utterly ridiculous budget plan," *The Washington Post* (February 19, 2016), https://www.washingtonpost.com/opinions/donald-trumps-utterly-ridiculous- budget-plan/2016/02/19/b6300002-d72b-11e5-be55-2cc3c1e4b76b_story.html; Linda Qiu, "PolitiFact's guide to the 2016 presidential candidate tax plans" (April 7, 2016), www.politifact.com/truth-o-meter/article/2016/apr/07/politifacts- guide-2016-candidates-tax-plans/; Tax Foundation, "Comparing the 2016 Presiden- tial Tax Reform Proposals," http://taxfoundation.org/comparing-2016-presidential- tax-reform-proposals; Trump: Make America Great Again! "Tax Reform That Will Make America Great Again," https://www.donaldjtrump.com/positions/ tax-reform.

34 Named after the Hoover Institution economists, Robert Hall and Alvin Rabushka, who developed it early in the 1980s. See William G. Gale, "Flat Tax," Urban Institute, http://webarchive.urban.org/publications/1000530.html.

35 FAIRtax, "How FAIRtax Works," https://fairtax.org/about/how-fairtax-works? gclid=CjoKEQjw-Mm6BRDTpaLgj6Ko4KsBEiQA5f2oE8vyNTC-S17 LiiCjZeuVLskk61gTVF4iorfkcUeXm_YaAs1x8P8HAQ.

36 Investopedia, "Value-Added Tax—VAT," www.investopedia.com/terms/v/ valueaddedtax.asp. Also see "Should the U.S. Adopt a Value-Added Tax?" *The Wall Street Journal* (February 18, 2016), www.wsj.com/articles/should-the- u-s-adopt-a-value-added-tax-1456715703.

37 Bartlett, Chapter 21; Kindle ed.

1 Carlyle coined the phrase in "Occasional Discourse on the Negro Question," as essay he wrote under the pseudonym "Dr. Phelim M'Quirk" for *Fraser's Magazine for Town and Country* vol. 40 (December 1849), 670-679; available online at https://babel.hathitrust.org/cgi/pt?id=inu.30000080778727;view=1up;seq=699.

2 Abraham Lincoln, "Second Annual Message" (December 1, 1862), The American Presidency Project, www.presidency.ucsb.edu/ws/?pid=29503.

3 Larry Diamond, "Liberation Technology," *Journal of Democracy*, 21:3 (July 2010), 70.

4 A remarkably thorough survey of "Comprehensive Solutions" for reduction of the American national debt is available at Peter G. Peterson Foundation, "Comprehensive Solutions," www.pgpf.org/finding-solutions/comprehensive-plans" and at "Tax Reform," www.pgpf.org/finding-solutions/tax-reform.

5 As a reminder, "Glass-Steagall" refers to four provisions of the Banking Act of 1933 that effectively barred deposit banks from engaging in investment banking. This institutional separation of deposit and investment activity was largely ended with the repeal of Glass-Steagall by the 1999 Gramm-Leach-Bliley Act.

6 For the origin of this *Russian* proverb ("Doveryai no proveryai"), see Suzanne Massie, "The Reagan Years 1984-88," www.suzannemassie.com/reaganYears.html.

7 Rebecca Thorpe, *The American Warfare State: The Domestic Politics of Military Spending* (Chicago: University of Chicago Press, 2014).

8 Paul M. Krawzak, "For CBO, Dynamic Scoring Is the Battle of Evermore," *Roll Call* (June 1, 2015), www.rollcall.com/news/for_cbo_dynamic_scoring_is_the_battle_of_evermore-242118-1.html.

9 The findings have also created considerable controversy among economists. Take note of Jacob Davidson, "How Much Does America's Huge National Debt Actually Matter?" *Time* (February 11, 2016), http://time.com/4214269/us-national-debt/?iid=sr-link1; Free exchange, "The 90% question," *The Economist* (April 20, 2013), www.economist.com/news/finance-and-economics/21576362-seminal-analysis-relationship-between-debt-and-growth-comes-under; and Thomas Herndon, Michael Ash, and Robert Pollin, "Does High Public Debt Consistently Stifle Economic Growth? A Critique of Reinhart and Rogoff," *Political Economy Research Institute Working Paper Series*, no, 322 (April 2013), 1-25, www.peri.umass.edu/fileadmin/pdf/working_papers/working_papers_301-350/WP322.pdf.

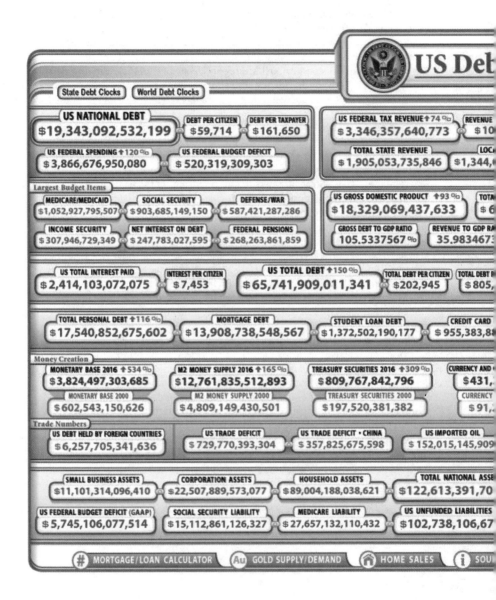

US Debt

US NATIONAL DEBT
$19,343,092,532,199

DEBT PER CITIZEN	DEBT PER TAXPAYER
$59,714	$161,650

US FEDERAL SPENDING ↑120%	US FEDERAL BUDGET DEFICIT
$3,866,676,950,080	$520,319,309,303

US FEDERAL TAX REVENUE ↑74%	REVENUE
$3,346,357,640,773	$10

TOTAL STATE REVENUE	LOC
$1,905,053,735,846	$1,344,

Largest Budget Items

MEDICARE/MEDICAID	SOCIAL SECURITY	DEFENSE/WAR
$1,052,927,795,507	$903,685,149,150	$587,421,287,286

INCOME SECURITY	NET INTEREST ON DEBT	FEDERAL PENSIONS
$307,946,729,349	$247,783,027,595	$268,263,861,859

US GROSS DOMESTIC PRODUCT ↑93%	TOTA
$18,329,069,437,633	$6

GROSS DEBT TO GDP RATIO	REVENUE TO GDP RA
105.5337567%	35.9834673

US TOTAL INTEREST PAID	INTEREST PER CITIZEN	US TOTAL DEBT ↑150%	TOTAL DEBT PER CITIZEN	TOTAL DEBT
$2,414,103,072,075	$7,453	$65,741,909,011,341	$202,945	$805,

TOTAL PERSONAL DEBT ↑116%	MORTGAGE DEBT	STUDENT LOAN DEBT	CREDIT CARD
$17,540,852,675,602	$13,908,738,548,567	$1,372,502,190,177	$955,383,8

Money Creation

MONETARY BASE 2016 ↑534%	M2 MONEY SUPPLY 2016 ↑165%	TREASURY SECURITIES 2016 ↑309%	CURRENCY AND
$3,824,497,303,685	$12,761,835,512,893	$809,767,842,796	$431,
MONETARY BASE 2000	M2 MONEY SUPPLY 2000	TREASURY SECURITIES 2000	CURRENCY
$602,543,150,626	$4,809,149,430,501	$197,520,381,382	$91,

Trade Numbers

US DEBT HELD BY FOREIGN COUNTRIES	US TRADE DEFICIT	US TRADE DEFICIT · CHINA	US IMPORTED OIL
$6,257,705,341,636	$729,770,393,304	$357,825,675,598	$152,015,145,909

SMALL BUSINESS ASSETS	CORPORATION ASSETS	HOUSEHOLD ASSETS	TOTAL NATIONAL ASSE
$11,101,314,096,410	$22,507,889,573,077	$89,004,188,038,621	$122,613,391,70

US FEDERAL BUDGET DEFICIT (GAAP)	SOCIAL SECURITY LIABILITY	MEDICARE LIABILITY	US UNFUNDED LIABILITIES
$5,745,106,077,514	$15,112,861,126,327	$27,657,132,110,432	$102,738,106,67

(#) MORTGAGE/LOAN CALCULATOR (Au) GOLD SUPPLY/DEMAND (🏠) HOME SALES (i) SOU

www.USDebtClock.org page, as captured on July 8, 2016 at 4:21 pm

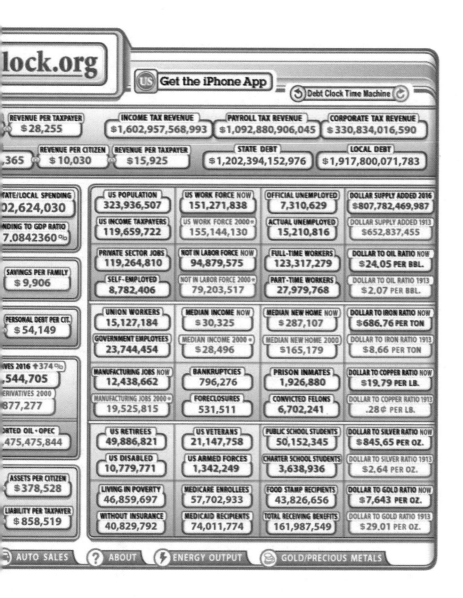

lock.org

US Get the iPhone App

Debt Clock Time Machine

REVENUE PER TAXPAYER $28,255

INCOME TAX REVENUE $1,602,957,568,993

PAYROLL TAX REVENUE $1,092,880,906,045

CORPORATE TAX REVENUE $330,834,016,590

,365 **REVENUE PER CITIZEN** $10,030

REVENUE PER TAXPAYER $15,925

STATE DEBT $1,202,394,152,976

LOCAL DEBT $1,917,800,071,783

TATE/LOCAL SPENDING 02,624,030

NDING TO GDP RATIO 7.0842360 %

SAVINGS PER FAMILY $9,906

PERSONAL DEBT PER CIT. $54,149

VES 2016 ↑374 % ,544,705

ERIVATIVES 2000 877,277

RTED OIL · OPEC 475,475,844

ASSETS PER CITIZEN $378,528

LIABILITY PER TAXPAYER $858,519

US POPULATION 323,936,507	**US WORK FORCE NOW** 151,271,838	**OFFICIAL UNEMPLOYED** 7,310,629	**DOLLAR SUPPLY ADDED 2016** $807,782,469,987
US INCOME TAXPAYERS 119,659,722	**US WORK FORCE 2000*** 155,144,130	**ACTUAL UNEMPLOYED** 15,210,816	**DOLLAR SUPPLY ADDED 1913** $652,837,455
PRIVATE SECTOR JOBS 119,264,810	**NOT IN LABOR FORCE NOW** 94,879,575	**FULL-TIME WORKERS** 123,317,279	**DOLLAR TO OIL RATIO NOW** $24.05 PER BBL.
SELF-EMPLOYED 8,782,406	**NOT IN LABOR FORCE 2000*** 79,203,517	**PART-TIME WORKERS** 27,979,768	**DOLLAR TO OIL RATIO 1913** $2.07 PER BBL.
UNION WORKERS 15,127,184	**MEDIAN INCOME NOW** $30,325	**MEDIAN NEW HOME NOW** $287,107	**DOLLAR TO IRON RATIO NOW** $686.76 PER TON
GOVERNMENT EMPLOYEES 23,744,454	**MEDIAN INCOME 2000*** $28,496	**MEDIAN NEW HOME 2000** $165,179	**DOLLAR TO IRON RATIO 1913** $8.66 PER TON
MANUFACTURING JOBS NOW 12,438,662	**BANKRUPTCIES** 796,276	**PRISON INMATES** 1,926,880	**DOLLAR TO COPPER RATIO NOW** $19.79 PER LB.
MANUFACTURING JOBS 2000* 19,525,815	**FORECLOSURES** 531,511	**CONVICTED FELONS** 6,702,241	**DOLLAR TO COPPER RATIO 1913** .28¢ PER LB.
US RETIREES 49,886,821	**US VETERANS** 21,147,758	**PUBLIC SCHOOL STUDENTS** 50,152,345	**DOLLAR TO SILVER RATIO NOW** $845.65 PER OZ.
US DISABLED 10,779,771	**US ARMED FORCES** 1,342,249	**CHARTER SCHOOL STUDENTS** 3,638,936	**DOLLAR TO SILVER RATIO 1913** $2.64 PER OZ.
LIVING IN POVERTY 46,859,697	**MEDICARE ENROLLEES** 57,702,933	**FOOD STAMP RECIPIENTS** 43,826,656	**DOLLAR TO GOLD RATIO NOW** $7,643 PER OZ.
WITHOUT INSURANCE 40,829,792	**MEDICAID RECIPIENTS** 74,011,774	**TOTAL RECEIVING BENEFITS** 161,987,549	**DOLLAR TO GOLD RATIO 1913** $29.01 PER OZ.

AUTO SALES ? ABOUT ⚡ ENERGY OUTPUT 😊 GOLD/PRECIOUS METALS

INDEX

A

Adams, John, 54, 58–61, 155–56, 290
Adams, John Quincy, 65
Administrative Procedure Act (APA), 172
Administrative State, 40, 77, 80
  careerism and fiefdoms in, 262–63, 267, 418
  growth of, 88, 109, 267
  regulations made by, 171–74, 182–85
  size of, 47, 183–85, 193
advisers, presidential, 100
Aesop, 254
Afghanistan
  money wasted in, 252, 254
  War in, 87, 136, 231, 236, 243, 271
AFL-CIO, 166
agencies
  created under New Deal, 97 (table), 98
  lawmaking power of, 98, 170
  present number of, 98
aging of population, 397
agribusiness, 313–17
Agricultural Adjustment Act (AAA), 200
Agricultural Adjustment Administration (AAA), 94, 312
Agriculture Department, 305, 308–9, 315–16
agriculture sector, 94–95, 118
  lobbying by, 312–18
AIG, 207

Air Force One, 55
Ajemian, Robert, 129
Alien and Sedition Acts, 60
Alien Enemies Act, 60
Allies (World War I), 206
all-volunteer force (AVF), 249, 268, 274
al-Qaeda, 236
America, welfare state of, 382
American dream, 362
American Recovery and Reinvestment Act (ARRA), 143, 220, 393–94
American Revolution, 228, 354, 391
Americans for Tax Reform, 443
antitrust legislation, 86
Arab-Israeli "Six-Day War" (June 1967), 114
armaments industry, 228–30
Armey, Dick, 314
arms race, 266
Arthur, Chester A., 69
Articles of Confederation, 54, 354, 391
atomic bomb, development of, 250
attorney general, 56
Austria-Hungary, 206

B

Babcock, Bruce, 317
Baker, James, 273
balanced budget Amendment, 418

balance of payments, adverse, 113–14, 116
Baltimore, Md., 310
bank deposits
  federally backed insurance on, 215–17, 416
  savings in, 139
banks, 66–67
  "bail out" of, 202, 416
  public insurance for, 201–2
  risky loans of, covered by FDIC, 215–17
  separation of commercial and investment, 133–34, 207, 216–17, 416
Barbary Wars, 244
Bartlett, Bruce, 354, 364, 374, 376, 382, 393, 402, 403, 405, 443
Barzun, Jacques, 404
Bear Stearns, 207
benefit-cost analysis, 147, 186, 189–92, 287
benefits, tax, concentrated and dispersed, 290
Bernanke, Ben, 205
Beveridge, Albert, 180
Bickley, James M., 443
big corporations and organizations, profiting from big government, 48, 420
big government
  conflicting attitudes re, 151–52
  origin in Civil War, 72
  origin in New Deal and World War II, 98–100

unsustainability of,
40–45
wartime powers of,
88–89
who profits from,
46–48, 420
big media, profiting from
big government, 48,
420
bill of rights, 156
Boehner, John, 293
bonds (treasury), 22, 73,
394
Bonner, William, and
Addison Wiggin,
28–29, 431
Bonus Bill of 1817, 163
bonuses, Wall Street, 218
Boomers, retiring, 23,
30–31, 34
Bosnian War, 243
Bradford, David, 374
Brandeis, Louis, 176
Bretton Woods system,
107–8, 112, 114–17,
120
Breyer, Stephen, 185, 435
Brinkley, Alan, 196
Britain, 90, 99–100, 114–
15, 206
Brito, Jerry, 437
Brook, Yaron, and Don
Watkins, 207
Brunori, David, 318, 439
Buchanan, James, 69
Buchheit, Paul, 439
Buckholz, Todd G., 432
budget (federal)
balancing, 107
deficits, 20, 21, 135
making of, 20
structure of (the pie),
10 (map), 159–61
surpluses, 133, 135
Budget and Accounting
Act of 1921, 20
budget authority, 232
Budget Control Act of
2011 (BCA), 233

budget discipline, 131
budget request, 20
Buffett, Warren, 9
Bulgaria, 206
bureaucracy, 185
Bureau of Labor Statistics
(BLS), 424
Burns, Arthur, 117
Burton, Bill, 142
Bush, George H. W., 127,
129–30, 134, 364
Bush, George W., 89, 135–
38, 186, 193, 219, 237,
244, 365
rating of, 138
business sector
attitude toward regula-
tion, 187–88
lobbying by, 318–26
regulation of, 189–92
support from govern-
ment, 188–89

C
cabinet, 56
capital gains, 133, 366
capitalism
democratic, 411
free-market failures of,
196, 205
careerism in government,
42–43, 48, 67, 102, 187,
262–64, 267, 303, 418
Carlucci, Frank, 273
Carlyle, Thomas, 413
Carlyle Group, 273–74
Carter, Jimmy, 120–22,
364
Cassius, Lucius, 289
Cato Institute, 319, 398,
432
caveat emptor (buyer
beware), 178
CCH Standard Federal
Tax Reporter, 350–51
Center for Responsive
Politics, 327
Center on Budget and Pol-
icy Priorities, 443

Centers for Disease Con-
trol and Prevention
(CDC), 305
central bank, 66–67
Central Powers (World
War I), 206
CEOs, compensation of,
166
charitable contributions,
384–86
charitable organizations,
423
Cheney, Dick, 273
Chicago Mercantile
Exchange, 118–19
chief executive and mag-
istrate, president as,
55, 57
Children's Health Insur-
ance Program (CHIP),
211
China, 22, 32–33, 394
Churchill, Winston, 100
Cicero, 46, 289
Cillizza, Chris, 334
Cincinnatus, L. Quintius,
53–54
Citizens Against Govern-
ment Waste (CAGW),
282, 295–96, 440
Citizens for Responsible
Government, 309
citizenship, 60
Citizens United decision,
333–35
Civilian Conservation
Corps (CCC), 94
Civil Rights Act of 1964,
108
civil service
careerism of, 42–43
reform in, 77
Civil War (American),
70–75, 237, 240, 356,
357–58
financing of, 73
Clay, Henry, 66
Cleveland, Grover, 69

Clinton, Bill, 130–35, 139, 211, 364, 365, 366, 423
  entourage of, on China trip, 54–55
Clinton, Hillary, 317, 324, 331, 333, 335, 345
  tax policy proposals, 406
Clintonomics, 130–31
Club for Growth, 432
Coalition for Fiscal and National Security, 432
Coblentz, E. D., 360
Coburn, Tom, 34–35, 255, 257, 432
cognitive dissonance, 149–52
Cold War, 122, 126, 230, 236, 245, 266, 362
Cole, Alan, 443
Cole, Tom, 293, 298
Commerce Clause, 176
Commission on Wartime Contracting in Iraq and Afghanistan, 276
Committee for a Responsible Budget, 432
Committee on Public Information (CPI), 88
commodity futures, 118
competition, 86, 177–78, 188
Competitive Enterprise Institute (CEI), 80, 181, 432
Concord Coalition, 433
Confederacy, financing of Civil War, 73
Congress, 62–63 (table), 84–85, 182–85
  careerism in, 42–43, 263–64
  partisanship and loss of mission in, 254
Congressional Budget and Impoundment Control Act of 1974, 20
Congressional Budget Office (CBO), 425, 435

Conn, Steven, 162
Connally, John, 117
conservation, 77–78
conservatives, 150, 420
Constitution, U.S., 42, 54, 153–58, 163–65, 391
  amendment of, by Article V, 153–54
  checks and balances in, discouraging war, 238–39, 243
  framers of, 153–54, 162–65
  goals of, 43
  Preamble to, 156–57
  taxation addressed in, 355–56
consumer confidence, 138
consumer rights, 188
consumption taxes, 410
Contract with America, 132
Coolidge, Calvin, 91, 228, 359
corporate taxes, 92, 125, 353
corporations, 189, 191
  personhood of ("are people"), 333–35
  personnel sharing with government, 273–74
  subsidies to (corporate welfare), 318–19, 320 (table)
corruption
  of the legislature, 246–47
  of unions, 327
cost-plus contracting, 273
Council of Economic Advisers (CEA), 111–12, 363
Cox, Christopher, 404
Cox, James M., 359
credit rating, U.S. government, 395–96
credit rating agencies (CRAs), 139, 217

credit scores, individual (FICO), 36
Crews, Clyde Wayne, Jr., 98, 181, 436
crony capitalism, 99, 188, 217, 274
Cruz, Ted, 346, 423
cui bono? (who profits), 46, 289
currencies
  basket of (IMF), 38
  devaluation of, 29
  futures speculation, 119
  gold-backed, 108
  loss of value through inflation, 29
  printing of, by government, 30, 73, 118

D

Dante, 368
Davidson, Jacob, 37
Debs, Eugene V., 84
debt
  personal, 419
  terror of, 15–48
debt ceiling, 23, 395–96
deceased persons, payments to, 310
deductions, tax, 373–74, 383
  itemizing of, 385
defense. See military
Defense Advanced Research Projects Agency (DARPA), 250–51
deficit spending (federal), 353
  advantages of, 28
  cutting, 396–401
  origin in Civil War, 73
  as percent of GDP, projected, 397
  three approaches to reducing, 396–403
Deming, William Edwards, 203

demobilization, failure to take place, after World War II, 241, 266
democracy
  direct, 93
  information and, 414–15
democratic capitalism, 411
Democratic Party, 65, 131–32, 423
  profiting from big government, 48–49
  and tax reform, 405
dependence on government, 99
dependents, 211
deregulation, 207
  financial, 138–39
derivatives, 139, 218–19
derivatives clearing organizations (DCOs), 218–19
Detroit, bankruptcy of, 222
Diamond, Larry, 414
Dickens, Charles, 17
Dillon, C. Douglas, 111–12
DiNapoli, Thomas P., 218
direct assistance, 93
direct taxation, ban on, in original Constitution, 355–56
disabled, 211
Disaster Relief Fund, 89
discretionary spending, 21, 30, 159–60
  cutting, 392–94, 399–401
distribution tables, 366–67
Dodd-Frank Wall Street Reform and Consumer Protection Act, 184, 202
Dole, Bob, 132
dollar

gold-backed, 108, 116–17
  as reserve currency, 37–38, 394
Domenici, Pete, 432
Doubleday, Frank, 180
draft, military, 274
Dudley, Susan E., 186–89, 436, 437
Durran, Dale, 306
Dust Bowl migratory farmers, 198

E

earmarking, 283–84, 296, 297 (table)
  banning of, 291–95
  hard and soft, 292
Earned Income Tax Credit (EITC), 311, 380–82
Economic Recovery Tax Act of 1981, 125
economics, science of, 413
economic welfare, as right, 93
economy, regulation of the, 177–78
education, 109
Edwards, Chris, 398, 433
Einstein, Albert, 349–52
Eisenhower, Dwight D., 71, 106–7, 111, 362
  Farewell Address, 71–72, 227–30
Eisenhower, Milton, 229
elected officials, careerism of, 42–43, 47
election of 1968, 116
election of 2016, 317–18, 335–45, 406
Elmendorf, Douglas, 437
embargoes, 99
Emergency Economic Stabilization Act of 2008, 202
employer-sponsored insurance (ESI), 383–84, 404, 416

energy sector, waste in, 329–31
England, Gordon, 261
entitlements, 30, 161, 201, 211–15, 416
  percent of budget for, 211
  reform of, 397
environmentalism, 77–78
Environmental Working Group, 317
environment sector, 331–33
Espionage Act of 1917, 88
estate taxes, 125
euro, 38
European Union, 19, 184
Evans, Diana, 285, 298, 440
excise taxes, 356, 358, 359
Executive branch, 171, 243
executive departments, 56
executive orders, 75
exports, not taxed, 355
externalities, 178

F

Fair Deal, 77, 105–6
FAIRTax, 409–10, 444
faith, 151–52, 203
Fannie Mae, 138, 139, 207
federal accounts, 18, 31
federal crimes, 169–70
Federal Deposit Insurance Corporation (FDIC), 94, 201–2, 215–17
Federal Disability Insurance Trust Fund, 31
Federal Election Commission, 336
Federal Emergency Management Agency (FEMA), 308
federal employees, 40, 159
  appointments of, 86
  number of (1.5 percent), 167
federal government

creation of, by the Constitution, 354–55
only 537 elected personnel in, 40
federalism, 176
Federalist Party, 59, 61, 76
Federal Register, 81, 173, 181
Federal Reserve Act, 85
Federal Reserve Bank of St. Louis, Economic Research (FRED), 426
Federal Reserve Board, 32, 85
Federal Tax Regulations, 350
fiefdomsm, 262–63
filing as individuals or married, 367
Fillmore, Millard, 69
financial crisis of 2007-2008, 134, 139–42, 207–8, 217
financial futures, 119
financial organizations, bailout of, 219, 416
financial repression, 402
First Amendment, 152
fiscal gap (of Social Security), 213
fiscal year (FY), 20
Fitch, 217
501(c)(4) groups, 334
FiveThirtyEight, 429
Flake, Jeff, 257, 441
flat income tax, 409–10
floating exchange rate system, 117
Food and Drug Administration (FDA), 305
Food and Nutrition Service (FNS), 310
Ford, Gerald, 120, 364
Ford, John, 197
foreign investors, public debt owned by, 32–33, 394
foreign policy, 99–101
France, 60, 90, 117, 206

Franklin, Ben, 369, 386
fraud, 214, 311, 401–2
Freddie Mac, 138, 139, 207
French Revolution, 59
fringe benefits, 384
"full faith and credit," 21

G

Gallup, 147–48, 198, 306–7, 430
Garfield, James A., 69
Gates, Robert, 261–62
general welfare, 43, 162–65, 397
generational accounting, 221–24
generational transfer payments, 214
Germany, 90, 206
Gilded Age, 79–80
Gingrich, Newt, 132
Ginnie Mae, 139
Glass-Steagall Act, 133, 201–2, 207, 216–17, 416
globalization, 184
The Godfather (movie), 283
gold, 108, 114–15
gold window, 112, 115–17
Gordon, John Steele, 72
Gore, Al, 131, 135, 423
government
  central, weak vs. powerful, 59
  faith in, 147–52
  limited, 65, 158
  proper and legitimate functions of, 390–91
  right-sized, 57–58, 165
  role and limits of, 43, 390–91, 417
  six duties of, in the Constitution, 147, 157, 161–62
  size of, 65, 158, 159
  three branches of, 171

Government Accountability Office (GAO), 310–11
"government is the problem," 39–40, 124
government offices (pre-Civil Service), 57
  partisan appointments to, 67
"government of laws, and not of men," 155, 290
government-sponsored enterprises (GSEs), 138
Gramm-Leach-Bliley Act, 133, 207
Grant, Ulysses S., 69
The Grapes of Wrath, 197
Great Depression, 16, 28, 92–99, 203–9, 242–43, 359–61
  ended with World War II spending, 205, 208
  mythology of, 195–210
Great Society, 77, 108–10, 113–14, 211
greenbacks, 73
Greenberg, Scott, 444
Greenspan, Alan, 85
gross domestic product (GDP), 36
Gulf War, 87, 129, 243
gun control, 293–94
guns and butter, 111–13, 137, 143

H

habeas corpus, 71
Haiti, 243
Halliburton, 273
Hall-Rabushka flat tax, 409
Hamilton, Alexander, 22, 56, 66, 76, 356
handouts, opposition to, 92
Harding, Warren G., 91, 230, 359

Harnitchek, Mark, 260
Harrison, Benjamin, 69
Harrison, William Henry, 68
Hatch, Orrin, 375
Hayes, Rutherford B., 69
"Hayseed Coalition," 95
Health and Human Services Department, 310
health care, demand for, 404, 417
health-care reform, 150–51, 383
health insurance, 383–84
Hearst, William Randolph, 360
Heller, Walter Wolfgang, 111–12
Help A Hipster (HAH), 301–4
Heritage Action for America, 433
Hill, Catey, 444
Homeland Security Department, 89, 184
home ownership
encouragement of, 373, 404
as investment, 139
Hoover, Herbert, 91–92, 205–6, 359
"hope and change" agenda, 142
Hospital Insurance (HI) Trust Fund, 212
housing and subprime mortgage bubbles (2007-2008), 133–34, 138–39
Housing and Urban Development Department (HUD), 139, 308
Hubbard, Glenn, 433
Humphrey, Hubert H., 116
Hussein, Saddam, 136, 140, 237

I
ideology, 86–87, 411
imports, 356–57
improper payments, 310, 401–2, 420, 422
income
cap on, restricting, 361
meaning of, undefined by IRS, 366
income tax, 72, 79, 85, 92, 353
alternatives to, 409
bracket creep, 363
exemption from (for 45 percent of filers), 380
flat, 409
history of, 357–65, 373
lottery model of, 379
marginal rates, 125, 166
top bracket, 360, 362
independent regulatory agencies or commissions (IRCs), 173
independent voters, 307
industrial production bubble, 206
inefficiency, 287–88
infinite-horizon fiscal gap, 221–24
inflation, 113, 363
caused by national debt, 46
rate of, 394
runaway, 396
sustained period of, 29, 39, 120–21, 123
Inflation Calculator, 426
information
available on the Internet, 413–15
resources for the reader, 424–45
information asymmetry, 178–79
information economy, 413–15
Inglis, Robert, 151
Inouye, Daniel, 291
insurance

government-provided, 416–17
public-sector, for certain private-sector enterprises, 201–2
interest payments on debt, 20–21, 30
considered mandatory, 391–92
interest rates, 21
bank deposits, ceiling on, 216
holding down (financial repression), 402
low, 139
rising, 29–30
internal improvements, 163
Internal Revenue Code, 350
Internal Revenue Service (IRS), 310–11
International Bank for Reconstruction and Development (IBRD), 108
internationalism
intervensionist, 86–87
public turn against, 89–90
International Monetary Fund (IMF), 38, 108
International Monetary Market (IMM), 119
Internet, 413–15
interstate commerce, 176
interventionist government, 76
"In the long run, we're all dead," 29
intragovernmental holdings, 18
Iran hostage crisis, 121
Iraq War, 87, 136, 140, 231, 236, 237, 243, 271
a war of choice, 239
ISIS, 15–16
isolationism, 78, 91
Italy, 90, 206

J

Jackson, Andrew, 65–67, 76
Japan, 22, 32–33, 394
Japanese internment in World War II, 101
Jefferson, Thomas, 56, 59, 60–64, 155–56, 163, 244, 306
"Jeffersonian point of view," 158
Jeffersonian Republicans, 59, 61, 65
job programs, 94
Johnson, Andrew, 69
Johnson, Gary, tax policy proposals, 407, 409
Johnson, Lyndon Baines, 108–16, 211, 362–63
Johnson, Simon, 393
Judicial branch, 171
judicial inefficiency, 190, 191–92
The Jungle (novel), 180
Juvenal, 201

K

Kane, Tim, 433
Kansas City, Mo., 309
Kelly, Brian, 289
Kelly, Sean, 293
Kelly, Walt (Pogo strip), 378
Kennedy, John F., 107–8, 111, 362
inaugural address, 87
Kennedy, Robert F., 116
Keynes, John Maynard, 28–29, 208, 219
Keynesianism, 208–9, 242, 362
Keyserling, Leon, 111
Kirk, Mark Steven, 292
Knox, Henry, 56
Korean War, 87, 106, 236, 243, 362
Kotlikoff, Laurence, 213, 221–24, 439
Kramer, Mattea, 433

Kristof, Nicholas, 326
Krugman, Paul, 118, 119, 143

L

labor sector, 30, 160
lobbying by, 326–29
labor unions, 326–29
Laird, Melvin P., 274
Landon, Alf, 199
Latin America, 78
League of Nations, 90
Lebanon, travel to, 305–6
Lebanon Crisis, 243
legislation, general interest, 286–88
Legislative branch, 171, 243, 246–47
surrender of war authority to President, 244–45
See also Congress
Lehman Brothers, 207
Lenahan, John, 372
Lend-Lease Act, 100
lettermarking, 292
Lever Food and Fuel Control Act of 1917, 88
Levin, Mark, 210, 213, 439
Lewinsky, Monica, 366
Lewis, Hunter, 441
liberals, 150–51, 420
Liberia, 243
Libya, 244
licenses and permits, 175
Light, Paul, 141
Lincoln, Abraham, 47, 56, 70–75, 356, 414
Ling, Pamela, 303
lobbying, 291, 312–32, 385
Lodge, Henry Cabot, 90
Lofgren, Mike, 437
log-rolling, 280–83
Long, Huey, 360
loopholes, tax, 377–86

M

Madison, James, 61, 65, 156, 157, 162–64, 244
mainstream media, 48
mandatory spending, 30, 160–61, 391–92
cuts in, 398–99, 398 (table)
Marcy, William L., 67
Marès, Arnaud, 393, 433
market failures, 178, 189, 191
Martin, William McChesney, Jr., 112
Mattera, Philip, 318, 441
Mattersdorf, Leo, 349–50
Matthews, Chris, 273
Mauzy, Stephen, 9
Maxey, Chester Collins, 279–83, 441
McCain, John, 141, 208, 254–55
McConnell, Mitch, 396
McKinley, William, 69, 76, 83
means testing, 210–11, 417
Meat Inspection Act, 181
meatpacking industry, 180
Medicaid, 30, 109, 211, 223, 311
medical programs, 110
Medicare, 109, 151, 161, 211, 212, 223, 376, 391–92, 397
as entitlement, 30
fraud and waste in, 214, 401–2
Part D prescription coverage, 223
Melamed, Leo, 118–19
Mellon, Andrew, 359
mercenary soldiers, 267–68
Merrill Lynch, 207
military. *See also* all-volunteer force
military budget

pork barrel politics in, 265–76

waste in, 275–76

military contractors, 241–42, 259–60

military defense, 417–18

military establishment, 227–30

an "amalgam of fiefdoms," 261–63

bad accounting practices of, 258–60

career in, 268

marketing and advertising to sports teams, 249–50

money wasted by, 249–52, 254–57

privatization of functions of, 274

research sponsored by, 250–51

size of, current, 40

size of, historically, 237–38

superfluous inventory of, 260

military-industrial-Congressional complex, 71–72, 228–30, 240–45, 419

beginning of, in World War II, 265–66

military industry, 228–30

built in World War II, 265–66

economic benefits of, 241–42

military spending, 126, 362

percent of budget, 230–35, 236–38, 260–61

percent of GDP, 230

pork barrel appropriations in, 245

Missouri, 309

mobilization/demobilization, 237–38

money market funds, 216

monopolies (trusts), 85

Monroe, James, 65, 78

Monroe Doctrine, 78

Moody's, 217

Moos, Malcom, 229

moral hazard, 202, 216, 217–19, 312–13

recommendations, 416

Moreno, Paul, 438

"morning in America," 122

mortgage-backed securities, 217

Mortgage Forgiveness Debt Relief Act of 2007, 366

mortgage interest deduction, 373, 404

mortgages, home, 373

Mr. Micawber, 17

Mullen, Mike, 34

multiplier effect, 220–21

municipalities, regulations of, 174–75

N

National Association of Manufacturers (NAM), 182, 438

National Comission of Fiscal Responsibility and Reform, 444

national debt, 14 (map)

avoiding, as promoting the general welfare, 164

current figure (June 2016), 144, 390

data on, sources, 427

defaulting on, 22, 396

defined, 18–19

historical view of, 24–25 (table), 74–75 (table)

history of, 359

how it can be paid, 28–31

how it got so big, 20–23

interest on, 20–21, 30

per capita historical view of, 26–27 (table)

political will to address, 393–94

ratio to GDP, 36–37, 390, 392

recent increases in, 134–35

repudiation of, 29

rise in, under Reagan, 126

as security threat, 34

servicing of, 20–21, 160, 391–92

size of, 16–48

three approaches to reducing, 396–403

tipping point of, when action must be taken, 389–91

unsustainability of, 46

why it got so big, 39–40

National Flood Insurance Program (NFIP), 308

National Industrial Recovery Act (NIRA), 94

National Institutes of Health, 301

National Performance Review (NPR), 131–32

National Priorities Project, 136, 427

National Recovery Administration (NRA), 94, 200

National Science Foundation, 306

Naturalization Act, 60

Naylor, Bart, 218

necessary and proper clause, 157

needs-tested programs, 397, 399

negative spending, 376–77

Netherlands, 373

New Deal, 42, 43, 77, 94–99, 105–6, 108

did not end the Great
Depression, 203–9,
242–43
effectiveness of, 95–99
mythology of, 196–210
New Democrats, 130–32,
364
New Freedom, 77, 85–86
New Frontier, 77
New Look, 107
New York City, 54
New York State, 311
Nixon, Richard, 116–20,
245, 364
non-delegation doctrine,
172
nonprofits, 384–86
North American Free
Trade Agreement
(NAFTA), 132, 134
northern states, 357
Nourse, Edwin, 111
nutritional programs, 110

O

Obama, Barack, 20, 36,
141–44, 193, 211, 219,
292, 294, 315, 331, 365,
393
Obamacare. *See* Patient
Protection and Afford-
able Health Care Act
Office of Information
and Regulatory Affairs
(OIRA), 186
Office of Management and
Budget (OMB), 427,
442
oil prices, 121, 129
omnibus appropriation
bills, 279–83, 285–86,
290–92, 294
the 1 percent, 119
O'Neill, Tip, 264
OpenSecrets.org, 427
opportunity cost, 164
Organization of Petro-
leum Exporting Coun-
tries (OPEC), 121

O'Rourke, P. J., 313–14,
352
Ottoman Empire, 206
outsider candidates, 65,
120

P

Pakistan, 307
Paltrow, Scot, 258, 442
Panama Canal, 78
panem et circenses (bread
and circuses), 201
Paperwork Reduction
Acts (1980, 1995), 186
Patient Protection and
Affordable Health Care
Act ("Obamacare"),
142, 184, 211, 383
Paulson, Henry, 219
PaymentAccuracy.gov,
428
payroll taxes, 210, 214–15,
353, 361, 381
Pelosi, Nancy, 219, 291
Pentagon, waste in budget
of, 275–76
the People, 157–58
Peter G. Peterson Founda-
tion, 434, 444, 445
Pew Research Center,
147–48, 430–31
phonemarking, 292
Pierce, Franklin, 69
Pigou, A. C., 178
Pigouvian tax, 178
Polidiotic, 427
political action commit-
tees (PACs), 328, 334
political donations,
317–318 (table), 321–
326 (table), 328–331
(table), 330 (table), 332
(table)
political parties
considered harmful, 58,
306–7
control of Senate and
House, 62–63 (table)

and government
appointments, 67
partisanship of, and
stalemate, 405–6
role in government,
48, 64
and tax reform, 404–6
politics of personal and
professional destruc-
tion, 421
Polk, James K., 68
polls, 429–30
on faith in government,
147–49
on government expen-
ditures, 198
on most important
problems, 15
on political parties,
306–7
on term limits, 103
popular democracy, 61
pork barrel politics, 245,
264–76, 279–99
examples of improper
payments, 309–11
examples of waste, 301–
9, 311–33
opposition to, 287
reforms attempted,
290–95
spending as percentage
of federal spending,
298–99
potholes, 309
pound, 38, 115
poverty, 108, 110
president, 55–57
approval ratings, 134
"bully pulpit" of, 77
as commander in chief,
239
and foreign policy,
99–101
image of, 121
imperial, 75, 121
power of, 70, 79
as technocrat, 129

war powers, 100–101,
244–45
prices
agricultural, 312
regulation of, 177–78
principle, appealing to,
404–5
printing of money, 30,
73, 118
private military company
(PMC), 267–73
misuse and waste of, in
Iraq and Afghanistan,
271–73
reasons for using,
274–75
privatization
in the military, 274
of some government
functions, 269–70
Progressive ("Bull
Moose") Party, 83
progressive tax, 356
progressivism, 76
public debt, 19
advantages of, 23, 28
percent of GDP, 221
who owns it, 31–33,
394
public works, 92
Public Works Administra-
tion (PWA), 94
Pure Food and Drug Act,
181
Pye, Jason, 170

Q

quarantine of industry,
191–92

R

Randolph, Edmund, 56
Reagan, Ronald, 39, 122–
27, 134, 269, 274, 364,
373, 418
inaugural address, 124
Reaganomics, 124–27
Reagan Revolution, 269

rebellion, Jefferson's
views, 156
redistribution of wealth,
131, 360–61
refunds on taxes, 311
regressive tax, 215, 353,
361, 410
Regulation Q, 216
regulations, 169–93
benefit-cost analysis of,
186, 189–92
cost burden of, 181
economic and social
types of, 177–79
in everyday life, 176–77
notice period and mon-
itoring ofw, 173–74
presumption against,
192
progressivism and? 76
size and scope of, 80–81
Reinhart, Carmen M., and
Kenneth S. Rogoff, 36,
390, 434
reinvention of govern-
ment (REGO), 131–
32, 391
relief programs, 94
religion, 152
representative govern-
ment, 61
Republican Party
opposition to Clinton,
131–32
opposition to FDR, 96
profiting from big gov-
ernment, 48–49
and tax reform, 404–6
research projects, 250–51
resources for the reader,
424–45
retirement age, 34, 215
revenue (federal)
historical view of,
24–25 (table), 74–75
(table)
loss of, through deduc-
tions, 373–74

per capita histori-
cal view of, 26–27
(table)
sources of, 353, 358
the rich (1 percent), 166
soaking the, 360–61
rights, government pro-
tection of, 190, 191
rivers and harbors,
improvement bills, 280,
288
robber barons, 79–80
robots, research into,
250–51
Rockefeller, John D., Jr.,
360
Roemer, Tim, 263–64,
442
Rogers, Mike, 294
Rogowski, Robert A., 98
Rome, ancient, 53–54,
153
Romney, Mitt, 333
Roosevelt, Franklin D.,
42, 43, 57, 93–102, 105,
198, 359, 360–61
criticism of, 96
Hundred Days, 94
ranking of, 101
Roosevelt, Theodore,
75–84, 180
Roosevelt Corollary to the
Monroe Doctrine, 78
Rumsfeld, Donald, 231
Ryan, Paul, 402

S

safety, regulation and, 179
San Bernardino terrorist
attack, 237
Sanders, Bernie, 317, 324,
331, 335, 345
tax policy proposals,
407–8
Sandy Hook school shoot-
ing, 294
savings accounts (in
banks), 139
Schiff, Peter, 37

scientific efficiency, 41–42
secession, 70–71
Second Bank of the
United States, 66–67
"Second Bill of Rights,"
106
security personnel,
269–70
Sedition Act of 1798, 60
Sedition Act of 1918, 89
Sekulow, Jay, 438
Selective Service Act of
1917, 88
separation of powers, 172
September 11, 2001, ter-
rorist attacks, 136, 231,
237, 244
sequestration, 10 (map),
233
Sessions, Jeff, 136
Shakespeare, 28, 368, 375
Shays' Rebellion, 156
siloed organizations, 262
Sinclair, Upton, 9, 180
sinkholes, 17–18
Sixteenth Amendment,
79, 353, 356, 358, 373
slavery, 70, 75, 282,
356–57
smoking cessation pro-
grams, 301–2, 305
Smoot-Hawley Tariff, 92
Snowden, Edward, 89
social regulation, 178–79,
183
social safety net, 210–11,
397, 417
Social Security, 30–31,
160, 210–15, 391–92,
397, 416–17
as entitlement, 30
future obligations, 23
as generational transfer
payment, 214
not "insurance," 214
solutions to underfi-
nancing of, 213
tax. See payroll taxes

Social Security Act of
1935, 210
Social Security Act of
1965, 109
Social Security Adminis-
tration, 310
75-year projection,
212–13
Social Security Trust
Fund, 19, 21, 31, 214
borrowing from, 22–23
Somalia, 132
southern states, 356–57
Soviet Union, 236, 245,
269
Spanish-American War,
78, 237, 243
special drawing rights
(XDR), 38
special interest groups,
124, 188, 189–92
spending (federal)
demanding the reasons
for, 422
failure to prioritize, 44
historical view of,
24–25 (table), 74–75
(table)
mortgaging the future
by, 123
paid for from revenues,
390
per capita histori-
cal view of, 26–27
(table)
percent of GDP, 96
reduction in, 126
"stealth" (through tax
expenditures), 386
See also deficit; surplus
spending within your
means, 17
spoils system, 67
sports teams, military
money to, 249–50
Square Deal, 77
stagflation, 30, 117–18,
364
Stalin, Joseph, 17

Standard & Poor's, 217,
395–96
standing armies, 238, 243,
419
"starving the beast," 137,
403
State Department, 56, 305
State Policy Network, 434
states
as laboratories of
democracy, 176
regulations made by,
174–75
rights and powers of,
158, 200, 354
statism, 72, 76, 242
statistics, use of, 431
Stein, Herbert, 212
Steinbeck, John, 197
Stein's Law, 212
Stiglitz, Joseph, 207
stimulus programs, 99,
143, 204–5, 219–21,
362–65
stock bubble (2000-2002),
133
Stockman, David, 95, 96,
112, 119, 205, 208, 210,
246, 402, 434
stock market, 138
stock market crash of
1929, 92, 359
strikes, 327
suboptimization of Amer-
ica, 44–45, 304
subsidies, agricultural, 94
Summers, Larry, 205
super-PACs, 335–45
supply-side economics,
125, 127, 136, 364
Supreme Court, 200
surplus (federal spend-
ing), 365
Surrey, Stanley S., 375
and Paul R. McDaniel,
445
surtaxes, 363
survivors, 211
Sutton, Willie, 166

swap lines, 114
Swine Odor and Manure
   Management Act
   (SWOMM) of 2009,
   285–86
Switzerland, 116–17, 373

T

Taft, William Howard,
   83, 358
Taliban, 136
tariffs, 72, 85–86, 92,
   356–57
taxation, 72, 92
tax bills, impact of,
   366–67
tax breaks, 378
tax code
   complexity of, 350–54,
      368
   Einstein's noncompre-
      hension of, 350–52
   sleight of hand in, 372–
      74, 386
tax credits, 310, 380
   refundable, 380
tax cuts
   Bush's, 136–38, 393
   history of, 359–65
   misleading, 376
   stimulus from, 220–21,
      362–65
   value of, if any, 137–38
   for the wealthy, 136
taxes
   cutting while in deficit,
      111–13, 136
   history of, in U.S.,
      354–65
   raising, 30, 106, 402–3
   revenues from, 353
   simple and transparent,
      goal, 353–54
   time period of comput-
      ing, 367–68
tax expenditures, 375–76,
   382, 403
   resources on, 428
   total of, 386

Tax Foundation, 445
tax neutrality, 403–5,
   409–11, 419
Taxpayers for Common
   Sense, 295
tax policy, as economic
   lever, 363
Tax Policy Center, 378,
   445
tax rate, statutory vs.
   effective, 378
tax reform, 403–6
   ideological dogma
      impeding, 411
   politicalization of, 405
Tax Reform Act of 1986,
   125
Taylor, Zachary, 69
Tea Party movement, 150,
   395
Tennessee Valley Author-
   ity (TVA), 95
Tenth Amendment, 76,
   158, 175, 200
term limits, 102, 103, 156,
   418
terrorism, 15–16, 142,
   236–37
Thatcher, Margaret, 269
Thompson, Ken, 311
Thoreau, Henry David,
   158
Thorndike, Joseph, 125
Thorpe, Rebecca, 238,
   241, 245, 418, 442
three-card monte, 371–72
tobacco industry, 305
Tobin, James, 111–12
Tocqueville, Alexis de, 69
Tonkin Gulf Incident, 113
"too big to fail," 217
trade
   collapse of, in Great
      Depression, 206
   deficit, 134
Treasury bills, 22, 394
Treasury Department, 56
TreasuryDirect.gov,
   428–29

Treasury securities, 21, 22
   safety of, in investors'
      opinion, 21
Treaty of Versailles, 90
trillion, size of number,
   16–17
Troubled Asset Relief Program (TARP), 143
Truman, Harry S., 102,
   105–6
Trump, Donald, 266, 324,
   335, 336, 346
   tax policy proposals,
      408
trust fund, 19
Twelfth Amendment, 60
Twenty-Second Amend-
   ment, 102
two-term tradition, 57,
   83, 96, 101–3
Tyler, John, 68

U

unemployment, 119–20,
   197 (table), 204
unemployment benefits,
   104 (map), 160
   as entitlement, 30
United Nations, 244,
   267–68
United States
   a broke nation, 221
   credit rating lowered,
      395–96
   a debtor nation (since
      1985), 45, 126
   an imperialist power, 78
   an international power,
      81
   who runs it (holders of
      public debt), 31–35,
      45
United States Agency for
   International Develop-
   ment (USAID), 305–6,
   307
United States Office of
   Government Ethics,
   442

USA PATRIOT Act, 89
U.S. Census Bureau, 429
U.S. Debt Clock, 16, 427
USGovernmentSpending.
 com, 429
U.S.-Mexican War, 237,
 243
U.S. Military Railroad
 (USMRR), 72
U.S. Postal Service work-
 ers, 40, 159
U.S. Public Interest
 Research Group, 309

V

Value-Added Tax (VAT),
 410, 419
Van Buren, Martin, 68
The Verdict (movie), 151
veterans, 233–35
Veterans Affairs, waste by,
 252–53
veto, 66–67
vice president, 60
Vietnam War, 87, 113,
 236, 243, 362
Vinnell Corporation, 274
"the vision thing," 129
Volcker, Paul, 117
"voodoo economics," 127
Voting Rights Act of 1965,
 108

W

Wackenhut, 270
wages and prices, freeze
 on, 117
Waldo, Dwight, 41–42,
 438
"walk and chew gum," 142
Wall Street, 111, 133, 202,
 208
 bonuses, 218
 and the financial crisis
  of 2007-2008, 217–18
The Wall Street Journal,
 445

War Department, 56
War of 1812, 243
War on Poverty, 109
War on Terror, 267
war powers, 88–89, 100–
 101, 244–45
wars
 of choice, 86–87, 136
 Constitutional imped-
  iments to waging,
  238–39
 cutting taxes while wag-
  ing, 136
 declared, 100, 238–39,
  243
 existential threats,
  236–37
 ideological, 86–87
 industrial, 240
 raising taxes to fund,
  106
 undeclared (lacking
  congressional dec-
  laration), 106, 113,
  136, 243–45
Washington, D.C., wealth-
 iest counties in suburbs
 of, 165–66
Washington, George,
 54–58, 356
 Farewell Address, 58,
  227–28, 238, 306
 precedent set by, as
  President, 55
 return to Mount Ver-
  non, 54
waste
 amount of, 311
 causes of, 303
 seven criteria of,
  282–83
Wastebooks, 257, 303, 310
Watergate scandal, 120
Watson Institute for International and Public
 Affairs, 231
Wattenberg, Ben, 198

wealth transfers, regula-
 tion and, 178
Webster, Daniel, 66
welfare state, 93, 382
 rolling back, 122
West Germany, 116
We the people, 31
Whig Party, 66
Whiskey Rebellion, 356
Wiggin, Addison, and
 William Bonner, 69,
 127
Williams, Ralph E., 229
Williams, Walter E., 162–
 63, 438
Wilson, James Q., 185,
 438
Wilson, Woodrow, 84–91,
 358
wine and viticulture pro-
 grams, 307
Wolf, Leon, 254
Woodford, Lindam,
 258–59
Works Progress Adminis-
 tration (WPA), 96
World War I, 86–90, 206,
 230, 237, 240, 243,
 358–59
World War II, 89, 99–100,
 105, 205, 208–9, 230,
 236, 240, 243, 265–66,
 361–62, 394

Y

Yemen, 251–52
yen, 38
Young, Don, 293
yuan, 38

Z

Zhou Xiaochuan, 38

PER CAPITA HISTORICAL REVENUE, SPENDING, AND NATIONAL DEBT
inflation-adjusted to 2009 dollars

Congress	Administration	Population in Millions[1]	Revenue	Spending	Debt
1–4	George Washington (1789–1797)	4.44	$121.62	$128.38	$299.55
5–6	John Adams (1797–1801)	5.08	$120.08	$114.17	$271.65
7–10	Thomas Jefferson (1801–1809)	6.12	$326.80	$212.42	$166.67
11–14	James Madison (1809–1817)	7.79	$270.86	$345.31	$275.99
15–18	James Monroe (1817–1825)	9.80	$391.84	$342.86	$228.57
19–20	John Quincy Adams (1825–1829)	11.64	$201.89	$143.47	$136.60
21–24	Andrew Jackson (1829–1837)	13.84	$460.26	$291.18	$0.00
25–26	Martin Van Buren (1837–1841)	16.37	$150.89	$177.76	$4.89
27–28	William Henry Harrison/ John Tyler (1841–1845)	18.44	$112.26	$125.81	$29.83
29–30	James K. Polk (1845–1849)	20.85	$142.93	$172.66	$47.00
31	Zachary Taylor (1849–1850)	22.49	$33.79	$46.69	$59.14
31–32	Millard Fillmore (1850–1853)	23.92	$143.39	$132.11	$58.11
33–34	Franklin Pierce (1853–1857)	26.61	$221.72	$201.05	$23.30
35–36	James Buchanan (1857–1861)	30.06	$168.00	$215.90	$43.58
37–39	Abraham Lincoln (1861–1865)	33.10	$211.18	$920.85	$635.05
39–40	Andrew Johnson (1865–1869)	35.91	$649.40	$887.77	$1,014.20
41–44	Ulysses S. Grant (1869–1877)	41.29	$1,199.08	$1,048.20	$995.88
45–46	Rutherford B. Hayes (1877–1881)	48.26	$522.17	$474.51	$870.29
47–48	James A. Garfield/ Chester A. Arthur (1881–1885)	53.14	$638.88	$456.15	$718.67
49–50	Grover Cleveland (1885–1889)	58.19	$595.98	$465.54	$634.65
51–52	Benjamin Harrison (1889–1893)	63.54	$632.51	$567.04	$554.93

1. Average of population for all years of the administration.